Amherst County, Virginia
In the Revolution

WINTON

Home of Col. Jasper C. I. U. L. W. I.

AMHERST COUNTY, VIRGINIA IN THE REVOLUTION

Including Extracts from the
"Lost Order Book"

1773–1782

by

Lenora Higginbotham Sweeny

HERITAGE BOOKS
2013

HERITAGE BOOKS
AN IMPRINT OF HERITAGE BOOKS, INC.

Books, CDs, and more—Worldwide

For our listing of thousands of titles see our website
at
www.HeritageBooks.com

A Facsimile Reprint
Published 2013 by
HERITAGE BOOKS, INC.
Publishing Division
5810 Ruatan Street
Berwyn Heights, Md. 20740

Originally published:
Lynchburg, Virginia
1951

— Publisher's Notice —
In reprints such as this, it is often not possible to remove blemishes from the original. We feel the contents of this book warrant its reissue despite these blemishes and hope you will agree and read it with pleasure.

International Standard Book Numbers
Paperbound: 978-0-7884-2261-4
Clothbound: 978-0-7884-6867-4

TO THE MEMORY OF MY
MOTHER
ALTHEA JANE HIGGINBOTHAM
Great-granddaughter of Colonel James Higginbotham
of the French and Indian War and the
Revolutionary War
and
FATHER
CYRUS AARON HIGGINBOTHAM
Great-great-grandson of Captain Aaron Higginbotham
of the Colonial Wars and the Revolutionary War

Contents

	PAGE
Introduction	IX
Preface	XI
Committee of Safety, and Minute Men	1
The First Rifle Company	9
Captain James Franklin's Company, later Captain Clough Shelton's Company	25
Revolutionary Officers, Amherst County Militia	31
Revolutionary Soldiers from Amherst County, comprising then the territory of the present County of Nelson	40
Captain Azariah Martin's Company of Militia	52
Captain William Tucker's Company of Militia	55
Regiment of Guards	57
Clothing and Beef for 16th Division	60
Disbursements to Wives, Widows and Orphans of Revolutionary Soldiers	61
Letter of Colonel William Fontaine Describing Surrender of Cornwallis	65
Letter of Colonel Hugh Rose to Governor Harrison	68
Claims for Property Impressed or Taken for Public Service	69
Extracts from Lost Order Book, 1773-1782	72
Applications, in National Archives, of Amherst Soldiers for Pensions	94
Soldiers of French and Indian War	188
Officers of Amherst Militia Before the Revolution	189
Appendix: The Will of Sarah Henry	191
Index	195

Introduction

The literature relating to the American Revolution is abundant. Many volumes have been printed on the subject: biographies and correspondence of the leading participants; elaborate productions on the social and economic life before and during the Revolution, issued separately, or as parts of general histories of the United States; studies of the campaigns and battles; many original documents, including proceedings of the Continental Congress, and journals of the legislative bodies of the colonies; and in addition to these more ambitious publications, there are innumerable essays and scattered contributions in periodicals and pamphlets about minor incidents, and about individuals whose achievements were not so conspicuous as those of the leaders. For understanding the participation of Virginia, so unflinching in her attitude toward the redress of grievances at the beginning of the Revolution, and so persistent in maintaining her duty, there is a dearth of publications about the events of that period happening in the Counties. The minutes of the Committee of Safety of only a few of the counties, Caroline, Cumberland, Isle of Wight, and Southampton have survived and have been printed. In such minutes we learn of the views not only of the affluent and socially prominent, but of all the inhabitants. The loss of the committee records of the other counties is deplorable, and may never be retrieved. Altogether the information in print is scanty about the origin, development, and support of the revolutionary spirit in local communities in Virginia. We would like to know more definitely who the real leaders were, whether entirely men of property, or a mixed group of prosperous planters and those less fortunate. We wish to know how faithfully and impartially the orders of the Conventions and of the General Assembly were enforced. Was the economic life of each county continued in its pre-war vigor, or was it seriously impaired? What supplies were furnished to the armies? With what degree of competence and efficiency were the duties of the members of the County Committee of Safety and of the County Court performed? To what extent was the local government in abeyance? Until we know the answers to such questions as these and to others, in the Virginia Counties, we cannot expect to draw tenable conclusions. This volume on Amherst offers us a vivid and full account of the contribution, to the successful outcome of the Revolution, of at least one county. Amherst, impinging upon the eastern slope of the Blue Ridge, was, in the Revolution, distinctly of frontier location; it was much larger than at present, including in its boundaries the present Nelson County. No such contribution as this could be prepared without the most painstaking and persistent examination of the County Court records. For many years this patient search has been carried on by Mrs. Sweeny in the congested court house under numerous inconveniences. Inevitably some of the important documents of the Revolutionary period were missing, or supposed to be missing. The author was not contented until she had examined all that had survived. She recounts in the preface her discovery of the lost orderbook for the years 1773 to 1782, an indispensable record of the privations and sufferings of the inhabitants. The extracts from the order-book printed in this volume inform us of the general conditions, including the claims for supplies furnished by the inhabitants, at times when the stock of food in the county was seriously depleted; and in general they present a picture of orderly procedure of local government. Highly valuable and impressive are the applications of individual soldiers when they asked for pensions, and which the author has copied from the originals in the National Archives. What examples of noble purpose, patriotic endurance, and willing sacrifice these exhibit. If we multiply by the number of counties, what Amherst gave in men and goods, and what she endured in this critical period, we may have some comprehension of the contribution of the entire Commonwealth.

E. G. SWEM

Williamsburg, Virginia.

Preface

Amherst County, including the present County of Nelson, was formed from Albemarle in 1761. It was named in honor of the British hero of Ticonderoga, General Sir Jeffrey Amherst. The first Court House in 1764 was surrounded by the plantation of John Loving, known as the "Nassau Tract." On this estate was an orchard of two hundred peach and one hundred apple trees.

The first Amherst Order Book (1761-1766) was not extant upon our first examination of Amherst records nor were three other Order Books: 1770-1773, 1773-1782 and 1794-1799. Several times we visited Amherst and searched for the missing volumes but to no avail.

Perhaps thinking about our ancestors who were at Yorktown with Washington drew us to the county once more, soon after the Sesqui-Centennial Celebration of 1931. In any event, it was only to hear again the old story that "The Order Book covering the Revolutionary period had either been destroyed or carried away during the Civil War." Somehow I could never accept this statement, and decided to make a diligent search for it under the seats of the Court Room, where I had been told by Miss Vera Joyner, Deputy Clerk of Amherst County, books and papers thought to be of no importance had been stored when the new Court House was built. After moving stacks of old ledgers and papers covered with the accumulated dust of years, peering through the misty cobwebs, lo! I spied "THE LOST ORDER BOOK!" With it was found a mass of papers containing, among other things, marriage bonds, unrecorded deeds and wills, and a number of chancery suits of the eighteenth century. One of them relates to a signer of the Declaration of Independence, Carter Braxton, and another to a private soldier who died in the Continental Army.

The discovery of this ancient volume fills an important gap in historical and genealogical records. It is the crystal ball into which we gaze to study life in Amherst during the Revolutionary War. It contains the names of officers commissioned by the Governor for the Militia of Amherst County, Virginia, after June, 1777; prior to this time the commissions were issued by the Committee of Safety.

Another interesting feature of this Amherst County Order Book 1773-1782 is a list of the names of soldiers who proved they had served in the French and Indian War under such officers as General Braddock, General Forbes, Colonel George Washington and Colonel

William Byrd, and were thus qualified to obtain bounty land allowed by the proclamation of the King of Great Britain in 1763.

Although in hiding for sixty years, this large leather-bound volume was in good condition, except for a few worm-eaten pages. Since its discovery it has been used by many people coming from almost all the United States searching for Revolutionary ancestors. It was restored by the Society of Sons of the Revolution in the State of Virginia in 1938.

In the meantime, the Clerk's Office was enlarged and changes were made in the Court Room, and those old Court papers were stored in an outbuilding in the jail yard. Mr. William E. Sandidge, Clerk of the Circuit Court, did not live to enjoy the spacious office of which he had dreamed. He was succeeded by his son, William E. Sandidge, Jr., third successive Clerk of that name descended from William Sandidge, an Amherst County soldier in the Revolution.

On our next visit to Amherst, Virginia, we found a new jail under construction, and papers scattered on the floor of the outbuilding mixed with plaster and mortar. While arranging them in a carton to take to the Court House so that my husband could help me examine them, I found three marriage bonds. I noticed a similar carton on top of the large wooden box containing the old Court papers. In attempting to put it on the floor, it slipped and fell with a thud. Glancing down, I was horrified to see—not papers—but dynamite! Losing interest in those precious old papers I ran to the Court House, where the Clerk reassured me there was no danger unless the fuse was lit.

Later the papers were arranged and stored in the utility room of the Court House. Finally, through the interest of Mrs. Philip Wallace Hiden, "Fairy Godmother" of the Virginia Records and a member of the Virginia State Library Board, who has preserved many of the Virginia Records, an order of the Court resulted in the transfer of the papers to the archives department of the Virginia State Library in Richmond.

In my endeavor to give a true presentation of the part the brave men from Amherst County took in gaining our Independence I had the advice and guidance of my late husband, William Montgomery Sweeny, who aided me in the laborious though fascinating research. The "Lost Order Book," 1773-1782, supplied much of the information, but we drew on other sources as well, including muster and pay rolls from the War Department in Washington, which were photostated for the purpose, and records in the Virginia State Archives. In the Pension Files of Revolutionary Soldiers we found names of persons who, in testifying for an applicant, proved their own service. Or, some deponent in his application for a pension mentioned names of soldiers who served with him. The material was edited by Mr. Sweeny, and we had arranged to have it published when the splendid work of Mr. John H. Gwathmey, *Historical Register of Virginians in the Revolution,* appeared, giving, as we thought, a complete list of "names and evidence of service of the Virginians who were in the Army, Navy and Marine Corps in the American Revolution." However, after finding there were eighty-five commissioned officers and many private soldiers of the Amherst County Militia whose names do not appear in any Virginia Index, I was prompted to carry this work to completion to do justice to the patriots of Amherst County.

If I have rescued one name from oblivion and restored it to the hearts and remembrance of descendants of the brave men from the Blue Ridge, I shall be glad.

I wish to express my deep appreciation to Dr. E. G. Swem, Librarian Emeritus of William and Mary College, for his kindly encouragement and helpful suggestions. I am grateful to my niece, Eleanor Kasehagen, for her assistance in preparing this manuscript for publication.

Among others I wish to thank Mrs. Margaret M. H. Finch, retired from General Reference Division, National Archives, Washington, D. C.; Mrs. James Claiborne Pollard, Librarian, Archives Division, Virginia State Library, through whose interest in old documents there are given herein the names of two invalid soldiers from the "List of Virginia Pensioners—1786" which she found while assisting in examination of the old Court papers I found in 1931; my nephew, Shields Johnson, for helpful suggestions; and my sister, Mrs. Carpenter-Holland-Griffith, Anglesey, Wales and Bedford, England, who gave encouragement to this work and inspiration to my life.

NORA HIGGINBOTHAM SWEENY

"Give Me Liberty, or Give Me Death!"

Committee of Safety, and Minute Men

In March, 1775, the Virginia Convention met in old St. John's Church, crowning a lofty hill above the falls of the James River, at Richmond, where it could deliberate with more freedom than in Williamsburg under Governor Dunmore's shadow. At this meeting Patrick Henry moved the organization of militia and that the "Colony be immediately put in a state of defense." The bold proposal roused the resistance of many of the firmest friends of the colonial cause, and the debate was fierce in the extreme. But the genius of Henry rose to the full demands of the occasion, and as the last thrilling exclamation, "give me liberty, or give me death!" fell on the ears of the House, all were infused with the spirit of the orator; the bill passed, and the Colony was at once placed in the attitude of defense.[1]

Almost at the moment Henry's tocsin "Liberty or Death!" had been echoed by the "shot heard 'round the world," a company of volunteer minute-men from Amherst, under command of Captain James Higginbotham, Lieutenant Joseph Cabell and Ensign Nicholas Cabell,[2] joined Patrick Henry at New Castle in response to his call for an armed force to march to Williamsburg, to extort from Governor Dunmore the powder which he had removed from the public magazine.[3] This was the first act of armed resistance to the British authority in the Colony of Virginia.

The Governor had converted his Palace into a garrison, fortifying it in the best manner he could, and surrounding it with artillery, but the presence of this force was so alarming to him[4] that early in the morning of June 8, 1775, while George Purvis, a soldier in Captain Higginbotham's Company, was standing guard, Lord Dunmore with his family took shipping and proceeded to Yorktown, where they went aboard the *Fowey* man-of-war.

A Scotch merchant, James Parker, writing from Norfolk, Virginia, June 12, 1775, to his friend, Charles Stuart, Edinburgh, Scotland, says: "You will see the Govr with his famillie on board the *Fowey* again, I do not think his Lady will return to Williamsburg. 'Tis said he will, provided the shirt men are sent away. These shirt men or Virginia uniform are dressed with an Oznaburg shirt over their cloaths, a belt round them with a Tommyhawk or Scalping Knife. They look like a band of Assassins and it is my opinion if they fight at all it will be in that way."[5]

---

[1]"Eminent Virginians" by R. A. Brock, Secretary of the Virginia Historical Society, Hardesty's *Historical & Geographical Encyclopedia* (1884), p. 348.
[2]See George Purvis' application for a pension.
[3]William Wirt's *Life of Patrick Henry* (1833), p. 156.
[4]H. J. Eckenrode's *The Revolution in Virginia*, p. 54.
[5]*Letters from Virginia*, 1774-1781, *Magazine of History*, III, p. 159, March, 1906.

Early in 1775, the Virginia counties each appointed a Revolutionary committee, composed of twenty-one of the most discreet, prominent and experienced men, to work with a definite aim. They were elected by the freeholders of the counties annually on court-days in November and December. "The committees began their work with great energy and admirable system. Counties were divided into districts and each district was assigned to a subcommittee of the county committee."[6] Amherst County was in Buckingham District, which was composed of Albemarle, Amherst, Augusta and Buckingham counties.

The first Committee chosen for Amherst:

Colonel William Cabell, of "Union Hill," Chairman

Zacharias Taliaferro
Ambrose Rucker
Alexander Reid
Roderick McCulloch
Col. James Nevil
Daniel Gaines
David Crawford
Col. John Rose
James Dillard, Sr.
William Horsley

Hugh Rose
John Dawson
John Digges
Benjamin Rucker
Col. Joseph Cabell
Gabriel Penn
Lucas Powell
Dr. James Hopkins
David Shepherd
Francis Meriwether[7]

Each district was required to organize a battalion of minute-men who were to drill and prepare themselves for regular service.

The committee for each county in a district was to appoint three of their number as deputies to meet in one general district committee to appoint the officers to command the company to be raised in that district, as well as to regulate matters pertaining to the minute-men from the same district. Deputies chosen from Amherst were William Cabell, of "Union Hill," John Rose,[8] of "Rose Isle," and Hugh Rose,[8] of "Geddes," with Zachariah Taliaferro, Francis

---

[6]H. J. Eckenrode's *The Revolution in Virginia*, p. 98.
[7]Alexander Brown's *The Cabells and Their Kin*, p. 100.
[8]Col. John Rose (b. Oct. 8, 1735; d. 1803) married his cousin Catherine Rose, daughter of Rev. Charles Rose, of Westmoreland Co., Va. Her will was proved in Fairfax Co., Va., 1808; Col. Hugh Rose, born in King George Co., Sept. 18, 1743, died at "Geddes," Amherst Co., Va., 1795, married Sept. 8, 1767, Caroline Matilda Jordan, daughter of Col. Samuel Jordan, of "Seven Islands," Buckingham Co.; and Col. Charles Rose (1747-1802) who married Sarah Jordan, were sons of Rev. Robert Rose, born Feb. 12, 1704, son of John and Margaret (Grant) Rose, of Wester Alves, Scotland, deduced in the fifteenth generation from Hugh Rose, of Geddes, who died in 1333. Rev. Robert Rose was ordained by the Bishop of London, and came to Va. about 1725. He was rector of St. Anne's Parish, Essex Co., 1725-1747, and of St. Anne's Parish, Albemarle Co., 1747-1751. He died in Richmond, June 30, 1751, and was buried in old St. John's churchyard. (W. G. Stanard: *Rose Family Chart*).

Meriwether and Ambrose Rucker[9] as alternates. The three former were present when the representatives from Buckingham District met for the first time September 8, 1775, at the house of James Woods in Amherst. John Nicholas was chosen Chairman and Charles Rose, of "Bellevet," Clerk, and the meeting proceeded to divide the districts according to the advice of the Convention.

Charlottesville was designated as the place of rendezvous for the reception and review of the regulars to be raised in the district, with the following officers: William Fontaine, Captain; John Marks, First Lieutenant; Thomas Hughes, Second Lieutenant; William Robertson, Ensign.

Albemarle, Amherst, and Buckingham were ordered to raise two companies of minute-men each, and Augusta, four. Each company was to consist of a captain, lieutenant, ensign, and fifty men organized into a battalion, which was to be commanded by the following officers: George Matthews, of Augusta, Colonel; Charles Lewis, of Albemarle, Lieutenant-Colonel; Daniel Gaines,[10] of Amherst, Major; and Thomas Patterson, of Buckingham, Commissary. These officers in turn appointed the chaplain, adjutant, quartermaster, surgeon and sergeant-major. Commissions were issued by the Committee of Safety.[11]

Men of the greatest consequence were appointed officers and they enlisted the men from the body of the militia.[12] Each man so enlisted was furnished one hunting shirt, a pair of leggins and proper arms at public expense, and until the latter were provided they took into service their own rifles for which they were allowed twenty shillings per year. After serving twelve months, sixteen minute-men were discharged from each company, according to the date of their enlistment, by the commanding officer or captain of the company and the like number the end of every year, whose place was supplied by new enlistment.[13]

---

[9]June 4, 1781, he was in the House of Delegates, as a member of the Legislative Body in Charlottesville, which dispersed precipitately when John Jouett, "Paul Revere of the South," warned them of Col. Tarleton's approach. His life was saved by his horse, a powerful hunter, trained to jump fences which he did that June day although his rider weighed over three hundred pounds. Woods' *The Rucker Family Genealogy*, p. 69.

[10]Son of Bernard Gaines (d. Richmond Co., Va., 1747) and his wife Elizabeth, and grandson of Col. Daniel Gaines of Essex Co., Va. Col. Daniel Gaines of Amherst married Oct. 6, 1777, Mary, daughter of Henry & Mary (Wyatt) Gilbert. Col. Gaines sold his estate in Amherst and removed to Wilkes Co., Ga. prior to Feb., 1794. (Deed Book E, p. 587).

[11]Peter Force's *American Archives*, III, Ser. IV, 393.

[12]William Waller Hening's *Statutes at Large*, IX, 18.

[13]*Ibid.*, p. 23.

Officers chosen for the Minute Companies of Amherst:[14]

Nicholas Cabell,[15] Captain
John Gilmer, Lieutenant
Benjamin Taliaferro, Ensign

Gabriel Penn,[16] Captain
David Shepherd,[17] Lieutenant
James Pamplin, Ensign

In compliance with the order of the Committee the minute-men met within three miles of Rockfish Gap, in the Blue Ridge, on November 17, 1775, and the battalion continued in regular service and training under the adjutant for twenty successive days. During this time they were paid and provisioned by the public and were liable to be called into regular service at any minute—hence their name, "Minute-men." After battalion duty, the several companies of each battalion in their respective counties were mustered and continued to exercise four successive days in each month, except December, January and February. Their flag bore the motto: *"Virginia for Constitutional Liberty,"* on the one side and on the other, *"Buckingham District."*[18] Their pay per day was, captain, six shillings; lieutenant, four shillings; ensign, three shillings. Of the non-commissioned officers and privates, a sergeant was to receive two shillings per day; corporals, drummers and fifers, one shilling and eight pence; and a private, one shilling and four pence. A captain was allowed to keep two horses, for which he received one shilling and six pence per day for forage, and for himself one shilling two and a half pence for rations.

Captain Cabell's Minute-men (or shirtmen, as the British designated the Virginia riflemen, who wore their hunting shirts) were engaged at the battle of Great Bridge, December 9, 1775, where the brave British Captain Fordyce fell pierced by fourteen bullets from the rifles of the mountaineers and by his conduct so excited the admiration of the Virginians that Colonel Woodford, of the Second Virginia Regiment, had him buried with the full honors due his rank.

"The battle lasted only about twenty-five minutes, but was very severe. The number of the enemy slain is not precisely known. Thirty-one killed and wounded fell into the hands of the patriots,

---

[14]*Gilmer Papers, Collections of the Virginia Historical Society,* New Ser. VI, 112.

[15]He was an original member of the Society of the Cincinnati in the State of Virginia.

[16]Son of George and Ann Penn; born July 17, 1741; married Sept. 20, 1761, Sarah, daughter of Col. Richard & Frances (Walton) Callaway of Bedford Co.; died in Amherst Co., 1798. (Ackerly & Parker, *Our Kin,* p. 189).

[17]Alexander Brown, in *The Cabells & Their Kin,* gives his name as Heffer; the *Gilmer Papers* state it was Slipper; recent research has proved that his name was neither Heffer nor Slipper, but *Shepherd.* See MSS. *Diary & Revolutionary Memoranda* by Dr. George Gilmer, Virginia Historical Society which gives his name as Shepher[d].

[18]*American Archives,* III, Ser. IV, 757.

and many were carried away by their friends. Gordon says their whole loss was sixty-two. They fought desperately, for they preferred death to captivity, Dunmore having assured them that, if they were caught alive, the savage Virginians would scalp them. It is a remarkable fact that not a single Virginian was killed during the engagement, and only one man was slightly wounded in the hand, notwithstanding two field-pieces upon the island hurled doubleheaded shot as far as the church, and cannonaded them with grapeshot as they approached their redoubt. The wounded who fell into the hands of the Virginians were treated with the greatest tenderness, except the Tories, who were made to feel some of the rigors of war."[19]

The Convention which met May 10, 1776, resolved that two battalions of six hundred and fifty men each be sent to the assistance of North Carolina. Amherst County's quota was one company of fifty men.[20] "Captain Nicholas Cabell, not having a full company, his men were united with those of Captain Gabriel Penn, who also had an imperfect company, and the whole was placed under command of the first named officer,"[21] Lt. James Pamplin, Ensign William Spencer and Sergeants Jesse Allen, Clough Shelton and Robert Horsley and was assigned to the Second Battalion, under Colonel Charles Lewis.

When the Convention met May 29, it decreed that the march of the minute-men ordered to the assistance of North Carolina be countermanded and the Committee of Safety were instructed to give such directions respecting them as they judged would be most beneficial for the public service.

The following extracts are from Colonel William Cabell's Diary: "July 20, 1776. Paid Col. Nevil £3 10 s. for a rifle furnished by Capt. Thomas's estate to Capt. Nicholas Cabell's company of minute-men." "Paid Joseph Cabell £10 2 s. for the guns he furnished Capt. Nicholas Cabell's company with."

A warrant was issued to Capt. Nicholas Cabell by the Committee of Safety, June 27, 1776, for £18 11 s. 11½ d. for arms, hunting shirts, and provisions to his minute company. June 28, Mr. Maupin was ordered to deliver Capt. Nicholas Cabell's Minute Company 56 canteens, 9 cartridge-boxes and one drum; also 4 rifles to be replaced by four other guns.[22]

On the 22nd of June, 1776, Capt. Cabell's company received the resolution passed by the Convention June 18th: "Resolved, that the two battalions of minute men and militia lately ordered to the assistance of North Carolina be called down to supply the place of

---

[19]Benson J. Lossing's *Pictorial Field-book of the Revolution*, II, 536.
[20]*The Cabells & Their Kin*, p. 149.
[21]See William Davis's application for a pension.
[22]*Calendar of Virginia State Papers*, VIII, 225, 228.

the regular forces as may be ordered to the Southward." Next day William Pollard carried their baggage to the river and they "set off" down James River by canoes to Westham, thence by land to Jamestown,[23] and were attached to the First Battalion commanded by Colonel Samuel Meredith, of Hanover, later of "Winton," Amherst County. While here part of the company was detached under Lt. James Pamplin, as guard to ammunition sent to Halifax, N. C.; after delivering it they returned to Jamestown. Shortly afterwards the regiment went to Richmond on board a schooner, where they were discharged Sept. 12, 1776.

A few weeks after Capt. Cabell's company returned home they were called out on the Indian Campaign; marched to Lynch's Ferry where they were discharged after twenty days service owing to a "great indisposition of the company."

"Oct. 2, 1776, Capt. Cabell delivered to Capt. Samuel Higginbotham for Capt. Sale, on Major James Franklin's order, seven pots and one kettle, six rugs, one tent, twenty-two rifles, and eight shot guns which his company of minute-men had when in the service."[24]

At this time a land bounty warrant of one hundred acres was promised to every Virginian enlisted on Continental Establishment, without limitation of service,[25] which so reduced the minute-men that at the next call, Capt. Samuel Higginbotham's company of militia was counted as minute-men and, under Col. Joseph Cabell, marched to Richmond where Capt. Higginbotham commanded the artillery. His lieutenant was James Ware and his ensign Joseph Staples. John, Josiah and William Giles (brothers), John, Peter and Howard Cash (brothers), and Dick McCary were among the privates in his company.

In October the House of Delegates ordered the Minute Companies dissolved, but their services were not dispensed with until the spring, when six regiments of regulars were raised to take their place.[26]

The minute-men were enrolled with the militia under the act passed by the General Assembly, May 5, 1777, viz.: "An act for regulating and disciplining the Militia," which required all free male persons, hired servants, and apprentices, between the ages of sixteen and fifty years "(except the Governour and members of the council of state, Congressmen, Judges of the Superior Courts, speakers of the two houses, treasurer, attorney general, commission-

[23]*The Cabells & Their Kin*, p. 149.
[24]Alexander Brown, in *The Cabells & Their Kin*, published in 1896, mentions the pay rolls of Captain Nicholas Cabell's Company of Minute-men as being then extant, presumably among the Cabell papers to which he had access when writing the book.
[25]Hening's *Statutes*, IX, 179.
[26]*Correspondence of Colonel Leven Powell*, p. 22.

ers of the navy, auditors, clerks of the council of state, of the treasury, and the navy board, ministers of the gospel who had taken the oath, postmasters, keepers of the publick jail and publick hospital, millers, except in Accomack and Northampton, persons concerned in iron or lead works, or persons solely employed in manufacturing fire arms, and military officers and soldiers) be formed into companies of not less than thirty-two nor more than sixty-eight, rank and file, and these companies shall again be formed into battalions of not more than one thousand, nor less than five hundred men, if there be that many in the county. Each company shall be commanded by a captain, two lieutenants, and an ensign; each battalion by a colonel, lieutenant colonel, and major, and the whole by a county lieutenant."[27]

This act does not seem to have become effective until August, when almost every free man over sixteen and under fifty years in Amherst took the oath of allegiance and was enrolled in the militia. They were separated into ten divisions and each man was given a number. When his number was called he served a three-months tour of duty or furnished a substitute.

Colonel William Cabell, Chairman of the Amherst County Committee, was the only member of the Committee of Safety chosen from the Piedmont Counties. It may be that the people of Amherst, since they were represented on the Committee of Safety for the Colony of Virginia by one of their most prominent citizens, felt duty-bound to aid the patriot cause to the uttermost by furnishing men and supplies to the cause of American Independence.

The eminent Virginian historian, Alexander Brown, in *The Cabells & Their Kin*, says, "The Militia of Amherst, from January, 1776, to January, 1781, numbered about 1200 men. Of these, about 350 had entered the Continental service, and about 200 of the remainder had seen actual service as Militia in the State service. But between January 4th and October 19th, 1781, probably every able man remaining in the County was employed in one way or another in the defense of the State. Old Amherst sent her men North and South, East and West. The soldiers from Amherst fought on all the important battlefields of the Revolutionary War: Great Bridge, Trenton, Princeton, Saratoga, Monmouth, Camden, Guilford Court House and Charleston." To these can be added Germantown, King's Mountain, Cowpens, Eutaw Springs and Savannah. They were with "Morgan's Riflemen" in 1775, when they joined General Washington, "then at Boston, and while riding along his lines, Washington saw them approaching. At the sight he stopped, the riflemen drew nearer, and their commander, stepping in front, made the military salute, exclaiming, 'General, from the right bank of the Potomac!' The effect of these words was remarkable. Washing-

[27]Hening's *Statutes*, IX, 267, 268.

ton dismounted, came to meet the battalion, and going down the line with both arms extended, shook hands with the riflemen one by one, tears rolling down his cheeks as he did so. He then mounted, saluted, and silently rode on."[28] In 1776 a volunteer company from Amherst marched to Charleston, South Carolina, and were under command of General Lee until the British withdrew from before that City in June, 1776.* A company of the gallant troops that followed General Wayne at Stony Point and Major Lee at Paulus Hook were nearly all from Amherst County. The soldiers from Amherst marched with General George Rogers Clark in the middle of the winter, through the "drowned lands" of the Wabash river, with water frequently up to their necks, to capture Vincennes, and they defended the Western frontier against depredations of the Indians.

---

[28]John Esten Cooke's *Virginia in the Revolution*, in *Harper's Magazine*. LIII, 14, June, 1876.

*See Thomas Bibee's application for a pension.

WASHINGTON AT VALLEY FORGE
As seen and described by Isaac Potts March, 1778. "General Washington's horse was tied to a sapling in a thicket. The General was on his knees praying fervently." From the bronze by J. E. Kelly, on the Sub-Treasury, Wall Street, New York.

The First Rifle Company

In January, 1776, the Convention of Virginia for the better protection of the Colony passed an ordinance for raising an additional number of forces, under which Amherst was required to furnish one company of expert riflemen, to act as light infantry, consisting of one captain, two lieutenants, one ensign and seventy-four non-commissioned officers and privates, to be ready for marching orders by the 25th of March, 1776. Colonel William Cabell, of "Union Hill," then serving on the Committee of Safety in Williamsburg, sent at once for his eldest son, Samuel Jordan Cabell, a student at William and Mary College, for assistance in recruiting the required company, which was duly completed, and on March 4th, the officers who had been selected by the county committee February 5th were commissioned and the company received into service by Colonel John Rose, of "Rose Isle," and Lucas Powell, of the Amherst County Committee.[29]

Samuel Jordan Cabell was commissioned captain, Alexander Rose[30] first lieutenant, Benjamin Taliaferro[31] second lieutenant, and James Barnett ensign; Matthew Snooks* and James Weeks, fifer and drummer; James Dillard, Jr., Samuel Ayres,[32] Ralph Jopling and William Coffee, sergeants; and John Jordan[33] cadet.

The company rendezvoused at old Key's Church, later known as Fairmount Church, in the present county of Nelson, and marched to Williamsburg, arriving March 24, 1776, after a march of twelve days. They were assigned to the Sixth Virginia Regiment, General

---

[29]Hening's *Statutes*, IX, 82; Brown's *The Cabells and Their Kin*, p. 177.

[30]Son of Col. John Rose, of "Rose Isle," Amherst Co.; promoted Captain, Sept. 17, 1776; retired with the rank of Major, Sept. 14, 1778.

[31]Son of Capt. Zachariah Taliaferro; married, April 8, 1782, Martha, daughter of David and Mary (Harvie) Meriwether, of Amherst Co.; removed to Wilkes Co., Ga., 1784, where he became a leading citizen. He died Sept. 3, 1821, leaving many descendants. Saunders' *Early Settlers of Alabama*, p. 250.

*Matthew Snooks was an indentured servant of Gabriel Penn, from whom he was purchased jointly by the commissioned officers of the company at £20. Hardesty's *Historical & Geographical Encyclopedia*, p. 408.

[32]Son of Thomas Ayres of Essex Co.; married in Amherst Co., Nov. 9, 1772, Rachel Morrison, widow of William Morrison, who died in Albemarle Co., 1761, and daughter of John and Frances (Riley) Higginbotham.

[33]Son of Matthew Jordan, will proved in Albemarle Co., Nov., 1769, and nephew of Col. Samuel Jordan, of "Seven Islands," Buckingham Co., and grandson of Col. Charles Fleming, of New Kent County.

Andrew Lewis's Brigade, on Continental Establishment, and officered as follows:

    Mordecai Buckner, Colonel
    James Hendricks, Major
    James Dillard, Jr., Sergt. Major; promoted from Capt. Cabell's Co.*
    Robert Rose,[34] Surgeon
    John Hawkins, Sutler
    Thomas Elliott, Lieut.-Colonel
    Simon Summers, Adjutant
    Rev. William Dunlap, Chaplain
    William Croker, Drum-Major
    Matthew Snooks, Fife-Major; promoted March 27, from Capt. Cabell's Co.*

Captain Cabell's riflemen were expert marksmen, many exceeding six feet in height and powerful in person, who from that period of boyhood when they could carry a rifle had been accustomed to make the wild turkey's head the mark for their bullets; and so steady was their aim and so sure their sight that a conservative historian of our day speaks of them as a "sturdy band of sharpshooters each man of whom, it was said, while marching at double-quick, could cleave with his rifle-ball a squirrel at a distance of three hundred yards."[35]

Each one of Cabell's men, "in addition to the rifle which he carried, was armed with a tomahawk and a long knife. He rammed his rifle-ball, moulded with his own hands, wrapped in its buckskin jacket, home to its powder with a long ramrod of native wood; and his flints were found among the hills and valleys of Virginia."[36]

The uniform of the officers consisted of a shirt ruffled at the hand, buckskin breeches, fastened at the knee with silver buckles, white broadcloth vest and blue broadcloth coat, over which they wore a tow linen or homespun hunting shirt, short and fringed, with the usual crimson sash over this and round their waist. From their belt hung their sword, tomahawk and shot pouch; sergeants were clothed in flannel shirts, buckskin breeches, over which they wore a hunting shirt trimmed in red, short and *plain,* with a small *white* cuff; drummers and fifers, similar with *dark* cuffs, and privates, *without* cuffs, fastened at the waist with a leather belt, from which hung a long knife, tomahawk and bullet-pouch. From his shoulder was suspended his powder horn. Officers, non-commissioned officers and privates alike wore buckskin leggins and moccasins and felt hats cut round, bound with black and brims two inches deep, cocked on one side, with a button, loop and cockade worn on the left. They were required to wear their hair short and as near alike as possible.

---

    *The Orderly Book of that Portion of the American Army stationed at or Near Williamsburg, Virginia Under the Command of Gen. Andrew Lewis from March 18th, 1776 to August 28th, 1776, pp. 7, 42.
    [34]Died Nov., 1793; son of Rev. Charles Rose, of Westmoreland Co.
    [35]John Fiske's *The American Revolution*, Vol. 1, 156.
    [36]Armistead C. Gordon's *Men and Events*, p. 10.

After the regiment was armed and equipped, they marched to Springfield in the vicinity of Williamsburg, where they entered camp and military training. While here they were engaged in several skirmishes with the Loyalists under Lord Dunmore, who had intrenched himself at Gwynn's Island and continued to ravage the banks of the rivers. On July 9, 1776, under General Lewis they shared in dislodging him from his stronghold. "The British not fancying a too close contact with the frontier riflemen, exclaimed as they came in sight, 'the shirt-men are coming!' when they, panic-stricken, precipitately evacuated the Island."[37]

For a month they guarded the coast to prevent Lord Dunmore's return, then marched to Williamsburg and encamped on the College grounds. They were ordered to Cross Creek, North Carolina, and marched to Jamestown where the orders were countermanded, as Washington was calling urgently to his native State for reinforcement in New York.

In the latter part of September, the Sixth Virginia Regiment, of which Mordecai Buckner,[38] of Essex county, was Colonel and James Hendricks[39] Lieutenant-Colonel (succeeding Lieutenant-Colonel Elliott, who was promoted Colonel of the Fourth Virginia Regiment, September 3, 1776), General Adam Stephen's Brigade, marched from Deep Spring Camp to the North. At Elizabethtown, New Jersey, they met Generals Washington and Putnam, who were retreating before the British. They joined in the retreat until finally the tired band of patriots put the Delaware River between themselves and the enemy. On Christmas Eve they recrossed the Delaware with Washington in command, and surprised the Hessians at Trenton.

"Colonel George Johnston, aide to Washington, tells us how Stephen's Virginians, consisting of the 4th, 5th and 6th Virginia Regiments, under General Greene, pursued the fleeing Hessians and surrounded them, causing the surrender of two of their regiments. The third, unable to escape, surrendered to General Sullivan's New England men."[40]

"A splendid flag, taken from the Hessians at Trenton, composed of two pieces of heavy white damask silk, bearing devices embroidered with gold thread, and the words For Our Prince and Country, in Latin, exquisitely wrought in needlework, was presented to Washington."[41]

---

[37]Draper's *King's Mountain and Its Heroes*, p. 382.

[38]Served as Capt. in Col. Adam Stephen's Regt. in the French and Indian War.

[39]Promoted August 13, 1776.

[40]Dr. Lyon G. Tyler, *The Richmond News Leader*, Richmond, Va., Aug. 7, 1931.

[41]Lossing's *The Home of Washington*, p. 102.

At the battle of Princeton, Benjamin Taliaferro, who had been promoted captain, captured, with his company, a British officer with his command; but when that officer approached, in his splendid regimentals, to surrender his sword, Captain Taliaferro being barefooted was too proud to meet him, and sent his lieutenant forward to receive it.[42]

Captain Cabell's company was one of the eight rifle companies personally selected by Colonel Daniel Morgan from the main army which formed the "500 picked riflemen"[43] sent by Washington to join General Gates at Stillwater, by whom they were ordered "to begin the game" at Saratoga and were at the surrender of Burgoyne. "It is said that when Burgoyne was introduced to Morgan, after the surrender at Saratoga, he seized him by the hand and exclaimed, 'My dear sir, you command the finest regiment in the world!' "[44]

After the return of Morgan's Regiment of Riflemen, and its junction with the main army, commanded by the illustrious Washington, a sharp conflict ensued between Morgan's Regiment of Riflemen and the First Battalion of light-infantry and the Thirty-third Regiment, commanded by Lord Cornwallis. Lieutenant Jordan, fighting in the most heroic manner, was severely wounded in the knee, and was saved from the general butchery by Captain John Nicholas and his lieutenant, Meriwether. They hoisted him on Captain Dandridge's horse, that carried him from the scene of defeat. "Four officers and thirty men fell before the unerring rifles of Morgan's corps, before they could be dislodged from their position, when they were compelled to retire before superior numbers."[45]

General Washington in his dispatch to Congress writes: "We lost twenty-seven men in Morgan's Corps, killed and wounded, besides Major Morris, a brave and gallant officer, who is among the latter."

They were with Washington at Valley Forge the never-to-be-forgotten winter of 1777-1778, during which time they were in several skirmishes. Lafayette was with them in one of the skirmishes near Philadelphia. "I never saw," said he, "men so merry, so spirited, and so desirous to go on the enemy, whatever force they might have."[46]

It was Morgan's Riflemen who retarded the progress of the British Army through the Jerseys and enabled General Washington to march his main army by Englishtown and obtain a position which gave him the power to bring General Clinton to a general engagement at Monmouth Courthouse, in which, it is believed, he would have been entirely successful had it not been for the flagrant

---
[42]Saunders' *Early Settlers of Alabama*, p. 250.
[43]Brown's *The Cabells and Their Kin*, p. 182.
[44]Appletons' *Cyclopaedia of American Biography*, IV, 396.
[45]Dawson's *Battles of the United States*, 1, 370.
[46]Gordon's *Men and Events*, p. 11.

disobedience of orders by General Charles Lee, who commanded the van of the American army.

Major Thomas Massie, aide to Colonel Morgan, in his application for a pension, says, "On that the 28th day of June, 1778 (an intense hot day), Gen. Washington ordered Gen. Lee to attack in full force. This the said Massie knows to be a fact, the orders having been communicated verbally by Gen. Washington through him the evening before. On Gen. Lee's approach the British Army drew up in order of battle. Gen. Lee ordered a retreat, which was done under slow, retreating fire for some time. Gen. Lee repeatedly sent orders to the officers commanding the several flanking corps not to advance and engage. This state of things continued until Gen. Washington came into the field himself, took command, arrested Gen. Lee, and retrieved the battle by bringing the troops into action. After the sun set the British Army gave way, and it being too dark for pursuit, the American Army lay on the field for the night with a view to renew the battle the next day; but the British Army in the night made a silent and rapid retreat leaving their dead and wounded. Col. Morgan, under whose command he, the said Massie, still acted, was ordered to pursue the British early next morning, but they could not be overtaken except two or three hundred stragglers that were captured. Pursuit was continued to Middleton Heights, immediately above Sandy Hook. After being there and thereabout for several days, the troops marched up by Spotswood to Brunswick bridge on the Raritan River. Here we had a *feu de joie* in honor of the victory at Monmouth. . . . The British embarkation of troops to our Southern States and other occurrences demonstrated their intention of moving the main seat of war there with a view to attempt the subjugation of those States, Congress determined to defend and save Charleston if possible and the ten old Virginia regiments were doomed to that service. Those ten regiments were then so much reduced in number that they were consolidated into eight regiments, March, 1780."[47]

Captain Cabell was promoted Major when only twenty-one years of age, for his gallant conduct at Saratoga, and in the winter of 1778 he was Brigade Inspector at Valley Forge.[48] He attained the rank of Lieutenant-Colonel and with his riflemen was with the Virginia troops under General Woodford who entered Charleston, South Carolina, on April 7, 1780, after a forced march of five hundred miles in twenty-eight days. He was taken prisoner at the

---

[47]Son of William Massie and grandson of Captain Thomas Massie, of St. Peter's Parish, New Kent County, who died about 1740; was born in New Kent County, August 22, 1747; educated at William and Mary College; recruited his company in New Kent County. He married Sarah, daughter of Bowler Cocke, of "Turkey Island;" died at "Levell Green," Nelson County, February 2, 1834. He was an original member of the Society of the Cincinnati in the State of Virginia.

[48]*Orderly Book of General Weedon*, p. 275.

fall of Charleston, May 12, 1780, and retained at Haddrell's Point; returned home on parole August 21, 1781; Brevet Colonel September 30, 1783; County Lieutenant, 1784. He was an original member of the Society of the Cincinnati in the State of Virginia. He died August 4, 1818, at "Soldier's Joy," Nelson County, and is buried there beside his wife (daughter of Col. John Syme) who died May 15, 1814.

Benjamin Taliaferro attained the rank of captain and was under Washington's command during the severe campaign of the Jerseys. Late in the war he served with that dashing partisan officer, Colonel Henry Lee, in many of his most successful exploits. He was one of the eighty-four captains taken prisoner at Charleston. He was permitted to return home on parole, and on September 30, 1783, he was made a Major by brevet.

John Jordan, who was promoted first lieutenant for his bravery at Chestnut Hill, where he was wounded, remained ill for months from the effects of the wound, recovering in time to participate in the Siege of Charleston, where he was taken prisoner. Soon after being exchanged he joined General Wayne in Georgia, where he was commissioned Captain and continued in service until discharged at Savannah, Georgia, June 23, 1782. After the close of the Revolution he attained the rank of Colonel and was elected to the office of Sergeant-at-Arms in the House of Delegates, which office he filled for many years.

"In the history of the war for American independence," says Gordon, in *Men and Events*, "no soldiers displayed more skill, more courage, more power of endurance or more patriotic loyalty to the American cause than did the Rifle Rangers of the Virginia Valley under Morgan."

A Muster Roll of Captain Samuel Jordan Cabells Comp^y of 6th Virginia Regiment of Foot in the United States of America Under the Command of Lieutenant Col^o James Hendricks for the Months of May and June 1777.

Samuel Jordan Cabell Captain Appointed 5th Feby 1776
Benjamin Taliaferro 1st Lt   On Command
John Jordan 2nd Lt Appointed 4th June
Commissioned

No	Sergeants	Appointed	Remarks
1	Ralph Jopling	20th Feby	Died 28th Jany 77
2	Samuel Ayres	19th Do	
3	Thomas Burfoot	9th Feby	
4	William Coffee	13th Do	Discharged 11th October
5	Edward Cox	28th Octo	

	Corporals		
1	Thomas Dickerson	4th March	
2	John Josling	28th October	
3	George Creasey	1st May	

Lancaster's Virginia Homes and Churches

SOLDIER'S JOY
Home of Col. Samuel Jordan Cabell, built in 1785

Amherst County, Virginia, in the Revolution 15

    Drums & Fifes
1 Matthew Snooks   14th Mch   Taken Prisoner Trenton
2 James Weeks   4th Mch   Left Capt Roses Compy 6th Virga
3 Ozborn Coffee   14th Mch   Reduced to the Ranks 1st June 1777
    Sick Mendem [Mendham]

1 John Carpenter   17th Feby
2 William Johns   4th Mch
3 Thomas Johns   4th Do
4 William Montgomery   7th Feby
5 John Bell   15th Do
6 William Johnson   } Supplied the Place of John
7 Benjamin Galloway   } West and Francis West
8 John Fitz Gerrell   9th Feby
9 Samuel Bell   26th Do
10 Joseph Welch   5th Do
11 Daniel Ramsey   4th Mch
12 Daniel Tyler   4th Do
13 Austin Smith   14th May   Sick Mendem [Mendham]
14 Reuben Seayres   5th Feby
15 Thomas Laine   8th Do
16 Stark Brown   4th Mch
17 Joshua Tuggle   4th Do
18 George Key   4th Do
19 Joseph Newman   4th Do
20 John Layne   17th Feby
21 William Hensley   11th October
22 William Burford   13th Augt   Sick Mendem [Mendham]
23 Thomas Gregory   24th Feby
24 Josiah Cheatham   24th Do
25 Bennoni Goldsmith   26th Do
26 John Welch   Supplied the Place of Daniel Damron

27 Thomas Smith   4th March
28 John Shenault   4th Do
29 William Brooks   9th Feby
30 Thomas McClain   7th Do   Left Sick Jerseys
31 Nathan Tate   5th Do   Left Sick Pensylvania
32 William Wray   6th Jany   Sick Mendem [Mendham]
33 William Higginbotham   6th Do
34 Samson Welch   6th Do
35 John Master   6th Do
36 Charles Eads   6th Do
37 Daniel Conner   17th Do
38 John Temples   17th Do   Sick Mendom [Mendham]
39 Joseph Staples   17th Do
40 John Phillips   28th Feby   Died July
41 John Tyree   28th Do
42 George Phillips   9th Mch   Sick Black River
43 George Campbell   28th Feby   Sick Mendom [Mendham]
44 John Murray   3rd March   Sick Mendom [Mendham]
45 Thomas Alfred   10th Do   Died 20th July
46 Thomas Becknal   20th Feby
47 John Phillips Jnr   10th Mch
48 Robert Hudson   9th Do
49 Joel Ramsey   9th Feby
50 John Davenport   13th Do
51 James Becknal   24th Feby   Died July
52 William Smith   4th Mch   Discharged 6th June 76

53 Josiah Jones*	14th May	Deserted 16th September
54 David Barnett*	14th Do	Deserted 16th Do
55 Joseph Canterbury*	9th Feby	Deserted 16th Do
56 Joseph Canterbury Jnr	10 Augt	Deserted 23rd March 77
57 Joseph Nail	18 Feby	Deserted from Willmington Hospital Pensl
58 Augustine Smith	4th Mch	Left sick Virginia
59 David Duncan Corpl	17th Feby	Died Jany 20th
60 John Dickerson	5th Do	Died 9th Jany
61 Samuel Staples		Supplied the Place of Thomas Smith Died 1st Feby
62 Benjamin Clark	5th Do	Died 9th Jany
63 Josephus Bailey	16th Do	Died 1st Feby
64 William Whorley	14th Mch	Died 20th Jany
65 Ptolemy Handsbrough	5th Feby	Died 28th Jany
66 Littlebury Coleman		Supplied the Place of William Higginbotham Died 28th Nov
67 John Welch	5th Feby	Died 1st March
68 Robert Pollard	4th Mch	Died 24th Jany
69 Benjamin Wright	5th Feby	Died Time Uncertain
70 Edmond Deavenport	24th Feby	Died 1st March
71 Absolem Stratton	4th Mch	Died 6th Feby
72 Achilles Deavenport	24th Feby	Dead
73 Samuel Gowing	4th Mch	Died 1st Feby
74 Robert Miller	5th Feby	Died 1st Do
75 George Munroe	9th Do	Died 10th April 77
76 Thomas Moody	12th Do	Died 16th Sept
77 Reuben Nevill	4th Mch	Died 10th April
78 Samuel McDowel	24th Feby	Died 1st Jany
79 John Tate		Supplied the Place of Dudley Wade Dead

Deep-Spring Camp, September 17, 1776

*Deserted last night from my company of Riflemen, the following soldiers: *Josiah Jones*, about twenty-two years old, six feet two inches high, well made, has short black hair, a very lively countenance, and when intoxicated very talkative and desirous of raising disputes; he carried away with him a hunting-shirt trimmed with red, a pair of leather breeches, several new shirts, and other things which I cannot recollect at present. *David Barnett*, aged twenty-one years, six feet four inches high, well made, has short black hair, a thin visage (occasioned by the ague and fever, which he had when he deserted,) is very serious, and speaks but seldom; he carried with him a hunting-shirt trimmed with red, a pair of leather breeches, a pair of new shoes, and several yards of linen, which I had delivered to him about two days before he deserted. *Joseph Canterbury*, aged twenty-eight years, five feet ten inches high, well made, has short red hair, reddish complexion, and a dejected look; he carried along with him a hunting-shirt trimmed with red, a gray-coloured broadcloth waistcoat and breeches, a pair of black stockings, two pair of shoes, and several yards of linen, which I had delivered to him a few days before he deserted. They went off indebted to the public store, and were raised and enlisted in *Amherst*, where I expect they will endeavour to get. Whosoever will deliver the said deserters to the commanding officer in *Williamsburg*, or safely contrive them to the Sixth *Virginia* Regiment at *New-York*, shall have £4 10s. for each, and all reasonable expenses paid.

Samuel Jordan Cabell,
Captain in the Sixth Virginia Regiment.

Force: *American Archives*, Vol. 2, Series 5, p. 362.

Amherst County, Virginia, in the Revolution

80 William Gillinwaters	26th Sept	Died 1st Feby	
81 David Bowles	26th Do	Died 1st Do	
82 James Vaughan	24 Feby	Died 7th Dec	
83 Bassalius Lovday	9th Do	Died 28th October	
84 Walter Lockert	4th March	Died Time Uncertain	
85 Reuben Griffin	5th Feby	Dead	
86 Moses London	5th Do	Died 28th Feby 77	
87 John Deaver	5th Do	Died 8th Sept 76	
88 William Steel	4th Mch	Died 8 November	
89 Mitchel Fland	4th Do	Discharged 5th October	
90 James Dillard	26th Feby	Prefered 17th Novr to 2nd Lt	
91 Jesse Cartwright	26th Feby	Inlisted in the Train of Artillery April 16th 76	
92 John Taylor	26th Do	Inlisted in the Marine service 6th May 76	

Augt 4th 1777 then Mustered Capt Cables Compy as specified in above Roll

A Dickey D. M. M.

A Pay Roll of Captain Samuel Jordan Cabells Compy of sixth Virginia Battalion of Continental Forces commanded by Lieutenant Colo James Hendricks for the Month of July 1777.

Names	Rank	Pay	Mo	Days	Dollars	Amount of Pay		
Samuel Jordan Cabell	Capt	1	July	1	40	15		
Benjamin Taliaferro	1st Lieut	ditto	Do		27	10	2	6
John Stokes	1st Do	ditto	Do		27	10	2	6
John Jordan	2nd Do	ditto	Do		27	10	2	6
Phillip Hockaday	2nd Do	ditto	Do		27	10	2	6
Samuel Ayres	Serjt	1	Do	1 Do	8	3		
Thomas Burfoot	Do	1	Do	1 Do	8	3		
Edward Cox	Do	1	Do	1 Do	8	3		
John Thomas	Do	1	Do	1 Do	8	3		
Littlebury Patteson	Do	28	Octr	3 Do	8	9		
Daniel Low	Do	1st	July	1 Do	8	3		
James Wash	Drumr	1	Do	1 Do	7 1/3	2	15	
John Gilliam	Do	1	Do	1 Do	7 1/3	2	15	
Thomas Dickerson	Corpl	1	Do	1 Do	7 1/3	2	15	
John Josling	Do	1	Do	1 Do	7 1/3	2	15	
George Creasey	Do	1	Do	1 Do	7 1/3	2	15	
James Hill	Do	1	Do	1 Do	7 1/3	2	15	
Joel Jones	Do	1	Do	1 Do	7 1/3	2	15	
John Carpenter	Private	1	Do	1 Do	6 2/3	2	10	
Thomas Johns	Do	1	Do	1 Do	6 2/3	2	10	
William Johns	Do	1	Do	1 Do	6 2/3	2	10	
William Montgomery	Do	1	Do	1 Do	6 2/3	2	10	
John Bell	Do	1	Do	1 Do	6 2/3	2	10	
William Johnson	Do	1	Do	1 Do	6 2/3	2	10	
Benjamin Golloway	Do	1	Do	1 Do	6 2/3	2	10	
John Fitz Gerrald	Do	1	Do	1 Do	6 2/3	2	10	
Samuel Bell	Do	1	Do	1 Do	6 2/3	2	10	
Joseph Welch	Do	1	Do	1 Do	6 2/3	2	10	
Daniel Ramsey	Do	1	Do	1 Do	6 2/3	2	10	
Daniel Tyler	Do	1	Do	1 Do	6 2/3	2	10	
Austin Smith	Do	1	Do	1 Do	6 2/3	2	10	
Reuben Seayres	Do	1	Do	1 Do	6 2/3	2	10	
Thomas Layne	Do	1	Do	1 Do	6 2/3	2	10	

Stark Brown	Do	1	Do	1 Do	6⅔	2 10
Joshua Tuggle	Do	1	Do	1 Do	6⅔	2 10
George Key	Do	1	Do	1 Do	6⅔	2 10
Joseph Newman	Do	1	Do	1 Do	6⅔	2 10
John Layne	Do	1	Do	1 Do	6⅔	2 10
William Hensley	Do	1	Do	1 Do	6⅔	2 10
William Burford	Do	1	Do	1 Do	6⅔	2 10
Thomas Gregory	Do	1	Do	1 Do	6⅔	2 10
Josiah Cheatham	Do	1	Do	1 Do	6⅔	2 10
Benoni Goldsmith	Do	1	Do	1 Do	6⅔	2 10
John Welch	Do	1	Do	1 Do	6⅔	2 10
Thomas Smith	Do	1	Do	1 Do	6⅔	2 10
John Shennault	Do	1	Do	1 Do	6⅔	2 10
William Brooks	Do	1	Do	1 Do	6⅔	2 10
Thomas McClain	Do	1	Do	1 Do	6⅔	2 10
Nathan Tate	Do	1	Do	1 Do	6⅔	2 10
William Wray	Do	1	Do	1 Do	6⅔	2 10
William Higginbotham	Do	1	Do	1 Do	6⅔	2 10
Samson Welch	Do	1	Do	1 Do	6⅔	2 10
John Master	Do	1	Do	1 Do	6⅔	2 10
Charles Edes	Do	1	Do	1 Do	6⅔	2 10
Daniel Conner	Do	1	Do	1 Do	6⅔	2 10
John Temple	Do	1	Do	1 Do	6⅔	2 10
Ozborn Coffey	Do	1	Do	1 Do	6⅔	2 10
Joseph Staples	Do	1	Do	1 Do	6⅔	2 10
John Phillips	Do	1	Do	1 Do	6⅔	2 10
John Tyree	Do	1	Do	1 Do	6⅔	2 10
George Phillips	Do	1	Do	1 Do	6⅔	2 10
George Campbell	Do	1	Do	1 Do	6⅔	2 10
John Murray	Do	1	Do	1 Do	6⅔	2 10
Thomas Becknal	Do	1	Do	1 Do	6⅔	2 10
Robert Hudson	Do	1	Do	1 Do	6⅔	2 10
Joel Ramsey	Do	1	Do	1 Do	6⅔	2 10
John Davenport	Do	1	Do	1 Do	6⅔	2 10
Benjamin Bristow	Do	1	Do	1 Do	6⅔	2 10
Archer Gilliam	Do	1	Do	1 Do	6⅔	2 10
James Brown	Do	1	Do	1 Do	6⅔	2 10
Joseph Green	Do	1	Do	1 Do	6⅔	2 10
Ebenezer Mann	Do	1	Do	1 Do	6⅔	2 10
Edward Patteson	Do	1	Do	1 Do	6⅔	2 10
John McCormmack	Do	1	Do	1 Do	6⅔	2 10
Archer Briant	Do	1	Do	1 Do	6⅔	2 10
George Blakey	Do	1	Do	1 Do	6⅔	2 10
John Williams	Do	1	Do	1 Do	6⅔	2 10
Jesse Low	Do	1	Do	1 Do	6⅔	2 10
John Stevens	Do	1	Do	1 Do	6⅔	2 10
John Adcock	Do	1	Do	1 Do	6⅔	2 10
James Wheeler	Do	1	Do	1 Do	6⅔	2 10
Richard Johnson	Do	1	Do	1 Do	6⅔	2 10
George Coats	Do	1	Do	1 Do	6⅔	2 10
John Lipford	Do	1	Do	1 Do	6⅔	2 10
George Damron	Do	1	Do	1 Do	6⅔	2 10
Gidion Crews	Do	1	Do	1 Do	6⅔	2 10
Austin Godsey	Do	1	Do	1 Do	6⅔	2 10
Robert Mann	Do	1	Do	1 Do	6⅔	2 10
William Blakey	Do	1	Do	1 Do	6⅔	2 10
William Godsey	Do	1	Do	1 Do	6⅔	2 10
James Crews	Do	1	Do	1 Do	6⅔	2 10
John Wheeler	Do	1	Do	1 Do	6⅔	2 10

Amherst County, Virginia, in the Revolution 19

William Moore	Do	1	Do	1 Do	6⅔	2 10	
David Gollihorn	Do	1	Do	1 Do	6⅔	2 10	
Thomas Alfred	Do	1	Do	1 Do	6⅔	2 10	Died 20th July as mentioned in last Muster Roll

Incorporated with my Compy the Compy formerly Commanded by Capt Patteson which consists of 2 Lieuts 3 Serjts I Drummer 2 Corpls and 27 Rk & file July 6th 1777

Saml Jordan Cabell Capt
6th Virga Regt

Pay Roll of Capt Samuel Jordan Cabell's Company of the Rifle Detachment Commanded by Colo Daniel Morgan for Three Months from the 1st of August to the 1st of November 1777.

Names	Rank	Commencent of Pay	Dollars per Month	Whole Pay in Dollars	Whole Pay in Virginia Currency £ S. D.	
Samuel Jordan Cabell	Capt		40	120	36	
Benjamin Taliaferro	1st Lieut		27	81	24 6	
John Stokes	1st Lieut		27	81	24 6	
John Jordan	2 Lieut		27	81	24 6	
Phillip Hockaday	2 Lieut		27	36	10 16	Killed at the Battle of Brandywine 11th of September
Robert Watkins	Ensign		20	60	18	Detached from the 4th Va
Samuel Ayres	Sergt		8	24	7 4	
Thomas Burfoot	ditto		8	24	7 4	
Edward Cox	Do		8	24	7 4	
John Thomas	Do		8	24	7 4	
Littlebury Patteson	Do		8	24	7 4	
Daniel Low	Do		8	24	7 4	
James Weekes	Drum.		7⅓	22	6 12	
Thomas Dickerson	Corpl		7⅓	22	6 12	
John Josling	Do		7⅓	22	6 12	
George Creasey	Do		7⅓	22	6 12	
James Hill	Do		7⅓	22	6 12	
Joel Jones	Do		7⅓	22	6 12	
John Carpenter	Private		6⅔	20	6	
William Johns	Do		6⅔	20	6	
Thomas Johns	Do		6⅔	20	6	
William Montgomery	Do		6⅔	20	6	
William Johnson	Do		6⅔	10⅔	3 4	{ Killed 19th of Sept. October 21 1777
Samuel Bell	Do		6⅔	20	6	
Benjamin Golloway	Do		6⅔	20	6	
Joseph Welch	Do		6⅔	20	6	

Name						
Reuben Seayres	Do	6⅔	20	6		
Josiah Cheatham	Do	6⅔	20	6		
Thomas Gregory	Do	6⅔	20	6		
Daniel Tyler	Do	6⅔	20	6		
John Shenault	Do	6⅔	20	6		
Thomas Smith	Do	6⅔	20	6		
William Brooks	Do	6⅔	20	6		
John Welch	Do	6⅔	20	6		
Austen Smith	Do	6⅔	20	6		
William Anflay	Do	6⅔	20	6		
John Bell	Do	6⅔	17½	5	6	8 Died at the Hospital Albany October 21st 1777
William Burfoot	Do	6⅔	20	6		
Ozborn Coffey	Do	6⅔	20			
George Key	Do	6⅔	20			
Benoni Godsey	Do	6⅔	20			
John Layne	Do	6⅔	20			
Thomas Layne	Do	6⅔	20			
Stark Brown	Do	6⅔	20			
Joshua Tuggle	Do	6⅔	20			
Joseph Newman	Do	6⅔	20			
John Fitsgerrald	Do	6⅔	20			
(illegible)	Do	6⅔	20			
William Wray	Do	6⅔	20	6		
William Higginbotham	Do	6⅔	20	6		
Samson Welch	Do	6⅔	20	6		
John Masters	Do	6⅔	20	6		
Charles Edes	Do	6⅔	20	6		
Daniel Connor	Do	6⅔	20	6		
John Temples	Do	6⅔	20	6		
Joseph Staples	Do	6⅔	20	6		
John Deavenport	Do	6⅔	20	6		
George Phillips	Do	6⅔	20	6		
George Campbell	Do	6⅔	20	6		
Thomas Becknel	Do	6⅔	16⅔	5	0	0 Died at the Hospital Albany 16th October
Robert Hudson	Do	6⅔	20			
John Phillips	Do	6⅔	20			
Joel Ramsey	Do	6⅔	20			
John Murray	Do	6⅔	20			
Thomas McClain	Do	6⅔		Not drawn for Muster		
Nathan Tate				” ” ” ”		
Daniel Ramsey	Do	6⅔	20	6		
John Tyree	Do	6⅔	17½	5	6	Died at Hospital Albany October 21st
George Blakey	Do	6⅔	20	6		
Benjamin Bristoe	Do	6⅔	20	6		
William Blakey	Do	6⅔	20	6		
Archer Gilliam	Do	6⅔	20	6		
Jesse Low	Do	6⅔	20	6		
John McCommack	Do	6⅔	20	6		
John Stevens	Do	6⅔	20	6		
John Lipford	Do	6⅔	20	6		
John Adcock	Do	6⅔	20	6		

Name				
John Wheeler	Do	6⅔	20	6
Archer Beard	Do	6⅔	20	6
Gidion Crews	Do	6⅔	20	6
James Crews	Do	6⅔	20	6
William Moore	Do	6⅔	20	6
George Damron	Do	6⅔	20	6
William Godsey	Do	6⅔	20	6
James Wheeler	Do	6⅔	20	6
Edward Patteson	Do	6⅔	20	6
Joseph Green	Do	6⅔	20	6
Ebenezer Mann	Do	6⅔	20	6
Robert Mann	Do	6⅔	20	6
John Williams	Do	6⅔	20	6
Richard Johnson	Do	6⅔	20	6
David Galliher	Do	6⅔	20	6
Austin Godsey	Do	6⅔	20	6
George Coats	Do	6⅔	20	6
James Brown	Do	6⅔	20	6

A Payroll* of Capt Benjamin Taliaferros Comp^y of detached Riflemen Commanded by Col^o Danl Morgan for the month of December 1777.

Names	Rank	For What Time	Dollars Pr month	Whole pay in Dollars	Casualties
Benj Taliaferro	Capt	1 Mo	40	83	The difference between
John Jordan	Lieut	do	27	27	Lts pay and Capts for 3
Robert Watkins	Ens	do	20	20	Months & 8 days included—from 23d September the date of my Commission
Saml Ayres	Serjt	do	8	8	
Thomas Burfoot	do	do	8	8	
Edward Cox	do	do	8	8	
Littleberry Patterson	do	do	8	8	
Danl Low	do	do	8	8	
John Thomas	do	do	8	8	
James Hill	Corpl	do	7⅓	7⅓	
Joell Jones	do	do	7⅓	7⅓	
Thomas Dickerson	do	do	7⅓	7⅓	
John Josling	do	do	7⅓	7⅓	
George Creasey	do	do	7⅓	7⅓	
William Johns	Privt	do	6⅔	6⅔	
Thomas Johns	do	2 do	6⅔	13⅓	Omited in Novem^r Pay-roll
John Shenault	do	1 do	6⅔	6⅔	
Josiah Cheatham	do	do	6⅔	6⅔	
Charles Eades	do	do	6⅔	6⅔	
John Demasters	do	do	6⅔	6⅔	
Saml Bell	do	do	6⅔	6⅔	
Will Montgomery	do	do	6⅔	6⅔	
Robert Hudson	do	do	6⅔	6⅔	
Joseph Staples	do	do	6⅔	6⅔	
Wm Higginbotham	do	do	6⅔	6⅔	
Danl Tyler	do	do	6⅔	6⅔	

*All of the men listed on this payroll, except Sergt. Thomas Burfoot, received the "Extra month's Pay allowed by the Honourable the Continental Congress." In addition, James Weeks, Drummer, & John Fitzgerald are listed as recipients of the extra pay.

Name					
Thomas Smith	do	do	6⅔	6⅔	
Benj Galleway	do	do	6⅔	6⅔	
John Carpenter	do	do	6⅔	6⅔	
Osburn Coffey	do	do	6⅔	6⅔	
Geo Phillips	do	do	6⅔	6⅔	
John Phillips	do	2 do	6⅔	13⅓	Omited in Novemr Pay-
William Brooks	do	1 do	6⅔	6⅔	roll
William Burford	do	do	6⅔	6⅔	
John Murrah	do	do	6⅔	6⅔	
Joseph Canterbury	do	do	6⅔	6⅔	
Stark Brown	do	do	6⅔	6⅔	
Geo Key	do	do	6⅔	6⅔	
John Deavenport	do	do	6⅔	6⅔	
Reuben Seayres	do	do	6⅔	6⅔	
John Welch	do	do	6⅔	6⅔	
Sampson Welch	do	do	6⅔	6⅔	
Joseph Welch	do	do	6⅔	6⅔	
Danl Ramsay	do	do	6⅔	6⅔	
Joseph Newman	do	do	6⅔	6⅔	
Thomas Gregory	do	do	6⅔	6⅔	
Benoni Goldsmith	do	do	6⅔	6⅔	
Joshua Tuggle	do	do	6⅔	6⅔	
Austin Smith	do	do	6⅔	6⅔	
Geo Campbell	do	do	6⅔	6⅔	
John Layne	do	do	6⅔	6⅔	
Thomas Layne	do	do	6⅔	6⅔	
Danl Connor	do	do	6⅔	6⅔	
William Ray	do	do	6⅔	6⅔	
Edward Patterson	do	do	6⅔	6⅔	
Jessee Low	do	do	6⅔	6⅔	
Geo Blakey	do	do	6⅔	6⅔	
Archibald Gillam	do	do	6⅔	6⅔	
John McCormack	do	do	6⅔	6⅔	
William Blakey	do	do	6⅔	6⅔	
James Brown	do	do	6⅔	6⅔	
Joseph Green	do	do	6⅔	6⅔	
Gidion Crews	do	do	6⅔	6⅔	
Geo Coats	do	do	6⅔	6⅔	
Ebenezar Mann	do	do	6⅔	6⅔	
John Stevens	do	do	6⅔	6⅔	
John Williams	do	3 do	6⅔	20	Omited in Novemr &
Archibald Beard	do	1 do	6⅔	6⅔	Decemr 1776
John Adcock	do	do	6⅔	6⅔	
James Crews	do	do	6⅔	6⅔	
William Moore	do	do	6⅔	6⅔	
Austin Godsey	do	do	6⅔	6⅔	
William Godsey	do	do	6⅔	6⅔	
Robert Mann	do	do	6⅔	6⅔	
David Galliher	do	do	6⅔	6⅔	
Geo Damron	do	do	6⅔	6⅔	
John Lipford	do	do	6⅔	6⅔	

661⅔ Equal to £198-10
Lawfull

E Excepted
Ben Taliaferro Capt

Capt Taliaferros Payroll for December 1777
661⅔ Dollars
Morgan's for Men of his Regt whose times are out

Amherst County, Virginia, in the Revolution

A Pay roll of Cap^n Benjamin Taliaferro's Comp^y of detached Riflemen Commanded by Col^o Danl Morgan, from the first day of February 78, to the expiration of their Service, including 15 days allowed them for going to Virginia.

Names	Rank	For what time months	days	Time discharg^d	Dollars P Month	Whole pay in Dollars	Casualties
Ben Taliaferro	Capt	1			40	40	
John Jordan	Lieut	1			27	27	
Saml Ayres	Serjt	1	4	19th Feby	8	9 8/72	
Edward Cox	do	1	9	24th	8	10½	
Littleberry Patterson	do		25	10th	8	6 68/72	
Danl Low	do	1		15th	8	8	
John Thomas	do		27	12th	8	7½	
James Hill	Corp^l	1	6	21st	7⅓	8⅚	
Joell Jones	do		27	12th	7⅓	6 54/72	
Thomas Dickerson	do	1	19	4 Mch	7⅓	12 6/72	
John Josling	do	1	1	16th Feby	7⅓	7 36/72	
George Creasay	do	1	1	16th	7⅓	7 36/72	
Thomas Johns	pri	1		15th	6⅔	6⅔	
Josiah Cheatham	do	1	9	24th	6⅔	8½	
Samuel Bell	do	1	11	26th	6⅔	9	
Wm Montgomery	do		22	7th	6⅔	4 68/72	
Danl Tyler	do	1	19	4th Mch	6⅔	10 40/72	
Thomas Smith	do	1	19	4th	6⅔	10 40/72	
Benj^a Gallaway	do		20	5th Feby	6⅔	4 32/72	
John Carpenter	do	1	2	17th	6⅓	7 8/72	
Osburn Coffey	do		28	13th	6⅔	6 16/72	
William Brooks	do		24	9th	6⅔	5 24/72	
Joseph Canterbury	do		24	9th	6⅔	5 24/72	
Stark Brown	do	1	19	4th Mch.	6⅔	10 40/72	
Geo Key	do	1	19	4th	6⅔	10 40/72	
Reuben Seayres	do		20	5th Feby	6⅔	4 32/72	
Joseph Welch	do		20	5th	6⅔	4 32/72	
Danl Ramsay	do	1	19	4th Mch.	6⅔	10 40/72	
Benoni Goldsmith	do	1	11	26th Feb.	6⅔	9	
Austin Smith	do		20	5th Feb	6⅔	4 32/72	
John Layne	do	1	2	17th Feby	6⅔	7 8/72	
Thomas Layne	do		23	8th	6⅔	5 8/72	
Edward Patterson	do		26	11th	6⅔	5 64/72	
Jessee Low	do	1	9	24th	6⅔	8½	
Geo Blakey	do		28	13th	6⅔	6 16/72	
Archibald Gillam	do		27	12th	6⅔	6	
William Blakey	do		29	14th	6⅔	6 40/72	
James Brown	do	1	1	16th	6⅔	6 64/72	
Joseph Green	do	1	1	16th	6⅔	6 64/72	
Gideon Crews	do	1	1	16th	6⅔	6 64/72	
Ebenezer Mann	do		24	9th	6⅔	5 24/72	
John Stevens	do		24	9th	6⅔	5 24/72	
John Williams	do		24	9th	6⅔	5 24/72	
Archibald Beard	do		26	11th	6⅔	5 64/72	
John Adcock	do		29	14th	6⅔	6 40/72	
James Crews	do		24	9th	6⅔	5 24/72	
William Moore	do	1	1	16th	6⅔	6 64/72	

Austin Godsey	do		29	14th	6⅔	6 40/72
William Godsey	do	1	1	16th	6⅔	6 64/72
Robert Mann	do		24	9th	6⅔	5 24/72
David Galliher	do	1	4	19th	6⅔	7½
George Damron	do		29	14th	6⅔	6 40/72
John Lipford	do		20	5th	6⅔	4 32/72

                                                            428 28/72

Errors Excepted

                        Ben Taliaferro Capt

Brought down   428 28/72
December Roll   661⅔
Januarys Payroll   499⅔

                    1589 42/72 Dollars

Equal to £476: 18: 4 Lawful money

Amherst County, Virginia, in the Revolution 25

Captain James Franklin's Company, later Captain Clough Shelton's Company

A Muster Roll* of Capt James Franklins Company of foot belonging to the 10th Virginia Regiment and now in the Service of the United States of America Dated, 1777.

Commissioned
November 19 1776

Capt James Franklin
1s^t Lieut Clough Shelton
2 Lieut James Dillard
Ensign William Powell

appointed

1	Reuben Thomas		Nov^m	24	
2	Thomas Wash	Serjents	Do	30	
3	William Jones		Dec^m	7	
4	Will. Johnson		Nov.	21	

1	Harrison Thomas		Nov^m	23	Sick Trenton
	Charles Jones	Corp^{ls}	Jan^y	7	
	Benj. Wash		Nov^m	30	

Fifes & Drums
Randolph Brown		Jan^y	1	th
George Reid		Do	1	Dece^d 16 May 1777
				Turn^d into ranks 28th March

Privates   Remarks

1	Thomas Croucher	Nov^m	21	hospital
2	Griffin Gibson	do	21	
3	James Byrnes	do	28	hospital
4	John Ware	do	30	Sick Virg^a
5	Robert Brown	do	30	Sick M. Town
6	George Peyton	do	30	Sick Trenton
7	James Peyton	do	30	hospital
8	Nicholas Jones	Dec^m	2	
9	John White	do	2	hospital
10	Thomas Jones	do	7	
11	Richard Harrison	do	14	
12	Isham Thacker	do	14	Deces^d 24 Ap^l
13	James Shasteen	do	16	deserted 8 Mar
14	Peter Diamond	do	24	do do do
15	Hugh Cameron	Jan^y	7	Sick Philad^d
16	Thomas Jones Gra^l	Dec^m	25	
17	John Guttry	Jan^y	20	Sick Virg^a

*Muster Roll July '77 same with following exceptions: Col. Edward Stevens in Command; William Powell, Ensign, Resigned 10th July; Reuben Thomas, Sergt., not on Roll; William Jones, Sergt., "Recruitg Virg^a"; Jeremiah Walker, Drummer; 44 privates; George Peyton "Dec^d by information 15th July"; Thomas Jones *"Grend."* Capt. James Franklin resigned; Clough Shelton was promoted Captain.

18	Thomas Winker	Feby	3	
19	Alexr McBride	do	3	
20	John Hadrick	do	11	deserted 21 May
21	William Henderson	Decm	2	Sick M. Town
22	James Smith	Novm	20	Deced May
23	William Aaron	do	20	hospital
24	Thomas Crawley	do	21	deced 23 Apl
25	William Hosack	do	22	
26	James Toner	do	22	
27	William Bailey	do	22	hospital
28	Henry Tuggle	Do	26	
29	Charles Tuggle	Do	26	
30	George Savage	Do	30	
31	Noel Battles	Decm	3	Guard
32	Shadrack Battles	do	3	Do
33	William Johnson Junr	do	5	
34	John Ominate	Novm	21	Sick M. Town
35	Francis Northcutt	do	23	Sick Baltimore
36	Joseph Sharp	Do	23	deserted 9 Mar
37	George Bond	Do	30	
38	Richard Bryant	Decm	4	Sick M. Town
39	William Brown	Novm	30	do do
40	John Layne	Decm	2	
41	Jeremiah Walker	do	2	
42	Joseph Newman	do	15	
43	George Hazele	Jany	2	
44	Jacob Hutz	do	3	
45	James Gowing	do	7	hospital
46	Henry Christian	Novm	22	Sick Virga
47	John Burnett	Decm	2	deserted 15 March
48	William Chandler	do	8	
49	William Beckham	do	14	
50	William Cunningham	do	20	deserted 21 May
51	John McCalver	do	20	Decd 11 Apl
52	William McManniway	Jany	4	hospital
53	Thomas Akins	do	11	life guard
54	John McManniway	Jany	23	hospital
55	Moses Wright	do	23	
56	Thomas Brummitt	do	19	Sick Philad
57	Jesse Johns	Feby	3	Deserted Feby 4
58	John Phelps	Decm	4	
59	William Phelps	do	4	
60	Tilmon Walton	Jany	1	Sent to M. Town
61	Andrew Night	do	1	th
62	Jeremiah Burnett	Decm	26	Deserted 15 March
63	William Brummitt	March	4	Sick Trenton
64	James Campbell	Decm	2	Deserted 9 March
65	Joseph Thomas	do	8	Do Do Do
66	John Bowman	do	24	hospital
67	James Simons	Jany	1	Do
68	Levi Thomas	Novm	26	

June 13 Then Musterd Capt James Franklins Company as Specified In the above Roll

Will Bradford Jun D.M.M.G.

A Muster Roll of Capt. Clough Sheltons Company of Foot Belonging to the 6th Virginia Regt Commanded by Col. William Russell for the Months of October and November 1778.

Commissioned March 1 77 Capt. Clough Shelton on furlow October 20th 77 2 Lt Nicholas Taliaferro

No.	Serjeants	Inlistment or Draught	3 Year	1 Year	Remarks
1	Tilman Walton	Jany 1 77	"		Sick in the Cuntry
2	William Johnson	Novr 21 76	"		
3	Charles Jones	Jany 7 77	"		
4	Thomas Jones	Feby 26 76	"		Promoted to Serjt Novr 1st
5	William Jones	Decr 7 76			Reduced to Private Octr 31

No.	Corporals				
1	John Ware	Novr 30 76			
2	Thomas Jones	Novr 25 76			Promoted to Serjt Novr 1st
3	Andrew Knight	Jany 1 77			Promoted to Corpl Novr 1st
1	Jeremiah Walker Drumr	Decr 2 76			Sick at Brunswick

1	William Jones	Decr 7 76	"		Reduced from Serjt Octr 31
2	William Hoesack	Novr 22 76	"		
3	Joseph Newman	Decr 15 76	"		
4	Joseph Thomas	Decr 8 76	"		on Duty
5	John Bowman	Decr 24 76	"		
6	Jacob Hutts	Jany 3 77	"		
7	Moses Wright	Jany 23 77	"		
8	James Simmons	Jany 1 76	"		
9	Richard Harrison	Decr 14 76	"		
10	Levy Thomas	Decr 11 76	"		
11	James Toner	Novr 22 76	"		
12	Thomas Moilos	Feby 17 78		1	on Duty
13	Thomas Brummit	Jany 19 77	"		
14	William Chandler	Decr 8 76	"		on Duty
15	John Omminate	Novr 21 76	"		
16	Shadrack Battles	Decr 3 76	"		
17	Andrew Knight	Jany 1 77	"		Promoted to Corpl Novr 1st
18	Thomas Jones	Decr 7 76	"		
19	Henry Harper	Feby 17 78		1	
20	Alexander Forbus	Augt 22 77	"		
21	Scott Martin	Augt 22 77	"		on Comd Brunswick
22	John Gue	Feby 17 78		1	on Comd West point
23	George Bonds	Novr 30 76	"		on Comd Fishkills
24	Edmond Grady	Jany 17 77	"		on Comd French Creek
25	Charles Tuggle	Novr 26 76	"		Sick at Brunswick
26	Noel Battles	Decr 3 76	"		Sick at Brunswick
27	Thomas Church	Feby 17 78		1	Sick at west Point
28	William Jones	Feby 17 78		1	Sick at west Point
29	John Crow	Feby 17 78		1	Sick at New winsor
30	James Campbell	Decr 2 76	"		Sick at New winsor
31	James Payton	Novr 30 76	"		Sick at Fishkills
32	William Beckham	Decr 14 76	"		Sick at Brunswick
33	Henry Tuggle	Novr 26 76	"		Sick at Brunswick
34	John McMannaway	Jany 23 77	"		Sick west Point
35	Jules Golden	Feby 17 78		1	Discharged Novr 14

Camp Middle Brook Decr 19th 1778 Then Mustered Capt. Clough Sheltons Company as Specified in the Above Roll

Jos. Clark D.M.M.

28   Amherst County, Virginia, in the Revolution

Muster Roll* of Capt Clough Sheltons Company of Foot Belonging to the 6th Continental Virginia Regt Comd by Col^o John Green for the Month of May 1779.

	Commiss^d	March 1st 77 Capt Clough Shelton Joseph Blackwell Com^{md} Sepr 14th 78 Lt Saml Baskerville			
No	Sarjeants	Inlistmts	War	Yrs	Remarks
1	Tilman Walton	Jany 1 77		3	
2	Charles Jones	Jany 7 77			
3	Thomas Jones	Decr 25 76			on Guard
4	William Johnson	Novr 21 76		3	on Furlough
	Corporals				
1	Andrew Knight	Jany 1 77		3	
2	Richard Harrison	Decr 14th 76			on Guard
3	William Yours	Jany 6 77			
4	Joseph Coleman	Sepr 15 77			
5	John Ellis	Jany 2d 77			on Furlough
6	John Ware		War		on Ditto
1	Jeremiah Walker Drumr	Decr 3 76		3	
	Privates				
1	Peter Francisco	Decr 15 76		3	
2	John Lowe	Feby 1 77			
3	Levy Thomas	Decr 11 76			
4	Edward Hix	Sepr 8 77			
5	George Robinson	Jany 11 77			
6	Thomas Smith	March 4 77			
7	Noel Battles	Decr 3d 76			
8	James Simmons	Jany 1 77			
9	Thomas Jones	Decr 7 76			
10	Alexander Forbus	Augt 22 77			
11	William Hosack	Novr 22d 76			
12	William Beckham	Decr 14 76			
13	Edmund Gready	July 17 77			
14	Henry Coke	Sepr 15 77			
15	William Cox		War		
16	John Saterwhite		do		
17	Joseph Thomas		do		
18	George Bond		do		
19	Charles Charity		do		
20	Samuel Goff		do		on Guard
21	Alexander Kent	Jany 27 77			on Ditto
22	John Loftis	Jany 8 77			on Ditto
23	Henry Walker	Decr 26 76			on Com^d
24	James Payton	Novr 30 76			on Guard
25	Henry Tuggle	Novr 26 76			on Com^d
26	John Amonnet	Novr 21 76			on Ditto
27	Moses Wright	Jany 23 77		3	on Guard
28	Paul Wright	Sepr 8th 77		3	on Ditto

*Muster Roll July '79 same except "Mustered Ramapau Aug 3, 1779." Aug. '79 same except Samuel Goff "Supposed killed at Paulus Hook Augt 18." Sept. '79 same except Col. was Samuel Hawes; Mustered "Camp Haverstraw Nov. 8th 1779." Nov. '79 same except "Camp Morris Town Dec. 1779, Sam. J. Cabell Lt. Col. & Sub. Inspr."; 50 privates; Edmund Grady, Sergt. in place of Thomas Jones.

Amherst County, Virginia, in the Revolution

No	Name	Date		Remarks
29	Charles Tuggle	Nov*r 26 76		on Com*d
30	John Bowman	Dec*r 24 76		on Ditto
31	John McManaway	Jan*y 23 77		on Guard
32	Scott Martin	Aug*t 22 77		on Com*d
33	Thomas Brummit	Jan*y 19 77		on Ditto
34	James Toner	Nov*r 22 76		on Ditto
35	James Campbell	Dec*r 2*d 76		Waggonner
36	David Akin	Dec*r 22 76		on Com*d
37	James Johnson	Dec*r 14 76		on Ditto
38	William Chandler		War	on Ditto
39	Joseph Newman		War	Guard
40	Shadrack Battles	Dec*r 3 76		on Furlough
41	Jeremiah Johnson	Dec*r 14 76		on Ditto
42	John McCraw	Jan*y 7 77		on Ditto
43	Thomas Scott	Jan*y 11 77		on Do
44	Drury Scott		War	on Ditto
45	John Branwood		do	on Ditto
46	Ellis Palmer		do	on Ditto
47	John Evans		do	on Ditto
48	John Scott		do	on Ditto
49	John McDowell		do	on Ditto
50	William Jones		do	on Ditto
51	Jacob Hutts		do 3	on Ditto

Smiths Clove June 12*th 1779 Muster*d Then Cap*t Sheltons Comp*y as Specified above   Jos. Clark D.M.M.

Muster Roll of Cap*t Clough Sheltons Company of Foot belonging to the 6*th Virginia Regiment Com*d by Col*o John Green for the Month of June 1779.

Commiss*d   March 1 1777 Cap*t Clough Shelton on Com*d Light Infantry
March 30*th 1777 Lt Joseph Blackwell
Sep*r 14 1778 Lt Samuel Baskerville

No	Serjeants	Inlistments	War Years	Remarks
1	Tilman Walton	Jan*y 1 77	3	
2	Charles Jones	Jan*y 7 77	3	
3	Thomas Jones	Dec*r 25 76	3	
4	William Johnson	Nov*r 21 76	3	Supposed with Gen*l Scott, Southward
	Corporals			
1	Andrew Knight	Jan*y 1 77	3	Light Infantry
2	Richard Harrison	Dec*r 14 76	3	Do Do
3	William Yours	Jan*y 6 77	3	
4	Joseph Coleman	Sep*r 15 77	3	
5	John Ellis	Jan*y 2 76	3	Supposed with Gen*l Scott, Southward
6	John Ware	War		Do Do
1	Jeremiah Walker	Drum*r Dec*r 3 76	3	
	Privates			
1	John Lowe	Feb*y 1 77	3	
2	Edward Hix	Sep*r 8 77	3	
3	George Robertson	Jan*y 11 77	3	
4	Thomas Smith	March 4 77	3	
5	Alexander Forbus	Aug*t 22 77	3	

#	Name	Date			Status
6	Edmund Grady	July 17 77		3	
7	Henry Coke	Sepr 15 77		3	
8	Alexander Kent	Jany 27 77		3	absent with Leave
9	John Loftis	Jany 8 77		3	
10	Henry Walker	Decr 26 76		3	
11	James Payton	Novr 30 76		3	
12	Henry Tuggle	Novr 26 76		3	
13	John Amonnet	Novr 21 76		3	
14	Paul Wright	Sepr 8 77		3	
15	Charles Tuggle	Novr 26 76		3	
16	John Bowman	Decr 24 76		3	
17	John McManaway	Jany 23 77		3	
18	Scott Martin	Augt 22 77		3	
19	James Campbell	Decr 2d 76		3	Absent with leave
20	William Cox		War		
21	John Saterwhite				
22	Joseph Thomas			3	
23	George Bond				
24	Charles Charity				
25	Samuel Goff		War		
26	Peter Francisco	Decr 15 76		3	Light Infantry
27	Levy Thomas	Decr 11 76		3	Ditto
28	Noel Battles	Decr 3 76		3	Ditto
29	James Simmons	Jany 1 77		3	Light Infantry
30	Thomas Jones	Decr 7 76		3	Do Do
31	William Hosack	Novr 22 76		3	Do Do
32	William Beckham	Decr 14 76		3	Do Do
33	Moses Wright	Jany 23 77		3	Do Do
34	James Toner	Novr 26 76		3	Do Do
35	William Chandler		War		Do Do
36	Joseph Newman		War		Do Do
37	David Akin		War		On Comd Trenton
38	Thomas Brummit	Jany 19 77		3	Do Do
39	James Johnson	Decr 14 76		3	Do Virginia
40	Shadrack Battles	Decr 3 76		3	on Furlough
41	Jeremiah Johnson	Decr 14 76			Do
42	John McCraw	Jany 7 77			Do
43	Thomas Scott	Jany 11 77		3	Do
44	Drury Scott		War		Do
45	John Branwood				Do
46	Ellis Palmer				Do
47	John Evans				Do
48	John Scott				Do
49	John McDowell				Do
50	William Jones				Do
51	Jacob Hutts				Do

Rows 41–51 "Do" column noted: Supposed with Genl Scott at the Southward

Smiths Clove July 9th 79 Mustered Then Capt Sheltons Company as Specified above

Jos. Clark D.M.M.

Revolutionary Officers, Amherst County Militia

The following procedure was used in commissioning officers for the Amherst County Militia: The County Court recommended men to the Governor and he issued commissions. When the commissions were returned to the County Lieutenant the prospective officers appeared before the Court and were sworn in. It seems that when officers were recommended they immediately assumed their duties.

The following is the form that was used in entering all these commissions in the Order Books 1773-1782 and 1782-1784:

At a Court held for Amherst County at the Court House the Second Day of June 1777——

Present

James Nevil	David Crawford	Gent. Justices
Zachariah Taliaferro	William Horsley	

William Harris Jr. Gent. appeared in Court and took the Oath of Lieut. of a Company of the Militia of this County as the Law Directs. Page 188

Court Held April 7, 1778

On the Resignation of Capt. James Dillard, John Christian is Recommended to his Excellency the Governour, as a proper person to Execute the said Office. Page 223

George Hilton recommended as First Lieut.	"
William Horsley Gent. recommended as Second Lieut.	"
Robert Christian recommended as Ensign	"

On the Resignation of James Nevil Gent. County Lieutenant, Joseph Cabell Gent. is Recommended to his Excellency the Governour, as a proper person to Execute the said Office. Page 223

John Rose Gent.	recommended as Colonel		"
James Higginbotham	"	" Lieut.-Colonel	224
Alexander Reid	"	" Major	"

Court held May 4, 1778

Richard Ballenger	recommended as Captain		Page 228
John Loving, Jr.	" " "		"
James Pamplin	"	" "	"
Robert Edmonds	"	" First Lieut.	"
William Bibb	"	" " "	"

William Spencer	recommended as First Lieut.	Page 228
Charles Ison	,, ,, Second Lieut.	,,
William Walton	,, ,, ,, ,,	,,
John Horsley	,, ,, ,, ,,	,,
John Matthews	,, ,, Ensign	,,
Abraham Seay	,, ,, ,,	,,
Richard Allcock	,, ,, ,,	,,
Charles Burras	,, ,, Captain	229
David Shelton	,, ,, ,,	,,
Joseph Tucker	,, ,, First Lieut.	,,
James Montgomery	,, ,, ,, ,,	,,
Wiatt Powell	,, ,, Second Lieut.	,,
James McAlexander Jr.	,, ,, ,, ,,	,,
John Franklin	,, ,, ,, ,,	231
Isaac Rucker	,, ,, ,, ,,	,,
Daniel Tucker	,, ,, Ensign	229
Robert Wright	,, ,, ,,	,,
Isaac Tinsley	,, ,, ,,	231
John Loving Jr.	qualified as Captain	,,
Charles Burras	,, ,, ,,	232
Richard Ballenger	,, ,, ,,	,,
John Christian	,, ,, ,,	233
William Bibb	,, ,, First Lieut.	231
Joseph Tucker	,, ,, ,, ,,	232
William Walton	,, ,, Second Lieut.	231
Wiatt Powell	,, ,, ,, ,,	232
John Franklin	,, ,, ,, ,,	,,
Charles Ison	,, ,, ,, ,,	,,
William Horsley Gent.	,, ,, ,, ,,	233
Isaac Rucker	,, ,, ,, ,,	,,
William Hansbrough Jr.	,, ,, Ensign	230
Abraham Seay	,, ,, ,,	231
Daniel Tucker	,, ,, ,,	232
John Matthews	,, ,, ,,	,,
Robert Christian	,, ,, ,,	233
Robert Wright	,, ,, ,,	,,
Richard Allcock	,, ,, ,,	,,

Court held July 6, 1778

Joseph Cabell Gent.	qualified as County Lieutenant	234
James Higginbotham	,, ,, Lieut.-Colonel	,,
Alexander Reid	,, ,, Major	,,
James Pamplin	,, ,, Captain	235
William Martin	recommended as Captain	236
William Harris	,, ,, ,,	,,
James Matthews	,, ,, First Lieut.	,,
Alexander Reid Jr.	,, ,, ,, ,,	,,

Amherst County, Virginia, in the Revolution 33

Young Landrum	recommended as Second Lieut. Page	236
Michael McNeely	" " " "	"
William Barnett	" " Ensign	"
William Martin	qualified as Captain	238
William Harris	" " "	239
James Matthews	" " First Lieut.	238
Michael McNeely	" " Second Lieut.	239
George Hilton	" " " "	235
John Horsley	" " " "	"
Lindsey Coleman	" " " "	"
James McAlexander Jr.	" " " "	"
Isaac Tinsley	" " Ensign	"

Court held August 3, 1778

James Turner	recommended as Second Lieut.	242
Patrick Rose Gent.	" " " "	244
William Montgomery	" " Ensign	242
David Shelton	qualified " Captain	241
James Montgomery	" " First Lieut.	"
William Banks	" " Ensign	242

Court held September 8, 1778

Charles Ellis	recommended as Second Lieut.	291
James Ware	" " " "	"
Edmund Powell	" " Ensign	"
Zachariah Taylor	" " "	"
Young Landrum	qualified as Second Lieut.	293

Court held October 5, 1778

On the Resignation of Capt. Joseph Crews, Henry Christian, Leroy Upshaw, Giddion Crews and Elijah Christian are Recommended to his Excellency the Governour as proper persons, the said Henry Christian to Execute the Office of Captain, Upshaw First Lieutenant, Crews Second Lieutenant and the said Elijah Christian as Ensign of a Company of the Militia of this County. Page 323

Phillip Thurmond	recommended as First Lieut.	"
Joseph Edwards	" " Second Lieut.	"
William Ware	" " Ensign	324
Henry Christian	qualified as Captain	"
James Ware	" " Second Lieut.	322
Edmund Powell	" " Ensign	"
Elijah Christian	" " "	324

November Court, 1778

John Horsley	recommended as First Lieut.	333
Richard Allcock	" " Second Lieut.	"

Steven Watts	recommended as Ensign	Page 333
Leroy Upshaw	qualified as First Lieut.	332

December Court, 1778

Giddion Crews	qualified as Second Lieut.	337

February Court, 1779

John Horsley	qualified as Lieut.	340
Richard Allcock	,, ,, ,,	,,
James Turner	,, ,, ,,	,,
Stephen Watts	,, ,, Ensign	,,
Zachariah Taylor	,, ,, ,,	,,

July Court, 1779

Azariah Martin	recommended as Captain	365
James Matthews	,, ,, ,,	,,
Claudeous Buster	,, ,, First Lieut.	,,
Young Landrum	,, ,, ,, ,,	,,
Thomas Morrison Jr.	,, ,, Second Lieut.	,,
William Hansbrough	,, ,, ,, ,,	,,
David Davis	,, ,, ,, ,,	366
David McAnally	,, ,, Ensign	365
Thomas Farrar	,, ,, ,,	365
Nicholas Moran	,, ,, ,,	366
James Matthews	qualified as Captain	367
Young Landrum	,, ,, First Lieut.	,,

August Court, 1779

Azariah Martin	qualified as Captain	369

September Court, 1779

Roderick McCulloch having Resigned his Commission as a Captain of a Company of the Militia for this County, Whereupon Philip Thurmond, Joseph Edwards, William Ware, and Peter Carter are Recommended to his Excellency the Governour as proper persons to Execute the Office, the said Thurmond as Captain, Edwards First Lieut., Ware Second Lieut., and Carter as Ensign of a Company of the Militia for this County. Page 374

Michael McNeely	recommended as First Lieut.	375
Thomas Ewers	,, ,, Second Lieut.	,,
James Henderson	,, ,, Ensign	,,
Thomas Morrison	qualified as Second Lieut.	,,

October Court, 1779

Nicholas Cabell Gent.	recommended as Colonel	380
Daniel Gaines Gent.	,, ,, Major	,,

February Court, 1780

Nicholas Cabell Esq. qualified as Colonel Page 398

May Court, 1780

George Penn	recommended as Captain			418
Josiah Ellis	,,	,,	,,	,,
Charles Christian	,,	,,	,,	,,
John Diggs	,,	,,	,,	,,
Patrick Rose Gent.	,,	,,	,,	,,
Young Landrum	,,	,,	,,	,,
James Ware	,,	,, First Lieut.		,,
Lindsey Coleman	,,	,,	,,	,,
Charles Ellis	,,	,,	,,	,,
James Turner	,,	,,	,,	,,
Charles Rose	,,	,,	,,	,,
William Horsley	,,	,,	,,	,,
William Hansbrough	,,	,,	,,	,,
Richard Powell	,,	,, Second Lieut.		,,
Edmund Powell	,,	,,	,,	,,
William Banks	,,	,,	,,	,,
Zachariah Taylor	,,	,,	,,	,,
William Montgomery	,,	,,	,,	,,
Thomas Dickerson Jr.	,,	,,	,,	,,
Robert Christian	,,	,,	,,	,,
Thomas Farrar	,,	,,	,,	,,
George Lee	,,	,, Ensign		,,
Caleb Higginbotham	,,	,,	,,	,,
George Phillips	,,	,,	,,	,,
Samuel Shackleford	,,	,,	,,	,,
Benjamin Moore	,,	,,	,,	,,
Charles Hay	,,	,,	,,	,,
Drury Christian	,,	,,	,,	,,
Hudson Martin	,,	,,	,,	,,

June Court, 1780

Hugh Rose Esq.	recommended as County Lieut.		422
Nicholas Cabell Esq.	,,	,, Col., First Bat.	,,
John Pope Jr., Esq.	,,	,, Major, First Bat.	,,
Daniel Gaines Esq.	,,	,, Col., Second Bat.	,,
Ambrose Rucker Esq.	,,	,, Lieut. Col., Second Bat.	,,
Gabriel Penn Esq.	,,	,, Major, 2nd Bat.	,,
Benjamin Rucker	,,	,, Captain	,,
John Hill	,,	,, ,,	423
Charles Ison	,,	,, First Lieut.	420
Isaac Rucker	,,	,, ,, ,,	422

Thomas Dickerson Jr. recommended as First Lieut. Page 423
Jacob Higginbotham   "   " Second Lieut.   420
Isaac Tinsley   "   "   "   "   422
Charles Hay   "   "   "   "   423
Reuben Harrison   "   " Ensign   419
James Manees Jr.   "   "   "   422
John Massey   "   "   "   423
Patrick Rose Esq.   "   " Lieut.-Col.,
                                        Second Bat.   422
John Diggs   qualified as Captain   421
George Penn   "   "   "   "
Charles Christian   "   "   "   "
Young Landrum   "   "   "   "
Lindsey Coleman   "   " First Lieut.   "
James Ware   "   "   "   "   "
William Horsley   "   "   "   "   "
William Banks   "   " Second Lieut.   "
Jacob Higginbotham   "   "   "   "   "
Thomas Ewers   "   "   "   "   "

John Loving, Jr., Patrick Rose, John Diggs, Young Landrum, John Jacobs, William Harris, Azariah Martin, James Pamplin and David Shelton Captains of the Militia and their Subalterns & Companys are Appointed of the first Battalion of this County being chiefly of Amherst Parish.   Page 421

Ambrose Rucker, David Woodroof, Samuel Higginbotham, Charles Burras, Philip Thurmond, George Penn, Josiah Ellis, Charles Christian, John Christian and Richard Ballenger Captains of the Militia and their Subalterns & Companys are appointed of the Second Battalion of this County.   Page 421

August Court, 1780

Hugh Rose Gent.   qualified as County Lieutenant   426
Daniel Gaines Gent.   "   " Col. of a Bat. of
                                      Militia   "
Patrick Rose Gent.   "   " Lt.-Col. of a Bat. of
                                      Militia   "
Ambrose Rucker Gent.   "   " Lt.-Col. of a Bat. of
                                      Militia   "
Gabriel Penn Gent.   "   " Major of a Bat. of
                                      Militia   "
Edmund Powell   "   " Second Lieut.   "
Richard Powell   "   "   "   "   "
James Henderson   "   " Ensign   425
Josiah Ellis   "   " Captain   426

September Court, 1780

John Pope Jr.	qualified as Major	Page 429
John Hill	" " Captain	"
Robert Christian	" " Second Lieut.	"
William Montgomery	" " " "	"

On Motion of Nicholas Cabell Esq., the Court Doth Certify that the said Nicholas Cabell, Early in this present Contest with Great Britain did Actual Service as Captain of a Minute Company, that since by Recommendation from this Court he Received a Colonels Commission in which Capacity the said Nicholas Cabell has acted some time past, that Lately this Court has recommended him to Executive as a proper person for Col. of the first Battalion, that in the Different Publick Capacities aforesaid in which he acted, this Court Entirely approves of his Conduct. Page 431

November Court, 1780

Benjamin Rucker	qualified as Captain	Page 436
Isaac Rucker	" " First Lieut.	"
Joseph Edwards	" " " "	437
William Ware	" " Second Lieut.	"
Peter Carter	" " Ensign	"

February Court, 1781

Charles Ellis	qualified as First Lieut.	Page 440
Elijah Christian	recommended as Second Lieut.	442
James Gresham	" " Ensign	"

March Court, 1781

Philip Thurmond	qualified as Captain	Page 442

May Court, 1781

Patrick Rose Gent.	recommended	as Col. of the First Bat.	446
John Pope Jr. Gent.	"	" Lt.-Col. of the First Bat.	"
William Cabell Jr. Gent.	"	" Major of the First Bat.	"
William Lee	"	" Captain	"
William Walton	"	" First Lieut.	"
Lewis Nevil	"	" " "	"
Abraham Seay	"	" Second Lieut.	"
William Martin	"	" " "	"
Pleasant Dawson	"	" " "	"
Terisha Turner	"	" Ensign	"

Reuben Harrison   recommended as Ensign   Page 446
Thomas Hawkins   ”   ”   ”   ”
James Foster   ”   ”   ”   ”

June Court, 1781

John Pope Jr.   qualified as Lt.-Col. of Militia of
                            Lower Battalion   450
William Cabell Jr.   ”   ” Major of Militia of
                            Lower Battalion   ”
Michael McNeely   ”   ” First Lieut.   449
Lewis Nevil   ”   ”   ”   ”   450
Charles Hay   ”   ” Second Lieut.   ”
Samuel Shackleford   ”   ” Ensign   ”
William Tucker   recommended as First Lieut.   451
William Haynes   ”   ” Second Lieut.   ”

August Court, 1781

William Martin   qualified as Second Lieut.   453
Charles Taliaferro Jr. recommended as Ensign   ”

November Court, 1781

Joseph Tucker   recommended as Captain   458
Reuben Jordan   ”   ”   ”   ”
Richard Taliaferro   ”   ” Lieut.   ”
Stephen Watts   ”   ”   ”   459
John Crawford   ”   ” Ensign   458
Robert Horsley   ”   ”   ”   459

May Court, 1782

William Cabell Jr.   recommended as Lt.-Col. of First
                            Battalion   504
James Pamplin   ”   ” Major of First
                            Battalion   ”
Gabriel Penn   ”   ” Lt.-Col. of Second
                            Battalion   ”
John Wiatt   ”   ” Major of Second
                            Battalion   ”
John Barnett   ”   ” Captain   503
Zacharias Taliaferro Jr. ”   ” Lieut.   ”
Charles Jones   ”   ” Ensign   ”

June Court, 1782

Stephen Watts   recommended as Captain   507
William Ware   ”   ”   ”   509
Robert Horsley   ”   ” Lieut.   507

Peter Carter	recommended as Lieut. Page	509
John Ware	” ” Ensign	507
Volentine (Valentine) Peyton recommended as Ensign		509

Court held July 1, 1782

William Ware	qualified as Captain	551
John Ware	” ” Ensign	”

Order Book, 1783-1784
August Court, 1782

Gabriel Penn Gent.	qualified as Lieut.-Colonel	7
Joseph Tucker	” ” Captain	1
Peter Carter	” ” Lieut.	3

September Court, 1782

James Pamplin	qualified as Major	22
Stephen Watts	” ” Captain	”
Robert Horsley	” ” Lieut.	”
Volentine (Valentine) Peyton qualified as Ensign		19

Court held December 2, 1782

Henry Turner	qualified as Ensign	71

Court held March 5, 1783

James McAlexander Jr.	recommended as Captain	106
Robert Wright	” ” Lieut.	”
Joseph Roberts	” ” Ensign	”

Court held June 2, 1783

David Saunders is Recommended to his Excellency the Governor as a proper person to Execute the Office of Captain of the Militia in this County in the Room of John Hill who hath Resigned. Page 122

Court held August 4, 1783

James McAlexander Jr. qualified as Captain	142

Revolutionary Soldiers from Amherst County, comprising then the territory of the present County of Nelson

Aaron, Benjamin
Aaron, William
Adkins, Absalom
Alcock, Richard
Alcock, William
Alford, John
Allen, Daniel
Allen, Jesse
Allen, John
Allen, Capt. John
Allen, Joseph
Allen, Samuel
Allen, William
Ampey, William
Arnold, Benjamin
Arnold, Hendrick
Baddow, Thomas
Bailey, Hezekiah
Bailey, William
Ballinger, Capt. Richard
Ballou, David
Ballou, John
Banks, Reuben
Banks, William
Barnett, Capt. James
Barnett, John
Barnett, William
Becknal, James (killed)
Becknal, John
Becknal, Micajah
Becknal, Thomas (killed)
Bean, Johnson
Bell, Henry
Bell, Samuel, Sr.
Bell, Samuel, Jr.
Bettysworth, Richard
Byas, John
Byas, Larkin
Byas, Obediah
Bibb, Henry
Bibb, William, Sr.
Bibb, William, Jr.
Biggs, John
Blackwell, David
Blaine, Ephraim
Blair, Allen
Bolling, Edward
Bolling, James
Bond, Charles
Bond, Nathan
Bond, Nathaniel
Bones, John
Bones, William
Bowles, Knight
Bowling, James
Bowling, John
Bowman, Drury
Bowman, John
Bowman, William
Brady, John
Brett, William
Brickley, William
Bridgewater, Jesse
Brooks, Benjamin
Brooks, John
Brooks, William
Brown, Andrew
Brown, John, Sr.
Brown, John, Jr.
Brown, Morris
Brown, William
Bryant, John
Bryant, William
Bullins, Isaac
Burden, Archibald
Burden, Henry
Burford, David
Burford, Capt. David
Burford, James
Burford, John

Burford, Nathaniel
Burford, William
Burks, Charles
Burks, John
Burks, William
Burnet, Isaac
Burrus, Capt. Charles
Burrus, Lieut. Joseph
Burrus, Joseph
Burrus, Thomas
Burton, James Halle*
Burton, Philip
Burton, William
Cabell, Col. John
Cabell, Col. Joseph, Sr.
Cabell, Col. Joseph, Jr.
Cabell, Capt. Nicholas
Cabell, Col. Samuel J.
Cabell, Col. William, Sr.
Cabell, Col. William, Jr.
Calbrath, William
Call, John
Camden, John
Camden, William
Cameron, Ambrose
Cameron, Duncan
Campbell, Ambrose
Campbell, Anthony
Campbell, George
Campbell, Henry
Campbell, James
Cannady, John
Canterbury, Jos., Sr.
Canterbury, Jos., Jr.
Carpenter, Benjamin
Carpenter, John
Carpenter, John
Carpenter, William
Carter, Abraham
Carter, Landon
Carter, Peter
Carter, William
Cartwright, John
Cartwright, Matthew
Cartwright, Peter
Cartwright, William
Cash, Benjamin

Cash, Howard
Cash, John
Cash, Joseph
Cash, Peter
Cauthorne, William
Childress, Abram
Childress, Benjamin
Childress, Henry
Childress, John
Christian, Capt. Chas.
Christian, Charles
Christian, Drury
Christian, Elijah
Christian, George
Christian, Henry
Christian, Capt. Henry
Christian, John
Christian, Capt. John
Christian, Robert
Clark, Benjamin
Clark, David
Clark, John
Clark, Nat
Clark, Nathaniel
Clark, William
Clarson, James
Clement, William*
Clough, John
Coleman, George*
Coleman, James*
Coleman, Littleberry*
Coleman, Lieutenant*
Conner, James
Coop, Adam
Cooper, Abraham
Cottrell, Gilbert
Cottrell, James
Cox, Archilaus*
Crawford, Joel
Crawford, John
Crawford, Nathan
Crawford, Nelson
Crawford, Peter
Creasy, Charles
Creasy, George
Crews, Gideon
Crews, Joseph, Sr.

Crews, Joseph, Jr.
Crittenden, Richard
Crowley, Thomas
Crutcher, William
Davis, Charles
Davis, Joel
Davis, Moses
Davis, Nathaniel
Davis, Richard
Davis, Thomas
Davis, William, Sr.
Davis, William, Jr.
Dawson, John
Dawson, Pleasant
Dawson, William
Depriest, John, Sr.*
Depriest, John, Jr.*
Derr, John*
Derr, Nat*
Derr, Will*
Diggs, Capt. John
Dillard, Capt. James
Dinwiddie or Dunwoody, John
Dinwiddie, Samuel
Dinwiddie, Will.
Dinwiddie, William
Diver, John
Dixon, William
Dodd, Josiah
Douglas, George
Duggin, Claiborne
Duggin, Daniel, Sr.
Duggin, Daniel, Jr.
Duggin, Duncan
Duggin, George, Sr.
Duggin, George, Jr.
Duggin, John
Duggin, Will.
Eades, Charles
Eades, Isaac
Edmonds, Charles
Edmonds, James
Edmondson, Robert
Edmondson, William
Edwards, Joseph
Edwards, Thomas
Edwards, William

Elder, Andrew
Ellis, Charles, Jr.
Ellis, Josiah*
Ellison, Francis
Enix, James
Eubank, John
Evans, Ben
Evans, William*
Ewers, John
Ewers, Thomas
Finnie, John
Finnie, Timothy
Finnie, William
Fitzgerald, James
Fitzgerald, John
Fitzpatrick, Samuel
Fitzpatrick, Thomas
Fitzpatrick, W.
Fitzpatrick, William
Forbush, W.
Fortune, Ben
Fortune, John
Fortune, Zachariah
Foster, James
Franklin, Major James
Franklin, Joel
Franklin, Lieut. John
Franklin, Samuel
Frayser, Philip
Frazier, Micajah
Frost, Joseph, Jr.
Fulcher, Richard
Furbush, George*
Furbush, Will.*
Gaines, Daniel
Galding, Julius
Galloway, Ben.
Garland, Thomas
Gatewood, Ambrose
Gatewood, John
Gatewood, Larkin
Gatewood, Richard
Gee, John
Gibson, Griffith
Gilbert, George
Gilbert, Henry
Gilbert, John Wyatt

Gilbert, Morris
Gilbert, Thomas
Gilliland, Hugh*
Giles, Josiah
Giles, Perrian, Jr.
Gillespie, Sherod
Gillespie, William
Gilmer, John
Glenn, Major John
Going, Phil.
Gooch, Philip
Goodrich, John
Goodwin, Micajah
Goodwin, Richard
Goolsby, James
Goolsby, John
Goolsby, William
Gosh, Thomas
Grattan, Robert
Graves, William
Gregory, Edward
Gregory, Fletcher
Gregory, John
Gregory, Thomas
Gresham, James
Griffin, Absalom
Griffin, John Murray
Griffin, Reuben
Griffin, Thomas
Grimes, Thomas
Guthrie, Moses
Guthrie, Nathaniel
Hall, John
Hall, William
Halliburton, James
Hambleton, Robert
Hamilton, James
Hamilton, William
Hamm, John
Hansborough, John
Hansborough, William, Sr.
Hansborough, William, Jr.
Hargrove, Hezekiah
Hardy, Andrew
Hardy, John
Harper, Edward, Sr.
Harper, Edward, Jr.

Harper, Henry
Harris, Matthew
Harris, William
Harris, Capt. William
Harrison, Richard
Harrison, William
Hartgrove, John
Hartless, James
Harvie, Daniel
Hawkins, Thomas
Hay, Charles
Hay, James
Henderson, Alexander
Henderson, James
Henderson, Ensign James
Henderson, Obediah
Henderson, Stephen
Henley, Leonard
Herd, John
Herndon, Owen
Higginbotham, A[a]ron
Higginbotham, Ben.
Higginbotham, Caleb
Higginbotham, Maj. James
Higginbotham, Joseph
Higginbotham, Capt. Samuel
Higginbotham, Sergt. William
Higginbotham, William
Hill, Isaac
Hill, Nat
Hill, William
Hilley, Thomas
Hilton, George
Hite, John
Hix, John
Hogg, John
Hollinsworth, Joseph
Holt, William
Hooper, William
Hopkins, James H.
Hopper, Thomas
Horsley, John
Horsley, Robert
Horsley, William
Horsley, Lieut. William
Houtchins, Charles
Houtchins, Edward

Houtchins, William
Huckstep, Samuel
Hudson, Reuben
Huffman, Frederick
Huffman, Henry
Hughes, John
Hughes, Will.
Hundley, Nehemiah
Hunter, Titus
Innis, John
Irvine, Christopher
Isham, Elijah
Ison, Charles
Ison, Elijah
Jacobs, John
Jocelin, John
Johns, John
Johns, Robert
Johns, Thomas
Johnson, John
Johnson, Snelling
Johnson, Tandy
Johnson, William
Jones, Ambrose
Jones, James
Jones, John
Jones, Josias*
Jones, Thomas
Jones, William
Jones, Zachariah
Joplin, Josiah
Joplin, Ralph
Joplin, Thomas
Joplin, Capt. Thomas
Jordan, John
Jordan, Reuben
Jordan, William
Jude, John
Key, Rice
King, Jacob
Kisterton, John
Knight, Andrew
Knuckolds, Robert
Lamont, John
Landrum, John
Landrum, Capt. Young
Lane, Charles, Sr.

Lane, Charles, Jr.
Lane, John
Lane, Joseph
Lane, Thomas
Lane, William
Lannum, Benedict
Lavender, Allen
Lavender, Charles, Sr.
Lavender, Charles, Jr.
Lavender, William
Lawless, Richard
Lawson, William
Leak, Mark
Leak, Samuel
Lee, Francis
Lee, Richard
Le Masters, John
Leslie, Robert
Lewis, John
Lively, Mark
Levy, Solomon
Lockhart, Walter
Loving, George
Lucas, Thomas
Lyon, Edward
Lyon, Nicholas
Lyon, Peter
Lyon, Will.
Mahone, Daniel
Mahone, William
Mantiply, Nathaniel*
Marksbury, Samuel
Marshall, William
Martin, Azariah
Martin, Capt. Azariah
Martin, James
Martin, John, Sr.
Martin, John, Jr.
Martin, William
Masters, James
Matthews, James
Matthews, John
Matthews, Joseph
Matthews, Thomas, Sr.
Matthews, Thomas, Jr.
Matthews, William
Mattox, Notly

Courtesy of Frick Art Reference Library

MAJOR SAMUEL MEREDITH, III
Painted by Samuel H. Dearborn
Owned by his great-great-granddaughter, Mrs. Howard Evans, Winton, Lexington, Kentucky.

Mayfield, George
Mayfield, John
Mays, Ben.
Mays, Elijah
Mays, James
Mays, Robert
McAlexander, Alexander
McAlexander, James
McAlexander, John
McAnnally, William
McCabe, Elijah
McCabe, James
McCann, James
McCarter, Robert
McClain, James
McCullock, Roderick
McDaniel, George
McDaniel, John
McKnight, John
McNeare, James
McNeely, Michael*
Megan, Merit
Megginson, Ben.
Megginson, Samuel
Megginson, William
Meredith, Samuel, Jr.
Miller, Alexander
Miller, Charles
Milstead, Zeal
Montgomery, David
Montgomery, James
Montgomery, Lieut. James
Montgomery, John
Montgomery, Thomas
Moran, John
Morris, John
Morris, Zachariah
Morrison, William
Morson, B.
Moss, Philip
Murray, John
Murray, Ransom
Murray, Richard, Sr.
Murray, Richard, Jr.
Murray, William, Sr.
Murray, William, Jr.
Murtar, Barnet
Neal, Joseph
Neighbors, Nat.
Nevil, James
Nevil, Reuben
Nightingale, Matthew
Noel, John
North, William
Nowland (Nowlin, Noland, Nowling), David
Nowland, James
O'Brian, James
Oglesby, Jesse
Oglesby, Richard
Ownby, Thomas
Page, James
Page, Joseph
Pagett, Edmond
Pamplin, Capt. James
Pamplin, Nicholas
Pannel (or Pannelle), Ben.
Parks, John
Parrock, Charles
Parrock, David
Parrow, Daniel*
Patterson, John
Patterson, Thomas*
Peacock, Edward
Pendleton, Benjamin
Pendleton, Edmond
Pendleton, John
Pendleton, Reuben
Pendleton, Richard
Pendleton, William
Penn, Gabriel
Penn, Capt. George
Penn, Philip, Sr.
Penn, Philip, Jr.
Penn, Rolly
Penn, Thomas
Perkins, Richard
Perkins, William
Peters, Richard
Peters, Samuel
Peters, William
Peyton, Charles
Peyton, Daniel
Peyton, George

Peyton, Henry
Peyton, James
Peyton, John, Sr.
Peyton, John, Jr.
Peyton, Lewis
Peyton, William, Sr.*
Peyton, William, Jr.
Peyton, William, minor*
Phillips, George
Phillips, Jacob
Phillips, Jeremiah
Phillips, John
Phillips, Leonard, Sr.
Phillips, Leonard, Jr.
Phillips, Mat.
Pierce, William (killed)
Poe, John
Pollard, Absalom, Sr.
Pollard, Absalom, Jr.
Pollard, James
Pollard, Robert
Pollard, William
Ponton, Joel
Pope, John, Jr.
Pope, Lt. Col. John, Jr.*
Powell, Ben.
Powell, Edmond
Powell, Francis
Powell, John, Sr.
Powell, John, Jr.
Powell, Nat.
Powell, Richard
Powell, William
Powell, Wyatt
Powell, Zachariah
Pratt, Thomas
Price, Thomas
Prior (Pryor), David
Prior (Pryor), John, Sr.
Prior (Pryor), John, Jr.
Prior (Pryor), Nicholas
Pugh, Willoughby
Pullins, Joseph
Purvis, George
Ramsey, James
Randolph, Henry
Ray, David, Sr. (killed)

Ray, David, Jr.
Ray, William
Redcross, John
Reid, Alexander
Reid, George
Reid, Jonathan
Renn, John (see Wrenn*)
Reynolds, Abraham
Reynolds, Patrick
Rice, Halman (Holman*)
Ricketts, Matthew
Roach, Henry
Roak, James
Roberts, Alexander
Roberts, Thomas
Roberts, Zachariah
Robertson, Robert
Robertson, Stephen
Robertson, Thomas
Robinson, Thomas
Rodes, Charles
Rodes, Captain Charles
Rogers, Ben.
Rose, Hugh
Rose, John
Rose, Peter*
Rosterson, John
Royalty, John
Rucker, A.
Rucker, Ambrose
Rucker, Isaac
Rucker, John (d. in service)
Rucker, John, Sr.
Rucker, John, Jr.
Rucker, Reuben
Ryan, Harris
Ryan, J.
Sandidge, William
Satterwhite, Francis
Saunders, Ben.
Saunders, David
Savage, James
Scott, William
Scruggs, Daniel
Scruggs, William
Seay, Abraham, Jr.
Shelton, Clough

Shelton, D.
Shelton, David
Shields, William
Shoemaker, John
Shoemaker, William
Shoemaker, Zedekiah*
Simmons, James
Simms, Charles
Simpson, David
Slatter, Tyne (Tyree*)
Slead, Will.
Smith, Alexander
Smith, Alexander or Austin
Smith, James
Smith, John
Smith, Johnson
Smith, Obediah
Smith, Thomas
Smith, Thomas "of Maryland"
Smith, Thomas, Jr.
Smith, William
Spencer, Samuel
Spencer, William
Staples, Joseph
Staples, Lieut. Joseph
Staples, Samuel, Jr.
Staten, Will.
Stevens, James
Stevens, John
Stevens, Thomas
Stoneham, Richard
Stovall, James
Stovall, Joseph
Stovall, Thomas
Stratton, Isaac
Stratton, John
Stuart (Stewart), Charles
Stuart, James
Stuart, John
Stuart, John
Stuart, Capt. John
Stuart, Swinney
Taliaferro, Ben.
Taliaferro, Charles
Taliaferro, Richard
Taliaferro, Capt. Richard
Tate, William, Jr.

Taylor, George
Taylor, Jesse
Taylor, John
Taylor, John*
Taylor, William
Taylor, Zachariah
Tennyson, Ignatius
Thomas, Cornelius
Thomas, John
Thompson, James
Thurman, Guthridge
Thurman, John
Thurman, Philip
Thurman, William
Thurtless, James
Tilford, David
Tilford, James
Tinsley, Isaac
Tinsley, James (son of Wm.)
Tomlinson, Ambrose
Trent, John
Trott, Joseph
Tucker, Charles
Tucker, Daniel
Tucker, Jesse
Tucker, John
Tucker, Joseph
Tucker, Matthew
Tucker, Thomas
Tucker, Capt. William
Tuggle, Charles
Tuggle, Henry
Tuggle, Joshua
Tuly, Charles
Tungett, Fielding
Turner, Henry
Turner, John
Turner, William
Tyler, John
Tyree, Zachariah
Upshur (Upshaw), John
Upshur (Upshaw), Leroy
Upton, Thomas, Jr.
Vaughn, John
Veale, Francis
Veale, Nathan
Veale, William

Via, David
Via, John
Via, William
Wade, Pierce
Walker, Jeremiah
Walton, Tilmon
Walton, William
Ware (or Weir), James
Ware, Mark
Warren, Burrus
Warren, James
Warwick, Abraham
Warwick, William
Waters, Francis
Waters, Moses
Watkins, Spencer
Watson, Edward
Watson, John
Watson, Lieut. John
Watts, Caleb T.
Watts, Thomas
Webb, Theodrick
Webster, William
Welch, Will.*
Wells, James
West, Bransford
West, Francis
West, John
Whitehead, John
Whitlor, John*
Whitten, Jeremiah
Whitten, John
Whitten, William
Wilburn, Richard
Wilburn, William
Wilcox, Edmund
Wilcox, Thomas
Williams, John

Williamson, William
Willis, John
Wilson, Matthew
Wingfield, John
Witt, Abner
Witt, Elijah
Witt, George
Witt, John
Witt, Lewis
Witt, Littleberry*
Witt, Will.
Wood, James
Wood, Jesse
Wood, John*
Wood, Robert
Wood, Silas
Wood, William
Woodroof, David
Woodroof, Capt. John
Woodroof, John
Woods, Josiah
Woody, George
Wrenn, John
Wright, Achilles
Wright, Andrew
Wright, Charles
Wright, Ellis
Wright, Francis
Wright, George, Sr.
Wright, George, Jr.
Wright, James
Wright, Jesse
Wright, John
Wright, Menos*
Wright, Moses
Wright, Robert
Wright, Thomas
Wright, Will.[49]

---

[49]Hardesty's *Historical & Geographical Encyclopedia, Special Edition,* pp. 409-411.

This list of "Revolutionary Heroes," compiled by "Alexander Brown, Esqr., a careful and devoted student of Virginia history," first appeared in *The Advance*, Lynchburg, Virginia, May 22, 1884. The editor states: "An incomplete list of those who served in the Revolutionary War from old Amherst County. Among them the great-grandfather of the writer, 'John Whitehead,' who served in the cavalry battalion of a Major Cabell."

*Names of soldiers added and corrections made from a photostat of a page of *The Advance* in possession of the author, through the courtesy of the New York Historical Society.

Additional Names of Amherst Soldiers Gathered from Miscellaneous Sources

Reuben Griffin, Amherst Co., Va., states in his will March 12, 1776; proved Sept. 1, 1777: "Having engaged in the Service of my Country and not knowing that it will please God that I shall return to the enjoyment of my worldly effects. . . ." (W.B. 1, p. 380).

Petitions of Amherst County: May 17, 1777 (A883). Charles Hay, William Johnson, Robert Horsley, Merritt Magann, John Woodroof, John Brown, Mitchell Floyd, Thomas Smith, Edmund Pendleton, Thomas Shelden, George Witt, Pearce Wade and John Guttery, ask reimbursement for expenses caused by sickness. They were soldiers in the State and Continental service in June and July, 1776, when taken ill and their expenses were £17, 15s, 2d and also £3, 9s, 6d for John Guttery. Allowed in the cases of the State troops and rejected in the cases of the Continentals. ("A Calendar of Legislative Petitions, arranged by Counties." 1908, p. 108, Va. State Library.)

Mordecai Brown, *Aud. Acct.* XXII, 20, Va. State Library.

Stephen Ham, Fifer 1776, *Military Accts.*, 1776, "War 22," p. 5, Va. State Library; private in Capt. Francis Taylor's Co., 2nd Va. Regt. His name first appears on the company pay roll March 28, to May 1, 1777; discharged March 12, 1778. (Adjutant General's Office, War Department, Washington, D. C.). His will was proved in Amherst Co., Va., Feb. 17, 1812. (W.B. 5, p. 59.)

Amherst Court March, 1784, Anthony Rucker, Deputy Commissioner of Provision Law for Amherst Co. for the year 1781 was allowed £50 for his service. (O.B. 1782-1784, p. 207.)

Amherst Court July, 1784, William Phillips proved he was heir at law to John Phillips a Continental Soldier who died in the Army, son of John Phillips of this county; William Tyree testified he was heir at law to Jacob Tyree a Continental Soldier who died in the Army, a son of Jacob Tyree of this county. (O.B. 1782-1784, p. 345.)

Oct. 4, 1784, Abner Witt heir at law to Charles Witt a Continental Soldier who died in the Army. (O.B. 1782-1784, p. 403.)

Amherst Court Nov., 1785, John Campbell, eldest brother & heir at law to George Campbell who died in the Continental Army. (O.B. 1784-1787, p. 367.)

Amherst Court, Sept., 1787, Mary Alford, sister & heir at law to Thomas Alford who died in the Contl. Army. (O.B. 1787-1790, p. 118.)

Reuben Tankersley, Rockbridge Co., Va., testified that his father, Richard Tankersley, managed Charles Rose's plantation while the latter & his wife were in Hanover Co. winter of 1780. After Christmas Richard Tankersley was called on a tour in the

Militia & his wife attended to Rose's affairs until he was discharged. (From a Suit in Chancery found with the Amherst Court papers in 1931.)

Bybie, Samuel
Carr, Nathaniel
Davison, Capt. John
Dawson, Robert
Eddes, William
Fasharn, Edward
Garland, Maj. Edward
Gillenwater, Joel
Griffin, Sherrod
Griggory, Jeremiah

Hardy, Charles
Hite, Patrick
Humphries, Thomas
Jackson, William
May, Lieut. Col. Charles
McKee, John
More, George
Miller, Francis
Quin, John
Sutlef, John

(Eckenrode's List of the *Revolutionary Soldiers of Va.*, Annual Report, Va. State Library, 1910-1911 & 1911-1912.)

Through the kindness of Mrs. Clyde W. Fisher, Palm Beach, Florida, the following is given from data collected by her father and uncle: Samuel Camp, born at Durham, Conn., May 14, 1753, son of Rev. Ichabod Camp, the first minister of Amherst Parish, married in Amherst Co., Va., Nov. 13, 1776, Mary, daughter of Gerrard & Ann (Stanton) Banks; died in Warren Co., Ga., 1824. Samuel Camp was assistant Quartermaster in Col. Gabriel Penn's Regt. He writes to his father from Albemarle Barracks 6 June 1779 and his family record shows that he was in Washington Co., Ga., Dec. 1, 1782. He received a grant of 287½ acres in Washington Co., Ga., for Revolutionary service. The Certificate reads: "GEORGIA—These are to certify, That Serjeant Samuel Camp of the Second Battalion of Continental Troops of the Georgia Line —is entitled to one Hundred & fifty acres of Land, as a Bounty, agreeable to an Act and Resolve of the General Assembly, passed at Augusta the 20th August 1781 and to one Hundred & fifty acres by a resolution of Congress of the 16th Sept. 1776, as P Certificate, Saml. Elbert, B.G. GIVEN under my Hand at Augusta the *8* day of *July* in the year of our Lord One Thousand Seven Hundred and eighty-*four*.
J. Houstoun"

Rev. Camp's record reads: "Moved with my family 6 June 1760 from Middletown, Ct. arrived at Wilmington, N. C. in nine days. * * * Moved with my family 6 May 1761 arrived at Cornwall, Va., *Lunenburg* 5 June 1761—Moved 22 March 1762 arrived at Amherst, Va. 1 April 1762. Moved 1 June 1778—Going down the Mississippi and Mary Anne died at Natchez—When he returned to and settled in Illinois." He was the son of John & Phoebe (Canfield) Camp, baptized Milford, Conn., Feb. 20, 1726; graduated from Yale in 1743; married first Content, dau. of Capt. Meacock Ward. She died Dec. 2, 1754. He died at Kaskaskia, Ill. in 1786.

There were three James Dillards living in Amherst Co. during the Revolution: Capt. James Dillard (b. 1727; d. 1794), son of Capt. James Dillard (d. 1768) of the French & Indian War; Capt. James Dillard, Jr., an officer in the Contl. Army; and Capt. James Dillard (b. 1744; d. 1823), son of Thomas & Elizabeth (Holliday) Dillard of Spotsylvania Co., Va.

Sept. 6, 1779, Cornelius Vaughan "intending shortly by God's permission to join the Grand Continental Army as a Soldier under General Washington," constituted Peter Carter his attorney, to sell lands in "Onslow County, North Carolina being the same which was granted to John Wallace by patent bearing date the 20th April 1745 at Newbern and containing 100 acres which was held since that Time by my Father Martin Vaughan and on his Death descended to me his Heir." He died of smallpox while in service. His will, dated Aug. 20, 1779, proved in Amherst Co., Va., Sept. 3, 1781. (W.B. 2, p. 23.)

John Howard, Contl. Soldier. Brown's *The Cabells & Their Kin*, p. 183.

January 23, 1781, "Geddes"—Col. "Hugh Rose to Col. Geo: Muter, recommending Mr. Lamont, the bearer to some easy duty in the service, on account of his recent recovery from illness of several months." *Calendar of Va. State Papers*, 1, 455.

The name of Benjamin Fry appears on the "LIST OF VIRGINIA PENSIONERS,—1786." Two names are illegible. From the following is gleaned one of the missing names: Amherst Court, April, 1784, *"John Brown* a Serjeant & Benjamin Fry a Soldier are considered by the Court as Pensioners." (O.B. 1782-1784, p. 116.)

Jan. 21, 1820—Lynchburg Press: Revolutionary Soldier, Mr. Micajah Carter in his 65 year, died on the morning of the 6th inst. at his residence in Amherst Co.

Captain Azariah Martin's Company of Militia

A Pay Roll of Capt. Azh. Martin's Compy. of Militia from Amherst County belonging to the 4th Regt. V. M. Commanded by Colonel Jas. Lucas, taken from ye 15th of June to ye 7th of Sepr. 1780 being Eighty four Days.

Name	Rank	Days	Pay P Day		Amount of Pay	Remarks
Azh. Martin	Capt.	84	@ 40	lbs Toba	3360	£42
Wm. Holt	Lieut.	84	@ 30	" "	2520	Sub. for 26 12 Wm. Bibb
Lee Royupshaw	Lieut.	61	@ 30	" "	1830 (as Ensign)	15 5
Jas. Alexander	Lieut.	30	@ 30	" "	900	3 Discharged
Jno. Martin	Serjt.	132	@ 10	" "	1320	
Jereh. Walker	Drm Major	132	@ 10	" "	1320	
Josa Tuggle	Corpol	132	@ 8½	" "	1122	
Saml. Bell	Private	132	@ 7½	" "	990	
Absom. Pollard	"	132	@ 7½	" "	990	
Saml. Dinwiddie	"	61	@ 7½	" "	457½	Dissarted[50] from ye Battle Cambden
Lane Carter	"	61	@ 7½	" "	457½	" "
Jas. Hopkins[51]	"	61	@ 7½	" "	457½	" "
Wm. Pierce	"	61	@ 7½	" "	457½	Mising from Battle
Wm. Forbus	"	61	@ 7½	" "	457½	Dissarted from hilsborough
Wm. Boulware	"	61	@ 7½	" "	457½	" "
Alexr. Forbus	"	61	@ 7½	" "	457½	" "
Jno. Henryplod	"	61	@ 7½	" "	457½	" "
Edwd. Bibey	"	61	@ 7½	" "	457½	" "
Nicos. Lyon	"	61	@ 7½	" "	457½	" "
Wm. Phillips	"	61	@ 7½	" "	457½	" "
Pleasant Dawson	"	61	@ 7½	" "	457½	" "
Wm. Murrah	"	61	@ 7½	" "	457½	" "
Wm. Bowman	"	61	@ 7½	" "	457½	" "
Robt. Tate	"	61	@ 7½	" "	457½	Mising from ye Battle
Owen Ohern	"	61	@ 7½	" "	457½	Dissarted from hilsborough
Jacob Pucket	"	61	@ 7½	" "	457½	" "
Heny. Mcclain[52]	"	61	@ 7½	" "	457½	" "
John Clifton	"	61	@ 7½	" "	457½	" "
John Bowman[53]	"	61	@ 7½	" "	457½	" "
( ) Miller	"	61	@ 7½	" "	457½	Mising from ye Battle
( ) ( )se	"	132	@ 7½	" "	990	taken Prisoner &————d
(Benj.) (B)rya(nt)[54]	"	61	@ 7½	" "	457½	Dissarted hilsborough
Jno Lobbing	"	61	@ 7½	" "	457½	"
Giddn Martin[55]	"	61	@ 7½	" "	457½	"
Thos. Church	"	61	@ 7½	" "	457½	"
Simn. Ramsey	"	61	@ 7½	" "	457½	"
Jno Cloe	"	61	@ 7½	" "	457½	"
Wm. Purkins	"	61	@ 7½	" "	457½	"
Thos. Gash	"	61	@ 7½	" "	457½	"
Thos. Price	"	61	@ 7½	" "	457½	"
Jos. Henderson	"	61	@ 7½	" "	457½	"
Robt. Grattan	"	61	@ 7½	" "	457½	Taken Prisoner, Return'd
Jno. Brown	"	61	@ 7½	" "	457½	Dissarted, at hilsborough
Bennet Henderson	"	61	@ 7½	" "	457½	" "
Jas Obryan	"	61	@ 7½	" "	457½	" "
Alexr. Pattern	"	61	@ 7½	" "	457½	Did not Rece. £50 Bounty Dissarted hilsborough
Wm. Marshall Amherst Sc	"	61	@ 7½	" "	457½	" "

This Day Azariah Martin made Oath before me, The Above Roll is true & Rightly Drawn off or that he Believes it to be so. Certified by me this 3d Day of June 1783   Jno. Diggs J. P.[56]

---

[50]"Deserter" written after a name in the original documents, must not be taken too seriously. Frequently a man absented himself to gather crops, to attend a sick wife, or to bury a child; but it is found that the soldier generally returned, and was again taken up on the rolls. *New York in the Revolution as Colony and State*, Introductory, Vol. 1, pp. 14-15.

[51]James Hopkins, Pittsylvania Co., Va., applied for a pension, Sept. 17, 1832: born Feb. 22, 1765. He enlisted in the spring of 1780 in Amherst Co., Va., served as a substitute for James Hopkins, Sr. as private in Capt. Azariah Martin's company, Col. Lucas's 4th Va. Regt., Gen. Stevens' Brigade. Rendezvoused at Hillsborough, N. C. where we remained sometime for the purpose of being disciplined, joined Major-Gen. H. Gates, Commander-in-Chief of the Southern Army, at Rugeley's Mills, on the morning of August 15th; rested the balance of the day and at one o'clock at night took off—the time of march to surprise the enemy before day, who marched at the same time. The two armies met on the middle ground and a sharp skirmish between the advance guards took place. That night the line was formed and the men stood under arms all night. Next morning, August 16th, the line was ordered to advance and a general engagement took place about the rising of the sun, which resulted in a shameful defeat of the Southern Army. There was no place designated in the event of defeat at which we should rendezvous; we lost all our baggage and were destitute of any clothing except what little we had on; separated from our officers and no means of subsistence. Under these appalling circumstances, although our term of service was nearly expired, a considerable number of the company to which he belonged, determined to make the best of their way home. After our return to Amherst County, a Court of inquiry convened and made an order that we should all be sent back and serve a tour of 8 months under command of regular officers. We were accordingly mustered and put under command of Capt. Pamplin, who marched us back to Hillsborough, where Gen. Greene's Army lay, and we were transferred to the command of Capt. Graves from the county of Culpeper, who was assigned to take command of the men sent back from other counties for the same offense. In a short time the army marched South. We passed through Salisbury and Charlotte and about the 1st of Jan., 1781, took up winter quarters on the North side of Cedar River, near Cedar Hills, S. C. In the month of Feb. there was an order issued for all men belonging to the "Eight Month's Company," as they were called, to be discharged except the young men who were to be retained till their term of service expired. This reduced the company considerably. Capt. Graves returned home with the men discharged and the balance retained in service, were placed under Capt. Webb, who, he understood, came from about Richmond, Va. Shortly after this Gen. Morgan defeated Col. Tarlton at a place called the Cowpens, and took a number of prisoners, and had to make a rapid retreat to keep them from being retaken by the enemy. As soon as Gen. Greene received the information he immediately marched off the army to cover Morgan's retreat and left this small company of "Eight Month Men" some of whom were stationed at the mills to guard and keep them employed grinding meal and flour for the use of the army, and some to guard the encampments. Finally Capt. Webb received orders to take charge of 8 or 10 wagons loaded with meal and flour and about 400 head of hogs to follow after the army, and were in fact in rear of both armies, when we reached Deep River, N. C., intending to go to Guilford Courthouse, but received intelligence that Cornwallis was at that place. We then changed our route, turned to the right, went to Halifax and Granville Counties and crossed Roanoke River at Taylor's Ferry, near which place in the County of Mecklenburg, Va., was a Commissary store where the Captain delivered the meal, flour and hogs, which we protected safely through a part of our country that at that time was literally speaking in the hands of the British and Tories. By this time our term of service was nearly expired, and we were permitted to draw up a petition and send it on by express to Gen. Greene, stating our situation—that we were almost naked, worn out with fatigue and praying him to send orders to the captain to discharge us, which he did, and we met the express in the county of Halifax, near Banister River, Va., where the company was discharged about the first of March, 1781. His claim was allowed. James Hopkins died in Pittsylvania Co., July 20,

1844. His widow, Mary Hopkins (second wife) was allowed pension on her application executed March 2, 1853, aged 92. Their eldest son Reuben Hopkins (b. 1798) in 1853 was Clerk of the Court of Pittsylvania Co., Va. She died May 31, 1853.

[52]Henry McClain, Nelson Co., Va., applied for a pension Oct. 6, 1832: born in Lancaster Co., Penn., May 10, 1750. While residing in Amherst Co., Va., enlisted and served as a private with the Virginia troops as follows: 2 months under Capt. Azariah Martin; marched to Hillsborough, then to Camden. The engagement in which Gen. Gates was defeated took place the following night. Before day they had orders to retreat. Col. Dameron, who had lost his hat, told them to escape the best way they could, which they did and set off in great confusion, and from there returned home as his company was not organized again. Some time afterwards the said Capt. Martin drew his pay for 2 months and gave it to him; three months under Capts. James Pamplin & John Graves; nearly three months under Capt. John Loving, Lt. Turner; marched to Williamsburg where his brother, James McClain, completed the rest of the 3 months tour. His claim was allowed.

[53]William Bowman, Washington Co., Ind., applied for a pension, April 5, 1833; aged 71. He volunteered in Amherst Co., Va., Sept., 1777, served 60 days as private in Capt. Nicholas Cabell's Co., Col. Joseph Cabell's Va. Regt. Enlisted about Aug. 1, 1780, served as a private in Capt. Azariah Martin's Co., and was in the battle of Camden under Col. Porterfield and Gen. Gates. They were attacked in the night, 16th of August, and the main battle was fought next morning. The greater part of the company to which he belonged were killed or wounded. Returned home and furloughed by the colonel of the county for 20 days; returned to Hillsborough & served as private in Capt. Thomas Threadgill's company, Lt. William Collins, Gen. Stevens' Brigade; discharged about April 1, 1781. Shortly afterwards he volunteered in April, 1781, & served 90 days as a private in Capt. Charles Christian's Va. Co., marched to Yorktown, was in the battle at that place & guarded prisoners taken there, to Winchester, Va., after which he was discharged. Claim was allowed. He died April 2, 1843.

[54]Benjamin Bryant, Warren Co., Ky., applied for a pension, July 23, 1832, aged 82 years and 9 months. While residing in Amherst Co., Va., vol. June, 1780, served 3 months as a private in Capt. Azariah Martin's Co., Col. Lucas' Va. Regt., and was in the battle of Camden under Col. Porterfield who was shot in the knee & died next day of the wound. Oct., 1780, served as private in Capt. John Graves' Co., Col. Lucas' Regt., was in a skirmish with the Tories at Island Ford on the Yadkin River. Discharged in Pittsylvania Co., Va., Feb., 1781. His first discharge was signed by Capt. Azariah Martin; second by Capt. John Graves. He moved to Greenbrier Co., Va., thence to Warren Co., Ky. Placed on Pension Roll Oct. 22, 1832; died March 6, 1835. His widow, Nancy (Gragg) Bryant, same place, Dec. 24, 1838, aged 83, applied for a pension. They were married in the fall of 1771, Augusta Co., Va. Reference is made to their children, 4 of whom were born prior to 1775. Her claim was allowed.

[55]Gideon Martin, Warren Co., Ky., applied for a pension July 20, 1832, aged 100; enlisted June, 1780, in Amherst Co., Va., and served three months as a private in Capt. Azariah Martin's Co., Col. Lucas' 4th Va. Regt., Gen. Stevens' Brigade, and was in the battle of Camden. Received no discharge for this tour, for when Gen. Gates was defeated, Capt. Martin's company joined in the retreat becoming so dispersed many got no discharge. He enlisted in the fall of 1780 and served three months as a private in place of Luke Powell, whom he had employed as a substitute in Capt. Graves' Co., under Capt. John Loving, and marched to Little York; discharged before Cornwallis surrendered. His neighbor, Benjamin Bryant, was on a tour with him under Capt. Azariah Martin. Claim was allowed.

[56]Miscellaneous papers "K 2" Archives Division, Virginia State Library.

Amherst County, Virginia, in the Revolution

Captain William Tucker's Company of Militia

A Pay Role of Capt. William Tucker's Compy. of Militia from Amherst County in The State of Virginia Joined The Army The 14th Day of January 1781—Discharged The 26th Day of March following. Seventy-two days.[57]

William Tucker	Captn.
Jos. Tucker	Lieut.
Danl. Tucker	Ensign
Patrick Reynolds	F. Master
Elijah Gillinwater	Assistant ditto
John Watson	Q. M. Sergt.

Sergeants

James Stewart	William Penn
Joseph Burrus	Larkin Gatewood
Joseph Higginbotham	Joseph Stovaul

Corporals

Richard Pendleton	Thomas Jones
George Duglass	Reubin Banks

Phillip Penn

Privates

Moses Waters	John Hamm
John Rowsey	Henry Childress
Francis Wright	William Powell
James Simmons	Nicholas Lyon
James Coleman	John Pryor
Reubin Pendleton	John Shoemaker
William Webster	James Pollard
Thomas Wilcox	Titus Hunter
Obediah Powell	James Savage
William Knight	William Goodwin
Edward Lyon	Thomas Powell
William Davis	John Childress
Henry Slaton	Richard Peter
Thomas Gilbert	Phillip Burton
John Kipias	William Asburey
Orstin Knight	Joseph Layne
Robert Johns	Edward Reoch
Nath. Gutrey	Dan Goode

[57]Miscellaneous papers "K 3" Archives Division, Virginia State Library.

Gilbert Cotrell
James Stovaul
John Taylor
George Taylor
James Peyton
David New
Francis Powell
William Graves
Thomas Penn
David Viar
John Upshaw
Burrus Warren
William Viar
John Brooks
John Waters
Hugh Gilliland

William Mahoon
James White
William Crutcher
William Williamson
John Stinnett
Zachariah Powell
Saml. Cook
Stephen Rickitts
Richard Gatewood
Benjamin Johnson
William Bryant
John Gatewood
Richard Goodwin
Negro Will Waginer
 (waggoner)

ALBEMARLE BARRACKS
View of the Encampment of the Convention Troops
From a picture in Aubury's *Travels*

Amherst County, Virginia, in the Revolution

Regiment of Guards

The British and German prisoners taken at the battle of Saratoga were called the "Convention Troops," and from the middle of January, 1779, until early in June, 1781, they occupied an encampment several miles from Charlottesville, Virginia, "upon the brow and slopes of a high hill" on the north bank of Ivy Creek. This location was on the estate of Colonel Harvie, and ever since has been referred to as "The Barracks."

The Albemarle Barracks Regiment was organized first for one year, and was regarded as a State Regiment or a Volunteer Independent Corps, but finding its services would be needed longer than at first anticipated, Congress adopted it as a Continental Regiment and declared the class of officers that should command it. At one time orders were given for its removal outside of the State, so that the Regiment was fully under the control of Congress as a Continental Regiment.

A pay Roll of Capt. Richard Taliaferro's[58] Co. of foot in the Regiment of Guards at Alb. B. whereof F. Taylor, Esq., Commanded for the months of April & May '79.

No.	Names	Rank	Commencement of pay 1779 Mo.	days	Pay & Subsistence Money/Mo. in Dollars	Amount of pay in Va. currency
	John H. Woodroof	Lt.	19 Apl. 2	11	36⅔	£22 0s. 0d.
1.	Henry Campbell	Corp.	— 1	11	7⅓	3 - -
2.	Hardin Woodroof	do.	— 2	—	7⅓	4 8 -
3.	Daniel Hilley	P.	— 2	—	6⅔	4 - -
4.	John B. Hare	do.	— 2	—	6⅔	4 - -
5.	John Everett	do.	— 2	—	6⅔	4 - -
6.	Jesse Tucker	do.	— 2	—	6⅔	4 - -
7.	Robert Brown	do.	— 2	15	6⅔	4 - -
8.	Richard Cawthorn	do.	— 2	—	6⅔	4 - -
9.	Robert Cawthorn	do.	— 2	—	6⅔	4 - -
10.	Charles Hutchens	do.	— .	—	—Not found	- - -
11.	Edman Fair	do.	— .	—	—Deserted	- - -
12.	John W. Kenney	do.	— .	—	Enlstd.C.Ser.	- - -
13.	Basdel Hollas	do.	— .	—	do.	- - -

I do swear that the within is a just & true pay Roll—paid to the U. S. or any individual to the best of my knowledge £58—5s.

John H. Woodroof

Sworn to before me this 7 June, 1779.

F. Taylor, Col. Reg. G.

---

[58]This copy of Captain Richard Taliaferro's Pay Roll was found with his widow's application for a pension: Nov. 28, 1838, Nicholas L. Martin, testified this was a true copy of the Pay Roll now in his possession as son & Exor. of his father, Hudson Martin, Paymaster of Regt. of Guards stationed at Albemarle Barracks during the Revolution. "Widow's File No. 11,597," *Bureau of Pensions*, Washington, D. C.

A Muster Roll of Capt. James Burtons Company in the Regiment of Guards at the Barracks in Albemarle County Commanded by Colonel Francis Taylor for the Months of March, April, May, June & July 1780.

Commissioned Officers { James Burton Capt. Commission dated 8th October 1779
William Kennady Ensn. Commission date 16 June 1780

No.	Sergeants	When enlisted	Time of Service	Remarks
1.	James Goodall	Feby 16, 1779	Stay of the	
2.	John Briant	" 10	Troops in	
3.	Roger Shackleford	" 17	Albemarle	
4.	Thomas Smith	" 17	Discharged 13 April 1780	
	Corporals			
1.	Richard Quinn	Feby 8		
2.	Hardan Woodroof	" 5		
3.	William Ballard	Apr. 4		Reduced to a private 1 June
	Drum Fifer			
	John Barnett	Jan. 27		
	Privates			
1.	Phillip Sutherland	July 26, 1779		
2.	Jidethon Canterbery	Jany 22		
3.	Ambrose Lucas	" 25		
4.	James Farguson	" 29		
5.	Jonathan Roach	" 26		
6.	John Young	" 20		
7.	James Haney	" 26	2 years	
8.	John Lain	" 26	2 years	
9.	Francis Williams	" 11	2 years	
10.	Stark Wright	" 2		
11.	Zacha Lucas	" 2		On Furlough
12.	Absalom Roach	" 13		
13.	Caleb Jinnins	" 3		
14.	William Haynes	" 9		
15.	James Jorden	Feb 3		
16.	Johnson Smith	June 6		
17.	David Roach	Jany 26		
18.	William Tinsley	" 21		
19.	John Flowers	Oct. 16		
20.	John Briant*	Jany 27	Stay of the	
21.	Samuel Arrington*	" 19	Troops in	
22.	Thomas Bibe*	" 22	Albemarle	
23.	John Everett*	Feb 22		
24.	Richard Cawthorn*	Mar 25		
25.	Robert Caathan*	" 25		
26.	John Via*	Feby 18		
27.	Daniel Hilley*	" 17		
28.	Gideon Via*	" 15		
29.	Littlebury Via*	Mar 18		
30.	Charles Lavender*	Jany 16		
31.	Zacha Briant*	Feby 17		
32.	John Gillenwater*	Mar. 19		
33.	Daniel Tylor*	Jany 30	11 Sept. 1780	

*Enlisted from Amherst County.

Amherst County, Virginia, in the Revolution 59

34. Jeremiah Wade*	Mar 30	12 Months	Discharged	8th April
35. Jeremiah Wade, Jr.*	Jany 25	"	Do	19 March
36. Robt Cawthan, Senr*	Mar [illegible]	"	Do	23 Do
37. Edward Helton*	" [illegible]	"	Do	8 April
38. Joshua Wade*	" 30	"	Do	8 April
39. James Evins*	Jany 18	Stay of the	Deserted	
40. Zacha Fortune*	Jany 23	Troops in	Discharged	5 April
41. Henry Campbell*	Apr 19	Albemarle	Do	1 June

1780 August the 1st day. Then Mustered the above Company as Specified
John Roberts Majr. Ry.
J. Burton Capt.

Sworn to before me this 8 day of August 1780
James Wood
Colo. Com.

LIEUT. COL. JAMES HIGGINBOTHAM'S PAY AND THE PAY FOR HIS BATTALION GUARDING THE "CONVENTION TROOPS"

United States Dr.

"October 22, 1779. Warr[an]t to James Higginbotham for his pay as Lieut. Colo. of the Amherst Militia guarding the Convention Troops, pr. Cert.,———£20."
"Aud. Acct. 1779-80, 132." Virginia State Library.

1779

Warrt. to Capt. John Jacobs for pay & of his Company of Amherst Militia guarding the Convention Troops P Pay Roll } £128-18-1
Warrt. to Cap: Ambrose Rucker for Do.   128-12-4
Warrt. to Cap: Charles Burras for Do.   107- " -3
Warrt. to Cap: William Harris for Do.   193- " -1
Warrt. to Capt. John Christian for Do.   109-18-7
Warrt. to Cap: David Shelton for Do.   196- 6 -1
Warrt. to Cap: David Woodruff for Do.   28- 2 -
Warrt. to Cap: John Higginbotham for Do.   145-10-2

Virginia State Library
Richmond, Virginia
Oct. 22, 1932

This is to Certify that the above was this day copied by photostat from an original document (Amherst Public Claims) now in the Archives Division of the Virginia State Library, which document was transferred to the library under authority of Acts of Assembly, 1918, Chap. 231.

Morgan P. Robinson,
State Archivist

Clothing and Beef for 16th Division

Among the papers of Col. James Higginbotham, I found the following relating to payments at some period in the Revolution:[59]

"John Higginbotham's part of Clothing, Beef, etc., for the 16th Division

	£ 52-8-0
Col. Rose	365-18-1
Lawrence Campbell	17-9-5
John Brown	11-13-6
Thomas Bailey	1-2-0
Benjamin Evans	0-3-2
Peter Cashwell	4-2-6
William Gatewood	3-14-5
James Higginbotham	45-12-4
Henry Garrett	1-7-0
Francis Lee	16-11-9
Thomas Landrum	21-2-2
Abraham Stratton	9-3
Henry Stratton	14-8
Isaac Stratton	14-8
Thomas Wortham	7-4
William Spencer	123-16-10
John Ware	9-19-4
John Lamont	9-10
Richard Bean	11-1
	£688-16-4

The above is each man's part of Clothing and Beef for the 16th Division.

The Clothing cost	239
The Beef cost	450
	£689"

---

[59] In possession of his great-great-grandson, Thomas Lee Higginbotham, Sandidge, Amherst County, Virginia.

Amherst County, Virginia, in the Revolution

Disbursements to Wives, Widows and Orphans of Revolutionary Soldiers

Amherst County, Virginia, Order Book, 1773-1782

Court held May 5, 1777

William Cabell, Gent. is Recommended to the Treasurer to Receive Twenty pounds for the Support of Wives and children of Such Poor Soldiers as have Enlisted in this County in the Service of the United States of America. Page 185

January Court, 1778

Ordered that John Rose, Gent. supply Ruth Canterberry with provisions on the Publick Account, until further order of this Court. Page 214

May Court, 1778

Joseph Cabell, Hugh Rose and Gabriel Penn Gentlemen are appointed to inquire into the Several Cases of the Wifes (sic) and Children of Soldiers that enlisted from this County, in the Continental Service, or into the Service of this State, and to furnish them with such necessarys as they shall think Reasonable, and to Render an Account thereof to this Court, agreeable to an Act of Assembly in that Case made. Page 232

August Court, 1778

John Rose, Gent. rendered Account for Three pounds Seventeen shillings and six pence for provisions furnished Ruth Canterbery the wife of a poor Soldier in the Continental Army which being Examined and approved by the Court, It's ordered that the same be Certified to the Treasurer for payment thereof.
Page 234

William Pollard produced his Account for £38 for boarding Mary Ann Nevil the widow of Reuben Nevil a poor Soldier, who lately died in the Continental Army, who has been long affected with a serious disorder as also her child five months which Account being Examined etc. Page 234

John Peters produced his Account for Twelve pounds for Boarding Mary Ann Nevil the widow of Reuben Nevil—It's ordered William Cabell pay the said Peters the sum of Twelve Pounds out of the Publick Money in hand for that purpose. Page 234

Edmund Wilcox produced his Account for Medicines and Attendance on Mary Ann Nevil (and her Child) which Account is ordered to be Certified to Doctor Rickman for his Approval.
Page 234

On the Motion of William Cabell Gent. And it appearing to the Court that he has but £8 10s. 6d. of the Public money in his hands, And by an order of the Court yesterday the said Cabell was directed to pay John Peters the sum of £12, for boarding Mary Ann Nevil and her Child two Months. . . . It's ordered that the said Cabell pay said Peters the aforesaid £8 10s. 6d. It is also ordered that the Balance of £3 9s. 6d. be Certified to the Treasurer for payment thereof.
Page 288

September Court, 1778

William Pollard's Account for boarding Mary Ann Nevil and her child for two months Amounting to £8 it's Ordered to be certified etc.
Page 289

October Court, 1778

William Harris Jun. presented his Account in Court amounting to fifteen Pounds Sixteen shillings and four pence Half Penny for Provisions furnished Ruth Canterberry the Wife of Joseph Canterberry Susannah Conner the Wife of Daniel Conner and ——— Jones the Wife of Thomas Jones, Poor Soldiers in the Continental Army, which being Examined and approved of by the Court It's ordered etc.
Page 322

Joseph Cabell presented his Account for £2 13s. 9d. for provisions furnished Mary Burnett the Wife of John Burnett a poor Soldier in the Continental Army which being Examined and approved of by the Court It's ordered etc.
Page 322

On the Motion of Edmund Wilcox, It's ordered that his Account for Medicine and Attendance on Mary Ann Nevil be paid with the Approbation of Doctor Rickman.
Page 325

February Court, 1779

William Cabell produced his Account amounting to £5 for provisions furnished Mary Burnett the widow of John Burnett decd. a poor Soldier who lately Died in the Continental Army which being Examined and allowed by the Court It's ordered etc.
Page 340

March Court, 1779

Hugh Rose Gent. presented an Account for £34 2s. for provisions furnished Susannah Conner which being Examined and approved etc.
Page 347

Court held May 3, 1779

Hugh Rose Gent. presented an Account for £39 10s. for provisions furnished Mary Burnett which being Allowed It's ordered etc.
Page 353

June Court, 1779

William Pollard presented his Account for £11 for boarding Mary Ann Nevil (and her Child) from the third Day of Aug., 1778 to the 27th Sept. following which being proved and allowed It's ordered etc.   Page 361

Adam Brown presented an Account in Court amounting to £56 for boarding Mary Ann Nevil (& her child) Seven Months to this Day which was allowed.   Page 362

November Court, 1779

Joseph Cabell presented his Account in Court amounting to £2 18s. for Salt furnished Mary Burnett.   Page 383

Gabriel Penn Gent. presented an Account in Court amounting to £18 15s. which sum he had paid for provisions furnished Betty Wilton the Wife of James Wilton a poor Soldier in the Continental Army, which the said Penn made Oath to, etc.   Page 383

Joseph Cabell Gent. presented an Account in Court amounting to £26 5s. which sum he had paid for provisions furnished Betty Wilton.   Page 383

August Court, 1780

On Motion of Cassie Hays, the wife of George Hays a poor Soldier in the Western Battalion of this State, and it Appearing to the Court that the said Hays has four helpless children and that they are in great Distress for the Common Necessaries of Life and that the said Cassie Hays is not of ability to provide it, whereupon William Cabell, Esq. is directed to give the said Hays three barrels of corn & 150 pounds of Beef.   Page 427

November Court, 1780

William Cabell, Esq. is allowed £105 for three barrels of corn furnished Mrs. Hays the wife of George Hays.   Page 435

February Court, 1781

Thomas Parrock is allowed £150 for 150 pounds of Beef which the year passed he furnished Cassie Hays and four helpless Children.   Page 440

Cassie Hays is allowed ten barrels of corn and 250 pounds of pork to support her and four helpless children for the present year.   Page 440

June Court, 1781

Thomas Parrock is allowed £562 and 10 shillings for 250 pounds of net pork furnished Cassie Hays and four children.   Page 451

September Court, 1781

It Appearing to the Court that Mary Biggs and three helpless children the wife and children of John Biggs, Jr. a Soldier in the

Continental Army is not of ability to support themselves it is ordered that they be furnished by one of the Commissarys of the Specie Tax of this County with four barrels of corn till the 18th day of May next it being one year and they are also allowed 50 pounds of net Pork for Each person Amounting in the like to Two hundred Weight.   Page 455

Ordered that William Cabell Esq. furnish Mary Biggs and her children for the term of 18 months with four hundred weight of Beef out of the County Beef in his hands in lieu of two hundred weight of net Pork allowed the said Biggs by a former order of this present Court.   Page 456

Letter of Colonel William Fontaine Describing Surrender of Cornwallis

October 26th 1781
Richmond

"Dear Sir,

Major Penn gives me an opportunity, the first I have met with, since the glorious event of congratulating you on the surrender of York, which I do with all imaginable cordiality. I had the happiness to see that British Army which so lately spread dismay & desolation thro' all our Country, march forth on the 20th instant, at 3-o-clock, thro' our whole army, drawn up in two lines, at about twenty yards distance, & return disrobed of all their terrors, so humbled & so struck at the appearance of our Troops, that their knees seemed to tremble, and you could not see a platoon that marched in any order. Such a noble figure did our army make, that I scarce know which drew my attention most. You could not have heard a whisper or seen the least motion throughout our whole line, but every countenance was erect, & expressed a serene cheerfulness. Cornwallis pretended to be ill, & imposed the mortifying duty of leading forth the captives on General O'Hara. Their own officers acknowledge them to be the flower of the British troops, yet I do not think they at all exceeded in appearance our own, or the French. The latter, you may be assured are very different from the ideas formerly inculcated in us, of people living on frogs and coarse vegetables.

Finer troops I never saw. His Lordship's defence, I think, was rather feeble—His surrender was eight or ten days sooner than the most sanguine expected, tho' his force & resources were much greater than we conceived. He had at least a fortnight's provisions, & 1000 barrels of powder left, besides a magazine, that 'tis supposed was blown up with design during the negotiations for the surrender. The whole of the prisoners of war amount to 6,800, exclusive of sailors and marines, which with the shipping belong to the French, & the refugees, merchants & followers of their army. The shipping of every sort is about seventy sail, tho' a great many are sunk. Of brass ordnance we have taken eighty odd—of iron 120—muskets, 7313 fit for service, besides a great number in unopened boxes & of old arms. Of horse about 300 accoutred: there must be more horse accoutrements, but I have not seen a particular return from Gloucester where the horse lay. The military chest amounts to only 800 guineas. Merchants' stores are subject to the preemption of our army at a reasonable price for such articles as suit them; the remainder they are allowed three months to effect the sale of, then are to give their parole and clear out. Tories are subject to be treated by our laws. The 20th of next month has been appointed for that purpose. A small proportion of officers are to remain with the prisoners, the rest are to be paroled to New-York. A flag ship is allowed Cornwallis, to carry him to New York, thence I believe he goes home. His flag ship is not to be searched—The officers retain their side arms & baggage & the soldiers their knapsacks. They marched out with drums muffled & colors furled & crossed. All property taken from the inhabitants by the British is liable to be claimed by them. In consequence Master Tarleton met with a most severe mortification, the day before yesterday. The Hero was prancing thro' the streets of York on a very fine, elegant horse, and was met by a spirited young fellow of the country, who stopped him, challenged the horse, & ordered him instantly to dismount. Tarleton halted & paused awhile thro' confusion, then told the lad, if it was his horse, he supposed he must be given up, but insisted to ride him some distance out of town to dine with a French officer. This was more, however, than Mr. Giles was disposed to indulge him in, having been forced, when he & his horse were taken, to travel good part of a night on foot at the point of a bayonet—he therefore refused to trust him out of his sight & made him dismount in the midst of the street crowded with spectators. Many such instances since have happened on the road. The people who have been insulted, abused, nay, ruined by them, give them no quarter— I have not seen the articles of capitulation, but have given you the substance, as well as I can recollect from such as have read them.

We are surely to have a garrison at York—whether French or American was not known, when I left York, the day before yesterday—some troops are to go Southward. 'Tis supposed the French fleet & most of their troops will go to the West Indies—Tho' all is conjecture & will probably remain so to all, but the Count de Grasse & Gen: Washington. The General has been aboard the Admiral for some days past, as I came away something of consequence I suspect, was projecting between them. The troops of Portsmouth are levelling, to prevent the British taking post there. Nothing certain of a British fleet. They have lost, 'tis said, Bengall & Madras in the East Indies, by the powerful exertions of Hyder Ali, in favour of the French. Cornwallis, I am well assured, previous to his surrender, acknowledged to the Secretary, that the Capture of his Army would put an end to the war. The same sentiment was expressed to me by two of his officers, & I learn from an intelligent inhabitant of York, generally prevailed among them.

That General Lesly with all the crew, perished in the passage from Wilmington to Charles Town, in the Blonde Frigate in ore est omnium.

I certainly embark for Europe the soonest a passage can be had, perhaps three or four weeks hence, tho' I believe I shall be forced to take the West Indies in the way & probably may winter there. My love to my good sisters & families. My best respects to Mr. Armistead & all my relations and friends in your country—Farewell—farewell!—The good Doctor, Parson Cole & all—I have commissioned a gentleman, to get Mr. Holmes a hat from York. Mrs. Walker has recovered her two negroes, & my mother her one.

The French fleet & all our troops are under sailing & marching orders. If Major Holston is with you, let him know Mr. Burrows from his state has his servant that he wrote about.

I enclose two yards of ribbon for my Sister Sarah & two for Sister Mary, or in her absence, little Bess—trophies from York—had the stores been open, I would have dealt more largely, tho' they are strictly guarded, & general orders against anything being sold 'till the Army is supplied—All health & happiness to you & yours, & all with you.

Your affectionate friend & Servant,

W. Fontaine."[60]

---

[60]*Calendar of Virginia State Papers*, II, 567.

William Fontaine, son of Rev. Peter Fontaine, was tutor at "Union Hill," when the Revolution broke out. His company attached to the 2nd Va. Regt. under command of Col. Woodford was in the battle of Great Bridge; he served throughout the War; promoted Colonel and was at the Surrender of Lord Cornwallis.

Col. William Cabell wrote in his diary, "October 29th 1781. Killed my stag, and invited company to rejoice over the surrender of Cornwallis and his army. On the 17th instant, Cornwallis and his army surrendered to his Excellency General Washington."

Letter of Colonel Hugh Rose to Governor Harrison

"Feb'y 20, 1782

Sir

Your Proclamation requiring the apprehension of the British Prisoners came lately to hand; Since which time I have not had an opportunity of communicating to your Excellency the situation of a few of these People now in this County, & therefore have not as yet executed your orders against them; not doubting that when you were informed that so far from being a great Prejudice & Annoyance of the Citizens, & an Injury to the Commonwealth, they are sober well disposed men, valuable artisans & highly agreeable to the People, that your Excellency would not object to grant them a Permit to remain in this County until called for to be exchanged; the greater part of them are Prisoners made at the Cow-pens, who with the permission of Governor Jefferson resided in this County from the 20th of last Feby, until the cartel was offerd. at James Town: during which time they found Connections by marriage and otherways, which render their Return to their several Corps so extremely disagreeable, that I am convinced had our Laws permitted their Denization, they would most cheerfully have become good & faithful Subjects to this Common-wealth, but the case being otherwise & Retaliation upon that score inadmissable, they were exchanged, were captured at York & as soon as opportunity offered made their escape to this County & immediately as upon the former occasion applied to me for Protection, which I readily granted, until I could procure a permit from the Executive; this I had expected very shortly to have obtained, as I was to set out from Richmond in a few Days; but unluckily I arrived there during the interregnum, which prevented me from making personal application.

I hope to meet with your Excellency's Approbation of my conduct in waiting for your further orders respecting the apprehension of men who are really useful & agreeable to the People in General.

    I am, with the highest esteem
     your Excellency's most obt & hbl Servt.

P.S. There are eight Prisoners two of them Germans, for whom Coll: Sam: Cabell gave a Rec't to their officer——

          H. R."[61]

---

[61]*Calendar of Virginia State Papers*, III, 69.

TUSCULUM

Home of Captain David Crawford, built about 1790.

Amherst County, Virginia, in the Revolution 69

Claims for Property Impressed or Taken for Public Service

Order Book 1773-1782, pages 474-500

At a Court continued and held for Amherst County the 2nd Day of April, 1782.

Present:

William Cabell	David Crawford	Gent. Justices
Ambrose Rucker	Gabriel Penn	
Zacharias Taliaferro	Nicholas Cabell	

Pursuant to a late Act of Assembly entitled "An Act for adjusting Claims for property impressed or taken for public service," the Court now proceeds to receive the Claims of Sundry inhabitants of the said County against this and the United States which are as follows (amount and date of the certificate is stated in the Order Book following the name of the claimant and the kind of claim) :[62]

Alford, William	Bean, Johnson	Brooks, James
Allen, Erasmus	Bell, Henry	Brooks, Robert
Allen, Samuel	Bell, Thomas	Brooks, William
Allen, William	Bethell, John	Brown, Adam
Arnold, Hendrick	Bibb, John	Brown, John
Ayres, Samuel	Bibb, Sarah	Burford, Daniel
Ballenger, Richard	Bibb, William	Burford, Daniel, Jr.
Banks, Linn	Blain, George	Burford, John
Barnett, James, Jr.	Bond, Nathan	Burford, Margaret
Barnett, John	Bowles, Knight	Burford, William
Barnett, Robert	Bowling, Robert, Est.	Burks, Charles
Barnett, William	Bowman, William	Burks, David

---

[62] The form used in the Order Book is: To Samuel Allen for 58 lbs. gun powder, Militia to Gen. Greene, per Cert., Feb. 24, 1781, £14 10s. To Adam Brown for 61 days service his Waggon, Team and Driver at York Town and with the Prisoners to Winchester, per Cert. Nov. 4, 1781, £30 10s. To William Cabell for 60 lbs. Bacon for the use of James Andersons Armoures, June 20, 1781, per Cert. £2 5s.; to ditto for paid Ezekiah Bailey for shoeing and removing State Waggon Horses, per Cert. 15s. 6d.; to ditto for 100 Bu. of Rye per Cert. Henry Martin Commissioner, Prov. Law, Oct. 20, 1780, £15. To John Depriest for half blooded Bay Horse, Impressed by John Stith, June 27, 1781, per Cert £50. To Thomas Horrell for two horse collars, Whites Dragoons, Feb. 25, 1781, per Cert. 3s. To William Loving for Boarding and nursing Arthur Williams one of Washingtons Dragoons, per Acct. July 9, 1781, £5 4s. To John Shields for 28 days service for his Waggon, team and driver to Carolina, Nov. 1, 1780, per Cert. £3 10s. To James Stevens for Beef, 600 weight of Blades for Major Nelsons Corps, Feb. 1, 1781, per Cert. 15s. To Wiatt Powell for dieting James Hall, a Continental soldier for during the War, from 27 March to May 6, 1781, per Cert. £3; to ditto for dieting 8 men one day, per Cert. June 10, 1781, Militia expecting Tarltons Light Horse 16s.

Burrus, Charles
Cabell, Nicholas
Cabell, William
Cammeron, Duncan
Camp, Samuel
Campbell, Lawrence
Campbell, Moses
Campbell, Tabitha
Carpenter, Thomas
Carter, Edward
Carter, Peter
Cartwright, John
Casey, Roger
Cash, Robert
Cash, Stephen
Cashwell, Peter
Chapple, William
Childress, Ann
Childress, Joseph
Christian, Charles
Christian, Henry
Christian, John
Christian, Robert
Clark, Nathaniel
Cockburn, George
Coleman, Benjamin
Coleman, Elizabeth
Coleman, George
Coleman, John D.
Coleman, Lindsey
Crawford, Ann
Crawford, David
Crawford, Nathan
Crews, James
Crisp, William
Crittendon, John
Davies, Henry L.
Davis, Israel
Davis, Richard
Davis, Robert, Est.
Dawson, John
Dawson, Martin
Depriest, John
Diggs, John
Dillard, James
Dillard, Joseph
Dillard, William
Dixson, William
Eades, Thomas
Edmonds, Samuel
Edmunds, John
Edwards, Joseph
Elliot, William
Ellis, Charles
Ellis, Josiah
Fitzpatrick, Thomas
Fitzpatrick, William
Forsyth, Benjamin
Franklin, Henry

Franklin, Henry, Jr.
Franklin, James
Franklin, Joell
Franklin, John
Fry, Benjamin
Gaines, Daniel
Galaspie, George
Galaspie, William
Gatewood, Larkin
Gilbert, Ezekiel
Gilbert, George
Gilmer, John
Gresham, James
Griffin, John
Hambleton, Archer
Hambleton, Luke
Hamm, Stephen
Hansbrough, Keziah
Harding, Edward
Harding, Groves, Est.
Hargrove, Hezekiah
Harloe, Nathaniel
Harris, Lee
Harris, Mathew
Harvey, Daniel
Harvie, Martha
Harvie, Richard
Hartless, Henry
Henderson, Alexander
Henderson, John
Henderson, Obediah
Hight, John
Higginbotham, Aaron
Higginbotham, Benjamin
Higginbotham, Caleb
Higginbotham, Francis
Higginbotham, Jacob
Higginbotham, John
Higginbotham, Joseph
Higginbotham, Moses
Higginbotham, Samuel
Higginbotham, William
Hill, James
Hill, John
Hill, Thomas
Hilley, Thomas
Hopkins, James
Horrell, Thomas
Horrell, William
Horsley, John
Horsley, William
Hudson, Joshua
Hughes, Moses
Hughes, William
Irving, Charles
Ison, Charles
Johnson, William
Johnston, John
Jones, Charles

Jones, Mary
Jopling, James
Jopling, John
Jopling, Josiah
Jopling, Thomas
Jordan, Reubin
Knight, John
Lackey, Samuel
Lee, William
Lively, Joseph
Lively, Joseph, Jr.
London, James
Loving, John
Loving, William
Lucas, Thomas
Lyon, Elisha
Lyon, John
Manees, James
Marr, John
Martin, Azariah
Martin, Henry
Martin, James
Martin, Jesse
Martin, John
Martin, Moses
Martin, Stephen
Mathews, James
Mayfield, Isaac
Mays, James
Mays, Joseph
Mays, William
McAlexander, James
McCary, Richard
McGehee, Samuel
McNeely, Michael
Melton, William
Meredith, Samuel
Merriwether, David
Merriwether, Francis
Miller, Alexander
Moore, Benjamin
Montgomery, David
Montgomery, James
Montgomery, John
Montgomery, John, Jr.
Montgomery, Joseph
Montgomery, Thomas
Montgomery, William
Moran, Nicholas
Morrison, James
Morrison, John
Morrison, Capt. John
Morrison, Thomas, Jr.
Murrey, James
Murrow, Richard
Nevil, James
Nevil, Thomas
Nicholas, John
Nightingale, Mathew

Amherst County, Virginia, in the Revolution

Oglesby, Richard	Rucker, William	Trail, James
Patton, Alexander	Sale, Cornelius	Trent, Henry
Penn, Gabriel	Sale, John	Trent, John
Penn, George	Sandidge, John	Tucker, Mathew
Penn, John	Sandidge, Pulliam	Turner, Henry
Penn, Joseph	Satterwhite, Francis	Turner, James
Perrow, Daniel	Saunders, Benjamin	Turner, John
Phillips, David	Seay, Abraham	Turner, Stephen
Phillips, Jacob	Shelton, Clough	Turner, Terisha
Phillips, William	Shelton, David	Turner, Terisha, Jr.
Phillips, Zacharias	Shelton, Richard	Tyree, Jacob
Powe, Thomas	Shepherd, David	Walton, William
Powell, Edmund	Shields, John	Ward, James
Powell, Lucas	Simpson, William	Ward, Nathan
Powell, Thomas	Smith, Jacob	Ware, Edward
Powell, Thomas, Jr.	Smith, John	Ware, James
Powell, Wiatt	Smith, Philip	Ware, William
Purvis, George	Snider, John	Warwick, Abraham
Raines, Ignatious	Sorrell, John	Watson, James
Reid, Alexander	Staples, John	Watts, Caleb
Reid, Alexander, Jr.	Staton, William	Wells (Wills), James
Reid, Martha	Stevens, James	West, Bransford
Reynolds, Charles	Stewart, John	West, Francis
Rhodes, Charles	Stovaul, George	Whilsett, William
Richardson, John	Stratton, John	Whittle, John
Rickets, Thomas	Street, Anthony	Wiatt, John
Ridgway, Thomas	Swinney, Moses	Wilcox, Edmund
Roach, Ashcraft	Taliaferro, Charles	Williams, Robert
Roberts, Henry	Taliaferro, Richard	Witt, John
Roberts, Joseph	Taliaferro, Zacharias	Wood, Josiah
Robertson, Thomas	Tennison, John	Woods, James
Rose, Charles	Thacker, Petter	Woods, Samuel, Est.
Rose, Hugh	Thomas, Cornelius, Est.	Woodroof, David
Rose, John	Thomas, Michael	Wortham, Thomas
Rose, Patrick	Thurmond, Phillip	Wright, Andrew
Rucker, Ambrose	Tiller, William	Wright, Archillis
Rucker, Anthony	Tilman, Daniel	Wright, Benjamin
Rucker, Benjamin	Tinsley, David	Wright, James
Rucker, Isaac	Tinsley, Edward	Wright, John
Rucker, Isaac, Jr.	Tinsley, Isaac	Wright, Robert
Rucker, John	Tinsley, John	Wright, Thomas
Rucker, John, Jr.	Tinsley, Joshua	

NOTE: A number of others are listed in Order Book 1782-1784 among them: "To Joseph Higginbotham Morrison for a blanket for a Contl. soldier proof made in Court, 12s.6d."

Biddle, Bee	Gilbert, Josias	Scott, John
Cabell, Samuel Jordan	Hay, James	Stadner, John
Campbell, Joell	Hilton, George	Talbert, Thomas Henry
Campbell, Neill, Est.	Howard, William	Wade, Ballenger
Carter, Solomon	Pattison, James	West, John
Christian, Drury	Pope, John	West, Thomas
Fox, Samuel	Powell, Richard	Wright, Isaac
Galt, William	Savage, James	

The complete entries were copied from Order Book 1773-1782 as well as Order Book 1782-1784. The cost of printing the details of the hundreds of claims is prohibitive.

Extracts from Lost Order Book, 1773-1782

At a Court held for the County at the Court house on Monday the Sixth day of December 1773 in the fourteenth year of the Reign of his Majesty King George the third

Present

William Cabell, Junr.	Cornelius Thomas	Gentlemen
George Stoval, Junr.	Ambrose Rucker	Justices

Ordered that William Spencer pay the following for attendance at Court as Witnesses for him against Drury Bowman: Charles Pattison 358 lbs. of Tobo. and two shillings for 5 days and 4 times traveling 21 miles from Buckingham, Robert Robertson 125 lbs. Tobo. for 5 days.

Michael McNeely appointed Surveyor of the road from the top of Dokes Gap to the upper end of Nathaniel Barnet's plantation.

Ordered that William Du Val pay James Dillard Gent. 475 lbs. of Tobo. for 19 days and James Christian 275 lbs. of Tobo. for 11 days attendance at Court as witness for him against William Philips.

Ordered that Joseph Price pay the following for attendance at Court as witnesses for him against William Howard: Moses Sweeney, 13 days 325 lbs. Tobo., Sylvanus Massey 7 days and 4 times traveling 20 miles from Buckingham 515 lbs. Tobo., Nathan Ayres 7 days and traveling 25 miles from Buckingham 475 lbs. Tobo., Charles Scott 4 days and traveling 70 miles from Cumberland 520 lbs. Tobo., James Hallyburton 7 days and 3 times traveling 20 miles from Albemarle 355 lbs. Tobo., Thomas Jopling 7 days 125 lbs. Tobo.

March Court, 1774

Eight entries of Land made by William Cabell Gent. Surveyor of this County before James Nevil Gent. a Justice of the Peace for said County were returned and Ordered to be Recorded.

James Higginbotham appointed Surveyor of the road from Gabriel Penns to Buffaloe River in the room of James Page.

On Motion of Edmund Wilcox it is ordered that Benjamin Pollard be recommended to Mr. Secretary Nelson as Deputy Clerk of this County Court.

November Court, 1774

On the motion of Stephen Ham praying the Court to Certify the Value of a negro woman named Jude who was late his property, and was Committed to the Gaol of this County charged with murdering a Negro boy of the said Stephen and wilfully burning the dwelling house of her said Master, but died before the day appointed for her trial, the Court are of the opinion that the said Jude was worth fifty pounds, which is ordered to be certified to the General Assembly.

Amherst County, Virginia, in the Revolution

Court held March 6, 1775

William Loving produced A Commission to be Captain of a Company of Militia of this County, and John Loving, Jr. a Commission to be a Lieutenant, who took the usual Oaths, to his Majesty's person & Government the Abjuration Oath, and Repeated and Subscribed the Test.

James Bell granted leave to Erect a Water Grist Mill on Rockfish River.

Court held July 3, 1775

Present his Majesty's Justices, to wit, James Nevil, George Stovaul, Jr., John Rose and Roderick McCulloch, Gentlemen.

The Gentlemen who were appointed to Examine the Records of this County Court this day returned the following Report, Agreeable to an Order of the Worshipful Court of Amherst County, we the subscribers have Examined the Clerks Office of the said County, and do find, that the Records of the said Court are completely brought up to the time, and the papers appear to us to be in good Order; Given under our hands this 18th day of December 1774. Signed Hugh Rose, Daniel Gaines—which is ordered to be recorded.

Deed of marriage contract between Cornelius Thomas, Gent. & Hannah Scott was proved by John Nicholas, Jr., Benjamin Jordan & William Cabell.

Members of a jury: Charles Rodes, William Wilson, Moses Clark, Samuel Reid, John Shields, George Campbell, Thomas Pannell, Thomas Shannon, Charles Patrick, Hugh Peasley, Sherod Martin and John McCue sworn to view and value the Damages that will arise in Erecting a water Grist mill (Francis Weathered) on Beaver Branch. Do find the lands of Claudious Buster will be damaged 20 shillings. 9th Day of May 1775 Present Ambrose Rucker Gentleman.

Nancy and Joanna Croxton Infant Orphans of Samuel Croxton* Decd. came into Court and made Choice of Mordecai Brown

---

*Son of John Croxton who died in Essex Co., Va., 1757 (Will Book 11, p. 42) and his wife Johanna. Samuel Croxton married Elizabeth——— and migrated to Bute Co., N. C. where he died in 1767. (Co. Court Minutes, 1767-1776, p. 1). His widow married prior to May, 1769, Mordecai Brown of Essex Co., Va. (Bute Co., N. C. Wills & Inventories 1760-1800, part 1, Alf-Hav. [C.R. 15,008] p. 387, Doc. 26). They moved to Amherst Co., Va. where her daughter, Nancy Croxton, married Dec. 4, 1775, Aaron Higginbotham, son of Capt. Aaron and Clara (Graves) Higginbotham. Aaron Higginbotham, Jr. served as a private in the Amherst County Militia in the Revolution; commissioned Ensign July 3, 1786, and Captain before his death in 1794. The date of her death, Nov. 11, 1823, is from a diary of Col. George Washington Higginbotham, in the possession of Thomas Lee Higginbotham, Sandidges, Amherst Co., Va. "Higginbotham Family of Virginia" by William Montgomery Sweeny, *William & Mary Quarterly*, XXVI, No. 4, 265; XXVII, No. 4, 297.

as their Guardian, George Gilbert and Henry Gilbert his security.

Deed of gift from Cornelius Thomas with the memorandum thereon indorsed to John, Norborn, Cornelius, Elizabeth, Lucy & Salley Thomas was proved by the witnesses, Lindsey Coleman, Thomas Jopling & James Nevil.

February Court, 1776

Milley Lavender, widow of William Lavender, granted Admr. of said Decedents Estate.

Upon the Petition of Daniel Will Jackson for his freedom, Its ordered that William Horsley, Gent. be summoned to appear here at the next Court, for Determination of same.

William Camden appointed Surveyor of the Road from Gabriel Penn's upper Quarter to Tribulation Creek.

Henry Landon Davies appointed Surveyor of the Road from Pedlar Tract to Harries Road.

Ordered that Absalom Reynolds & Wm. Cannon Reynolds two poor orphans be bound out by the Church Wardens.

Mordecai Brown is appointed Surveyor of the Road from Thomas Lumpkins to Rose's Road and it is ordered that he with his and the Male Labouring Tithables of the Estate of Baylor Walker, decd., Thomas Lumpkins, George Gilbert, James Lively, John Livingston & John Davis keep the Road in repair according to Law.

Ordered that the Male Labouring Tithables of Henry Gilbert & John West do keep the Road in repair from the fork of Braxtons & Harvies Road to the forks of Higginbotham's Road under Henry Gilbert Gent. Overseer.

Hugh Rose Gent. produced a Commission appointing him Sheriff of the County. Security, Gabriel Penn, Edmund Wilcox, Joseph Cabell & John Rose Gent.; Gabriel Penn and Joseph Tucker qualified as Under Sheriffs.

Amherst County   Dr.
By 2554 Tithables at 1/2 per Pole   £148 19s. 8d.

June Court, 1776

John Rose, Gent. qualified as Vestryman.

Will of Richard La Master, Decd. presented in Court by Abraham LaMaster, and proved by David London, a witness thereto & ordered to be recorded.

Ordered that the Gentlemen that took the List of Tithables, last year do the same the ensuing year, Except William Horsley & Hugh Rose, Gents.

Ordered that James Dillard Gent. take the List of Tithables in the Bounds of William Horsley Gent., Daniel Gaines Gent. in the Bounds of Hugh Rose Gent. & Ambrose Rucker Gent. in the Bounds of Daniel Gaines Gent.

Ordered that the Widow of John Lavender be Summoned to appear here at the next Court to Declare whether she will take upon herself the Admr. of the said Decedents Estate.

July Court, 1776

In Obedience to an Order of the last Convention to Enable the Present Magistrates and Officers to Continue the Administration of Justice, and for settling the General Mode of proceedings in Criminal & other cases till the same can be more amply provided for, William Cabell, Esq. the first nominated Gentleman in the Commission of the Peace for the County having first taken the Oath prescribed by the said Ordinance which was administered to him by Zacharias Taliaferro and Ambrose Rucker Gent. whereupon the said William Cabell, Gent. proceeded to administer the same Oath to the said Zacharias Taliaferro, Ambrose Rucker, Alexander Reid, Jr., Roderick McCulloch, James Nevil, Daniel Gaines, David Crawford, John Rose and James Dillard, Gentlemen.

Edmund Wilcox, Clerk of the Court took the said Oath prescribed by the aforesaid Ordinance of Convention.

Hugh Rose Gent. qualified as Sheriff; John Dillard, William Loving, John Penn and Joseph Penn qualified as Under Sheriffs.

Ordered that Henry Bell Captain of a Patrole be allowed 540 lbs. Tobo. for his and Company's Service, and that they be paid according to Law.

August Court, 1776

Charles Rose, Gent. took the Oath as an Attorney as directed by an Ordinance of the Last Convention.

William Cabell, Joseph Cabell, Hugh Rose, John Dawson & James Dillard qualified as Vestrymen.

Nathaniel Mantiply is appointed Overseer of the Road from Capt. Gabriel Penn's to Saint Marks Church, in the Room of John Wright.

Deed from Ichabod Camp to Peter Joyner was ackd. & ordered to be recorded.

Ordered that Ambrose Mills, son and Heir at Law of William Mills, Decd. be Summoned to Appear here at the Next Court, to Declare whether he will take upon himself the Admr. of the Estate of Mary Mills, Decd.

September Court, 1776

Henry Landon Davies, Gent. granted leave to Erect a Water Grist Mill on Salt Creek.

Court held October 7, 1776

James Hill appointed Overseer of Harris Creek Road in Room of Henry Franklin Jr.

Ordered that James Higginbotham, Roderick McCulloch, Jacob Smith and William Spencer (or any three of them) divide the Estate of Cornelius Thomas, Gent. Decd.

Will of Battaile Harrison, Decd. was presented in Court by Reubin Harrison, son and Heir at Law of the said Decd. and proved by the Oaths of Ambrose Tomlinson, William Whitten and Richard Shelton.

November Court, 1776

Meritt Magann qualified as Under Sheriff.

Daniel Gaines, Ambrose Rucker & Alex. Reid, Jr. Gent. recommended as Sheriff for the Ensuing Year.

John Staples, son and heir at Law of Samuel Staples, Decd. appeared in Court and gave his consent to the appointment of Charles Irving as Admr. of the Estate of Samuel Staples, Decd. Security Charles Rose and Edmund Wilcox.

Court held January 6, 1777

James Higginbotham produced his Commission to be Surveyor of this County whereupon he took the Oath prescribed by Law, and It's Ordered that he give Bond with two good Securities in the Clerk's Office before the Next Court.

Thomas Johns appointed Admr. of the Estate of William Johns, Decd. Security Dudley Gatewood & John Penn.

Ordered that William Galt be summoned to appear here at the next Court to show whether he has heretofore uniformly shewed a friendly Disposition to the American Cause.

Court held February 3, 1777

Ordered that the Road leading by the House kept by Charles Ashley be Discontinued, for the present, till the Court shall be satisfied that there is no infection of the Small pox to be taken from his family, and It's ordered that Richard Murrow and Charles Statham run a strong fence across said Road at Each end of the Lane and open a new way through the plantation up the Branch on the South Side of the said Ashley's Dwelling House, and that the necessary expenses be paid by the public.

William Galt Assistant Storekeeper for Cunningham & Compy. Merchants of Glasgow, Appeared agreeable to a Summons of this County Court and on hearing, It's the Opinion of the Court, that the said Galt has not heretofore uniformly Manifested a friendly disposition to the American Cause, which is ordered to be certified to his Excellency the Governour.

Will of Benjamin Cash, Decd. was presented in Court by Robert Cash & Richard Ballinger, Exors. & Nancy Cash, Widow & Extrix. and proved by the oaths of Hendrick Arnold, Francis Satterwhite and Nancey Higginbotham, witnesses.

Know all Men by these presents that we James Higginbotham Joseph Cabell & Edmund Wilcox, are held & firmly bound to the Commonwealth of Virginia in the just & full Sum of Five hundred pounds Current Mony of Virginia to which payment well & truly to be made to the said Commonwealth we bind ourselves, our Heirs Executors & Administrators jointly & severally firmly by these presents As Witness our hands & Seals this 21st Day of January, in the year of our Lord 1777.

The Condition of this Obligation is such, that, whereas the above bound James Higginbotham is appointed Surveyor of the County of Amherst by Commission from the President & Masters of the College of William & Mary bearing Date the third day of December last, now if the said James Higginbotham shall truly & faithfully execute the said office of Surveyor of the said County of Amherst, & in all other things do as by law required; then this Obligation to be void, otherwise to remain in full force power & Virtue.

Signed Sealed & delivered
in presence of us.
Test
S. Ger mills

James Higginbotham

Jos. Cabell

Edm. Wilcox

Major James Higginbotham's Bond as Surveyor of the County of Amherst by Commission from the President & Masters of the College of William & Mary, December 3, 1776.

Ordered that David Shelton, David Woodroof, Martin Dawson & Joseph Goodwin View a way for a Road from Grahams Bridge to Capt. Henry Trents Ferry Landing.

Daniel Gaines, Gent. produced his Commission as Sheriff & qualified according to Law. William Loving, John Penn, Joseph Penn & John Dillard qualified as Under Sheriffs.

Ambrose Rucker qualified as Vestryman.

Court held March 3, 1777

A Report of a way from Perrion Giles on Indian Creek into the Road that Leads by Maple Run Church was returned as followeth: To wit 1 Feb. 1777, Beginning at the said Giles thence down Indian Creek, as the way now is to a plantation of Gilbert Hay's, where Francis Satterwhite now lives, turning round the lower end of his fence thence Rising a hill to the Top, from thence down said Ridge to a Branch running through a plantation of Mr. Patrick Rose where William Williams formerly lived thence through the woods to a School house where William Hay now keeps School from thence into a patch that leads to the Church, and are of the opinion that it is the nearest and best way that can be—John Sale, Nicholas Wren, Bartholomew Ramsey.

James Savage appointed Surveyor of the Road in Room of David Tinsley.

John Sandidge Appointed Surveyor of the Road in Room of James Smith & It's ordered that he with Philip Peyton, Joseph Milstead, John Swinney, John Matthews, Nicholas Prior and John Peyton keep the road in Repair.

James Bolling produced his Accounts for Guarding the Highland Prisoners of War* for Ninety four Days, which is Ordered to be Certified to his Excellency the Governor.

Richard Murrah produced his Account for Conveying & Guarding the Highland Prisoners of War nine miles, with an Assistant & two horses which is Ordered to be certified to his Excellency the Governor.

---

*"James Barron, captain in the Virginia Navy, dealt Dunmore a heavy blow by capturing a transport, filled with Highlander troops bound up the Bay for Gwynn's Island." Eckenrode's *The Revolution in Virginia*, p. 94.

June 24, 1776, Col. Christian laid before the Committee of Safety a General List of the Highland Prisoners taken by Capts. James & Richard Barron in the Ship Oxford, and also an allotment of them into fourteen divisions.

The General Convention ordered that they be immediately sent to fourteen different Counties and held as Prisoners of War, giving their parole to the said Committee not to depart without permission.

Allotment No. 3—To Amherst: Allan McCaskel, Murdon Campbel, John Morison, Ronald McCuagg, Patrick McCleod, Peter McCriman, Angus McLeor, Alexander McCleod, Neil McIntosh, Finley McLenin, Alexander McDowel, Kennith McCleod & Neil Beaton—13. 1 Woman. *Tyler's Quarterly Magazine*, Vol. V, No. 1, pp. 59-63.

Amherst County   Dr.
  To Samuel Davis Captain of a Patrole for his & Companys service £10 3s. 4d.
  To Henry Bell Captain of a Patrole for his & Companys service £4 10s.
  To Daniel Burford, Jr. Capt. of a Patrole for his & Comps. service £4 6s. 8d.
  To John Depriest for Bringing up the Ordinance of Convention £2 0.

  Samuel Higginbotham Appointed Surveyor of the Road in the Room of Philip Smith.
  Ordered that the Sheriff Collect one Shilling (or 6 lbs. of Tobo. in lieu thereof) a Pole from the Inhabitants of this County it being the County assessment.
  John Rose, Gent. appointed Treasurer for the Ensuing Year.
  Roderick McCulloch, Charles Taliaferro, Benjamin Higginbotham, George McDaniel Appraisers of the Estate of Neill Campbell, Decd.

Court held April 7, 1777

  On Motion of Peterfield Trent praying leave to Inoculate the slaves on his Estate in this County, It's the opinion of the Court that It's not necessary at present.

Court held May 5, 1777

  Joseph Cabell, John Diggs, Henry Landon Davies, Gabriel Penn, Benjamin Rucker, Richard Shelton and John Dawson recommended as proper persons to be Added to the Commission of the Peace for this County.
  Roderick McCulloch and Francis Merriwether, Gent. recommended as Coroner.
  John Ryan and Richard Murrah qualified as Constables.

Amherst County   Dr.
  To Richard Murrah Captain of Patrole for his & Companys service to April, 1777, 300 lbs. nett Tobo.
  To Jacob Webb Captain of Patrole for his & Companys service to April, 1777, 60 lbs. nett Tobo.
  To Henry Bell Captain of Patrole for his & Companys service 200 lbs. nett Tobo.

  Lucy Thomas Infant Orphan of Cornelius Thomas Decd. chose John Henderson, Jr., Guardian.
  Mary Johnson Infant Orphan of Jonathan Johnson, Decd. made choice of Thomas Moffitt, Guardian; Snelling Johnson, Phillip Johnson and Frances Johnson Infant Orphans of Jonathan Johnson, Decd. made choice of Charles Burruss as their Guardian.
  John Campbell Infant Orphan of George Campbell, Decd. chose Thomas Pannell, Guardian.

John Duncan appointed Admr. of the Estate of David Duncan, Decd.

Court held June 2, 1777

Ambrose Rucker, Charles Rose, Francis Merrewether & Thomas Jopling are appointed to Receive the public Salt for the use of the Inhabitants of this County, Each 33 bu., Except Charles Rose who is to Receive 34 bu., which is to be distributed at one a head, and It's Ordered that the said Gentlemen Employ some person to bring the same from Richmond, etc.

John Phillip qualified as Constable.

John Jacobs Appointed Surveyor of the Road from the lower part of Doake's plantation in Rockfish Settlement to the Road that leads to Col. Rose's Mill.

Court held July 7, 1777

A New Commission of the Peace and Commission of Oyer & Terminer was presented in Court, whereupon James Nevil and John Rose, Gent. Administered the Oath of Fidelity to William Cabell, Gent. and then the said William Cabell, Gent. administered the said Oath to James Nevil, John Rose, James Dillard, Hugh Rose, Ambrose Rucker, Alex. Reid, Junr., William Horsley, Joseph Cabell, Gabriel Penn, Benjamin Rucker and John Dawson, Gent. and then the above Gentlemen took the Oaths of the Peace and Oyer and Terminer as prescribed by Law.

James London Heir at Law of Moses London, Decd. ordered to appear at next Court and declare whether he will become Admr. of said Decedents Estate.

Charles Rose, Gent. produced a Commission from his Excellency the Governour Appointing him Deputy Atty. for this County whereupon the said Rose took the Oath prescribed by Law.

Court held August 4, 1777

Present: William Cabell, James Nevil, James Dillard, William Horsley, Joseph Cabell, Gabriel Penn, John Dawson, Benjamin Rucker, Gentlemen Justices.

Zacharias Taliaferro and John Diggs, Gent. took the Oath of a Justice and Oyer and Terminer.

Alex. Reid, Junr., John Diggs and John Dawson Gentlemen are by the Court appointed to administer the Oath of Allegiance prescribed by the Act of Assembly to the Inhabitants of this County Residing in the following bounds: between the County Line, the Blew Ridge, the Mountains Dividing the waters of Rockfish and Tye Rivers, the Dutch Mountains, to Rockfish River, and down the same to Green Creek, and you are enjoined to return to this Court a List of all those who do take, as well as those who refuse to take the aforesaid Oath by the Tenth Day of October next.

Richard Tankersley Lyon, orphan of John Lyon, Decd. chose Samuel Anderson, Guardian.

Admr. granted Alexander Chisnal on the Estate of Moses London, Decd.

Daniel Gaines, John Hardwick & Stephen Ham appointed Apprs. of the Estate of Merritt Magann, Decd.

William Cabell and James Nevill, Gent. are appointed to administer the Oath of Allegiance to the Inhabitants of this County Residing in the following bounds: between the Fluvanna River, Rockfish River, the Dutch and Findley's Mts. and Tye River and you are Injoined to Return to this Court a List of all those who do take, as well as those who shall refuse to take the aforesaid oath by the 10th October.

James Dillard and William Horsley, Gent. are appointed (same as above): The Fluvanna River, from the mouth of Tye River up to Stovall's Ferry, from thence along the Road to Maganns, from thence to Buffaloe at George Penn's Mill on Buffaloe River, thence down the same to Tye River thence down Tye River to Fluvanna River, and you are Injoined (same as above).

John Rose and Zacharias Taliaferro, Gent. are appointed (same as above): Between Tye River at Findley's Mt. to the Mouth of Piney River, thence up Piney River to the Blew Ridge, to the Mts. that divides the waters of Rockfish & Tye Rivers & down the said Mts. to Findley's Mt. to the beginning at Tye River, and you are Injoined (same as above).

David Crawford, Ambrose Rucker, Roderick McCulloch, Benjamin Rucker, Richard Shelton, Hugh Rose, Joseph Cabell and Gabriel Penn, Gent. are appointed to Administer the Oath of Allegiance prescribed by Act of Assembly to the Inhabitants of this County Residing out of the Bounds that is already laid off for that purpose and you are Injoined (same as above).

September Court, 1777

Ordered that the Sheriff of this County Take Thomas Moffitt if he be found within his Baliwick and him Safely keep, for Demeaning himself as an Enemy to this Commonwealth, and for Endeavouring to stir up the people to Resist the Government and Excite Tumult and disorder in this State, and if the said Thomas Moffitt shall refuse to give Security in the penalty of £500 to appear here at the next Court, to Answer the premises, as well as for his future good behaviour towards the good people of this Commonwealth, and that he do not violate in the meantime the laws of this State that then the Sheriff is hereby commanded to Raise to his assistance the posse of this County, to compel the said Thomas Moffitt to a due obedience of this order.

Ordered that the Sheriff of this County Take Augustine Smith (same as above).

John Campbell, William Hooker, James Hambleton and Philip Ryan summoned to appear as witnesses against Augustine Smith.

John Campbell, Joseph Magann, David Woodroof, James Nevil, Martin Key (overseer for Richard Jones) and Joseph Goodwin summoned as witnesses in behalf of the Commonwealth against Thomas Moffitt.

Court held October 6, 1777
The Commonwealth Agst. Augustine Smith
On Information of Releasing a
Deserter, etc.

This day came the Commonwealth by Charles Rose their Atty. as also the said Smith in his own proper person, came also a Jury to Wit: Lawrence Campbell, James Stevens, Linn Banks, Richard Oglesbey, Noell Johnson, George Penn, Moses Hughes, Mathew Nightingale, Richard Murrah, James Matthews, William Martin & John Barnett who being Elected tried & Sworn upon their Oath do fine the said Augustine Smith £25 current money of Virginia and the costs of this prosecution.

David Crawford, Roderick McCulloch, Gent. took the oath as Justice of Peace.

John Meritt qualified as Constable.

Court held January 5, 1778
Present: Ambrose Rucker, John Diggs, Alex. Reid, Jr., Gabriel Penn, Roderick McCulloch, Joseph Cabell & John Dawson, Gentlemen Justices.

William Loving is sworn as Deputy Clerk.
The Commonwealth of Virginia
Agst.
Thomas Moffitt

For Maliciously & advisedly by word & open Deed endeavouring to excite the people of this County to resist the Government of the Commonwealth.

Came as well the Commonwealth by Charles Rose their Atty. as the said Moffitt in his own proper person, came also a Jury to Wit: Benjamin Moore, William Martin, William Spencer, Noell Johnson, John Stewart, Joseph Dillard, Linn Banks, Samuel Allen, James Higginbotham, Joseph Edwards, William Walton and John Sale who being Elected tried and sworn upon their Oaths do fine the said Thomas Moffitt £5 and payment of costs of Court.

It is Ordered that Thomas Moffitt pay Micajah Goodwin and Caleb Ralls 25 lbs. of Nett Tobacco for their Attendance at Court one day as a Witness for the said Moffitt at the suit of the Commonwealth.

Henry Landon Davies, Gent. took the oath of Justice of the Peace.

April Court, 1778

Agreeable to a Recognizance Entered into by Julius Galdons, and William Walton his Security, for the sd. Galdons appearance here at this Court this day to Answer the Complaint of James Ward for breach of the Peace, the sd. Galdons Appearing here accordingly, and his being a Soldier in the Continental Army, was Delivered into the custody of James Dillard Jr. one of the Continental officers.

Mary Montgomery, widow and Admx. of James Montgomery, Decd. appeared in Court and renounced the administration of the said Decedents Estate.

On the Resignation of Charles Rose, Gent. Deputy Attorney for this County Thomas Miller, Gent. is Recommended to his Excellency the Governour as a proper person to Execute the said office.

Thomas Moffitt licensed to keep an Ordinary at his house for one year with Joseph Cabell, Gent. Security.

May Court, 1778

A Report for a new way for a Road from the Old Muster Ground above John Peyton's to the Road below John Peyton's was this Day returned to Court.

John Phillips qualified as Deputy Sheriff.

A Grand Jury for the Body of this County to wit: Alexander Reid, Foreman, Charles Burrass, Edmund Powell, William Hughes, Noell Johnson, Reubin Harrison, George Gilbert, William Spencer, James Christian, Drury Christian, Richard Powell, Josiah Gilbert, Thomas Jopling Jr., Thomas Hawkins, Joseph Tucker and Richard Oglesby.

Robert Barnett Orphan of Joseph Barnett, Decd. appeared in Court and chose Alexander Reid, minor, Guardian.

John Mayfield (son of Isaac) is Appointed Surveyor of the Road from Samuel Higginbothams to an old Plant patch on the Road near Neill Campbell's plantation and it is ordered that he do with the Gang formerly under John Higginbotham, Jr. Surveyor keep the said Road in repair.

July Court, 1778

Daniel Gaines, Gent. qualified as Vestryman of the Parish of Amherst.

The following granted licenses to keep an Ordinary: Charles Ashley, George Blaine and William Depriest.

Daniel Gaines, Gent. qualified as a Justice.

Joel Crawford informing the Court that he Intends soon to visit the Southern States of America and may proceed as far as the State of Georgia and that he would be willing to have the Opinion of this Court touching his Character, etc.

August Court, 1778

Joseph Cabell, Gent. Appointed Guardian of Joseph Cabell Meggenson.

John Diggs, Gent. qualified as Vestryman of Amherst Parish.

Ambrose Rucker, Gent. Sheriff with Edmund Wilcox, Gabriel Penn, Daniel Gaines, Benjamin Rucker, Joseph Cabell, Isaac Rucker, Anthony Rucker and John Penn his Securities Entered into and Acknowledged their bond in the Penalty of £6000 for the said Ambrose Rucker's faithful Collecting the Taxes for the present year.

John Merrit licensed to keep an Ordinary at his House.

Richard Gatewood qualified as Constable.

On the motion of Gabriel Penn, Gent. Its ordered that Weights and Measurers belonging to this County that is in the said Penn's care be Removed to this Court House, and William Powell take charge of them.

October Court, 1778

Thomas Ware Orphan of Robert Ware, Decd. chose James Henderson, Guardian.

A Petition for the Division of Amherst Parish was presented in Court and Ordered to be certified.

Will of William Johnson, Decd. was proved by the Oaths of Aaron Higginbotham, William Guttery and Thomas Dawson, witnesses.

A Petition for the Support of the Clergy was presented in Court and ordered to be Certified to the General Assembly.

November Court, 1778

The following granted licenses to keep an Ordinary: Obediah Henry Trent at Trent's Ferry; William Powell at the Court House; William Kyle at his house.

Francis & Richard Lee orphans of Ambrose Lee, chose George Penn & George Lee their Guardians.

December Court, 1778

Mary Parks, widow and Executrix of William Parks, Decd. granted Adm. on his Estate with Martin Dawson and Joseph Tucker Security.

The following licensed to keep Ordinaries: John Peyton and Jacob Brown.

William Brown Christian orphan of John Christian, Decd. chose Henry Christian, Guardian.

February Court, 1779

Abraham Warwick licensed to keep an Ordinary at Findley's Gap, John Staples Security.

Henry Martin and James Hopkins recommended as Justice of the Peace.

March Court, 1779

Ambrose Rucker, Hugh Rose, Daniel Gaines, David Woodroof and James Dillard, Gent. qualified as Vestrymen of Lexington Parish; Nicholas Cabell, John Rose, Patrick Rose and John Dawson, Gent. qualified as Vestrymen of Amherst Parish.

April Court, 1779

Josiah Ellis, Joseph Goodwin, Richard Ballenger, Robert Christian, Samuel Higginbotham and Gabriel Penn qualified as Vestrymen of Lexington Parish; Charles Rose, Lucas Powell, William Cabell, William Bibb and Zacharias Taliaferro qualified as Vestrymen of Amherst Parish.

May Court, 1779

Amherst County   Dr.

To Joseph Stark as Adjutant for one years service   £50 0 0
To James Reid, Junr. for one years service as Adjutant   50 0 0
To Moses Wright for one Wolf's head 100 lbs. Tobo.
To Ambrose Rucker Gent. Sheriff for his Publick Service   20 16 0
To Edmund Wilcox, Clerk for his Publick Service   20 16 0
To Thomas Miller, Deputy Attorney for this County   30 0 0

William Powell presented his Accounts against United States amounting to £45 13s. 4d.

James Nevill, Esq. qualified as Vestryman of Amherst Parish.

Resignation of Thomas Miller, Gent. as Deputy Atty. for Amherst County.

June Court, 1779

Richard Shelton qualified as Vestryman of Lexington Parish.

James Reid, Jr. Esqr. produced a license to practice as an Attorney.

July Court, 1779

John Lawrence licensed to keep an Ordinary at his house. Ezekiel Gilbert Security.

William Bryan and Ann Purkins Bryan Orphans of Benjamin Bryan, Decd. chose James Watson their Guardian.

Abigail Hardwick Wade & Lucreasy Wade Orphans of Pearce Wade, Decd. chose Richard Ballinger their Guardian; Security Francis Satterwhite; Clary Wade Orphan of Pearce Wade, Decd. chose David Woodroof, Guardian.

August Court, 1779

Nicholas Cabell is allowed to keep one Boat and two hands at his Ferry.

James Ware informing the Court that he Intends soon to visit the Southern States of America, and may proceed as far as the State of Georgia, and that he would be willing to have the Opinion of this Court touching his Character.

David Shepherd, Gent. recommended as Escheator of this County.

On Petition of Jeremiah Wade Orphan of Pearce Wade Decd. attested by three witnesses setting forth that he is a Soldier at the Albemarle Barracks and cannot personally attend to make choice of a Guardian but in his said Petition make choice of Ballinger Wade, Richard Ballinger Security.

September Court, 1779

David Shepherd,* Gent. qualified as Escheator, John Wiatt Security.

Thomas Miller, Esqr. qualified as Deputy Attorney of this County.

On the Motion of Matthew Tucker against John Woodroof an Officer who Enlisted Jesse Tucker a Son of the said Matthew Tucker into the Service of this State as a Soldier, It appearing to the Court that the said John Woodroof had notice of this Motion and that the said Jesse Tucker was just past 14 years of Age, therefore the said Jesse Tucker is Considered to be Altogether under the protection of the Civil Government and that the said Enlistment was Illegal, and the said Jesse Tucker is Discharged from any obligation thereof, the Enlistment being without the Consent of his Father.

Lucas Powell is appointed Guardian of Robert, Coatney & Charlotte Cooper, Orphans of Phillip Cooper, Decd.

October Court, 1779

The Jurors Inquest that was taken in this County on Walter Kings and John Harmers Estates being Subjects to the King of Great Britain was this day Returned and ordered to be Recorded.

On motion of James Lewis who Intermarried with one of the Daughters of Cornelius Thomas, Decd. Roderick McCulloch, James Higginbotham and Thomas Jopling are appointed to divide the Estate of sd. Decedent between the four orphans.

James Nevil and Hugh Rose, Esqrs. are appointed Commissioners of this County agreeable to an Act of Assembly for Levying a Tax payable in certain Enumerated Commodities.

---

*The sale of sequestered property began in 1779. The escheator from Amherst paid £454,709 into the auditor's office from the sale of Loyalist property. (Harrell's *Loyalism in Virginia*, p. 95).

On the Motion of Benjamin Bryant to have his Son Zacharias Bryant Discharged from his Enlistment with James Warren to Serve as a Soldier at the Barracks and it appearing to the Court that the said Benjamin Bryant had apply'd to the Commanding Officer that was at the Barracks to Call a Court of Inquiry, to inquire into the Age of his said Son Zacharias, which it appeared the said Officer Refused to do. Whereupon the said Bryant produced Several Depositions and Witnesses being Sworn and Examined, It appears that the said Zacharias Bryant was but 15 years old the 4th Day of Last June. Therefore under the protection of the Civil Government and that the said Enlistment was Illegal, and that the said Zacharias is discharged from any Obligation thereof, the said Enlistment being without the Consent of his Father.

Thomas and Richard Gilbert Orphans of Henry Gilbert, Decd. made choice of Daniel Gaines, Gent. their Guardian.

Ordered that James Nevil, Thomas Jopling, James Matthews and Richard Murrow or any three of them, being first sworn do view the Road from Saint Johns Church to Abraham Warwicks and a new way for a Road from said Church to said Warwicks and report thereof to the Court.

Margaret Meredith, widow of Rice Meredith, Decd. granted Admr. of said Decedents Estate; Bondsmen Hugh Rose and James Higginbotham, Esqrs.

November Court, 1779

The following persons were Sworn as a Grand Jury for the Body of this County to-wit: Lucas Powell, Foreman, Nathan Crawford, William Bibb, Nicholas Wren, Abner Witt, Richard Oglesbey, Noell Johnson, John Cartwright, William Lee, James Watson, Lindsey Coleman, Nicholas Moran, James Hopkins, Robert Wright, Linn Banks, George Gilbert, James London and John Turner.

Henry Martin qualified as Vestryman of Amherst Parish.

William Boothe and Judith, his wife, John Richardson and Mary, his wife, Robert Johns, William Johns, Jesse Johns, Nathaniel Booth and Elizabeth, his wife, Martha Johns an Infant by John Richardson, her next friend, Francis Johns, John Alexander Johns, Nancy Johns, Salley Johns and Bartlett Johns, Infants by William Booth their next friend, Plfs.—Against—Mary Johns, Admx. of Robert Johns, Decd., and Thomas Johns Heir-at-Law of the said Deceased, Dfts.—In Chancery—Mary Johns, Admx. ordered to make an Acct. of the Estate of Robert Johns, Decd. on Oath before Drury Christian, Charles Christian, John Christian (Buffaloe), and they will have authority to divide the Estate of her said Husband having regard to her Dower.

December Court, 1779

The following licensed to keep an Ordinary: Samuel Camp at

the place where Gabriel Penn lately lived, Security Edmund Wilcox; William Powell at the Court House, Security Lucas Powell.

February Court, 1780

Gabriel Penn, Gent. presented in Court a Deed with the Certificate of acknowledgement thereof annexed from John Barnes & Ann his wife of the State of New York to the said Penn, and on his motion, ordered to be recorded.

On the motion of Daniel Gaines, Gent. High Sheriff, John Loving, Jr. and Joseph Penn qualified as Deputy Sheriffs.

Ambrose Rucker, Gent. qualified as a Justice of the Peace.

John Lackey, Jr. ackd. his Deed to William Morrison, and it was ordered recorded.

March Court, 1780

Cornelius Vaughan in the service of America, Pltf. by Peter Carter his Attorney Against Joseph Edwards and Nelly, his wife, William Edwards and Anne, his wife and John and Mary Vaughan Infants, Dfts. Joseph Edwards is appointed Guardian to the Defendants John and Mary to Defend this Suit—Decreed that David Crawford, Roderick McCulloch and Matthew Tucker do Divide among the Pltf. & Dfts. the Slaves in the Bill Mentioned, etc.

William Burton Orphan of William Burton, Decd. chose George Penn, Guardian.

Court held April 3, 1780

The following licensed to keep an Ordinary: John Henry Goodwin at his house near Lynch's Ferry; Samuel McGehee at his house near Rose's Mill.

The Several Ferry Keepers in this County are authorized to Receive for the Services performed at their Respective Ferries 24 prices on what was Established by Law.

The Court proceeded to Rate the Prices to be paid for Diet at the Ordinarys* in this County, to wit

A Warm Diet	£2	10	0
A Cold Diet	1	10	0
Good Whiskey by the Gill	1	10	0
West India Rum by the Gill	2	2	0
Good Brandy by the Gill	1	16	0
Three Gills of Rum made into Toddy	8	8	0
Three Gills of Brandy made into Toddy	7	4	0
One Quart of Whiskey Bumbo	4	16	0
A Night's Lodging with Clean Sheets on a Feather Bed		12	0

---

*That the taverns of colonial Virginia left something to be desired I gather from Anburey's "Travels in America," where he says: "We stopped at a tavern, which in this country is called an 'ordinary,' and believe me it was."

Stabledge for a Horse Twelve Hours	12	0
Pasturage for a Horse Twelve Hours	12	0
Corn or Oats by the Gallon	2 0	0
Fodder by the Bundle	4	0
Cyder by the Gallon	2 0	0

Court held May 1, 1780

The following licensed to keep an Ordinary: Jacob Brown and William Whitsill.

Members of a Grand Jury: William Spencer, Foreman, Charles Christian, John Tinsley, Richard Powell, Noell Johnson, Levy Baldock, Joel Campbell, Joshua Hudson, Johnson Bean, John Witt, Nicholas Moran, John Barnett, Thomas Hawkins, John Montgomery, Lee Harris, Robert Wright, John Cartwright and William Horrell.

Amherst County   Dr.
    To John Stratton for Bringing the Acts of Assembly from Williamsburg £20.

Daniel Gaines, Gent. Sheriff with Zacharias Taliaferro, Ambrose Rucker, Gabriel Penn, George Penn, Hugh Rose & Charles Rose, Gent. his Securitys entered into and acknowledged two Bonds in the penalty, one for £30,000 with the Condition that the said Gaines do collect and Settle with the Commissioners and pay into the Treasury all the Money and Tobo. he shall Collect Agreeable to the Act of Assembly Entitled an Act for Establishing a fund to Borrow money for the use of the United States and for other purposes and the other in penalty of £50,000 for said Gaines to Collect and pay the Taxes for the Present year agreeable to the Act of Assembly for raising a supply of money for publick expenses.*

Ambrose Rucker, Gent. is appointed Surveyor of the Road from Rutledges to his own Meadow, and it is ordered that he do with his own Male Labouring Tithables, John Rucker, Benjamin Plunket and their Male Labouring Tithables, and the Male Labouring Tithables of Harvies Estate and Susannah Rucker at Pauls Mountain keep the said Road in repair according to Law.

Robert Cash ackd. his deed to Reubin Rucker and Tamasen the wife of Robert Cash released her right of dower.

June Court, 1780

A Power of Attorney from Robert Johnson to Edmund Wilcox, David Crawford & James Higginbotham was proved by the witnesses: William Payton & Isaac Wright.

John Depriest licensed to keep an Ordinary at the Forks of the Road below George Blains leading to Lovings Gap.

---

*For depreciation in currency see Lossing's *Field-Book of the Revolution*, Vol. 1, p. 319.

Court held August 7, 1780

Thomas Lewton Committed to the Gaol of this County on Suspicion that he was a Deserter on hearing It appears to the Court that the said Lewton is a prisoner of War on Parole Taken in Col. Bufords Regiment, whereupon the said Lewton is Discharged.

John Huffman, John Quinn and Peter Swindall who were committed to Gaol of this County on Suspicion that they were Deserters on hearing were Discharged.

October Court, 1780

Will of Edward Cox, Decd. presented by Benjamin Cox & Hendrick Arnold Exors.; proved by William Oglesby, Benjamin Cox & Ann Lively, witnesses.

Margaret Cox appointed Guardian of Clary Cox, Orphan of Edward Cox, Decd. Security, Samuel Higginbotham.

November Court, 1780

The Grand Jury being called and a sufficient number not appearing, they are Excused. "It appearing to the Court that several of them are now on their Tower of Duty as Militia Men."

February Court, 1781

Alexander Reid, Jr. Sheriff with James Nevil, Wm. Spencer, James Dillard, Gabriel Penn, John Pope, Jr., John Loving, Jr., Edmund Wilcox, Joseph Higginbotham Morrison, Samuel Higginbotham and Hugh Rose Gent. his Securitys Entered into and Ackd. their Bond in the penalty of £100,000 for the said Reid Collecting and Paying Taxes agreeable to the first Payment thereof as by an Act of Assembly Entitled an Act for Calling in and Redeeming the money now in circulation and for emitting and finding new Bills of Credit, according to the Resolutions of Congress of the 18th of March Last.

On the Motion of Alex. Reid, Jr. Sheriff John Loving, Jr. and Joseph Higginbotham Morrison *is* admitted and sworn as Under Sheriffs.

On the motion of William Loving the mark of his stock is admitted to Record, which is a crop and overkeel in Each Ear.

On motion of Joseph Clay formerly a citizen of the State of South Carolina who hath Removed 34 of his slaves from that State, it is ordered that their names and sex be recorded.

On the motion of John Habersham formerly a citizen of the State of South Carolina who hath removed his slaves from that State, 62 in number, etc.

The Will of Samuel Woods, Decd. was presented in Court by James Brooks, Exor. Security, Joseph Higginbotham Morrison, Samuel Lackey, Alex. Reid, Jr., Alexander Miller, William Barnett, William Harris, Joseph Roberts and John Loving, Jr.

Henry Martin and Gabriel Penn Gent. Commissioners for this County agreeable to the Act of Assembly for providing a supply of Provisions and other necessities for the use of the Army is allowed four per cent on the Account of the Commodities they procured for the use of the said Army which is ordered to be certified to the Auditor of Publick Accounts.

Nicholas Cabell, Patrick Rose and Samuel Meredith Gent. are Recommended to his Excellency the Governour as proper persons to Execute the Office of a Justice of the Peace for this County.

Court held March 5, 1781

On the motion of William Saunders formerly of the State of South Carolina who hath removed his slaves, 26 in number, from that State, it is ordered that their names and sex be recorded.

May Court, 1781

On motion of William Thompson (same as above—14 slaves named).

On motion of Thomas Powe (same as above—7 slaves named).

The Different Ferry Keepers in this County are allowed to Receive at their Different Ferrys four Dollars for the passage of a man and four for a horse, and so in proportion for other Services performed at their said Ferrys.

George Purvis is allowed £80 for setting up 8 Flower Bbls., which is ordered to be certified to the Auditor's Accounts for payment.

John Griffin allowed £253 6s. 8d. for carpenters work done on a granary and ordered, etc.

On the Resignation of John Rose, Gent. one of the Commissioners of the Specific Tax, William Loving is appointed a Commissioner of the said taxes in the said Roses place.

William Loving Commissary in the Lower District of this County is allowed £1056 9s. for his Services as Commissary for 1780, and for having the wheat Ground and Barrelled up and finding provision for the Cooper which is ordered to be certified to the Auditor of Publick Accounts for payment.

Ordered that Each Tithable in this County pay to the Sheriff 8s. per Pole being the Levy this day Assessed.

Alexander Reid, Jr. qualified as Sheriff. Samuel Higginbotham qualified as Deputy Sheriff.

June Court, 1781

John Penn Commissary in the Upper District of this County is allowed £1080 16s. 3d. for his Services in 1780 for having wheat Manufactured and Barrelled up and for a quantity of nails for the use of the Granary which is ordered, etc.

William Horsley Gent. appointed to take a List of Tithables in the following Bounds: from the Fluvanna River along the Parish

Line to Tye River, Down Tye River to the Fluvanna and up that to the Parish Line.

August Court, 1781

William Loving licensed to keep an Ordinary at his house; Joseph Higginbotham Morrison his Security.

Henry Martin and Gabriel Penn, Gent. are appointed to inspect the packing and weight of Pork, Beef, and Flour, and also inspect the filling of all Tar Pitch and Turpentine packed or filled for Sale or Exportation in this County Agreeable to the Act for the inspection of Pork, Beef, Flour, Tar, Pitch and Turpentine.

September Court, 1781

Samuel Meredith and William Cabell, Jr. Gent. are appointed Commissioners of the Specific Tax.

Will of Cornelius Vaughan presented in Court by Peter Carter and his widow, Ann Vaughan refused to qualify as Extrx.; Peter Carter appointed Exor.

November Court, 1781

On the Motion of William Thompson who had lost part of one of his ears, praying to have the Occasion thereof admitted to Record whereupon James Dillard, Jr. and James Dillard minor being first Sworn & Examined it appears to the Court that it was bit off by a man the said Thompson was fighting with.

John Witt, Jr. licensed to keep an Ordinary; Security, Thomas Evans.

December Court, 1781

On the motion of William Bracey formerly a citizen of the State of South Carolina who hath lately removed his slaves from that State, it is ordered that their names and sex be recorded.

James Nevil guardian to Richard & Harding Woodroof Orphans of David Woodroof, Decd. presented his Accts. of the orphans estate.

February Court, 1782

James Hopkins one of the Gentlemen in the Commission of the Peace for this County appearing in Court and refusing to take an Oath, Declared that Religious Scruples to be the true and only Reason of such Refusal whereupon the said Hopkins took the Solemn Affirmation of Allegiance to this State, also of a Justice of the Peace and of Chancery and also that of a Commissioner of Oyer and Terminer.

Revd. Benjamin Coleman (a Baptist Minister) is Licensed to celebrate the Rites of Matrimony.

March Court, 1782

James Nevil, Henry Martin and John Barnett are appointed Commissioners for the First Battalion for this County to ascertain

Value of Lands if it is necessary to sell for Ready money and name of each proprietor and return the same to the Clerks Office before June Next.

Anthony Rucker, William Ware and Roderick McCulloch are appointed Commissioners for the Second Battalion to Ascertain Value of Land (same as above).

Wiatt Powell licensed to keep an Ordinary at New Glasgow; Security, Charles Burrus.

William Loving and John Penn are appointed Commissioners of the Specific Tax for this County.

On the motion of Thomas Jopling (her father) Jane Davis, widow of Robert Davis, Decd. is granted Admr. of his Estate.

James Nevil, Gent. is Appointed in the first hundred of this County to take a list of all the Male Tithables above the Age of 20 and of the Names of all Slaves Specifying to whom they belong also the number of Cattle, Horses, Mares, Colts, and Mules, Wheels for Riding Carriages, Billiard Tables, and Ordinary License that is Resident in said Hundred which said Enumerated Articles are to be Placed under the Names of Persons to whom they belong and Return a fair List thereof together with the Vouchers with them taken to the Clerk of this County on or before the first Day of June Next.

The following are appointed same as above: John Diggs, Gent. in the second Hundred; William Horsley, Gent. in the third Hundred; Zacharias Taliaferro, Gent. in the fourth Hundred; James Dillard, Gent. in the fifth Hundred; Henry Landon Davies, Gent. in the sixth Hundred; Gabriel Penn, Gent. in the seventh Hundred; Roderick McCulloch in the eighth Hundred.

Thomas Becknall and Elizabeth, his wife made it Appear to this Court that the said John Becknall, their son, is Heir at Law to their Deceased sons, James & Thomas who died in the Continental Army.

April Court, 1782

George Muter, Gent. presented License to practice Law & took the oath of Allegiance to this State and also that of an Attorney.

Daniel Gaines & Nicholas Cabell, Gent. took the oath of Allegiance to this State as also of a Justice of the Peace in Chancery and a Commissioner of Oyer & Terminer.

May Court, 1782

The Will of Robert Howard Cash, Decd. presented in Court by Tamsey Cash, widow and Extrix. and Hendrick Arnold and Samuel Higginbotham Exors.; proved by the oaths of Caleb Higginbotham, Charles Burrus & Thomas Powell witnesses.

Nathan Crawford, Michael McNeely, Joseph H. Morrison and Alexander Reid (or any three of them) appointed to appraise the Estate of Alexander Miller, Decd.

June Court, 1782

Jacob Higginbotham appointed Surveyor of the Road in Room of John Mayfield.

William Higginbotham appointed Surveyor of the Road in Room of Patrick Lowry.

John Sandidge is appointed Surveyor of the Road from Swaping Camp to Horsley's Creek.

Letters of Admr. granted Mary Ann Franklin, widow of Henry Franklin, Jr., Decd. Security Richard Ballenger & John Franklin.

July Court, 1782

Certificate from under the hand of the Rev. Mr. Benjamin Coleman of the 5th of May, 1782 Certifying that he joined together in the Holy State of Matrimony to wit,

> Goolsbey Childress to Nancey Swinney, Feb. 28, 1782*
> Landon Carter to Mary Goodrich, March 22, 1782*
> William Carter to Katy Williams, April 4, 1782
> Joseph Ballinger to Tabitha Ballew, April 4, 1782
> John Gue to Peggy Whitten, April 9, 1782*
> James Goolsbey to Nancey Matthews, April 18, 1782*
> James Chastaine to Phebee Pagett, April 18, 1782*

"This is to Certify that Angus Forbes* and Mary Lee Came to me on Nov. 20, 1780 to Marry them and that they are Lawful married. Given under my hand this 30th Day of June 1782. W. Irvin V.D.M." (Rev. William Irvin.)

Certificate from under the hand of the Rev. Mr. Benjamin Coleman, June 30, 1782, Certifying that he joined together in the Holy State of Matrimony to wit,

> Edward Ware Jr. to Sally Thurmond, May 7, 1782.
> John Bush to Mary Tilman, May 9, 1782.

---

*There was no known record of these marriages in Amherst Co., Va. until I found this Order Book in 1931.

Applications, in National Archives, of Amherst Soldiers for Pensions

AARON, WILLIAM,—Franklin Co., Ga., Oct. 9, 1832, aged 79 or 80: enlisted Nov., 1776, under Lt. Cluff (Clough) Shelton, Capt. James Franklin, Col. Stevens' 10th Va. Regt. Contl. Line, and marched to Head Quarters at Bound Brook, N. J. Was ill in hospital at Mendon, N. J., and later joined Head Quarters at Germantown, but owing to ill health was furloughed by Gen. Muhlenberg. His term expired before he recovered and he was discharged by the General. Certificate of Pension April 16, 1833. He died in Franklin Co., Oct., 1841. May 28, 1857, Rebecca (Rudd) Aaron, his widow, applied in Whitfield Co., Ga., aged 71, stating they were married Nov. 3, 1829. Pensioned under Act. Feb. 3, 1853.

ALFORD, JOHN,—Davidson Co., Tenn., Sept. 8, 1832: b. Frederick Co., Va., May 8, 1760; drafted Amherst Co. 1778, under Capt. David Shelton as guard to British prisoners at Albemarle Barracks, about 45 miles from his home; three months tour 1780, James Pamplin, Capt., Charles Jones, Lt., Col. Lindsey's Regt.; marched 1781 under Capt. James Barnett to Little York, discharged just before Cornwallis surrendered. Placed on Pension Roll, March 16, 1833. Last payment April 24, 1837.

ALFRED, THOMAS and KENNEDY, JESSE,—Mrs. Susannah Alfred applied from Amherst Co., Va., March 25, 1847, aged 83, on account of the services of her husbands, Thomas Alfred and Jesse Kennedy. She alleged that Thomas Alfred was in the battle of White Plains and afterwards enlisted in sea service under his uncle, Capt. Hartshorn, and was in this service at the capture of Cornwallis. Her husband Jesse Kennedy served 1775 or 1776, as minute-man for several mos. under Capt. Samuel Cabell, and while in this service he enlisted in the regular service for two or three years under sd. Capt.; that he afterwards served a tour at Albemarle Barracks. She was m. in Oct., 1780 to Jesse Kennedy, and both were residents of Amherst Co. He d. 1799 or 1800. She m. April 2, 1805, Thomas Alfred, who d. in said Co. 1832. Charles Mays, same place, Sept. 8, 1848, aged 62, testified his father, Joseph Mays, decd. of Amherst and his brother, George Mays, of Ga., decd., enlisted with Jesse Kennedy & were transferred to Capt. Pannell's Co., Col. Samuel Elbert's Regt., marched to Ga. John Newman was in same company there. His father, Joseph Mays, had 350 acres allowed him for his service in Ga. Jesse Kennedy, James Dillard, John Phillips, John Tyre, Robin Hudson and William Johnson marched North under Capt. Samuel J. Cabell in 1776.

Her claim was not allowed as she failed to furnish proof of the alleged service.[63] (M.L.B. Amherst Co., Va.: "Jesse Kennedy & Susannah Dillard, Oct. 17, 1780. Consent of her father, Joseph Dillard"; "Thomas Alfred & Susanna Kennedy, April 5, 1805").

ALLEN, WILLIAM,— Nelson Co., Va., Sept. 25, 1832; b. Albemarle Co., Oct. 3, 1749, in that part later Amherst and then Nelson. Enlisted June 16, 1779 as private in Capt. Porter's Co., Col. Fontaine's Regt. of Guards at Albemarle Barracks, later commanded by Col. Taylor and known as the "Convention Guards," marched as guard to prisoners when they were moved to Winchester. An officer at the Barracks, James Garland, was killed by a young man on Post named Mansfield.[64] Spotswood Garland, Nelson Co., testified to the following return made by Capt. Porter to Hudson Martin, then Paymaster of the Regt. of Guards appointed by Patrick Henry, Esq., Governor of Virginia: "William Allen was furnished 1 coat, 1 vest, 2 pr. breeches, 4 shirts, 3 pr. stockings, 7 pr. shoes, 1 hat, 1 stock, 1 pr. buckles, 1 blankett, 1 pr. overalls & 1 hunting shirt while in service." Samuel Arrington, Nelson Co., testified he also was at the Barracks; William Fontaine commanded the Regt. for a short time; Francis Taylor commanded thereafter.

Dolly Allen, widow of pensioner (his 2nd wife) applied May 31, 1854, from Kanawha Co., Va., aged 68, stating her husband died March 6, 1838, at Nelson Court House, Va. William H. & Landon C. Allen were with their mother when she applied, & they testified the accompanying leaf was torn out of the Family Record made by their father:

> William and Dolly Allen, his wife, were married December 16, 1807.
> Barbara L. Allen, b. Dec. 14, 1808
> George W. Allen, b. March 26, 1810
> Jesse J. Allen, b. July 16, 1813
> William H. Allen, b. June 14, 1816
> Landon C. Allen, b. June 6, 1819
> Sally B. Allen, b. May 9, 1822
> James M. Allen, b. July 8, 1825 [living in Kanawha Co., 1855]
> Elizabeth M. Allen, b. April 14, 1828
> Andrew Jackson Allen, b. June 10, 1831

---

[63] Among the old court papers of Amherst Co. which I found in 1931 was the declaration made by Thomas Alfred, May, 1822, aged 69, by occupation a miller. "He enlisted as private in Contl. Service 1777 under Capt. David Earle, Col. Marshall's 3rd Va. Regt., for during the war." He was in the Battle of Brandywine, several skirmishes and the Siege of York and was honorably discharged after the surrender of Lord Cornwallis. His family consists of his wife and himself, both being infirm.

[64] Lawrence Mansfield. Woods' *Albemarle County in Virginia*, p. 44.

In 1851, John Allen, son of the soldier, was living in Nelson Co., Va. Dolly Allen's application was allowed; in 1866, she was living in Kanawha Co., then West Va.

AMMINET, JOHN,—Madison Co., Ala., Oct. 19, 1832; aged 79: enlisted Summer 1776, in Capt. John Perkins' Co., afterwards commanded by Capt. Thomas Balew, and was in "Christian's Campaign against the Indians"; discharged Nov. 20; again enlisted Nov. 21, 1776, under Capt. James Franklin & served in 10th Regt. under the following officers: Col. Stevens, Lt. Clough Shelton, 2nd Lt. James Dillard, Ensign James Powell. Later Col. Green commanded and at one time was under command of Gen. de La Fayette; when discharged, Dec. 1, 1779, Regt. was under command of Col. Samuel Hawes. Resided in Buckingham at date of enlistment, but enlisted in Amherst. Was at Germantown and was one of 300 men under command of Major Lee who attacked a British fort at Paulus Hook in the night and took 168 prisoners as was stated to him at the time—with which enterprise Congress was so well pleased that they voted $40 to each of the privates engaged in it—but which he never received. Was placed on Pension Roll Jan. 3, 1833; d. March 30, 1833.

ARNOLD, BENJAMIN,[65]—Warren Co., Tenn., Jan. 31, 1833: b. Buckingham Co., Va., Jan. 28, 1762; served 3 mos. 1779 in militia under Capt. Ford to guard Arrington's Station against the Indians; enlisted under Capt. McDowell, at the residence of Charles Moore, on Tiger River, Lawrence Co., S. C., Major James McDowell, Col. Cleveland, Gen. Morgan, and was in the battle of the Cowpens. The battle commenced shortly after sunrise, Jan. 17, 1781. He has a distinct recollection of the date, on account of it being the first battle in which he was engaged. Remembers seeing Col. William Washington, who commanded the Light Horse; 630 British were killed and taken prisoners. Marched as guard to prisoners to Beatty's Ford and was fired on while crossing by the British under Cornwallis, who had pursued the Americans. A message was sent informing him that if he did not desist all the prisoners would be put to death, and there was no more firing. 1781, removed with his grandfather, with whom he resided, his father being dead, to Henry Co., Va.; from there went as substitute for a man named Cox, Dillard was Lieut., Capt. George Hariston's

---

[65]Benjamin Arnold married Mary Ann, widow of Henry Franklin, Jr., and daughter of Capt. Aaron & Clara (Graves) Higginbotham. Clara Graves was a daughter of Francis Graves, Jr. (will probated in Essex Co., Va., 1748), and granddaughter of Francis Graves, Sr., son of Capt. Thomas Graves, who came to Virginia in 1607, and was Representative from Smythe's Hundred to the First Legislative Assembly in America held at Jamestown, 1619. *William & Mary Quarterly*, XXVI, 266; "Capt. Thomas Graves & Some of His Descendants," by William Montgomery Sweeny, *Ibid*, 2nd Ser. XV, 385.

Co.; after receiving discharge for this tour went as substitute for his uncle, Hendrick Arnold, of Amherst, who had been drafted, and he marched under Capt. David Woodroof towards Little York; Col. Meriwether and Samuel Higginbotham was Major in the regiment. Before reaching the main army news was received of the surrender of Cornwallis, when they wheeled and marched to Amherst C. H. & discharged. He lived in Amherst 15 or 16 miles from the C. H. for 10 years after the Revolution; in Henry Co., Va., 15 years, then removed to Rowan Co., N. C., and lived there 5 years, then removed to S. C. After 12 years, removed to Warren Co., Tenn. Lived in Illinois 2 years. Claim was allowed.

ARRINGTON, SAMUEL,—Nelson Co., Va., Aug. 22, 1843, aged 81: enlisted Amherst Co., Va., Feb. 17, 1779, marched to Albemarle Barracks, served under Capts. Jesse Allen, John Woodroof and James Burton and Col. Francis Taylor in the Virginia Troops as guard to the British Prisoners taken at the surrender of Burgoyne; when the prisoners were removed to Winchester, he acted as guard to that place where he was discharged May 22, 1781; enlisted June 30, 1781, under Capt. John Christian, Col. Richardson's Va. Regt., was in service in the lower part of the state and at the siege of Yorktown and after the surrender of Cornwallis, marched in Capt. John Stewart's Co., Col. Vance's Va. Regt., to Winchester as guard to British Prisoners taken at the surrender and was discharged Nov., 1781. Fellow soldiers in Capt. Allen's Co. were John, William and Gideon Via and James Evans. His pension was allowed. Died Aug. 10, 1849.

BAILEY, PHILIP, Sr.,—Bedford Co., Va., March 26, 1833: b. Goochland Co., Va., 1749; drafted from Amherst Co., under Samuel Richardson. He hired a substitute, John Oglesby, as he was a poor man and having tobacco growing upon rented land was fearful if he left it at this time he would lose the crop; drafted again and met the rest of the men at Amherst Old Court House, the place of rendezvous, marched under Capt. William Penn, Lt. John Penn, Col. John Pope, to mouth of Rockfish River. Discharged after 2 mos.; vol. next tour under Capt. William Harris. Since the Revolution lived in Amherst 6 years, Bedford 4 years, Campbell 4 years then returned to Bedford Co., Va., where he has lived ever since. Conny Witt testified that during the Revolution she lived neighbor to Philip Bailey. He was in the same service with her father. Claim was allowed.

BAILEY, WILLIAM,—Smith Co., Tenn., Dec. 26, 1836: b. Albemarle Co., Va., Dec. 24, 1756; enlisted 1778, under Capt. Christian, Lts. Byron & Burrus, Col. Meriwether's 4th Regt. Va. Line, Gen. Sumter's Brig. Marched to North Carolina, thence to Petersburg, Va., and after serving two years, furloughed early in

1780 and returned home. The militia was laid off into divisions, part to remain at home attending to agricultural pursuits and the balance engaged in duties of field or camp. During his furlough declarant was considered a minute-man and liable to be called into service upon a minute's warning. Called out in Feb., 1781, served in Capt. Woodroof's Va. Co., in a part of the main army under Gen. Washington, and was at the siege of Yorktown and surrender of Cornwallis; discharged latter part of 1781. Removed from Amherst Co., Va., to Smith Co., Tenn., 1817. His pension was allowed. He died Jan. 4, 1837. Bartholomew Stovall, a Revolutionary pensioner of Sumner Co., Tenn., testified 1837, he knew William Bailey at the time he enlisted in Amherst. James Cawthorn, Smith Co., Tenn., made affidavit April 3, 1837, that he was well acquainted with Jonathan Bailey, Wyatt Bailey, Susan Shepherd, Lucinda Horseley, Saluda Walker and Sarah Wilkerson, who constitute all the children and heirs of William Bailey.

BALDOCK, RICHARD,—Monroe Co., Ky., March 15, 1841, aged 78: substituted 1780, or 1781, for Levi Baldock who was drafted under Capt. William Penn & William Savage, Lt., William Johnston, Ensign, for six months as guard to the Magazine at New Glasgow, Va. Rejected. Remarks in case, did not serve 6 months.

BANKS, WILLIAM,—Putnam Co., Ind., Oct. 22, 1832: b. Culpeper Co., Va., June 3, 1761 or June 23, 1762; enlisted as Sergt. for 6 months tour, March, 1781, Capt. James Pamplin, Lt. Horsley, Ensign William McNeece, Col. Richardson's Va. Regt.; served under Gen. Lafayette, Gen. Muhlenberg's Brig. After the Revolution removed to Ky., and then to Putnam Co., Ind. Placed on Pension Roll Oct. 29, 1833; died Sept. 5, 1839. Elizabeth Banks, soldier's widow, was allowed pension on application executed April 26, 1855, at which time she resided in Putnam Co., Ind. They were married in Garrard Co., Ky., Dec. 10, 1801, by "one Randall Hall." She was living in 1863. Daniel P. and Wesley J. Banks testified May 11, 1855, Putnam Co., Ind., "these leaves were torn out of the Family Bible of our father and mother":

> William Banks, b. June 23, 1762: m. Elizabeth Brown, b. July 27, 1781.
> Nancy Banks, born August 4, 1802, died January 22, 1827.
> Frances Banks, born June 16, 1805, died October, 1806.
> Mary Banks, born February 15, 1807, died February 12, 1846.
> Elizabeth Banks, born February 8, 1809.
> Daniel P. Banks, born September 30, 1810.
> William S. Banks, born February 2, 1814.
> Emily A. Banks, born December 19, 1815.

Almirium Banks, born February 5, 1818, died September 4, 1847.
John Smith Banks, born March 7, 1820.
Joseph R. Banks, born July 15, 1823, died December 4, 1846.
Wesley J. Banks, born July 28, 1825.
John Banks and Louisa, his wife, married November 21, 1843.
Emily A. Banks, Jun., born May 10, 1845.

BARNETT, JAMES,—Madison Co., Ky., July 12, 1828: appointed Ensign Feb. 5, 1776, served in Capts. Samuel Cabell's and Peter Dunn's companies, Col. Mordecai Buckner's 6th Va. Regt.; commiss'd. 1st Lt. Jan. 6, 1778, Capt. Dunn's Co., Col. Febiger. At Capt. Dunn's death commanded his company until the reduction of the Regt. at White Plains, when the 2nd and 6th Va. Regts. were united. Capts. Dunn's & Hopson's companies were united and the command given to me; attached to Col. Febiger's 2nd Va. Regt. Sept., 1778, returned to Va. as supernumerary officer. Called into regular service 1780, as captain, by Col. Hugh Rose, County Lieut., attached to Col. Dick's Regt. by order of Gen. La Fayette until end of war.

Col. William Montgomery, Lincoln Co., Ky., Aug. 8, 1828: raised in Amherst Co., Va., and intimately acquainted with Col. James Barnett under whom I enlisted Feb. 14, 1776, in Capt. Cabell's Co., and marched to Williamsburg; attached to Col. Buckner's Regt.; marched to Trenton, N. J., thence to Elizabethtown and met Gen. Washington retreating with Putnam; joined their retreat before the British until we crossed the Delaware at Trenton and marched up said river to Cold Camp, crossing the river Christmas Day, took the Hessians at Trenton by surprise. After killing many, taking others prisoners, recrossed the Delaware, marched to Trenton, then to a small town in Jersey & was under arms two days and nights successively; following day the British came on, we retreated to Trenton, and after a hard scrimmage, crossed a creek and lay on the east bank until 10 o'clock at night. Washington with his small army took a circuitous route & fell upon the British at Princeton, taking about 300 prisoners & marched to Morristown. Shortly after this Barnett was promoted second lieut. and in the spring attached to Morgan's Riflemen. I was inoculated in Whippeny Town, N. J., and Barnett at Wilmington, Del. In the spring we met in Jersey and saw no more of each other until we had taken Burgoyne at Saratoga & returned to White Marsh, Pa., where we had a scrimmage with the British at Chestnut Ridge. Our time expired in March, & Capts. Rose and Barnett marched us back to Amherst. Barnett returned to the army in Jersey, remaining a considerable time, returning home as captain supernumerary officer of the Contl. Army. I was appointed lieut. in the Militia and acted as a volunteer & Barnett as a supernumerary officer, until the capture of Cornwallis. I was 19 years old at the time of the battle of the Point, 1774, where Barnett was wounded.

Daniel Barbee, Danville, Ky., Aug. 18, 1828, testified he became acquainted with Barnett at the taking of the Hessians at Trenton, while serving as Sergt. under Capt. Richard Taylor, Col. William Washington's 1st Va. Regt. Col. Barnett moved to Ky. 1786. James Barnett died Aug. 27, 1835, in 86th year, and his widow, Marcey Barnett, applied Madison Co., Ky., Jan. 15, 1839, aged 71. They were married at the home of her father, Nathan Hawkins, Madison Co., Ky., March 4, 1790, by Alexander McKey. Both pensions were allowed.

BARNETT, JAMES P.,—Lincoln Co., Ky., Oct. 22, 1832: b. Amherst Co., Va., 1762; enlisted Amherst, 1780, as substitute for his father, John Barnett, under Capt. John Leak, Lt. John Jones, Col. Martin, to guard Public Magazine, Guilford, N. C. While residing in Guilford Co., N. C., where he was taken as a boy, vol., March, 1781, 3 mos. under Capt. John May, Col. Martin, and was in the battle of Guilford Court House. Directly following this service moved to Logan's Fort, Ky., and vol. for 1 mo., 1782, marched to English Fort & the Cumberland Mts., to guard emigrants from Va. to the interior of Ky.; June or July 1 mo. under Capt. Robert Barnett, Col. Benjamin Logan; immediately following, 1 mo. under Capt. Kirkum, Col. Jack to guard the salt works at Bullits Lick; 2 mos. under Capt. Robert Barnett, Col. Logan, was in Gen. Clark's Expedition up the Miami River and in the battle of Shawnee Town; winter, 1782, 1 mo. under Capt. John Woods; May, 1783, 1 mo. under Capt. Robert Barnett, Cols. Logan and Isaac Shelby on an expedition against the Indians on Sandy River. His pension was allowed. Died March 31, 1834.

BEAN, RICHARD,—Lewis Co., Ky., Sept. 26, 1832: b. Northumberland Co., Va., Aug., 1752; enlisted Bedford Co., Va., 1776, under Capt. William Campbell, Lts. Daniel Trigg and Alex. Cumings, George Lambert, Ensign, Col. Henry, Lt. Col. Christian, marched to Williamsburg and Gwynn Island against Dunmore. Discharged 1777. Same was lost while ill at his mother's in the Northern Neck. Fellow soldiers: John Donelly, Fifer Major; Andrew Locke, Drummer; Henry Ayres, Samuel Bartor, Frederick ODaniel, & Henry Scrags, Sergts.; William Lee, Jesse Coper, Andrew Wright, Stephen Mitchell, Spencer Morgan, Charles McFagin, John Arter, Charles Nicholas, William Smith, Michael Garsh, Ellison Smith, John Everett, Bailey Harril, Andrew Rogers & Robert Mitchell. Residing in Amherst when drafted for second tour at Key's Gap, by Col. Gaines & served under Capts. Ewell & Scott, Major Finley. Served 7 mos. & hired a substitute "Sergeant Jones."

Discharged by Col. Febiger. Jacob Dooley, Madison Co., Ky., testified he served with Richard Bean in the 1st Va. Regt. under Capt. William Campbell. His pension was allowed.

BIBEE, THOMAS,—Cocke Co., Tenn., March 1, 1834: aged "about 100 years"; b. in Goochland Co., Va., and moved to Amherst Co. before the Revolution where he vol. Feb., 1776 under Capt. Higginbotham and marched to Charleston, S. C., to aid in repelling the British who were then about to invade that State. The declarant marched under Capt. Higginbotham in a southerly direction, crossed Fluvanna River in Va., Pedee River in N. C. & Santee River in S. C. and joined the American Army under Gen. Lee and served five months under Capt. Higginbotham guarding the City of Charleston until the British Fleet and Army withdrew from before the City, having failed in the attack made upon the Fort on Sullivans Island. Gen. Moultrie commanded the Fort on the Island and successfully resisted the attack of the British. Gen. Lee commanded the Troops on the mainland. In the month of July, 1776, declarant received a written discharge from his captain in the City of Charleston and returned home to Amherst, which discharge he has since lost. He served 5 mos. for which he never received any pay. Feb., 1779, vol. for 6 mos. under Capt. Reid, marched to Charleston, S. C., and joined Gen. Lincoln near Charleston—attached to Gen. Morgan's Va. Brig.—Col. Washington—Gens. Moultrie & Armstrong. In the attack upon the British under Col. Maitland at Stono. "A considerable number of our men being killed." Discharged Aug., 1779, Charleston, S. C. Shortly after returning home enlisted as substitute for one Johnson & marched South; served under Gen. Lincoln until just before taking of Charleston by the British; discharged March, 1780 & returned home. Before the termination of the Revolution he was excused from Military duty on account of his age. Moved to N. C. on the Yadkin River, thence to Burke Co., then Rutherford Co., thence to Buncombe Co., then removed to Cocke Co., Tenn., where he lives with his step-son. His claim was allowed.

BLAINE, GEORGE,—Nelson Co., Va., March 26, 1851: Rachel Blaine, aged 78, widow of George Blaine who died May, 1817, applied for a pension which was due on account of his service in the Revolutionary War. He was enlisted by Capt. Jacob Brown recruiting officer in Amherst Co., and served 18 mos. in the South; battles of King's Mt., Cowpens, Guilford Court House, and in a campaign near Jamestown, Va. M.L.B. Amherst Co., Va., March 3, 1790: George Blaine, widower & Eles Steven Rachel Masters, spinster. The claim was not allowed as she failed to furnish proof of the alleged service of George Blaine as required by the pension law under which she applied.

BLAIR, ALLEN,—Amherst Co., Va., Oct. 15, 1833: b. near Rockfish Gap (now Nelson Co.) July 8, 1754; drafted under Capt. Young Landrum, but engaged William Bowman as a substitute; in 1781, on Guilford Expedition under Capt. Young Landrum;[66] there saw Gen. Edward Stevens badly wounded. Capt. William Turner was Orderly Sergt. on this expedition; again drafted July, 1781, under Capt. John Loving & marched to Williamsburg. Capt. Turner testified he served as Sergt. and Blair as private in Capt. Landrum's Co. on the Guilford Expedition. Claim was allowed. He d. April 23, 1835. Mary Ann (Staples) Blair, soldier's widow, testified Amherst, Aug. 21, 1838, aged 76, that they were m. Dec. 22, 1778. A son, John S. Blair, was living in Lynchburg, Va., in 1838.

BOND, RICHARD,—Franklin Co., Ga., Sept. 10, 1832; aged 69: private, 1777, under Capt. David Shelton & Col. Richardson at Albemarle Barracks; drafted 1779, Orderly Sergt. & marched under Capt. Higginbotham to the mouth of Gillie's Creek below Richmond & discharged; drafted 1780, under Capt. Higginbotham as Orderly Sergt. & marched to New Glasgow in Lower Amherst; served 3 mos. & discharged. Substitute for his father, Nathan Bond, 1781, under Capt. James Franklin, Maj. Gabriel Penn & Col. Rose on Guilford Expedition. "At Guilford there was a dispute as to who should command, and with Gen. Greene's permission, we chose Capt. James Dillard, of Col. Lynch's Regt." Afterwards served a tour in the infantry riflemen attached to Washington's Light Horse. Placed on Pension Roll, July 30, 1833.

Richard Bond, Cobb Co., Ga., Nov. 3, 1851, applied for a pension for the heirs of his father, Richard Bond, who d. Jan. 31, 1837. His mother, Susannah Bond, d. Nov. 6, 1843. They were m. in Amherst Co., Va., 1783, and left the following children: Sarah Crider (widow of John Crider) b. Feb. 28, 1784; Richard Bond, b. Dec. 6, 1788; Sophia Hendricks, formerly Sophia Bond, b. 1793; Frances Santin, formerly Frances Bond, b. 1794; Lindsey Bond, b. Feb. 28, 1801. Following is from an almost illegible Bible Record: Permele Bond, b. May 22, 1786; Elizabeth Bond, b. Feb. 12, 1791.

BOWLING, EDWARD,—Clarke Co., Ga., Nov. 21, 1832: b. St. Mary's Co., Md., Aug. 25, 1744; moved to Amherst Co., Va., where he entered the service in three separate tours of 6 months;

---

[66]"Feb. 27, 1781. Capt. Landrum with about 30 men, who had been at the mouth of Tye River, from Friday last, marched by my home on their way to join Gen. Greene to the Southward. The remainder of the lower Battalion were ordered to Stovall's Ferry, at least 50 miles out of their way, to Moore's Ordinary in Prince Edward, where they were ordered to Rendez-vous. Strange orders and conduct when the enemy are almost at our doors." William Cabell's Diary, The Cabells & Their Kin, p. 113.

vol. as Sergt. in Capt. Richard Ballenger's Co. of Infantry & was at the battle of Guilford Court House. In Siege of York under the command of Gen. Washington. Some years after the Revolution he moved to Clarke Co., Ga. Thomas Simonton & John Gardner, of Clarke Co., testified James Bransford, an old and respectable citizen formerly living in same county, said he knew Edward Bowling in the Revolution; that Bowling gave Bransford his spoon, tray & Sifter when he quit the Army at Little York. Allowance ended March 4, 1833.

BOWLING, JAMES, Sr.,—Amherst Co., Va., Aug. 20, 1832: b. St. Mary's Co., Md., 1752; enlisted in Amherst fall of 1775, under Capt. William Fontaine, 2nd Va. Regt., Col. Woodford, Lt.-Col. Charles Scott, Maj. Hardiman, 1st Lt. John Marks, 2nd Lt. Thomas Hughes of Augusta Co., Ensign Robertson of Augusta Co. The company was raised in Amherst, Albemarle, Augusta and Buckingham; was at battle of Great Bridge, Dec. 9, 1775, when Lord Dunmore was defeated. We pursued the retreating army and took possession of Norfolk after compelling Lord Dunmore and his troops to evacuate and take shelter on their shipping. While we were in Norfolk the enemy set fire to the Town, partly destroying it. We remained in Norfolk during the winter, and burnt the remaining part as we were leaving, in order to render it useless for the enemy. Discharged, Williamsburg, April or May, 1776. Served at Albemarle Barracks under Capt. William Thurmond & at York Town under Col. Meriwether. Placed on Pension Roll Oct. 26, 1832; d. March 12, 1836. Letty M. Bowling, widow of James Bowling, aged 76, applied Amherst, Sept. 4, 1838. They were married April 7, 1777, by Rev. Kemp. The banns were published in the different churches of Amherst Co., as the law required: Pedlar, Maple Run & Keys Church. All the records of the churches have been destroyed. Bible Record: James Bowling and Letty More Gillaspie were married April 7th 1777.

Dec. 17, 1838, Samuel M. Garland, Clerk of Amherst Co. testified that they were married April 7, 1777—after third publishing of the banns without license from the Clerk, or marriage bond—a mode of celebrating the rites of matrimony then & now lawful in Virginia.

BOWMAN, JOHN,—Roane Co., Tenn., Oct. 21, 1822, aged 70: b. in Amherst Co., Va., where he enlisted March, 1777, in Capt. Clough Shelton's Co., Col. Edw. Stevens' Regt., Gen. Scott's Brig.; in battle of Germantown; from there to winter quarters at Valley Forge, and while there was on duty at a village called Penny packd and in a scrimmage with the British he and 14 others were taken prisoners & carried to Philadelphia & then to New York, and was a prisoner of war when the battle happened at Monmouth. Shortly afterwards exchanged & joined my Regt. at Brunswick. At battle of Stony Point and continued a private soldier in 10th Va. Regt. for 3 years; discharged at Burlington by Lt. James Dillard, Capt. Clough Shelton & Col. Ed. Stevens. His family consisted of himself, wife, Barsheba, aged 60, son Lewis, aged 19, and dau. Sally, aged 24. He died May 25, 1841. His widow, Barsheba (Hooper) Bowman, applied Oct. 2, 1843. They were married 1785. Both pensions were allowed. She died 1860.

BROWN, JOHN,—Shelby Co., Ky., July 11, 1853, Nancy (Glenn) Brown, aged 81, widow of John Brown, applied, stating on account of disability resulting from a wound in the elbow, which was shot to pieces in the battle of Saratoga, her husband was pensioned from Dec. 1, 1811, while residing in Woodford Co., Ky., where he died Aug. 20, 1822, and refers to his application in Washington for particulars. They were married in Woodford Co., Ky., March 23, 1806, by Rev. Isaac Crutcher. Issue: George, Lucinda, Nancy, Maurice, Joshua and Sydney Scott Brown. John Brown's pension papers could not be found on file, although he had received a pension, and as all the soldiers with whom he had served were dead, his widow tells what she remembers he stated in his lifetime: "While a resident of Amherst Co., Va., he entered service as a private in the Virginia troops soon after the battle of Lexington. He was in the battle of Bunker Hill, marched to Canada, was at the storming of Quebec, spent the winter there, after which he returned to the Main Army under Washington and was placed in a company of picked men as Sergt. under Morgan. While serving in line of duty in the fall of 1777, was in the battle of Saratoga in which he was shot in the elbow. Feb. 21, 1854, Mrs. Susannah Waugh, born in Amherst Co., Va., 1761, wife of George Waugh, an old settler of Gallia Co., Ohio, testified her brother, John Brown, left Amherst with three of his brothers and after more than two years service returned home wounded. Anderson Brown, Marion Co., Mo., July 18, 1854, aged 63, testified he was the son of John Brown and his first wife whom he married January, 1778. His mother d. 1805, and his father then married Nancy, widow of Tyra Glenn; her maiden name was Cloak. His father was Sergt. in Daniel Morgan's Riflemen, and was shot through his left elbow during the first day's battle near Saratoga, a short time before the surrender of the British General Burgoyne and his army. He was in the hospital for some time and when able to travel returned home. His father drew a pension allowed disabled soldiers. The widow's claim was not allowed as she failed to furnish proof of six months service. On her application, April 12, 1855, for bounty land, also, which was due on account of the Revolutionary War Service of her husband, she was allowed 160 acres on Warrant No. 30702, under Act of March 3, 1855.

BROWN, STARK,—Walton Co., Ga., Aug. 20, 1832: b. July 6, 1756; enlisted March 1, 1776, Capt. Samuel Cabell, Col. Mordecai Buckner's 6th Va. Regt., Gen. Lee. Marched to Williamsburg, thence to Gwynn Island. Returned to Williamsburg, marched north and joined Gen. Washington and was in the battle of Trenton and Princeton. Inoculated for smallpox, and when fit for duty joined Gen. Washington at Middlebrook. Detached, June 10, 1777, from the main army and placed under command of Col. Daniel Morgan, Lt.-Col. Butler, Major Morris, Capt. Cabell, as one of the Regt. of Riflemen. Marched to King's Ferry upon the Hudson and sailed up the Hudson to Albany; marched to Stillwater and was in the engagement with Gen. Burgoyne; thence marched in pursuit of sd. Burgoyne to Saratoga, where the enemy surrendered, Oct. 17, 1777; marched to Albany and by land to Trenton, and Col. Morgan's Regt. of Riflemen was stationed upon the line until Gen. Washington built his huts at Valley Forge; deponent was then quartered at a village called Whitehorse, about 24 miles from Philadelphia, where he was discharged, March, 1778. Cert. of Pension issued Jan. 2, 1833.

Dosha Wood, Henry Co., Tenn., Sept. 8, 1846, aged 66, applied as only living heir of Stark Brown, who d. Feb. 5, 1840, in Walton Co., Ga. Her father served as Orderly Sergt. She m. at the age of 19, James Wood, who is now dead. Her sister Matilda m. John Stokes—both now dead. Her brother, Meredith, died 18 years ago. Stark Brown m. Tabitha Reynolds, May 8, 1779.

Note: September Court, Amherst Co., 1782.

Order to summon James Gatewood, Guardian of *Stark Brown*, orphan of William Brown, decd. (of Essex Co., Va.) to Render an Account of sd. Orphan's Estate Dismissed.

BRIANT, JOHN,—Lincoln Co., Ky., Aug. 10, 1818: enlisted under Capt. Jesse Allen as Sergt. "for as long as the prisoners remained at the Barracks." Served nearly three years in the Regt. commanded by Col. Francis Taylor. John Warren testified he saw him in service at the Barracks. Sept. 19, 1820, John Briant, aged 69, appeared in Garrard Co., Ky., Court and declared he was a single man, and the same John Briant who was pensioned Aug., 1818 in Lincoln Co., Ky.

BRIANT, ZACHARIAH,—Daviess Co., Ky., Oct. 11, 1832, aged 67: enlisted Feb. 17, 1779, in Regt. Va. State Troops under Capt. Jesse Allen, Col. Francis Taylor, & was in service at Albemarle Barracks until 1781, guarding British prisoners; marched to Winchester with them and returned to the Barracks & discharged; two years service. Substituted then for James Stewart, Militia man drafted to go to the Siege of York and was enlisted in New Kent Co. for during the War by Capt. Meeky, of Albemarle or Louisa Co., and was a regular soldier under furlough at the cessation of hostilities. John Briant, now dead, was a fellow soldier at the Barracks. William Carter, of same county, was a fellow-soldier, 1779-1780. Raised in Amherst Co., Va.; removed in 1800 to Mercer Co., Ky., then to Washington Co. until 1818, then removed to Daviess Co. Feb. 25, 1837, Zachariah Briant, Spencer Co., Ind., made oath that he was the same person who was pensioned in Daviess Co., Ky., at $80 per annum, under Act of June 7, 1832, and desired to have his Certificate transferred to Indiana, as most of his family resided there.

BURFORT, TANDY,—Powhatan Co., Va., Aug. 15, 1832: b. Goochland Co., 1761; drafted Amherst, 1778, marched under Capt. John Trent against the Indians on Holston; took fever after 6 weeks and furloughed; again drafted under Capt. Nicholas Cabell & served around Richmond. Rejected.

CABELL, COL. NICHOLAS,—Nelson Co., Va., Feb. 3, 1855, Col. Edward A. Cabell testified "a trunk of old papers belonging to the late Judge Cabell was sent up from Richmond to his brother Joseph, who turned them over to me for examination. I found a number which go to show that my grandfather, Col. Nicholas Cabell, rendered military service during the Revolution, which should entitle his descendants to further compensation from the Government. It appears from them, that in the year 1775-6, he raised 2 companies of minute-men, the first perhaps as a volunteer Recruiting Officer, the second certainly by appointment—that he marched with the latter company to Manchester, Jamestown & Williamsburg; & that his company didn't return until late in the month of September." Joseph C. Cabell, only living child of Col. Nicholas Cabell, authorized his nephew, Nathaniel Francis Cabell, to act as his agent to collect & apply papers for the Pension Declaration. Family Record in possession of Joseph C. Cabell: "Nicholas Cabell, 4th son of Dr. William & Elizabeth Cabell, b. Oct. 29, 1750; m. Hannah, dau. of Col. George Carrington, April 16, 1772; d. Aug. 18, 1803. Mrs. Hannah Cabell d. Aug 7, 1817, aged 67."
N. Francis Cabell testified Col. Nicholas Cabell left six children. He sent the following proof of his service: Sept. Court, 1780. Copy of the Court record stating he served as Capt. of minute-men. Extract from a letter of Col. William Cabell, Sr., addressed to Col. Hugh Rose, Aug. 1, 1780: "N. Cabell early in the present dispute was appointed Capt. of a Minute Company in which capacity he was called into service for some considerable time, after which he had an appointment by the General Assembly of Lt.-Col. in State service, but as the Regt. was not raised he was not called for duty, & it is not long since that he was recommended by our Court as a proper person to be Colonel of the Militia, in which character he has since acted & as far as I have been informed with the approbation of the people."

CAMPBELL, ANTHONY,—Russell Parish, Bedford Co., Va., Jan. 28, 1833: b. Caroline Co., Va., Feb. 6, 1761; enlisted Amherst Co. Aug., 1779, as private under Capt. Reuben Jordan, Lt. Roger Shackleford, Col. Taylor, Albemarle Barracks. Drafted Jan. 10, 1781, Capt. Richard Ballinger, Lt. Thomas Jones, Ensign John Matthews. When Tarleton came to Charlottesville, summer of 1781, was drafted July 4, and marched to Williamsburg, joined Gen. Stevens; field officers, Col. John Pope, Major William Cabell, Capt. Diggs, Lt. Charles Eads, Ensign Barnett. When he returned home was placed in Col. Meriwether's Regt., Hardeman, Major, and was in an engagement under Gen. Stevens at James Town. Discharged by Col. Peter Rose in Amherst. Removed to Bedford, 1790. Dec. 24, 1832, James Cottrel, aged 80, Bedford, Va., testified he served a tour Jan., 1781, under Capt. Richard Ballinger with Campbell. Claim allowed.

CAMPBELL, HENRY,—Nelson Co., Va., Nov. 30, 1832: b. in Amherst, Feb., 1764, in the part which became Nelson; 1781, on Guilford Expedition, under Capt. James Dillard. At Siege of York Town under Capt. John Loving, Gen. Lawson and Col. Richeson; John Campbell was a fellow soldier on this 4 mos. tour. Sarah Campbell, same place, applied Oct. 31, 1839, widow of pensioner, who d. Jan. 13, 1835, testified they were m. May 19, 1786, by Rev. Benjamin Coleman.

CAMPBELL, JOHN,—Amherst Co., Va., June 18, 1833: b. Albemarle Co., 1750; removed to Amherst when a boy where he has lived ever since. Private, 1781, Capt. James Dillard's Co., on Guilford Expedition; Henry Campbell was a fellow soldier. Placed on Pension Roll Sept. 6, 1833. His widow, Frances Campbell, applied Oct. 13, 1841, aged 80. Benjamin Campbell & William Wright, his neighbors, stated he d. Jan. 29, 1838, and his son, Wyatt Campbell, testified there was no other record of his father's death. William Tucker, aged 63, testified he went to school with their children, Betsey & Nancy, previous to his moving to Powhatan Co. in 1796.

CAMPBELL, LAWRENCE,—Green Co., Ky., Sept. 17, 1832: b. Nov., 1763; drafted Amherst Co., Va., 6 mos. as private in Capt. George Penn's Co., Col. Scott's Regt., to guard County Stores at Charlottesville. His neighbors, Col. William Barnett, Carter Hubbard & Armstrong Kerr, testified to his character and service in the Revolutionary War. Placed on Pension Roll April 12, 1833.

CARPENTER, BENJAMIN,—Schuyler Co., Ill., Sept. 3, 1832, age 78: enlisted Amherst Co., Va., May, 1776, Sergt. under Capt. Joseph Cabell, Lt. Nicholas Cabell, Ensign Nathan Crawford, Col. Mason's Regt. Was in engagement at Long Bridge, on York River, in which Capt. Fordyce, the British commander, was killed. Second tour under Capt. James Higginbotham, Lt. Samuel Higginbotham[67] & Ensign James Pamplin, Col. Mason; third tour, under Capt. Wm. Harris, Lt. Charles Eads, Ensign Tilman Walton, stationed at Four Mile Run, on James River; later in Richmond guarding prisoners taken at battle of King's Mountain; fourth tour, under Capt. James Montgomery, Lt. Tilman Walton & Ensign Robt. Montgomery. The company joined Gen. Lafayette about the first of June at Deep Run Church, Va., and continued with the army until Cornwallis was taken at York Town, and was present at the surrender. In 1790, removed to Tenn. & later to Illinois. Placed on Pension Roll, Oct. 9, 1833.

CARPENTER, WILLIAM,—Wayne Co., Ky., Aug. 28, 1832: b. Rockfish River, Amherst Co., Va., March 19, 1761, where he vol. as private to guard prisoners at Albemarle Barracks; drafted, 1780, under Capt. William Harris, Lt. Wm. Montgomery,—"we met at one old Mr. Joplin's, on Rockfish River, and marched to Richmond, and acted, I think, under Col. Aaron or Joseph Higginbotham. Was in no engagements, but kept guard up and down James River, Malbon Hills & Hickory Neck Church; discharged at Richmond by our Captain and each man had his expenses home." Drafted after Christmas in Capt. Tilman Walton's Co.; marched against Cornwallis & Tarleton under Gen. Wayne & Gen. Lafayette "where I first saw him." The army split into several large detachments. some marching towards Norfolk and some up the River. Cornwallis marched over Chickahominy Bridge & tore it up and camped a while in Half Mile of James River; 250 with our company, were ordered to repair the bridge, which we did, and just as we had finished and were cleaning the mud off of our breeches, Gen. Wayne, with 4000 men, as I understood, passed in pursuit of Cornwallis & marched up the hill & fired upon the enemy. We were commanded to guard and keep the bridge, which we did. After a hard battle with Cornwallis, Gen. Wayne retreated back over the bridge and in the rear of them, Tarleton, with his Light Horse and with Horns blowing, came up. Under command of Capt. Walton, we fired our Rifles and kept them off Wayne's Army, and they retreated, Col. Tarleton having two horses shot from under him, as we heard. We then retreated about three or four miles back to the Army. Shortly afterwards, Cornwallis & Tarleton marched to Little York, where we were commanded to march, & endeavored to keep them there.

---

[67]Sept. 18, 1777. "Mr. Samuel Higginbotham having produced the Treasurers Receipt for One hundred & thirty Six pounds sixteen Shillings returned by him & also two bonds of Lieutenant David Bellews for fifty pounds each, being in full for so much advanced by the Board to the County Lieutenant of Amherst for the purpose of recruiting Men for the Service of this State; it is ordered that the said Mr. Higginbothams Bond, which he gave to the aforesaid County Lieut. be Cancelled." *Journals of the Council of the State of Virginia*, 1, 492.

Shortly afterwards I was taken sick & lay 18 days out of my senses in the Hospital. When able to travel, with the balance of the sick was ordered home—many died on the Road. After the Siege of York, our Captain said we had done our duty and we were discharged. Removed to Knox Co., Tenn., 1806, where he lived 18 or 19 years, and then to Wayne Co., where he was inscribed on the Ky. Pension Roll, March 1, 1831. He d. Sept. 14, 1835, in Adair Co., Ky., and his widow, Mary Carpenter, applied Sept. 24, 1840, aged 73; they were m. in Augusta Co., Va., Jan. 9, 1786. Mrs. Elizabeth Luttrell, Knox Co., Tenn., Sept. 24, 1843, aged 70, widow of William Luttrell, formerly of Amherst Co., Va., whence they moved 30 years ago, testified she was present when Parson Brown married Mary or Polly Strickling & William Carpenter. Mary Carpenter d. Oct. 20, 1846, and Dec. 16, 1857, Mary, wife of McFarlane Canterberry, aged 56, of Adair Co., Ky., applied, stating that Rebecca Pratt, Susan Ore, Nancy Money & deponent were the only surviving children of William & Mary Carpenter. Claim was rejected for lack of proof of the marriage.

CARTER, WILLIAM,—Ohio Co., Ky., Nov. 5, 1832: b. Aug. 21, 1760, in what is now Amherst Co., Va.; entered service after Burgoyne's defeat as a substitute under Capt. Philip Thurmond, Lt. Joseph Edwards, to guard prisoners at Albemarle Barracks, under Col. Francis Taylor. Substituted for 3 mos., Aug., 1779, under Capt. John Christian, Lt. James Ware & Ensign Travis Chambers; 1780, drafted under Capt. Richard Taliaferro, was crippled in the knee and furloughed. After returning to Amherst, said Captain raised a vol. company and he enlisted. Drafted Feb., 1781, under Capt. James Dillard, marched in company with Capt. James Franklin (there being two companies from Amherst) to join Col. Gabriel Penn and Col. Hugh Rose, at Stovall's Ferry, on the James River, where they rendezvoused. Arrived at Guilford day after the battle & was attached to Col. Buford's Rifle Regt. with 10 or 12 others of his company. He was taken sick with pleurisy, furloughed and returned home. He passed Gen. Greene's Army and was ordered to take a waggon and aided to Surry Town on Dan River, where he was in a hospital a few days. Same year marched against Cornwallis under Capt. Samuel Higginbotham, south side of James River to Carter's Ferry, crossed over[68] and marched to New Kent Co., where they halted and were joined by other troops. Enlisted here under Capt. Meeky for during the war, consequently furloughed for 90 days. Returned home and made preparations for service during the war, but before the time expired, Cornwallis sur-

---

[68]April 29, 1782. Claim of John Woodson (Carter's Ferry) for £1-7-3 for ferriage 80 men, 9 horses & 2 waggons and teams under command of Capt. Saml. Higginbotham, in Continental service, on their way to join the Army under Major-General Marquis De La Fayette, 6 Aug. 1781. Cumberland Co., Va., *Order Book*, p. 212.

rendered. He removed in 1802, to Carter Co., Tenn., and in the fall to Washington Co., Ky.; in 1805, to Ohio Co., Ky., where he died Oct. 14, 1842. Sarah (Williams) Carter, pensioner's widow, applied Dec. 13, 1853, aged 74. They were m. in Breckenridge Co., Ky., about Jan. 15, 1809, by Rev. Walls, a Methodist Minister. She applied from the same county, April 5, 1859, for Bounty Land, under the Act of Feb. 3, 1853, which was allowed.

CARTWRIGHT, JUSTINIAN, or JESSE,—Caldwell Co., Ky., April 27, 1819: b. Feb. 22, 1752; enlisted Feb. 26, 1776, as Sergt. in Capt. Samuel J. Cabell's Co. of Riflemen, Col. Buckner's Va. Regt. Contl. Troops. May following, by order of Gen. Charles Lee, transferred to Capt. James Innes' Co., Col. Harrison's Artillery Regt., was in the battle of Monmouth and many skirmishes. In 1780 or '81, he became impaired in health and furnished a substitute at the enormous sum of $500, equal to silver, on which he was discharged by Gen. Charles Scott. On moving to Ky., 1782, left discharge with Hon. John Marshall, now Chief Justice of the Federal Court. Placed on Pension Roll, June 5, 1819; d. Dec. 27, 1832.

Nov. 17, 1846, James A. Cartwright, Caldwell Co., Ky., in order to secure a pension for the heirs, testified that his father enlisted under Capt. Samuel Cabell, of Morgan's Va. Rifle Corps, on Contl. Estabmt. & was transferred to Capt. James Innes' company & was engaged in the battle of Monmouth. Discharged Dec. 28, 1780. His father married in 1777, Frances Gillaspie who d. the latter part of 1818. He left the following children: James A., Nancy S., Henry L., Winnefred, Sally m. Leonard Brown, residents of Caldwell Co., Ky., Polly M. m. Elisha Thurman, Livingston Co., Ky., Bennett G., Levin L., residing in Mississippi, Justinian, Terresa m. Tutt Brown.

CARTWRIGHT, PETER,—Sangamon Co., Ill., Nov. 19, 1852, Rev. Peter Cartwright,[69] son and only surviving child of Peter and

[69]This was the celebrated Peter Cartwright "the Backwoods preacher." He was an original character of whom many anecdotes are told. In 1846 he ran for Congress, his opponent being Abraham Lincoln. "It is related that during this campaign, Lincoln made a speech in a town where Cartwright had an appointment to preach in the evening, and that Lincoln attended the service at night, sitting in the rear of the room. At the close of the sermon, Cartwright called upon all who expected to go to Heaven to rise, and all rose except Lincoln. Then Cartwright, following the well-known evangelistic method of the period, asked all who expected to go to hell to rise. Still Lincoln remained seated. Cartwright never hesitated to be personal in his applications and appeals. He leaned across the pulpit and said, 'I have asked all who expect to go to Heaven to rise, and all who expect to go to hell to rise; and now I should like to inquire, where does Mr. Lincoln expect to go?' Lincoln rose, saying that he had not expected to participate in the service otherwise than by his presence, but since Mr. Cartwright insisted on knowing where he expected to go, he would answer, 'I expect to go to Congress.'" Barton's *The Life of Abraham Lincoln*, 1, 277-278.

Christian Cartwright, testified his father d. in Caldwell Co., Ky., 1809 or '10; entered service from Amherst Co., Va., about the year 1777 or '78. He heard his father say he was in the battle of Brandywine, where he lost two brothers, and that he married, Feb. 27, 1787, Christian Garvin, in Amherst Co. They moved to Kentucky in 1791. Shortly afterwards their home burned, and the Family Bible was destroyed. They had the following children: Rosanna, Peter and Polly Cartwright, all dead except deponent. Mother d. in Caldwell Co., Ky., Dec. 23, 1838. Neither parent ever applied for a pension. Oct. 18, 1852, Mrs. Sophia Wilcox & John Rucker testified Peter Cartwright was the son of Peter Cartwright, the Revolutionary soldier and his wife, Christian Garvin; their other children, Rosanna Vineyard & Polly Pentecost, and his widow, Christian Cartwright, being dead.

CASH, BARTLETT[70],—Amherst Co., Va., Oct. 15, 1832: b. Albemarle Co., Dec. 18, 1757; vol. in 1776, served 3 mos. in Capt. John Sale's Co., Lt. James Franklin, Col. Christian's Va. Regt., marched to the western frontiers of Virginia to protect the country from the depredations of the Cherokee Indians; 1781 on Guilford Expedition under Capt. James Franklin, where he was placed in Capt. Young Landrum's Co., Col. John Holcombe's Va. Regt. Benjamin Higginbotham stated he was raised in same county and neighborhood and knew his statement to be true. Claim was allowed. He d. April 11, 1835. Soldier's widow, Elizabeth, was allowed a pension on her application executed Oct. 11, 1841, while residing in Amherst Co., Va.

Bible Record: Bartlett Cash was born Dec. 18, 1757; Elizabeth Cash, his wife, was born Jan. 15, 1764. Bartlett Cash and Elizabeth, his wife, were married Feb. 14, 1781.

Children: Joel Cash was born April 30, 1783; Frances Cash was born Aug. 15, 1785; John Cash was born Feb. 19, 1788; Willis Cash was born July 23, 1790; Mary Ann Cash was born June 5, 1793; Nancy P. Cash was born July 29, 1796; Henry W. Cash was born March 5, 1801; William P. Cash was born June 16, 1803.

William P. Cash and Elizabeth, his wife, were married Dec. 3, 1823. Jefferson R. Cash was born Dec. 3, 1825.

Children of David and Nancy P. Moore: William Moore was born July 27, 1822; Bartlett Moore was born Sept. 23, 1823.

CASH, JOHN,—Living in Jackson Co., Ga., 1832, where he had resided 32 years: b. Amherst Co., Va., Feb. 1, 1760; enlisted, age 16, under Capt. James Franklin, Col. Samuel Cabell; was at

---

[70]The list of pensioners printed in 1834-35, erroneously states his service was with "North Carolina Militia."

Siege of Yorktown. Rejected as he failed to furnish proof of service.

CASH, JOHN,—Henry Co., Ga., Nov. —, 1832: b. Albemarle Co., Va., April 5, 1757; entered service under Capt. John Sale, Lt. James Franklin, Ensign Jesse Allen; on Cherokee Expedition; marched by Big Lick, Botetourt Co., English Ferry on New River to the Holston River about the Long Islands, where the country generally had been scared by large forces of Indians. We formed what was called a Ranging or Scouting party. There was a skirmish at Fort Chissell and we were in severe engagements; burned the Indian towns and drove the scattered Indians away. On returning home after 3 mos. tour, deponent and his brother Peter marched under Capt. James Pamplin, 1 mo. tour Albemarle Barracks. Col. Taylor was in command of the garrison. Again deponent served in second division (they were counted minute-men) under Capt. Samuel Higginbotham, Lt. James Ware, Ensign Joseph Staples—privates, John Giles, William Giles & Joseph Giles (three brothers), William Venison, William Tyra, Dick McCary—marched through Albemarle, Fluvanna & Goochland counties to Richmond and took charge of the artillery. Capt. John Barnett's Co. from the Lower Battalion of Amherst accompanied Capt. Higginbotham's Co. to Richmond; thence marched to Petersburg. Higginbotham's Co. remained in Richmond until the expiration of the tour and were discharged by company. Next tour under Capt. James Pamplin, joined Gen. Lawson at Ground Squirrel Bridge, was in hearing of the firing of the battle of James Town; night after the battle we marched by Moonshine to the battle-ground, were fired upon and retreated past Hickory Neck Church, where wounded persons were receiving aid. From there to Malbon Hills, Richmond & New Castle, upon Pamunkey River, where we met Col. Samuel Cabell lately exchanged from British confinement. Before they got to James Town, the Army prepared for battle at Big Springs, McNeece, the officer who commanded the proportion to which he & his brother Peter belonged, slipped off home to Amherst, which gave the parade field the name of "McNeece's field." About this time Gen. Lawson, for some misconduct, was deprived of his sword & his command given to Gen. Stevens. There was a suspicion against Gen. Lawson that he held back from the battle; he did lie by during the day & march the whole night in confusion. From New Castle deponent was marched towards York. A relief from Amherst overtook them at Prickly Pair old field, where he was discharged with others Aug. 14th immediately preceding the capture of Cornwallis. Fellow soldiers: Bartlett Cash, Howard Cash (now living in Habersham Co., Ga.), Joseph Bond, John Smith, James Ware, decd., Edmund Hodges & David Ballew.

Pensioner d. Aug. 13, 1836, and March 15, 1845, Lucy (Campbell) Cash, his widow, applied from Pike Co., Ga. She was b. March 3, 1760; m. Jan. 23, 1782; their banns were published at the house of Charles Rose, Amherst, Va., by a traveling minister. They lived seven years in Amherst, moved to Bedford Co., Va., then to Elbert Co., Ga., about 1802, where the Family Bible was destroyed when their house burnt. March 16, 1853, Nancy Cash, of Spalding Co., Ga., aged 61, James Cash, b. Nov. 6, 1784 & Mary Cash, aged 52, testified their mother d. Jan. 23, 1848; their brother, George Cash, d. Aug. 14, 1848, and Stephen Cash, of Miss., has since died and they are the only living heirs. Allowed.

CASH, PETER,—De Kalb Co., Ga., Nov. 15, 1832: b. Feb. 21, 1759; enlisted at age of 18 in company with his elder brother, John Cash, under Capt. John Christian, Lt. Benjamin Taliaferro, Roger Shackleford, Orderly Sergt.; 2nd tour, same year, under Capt. Charles Christian, brother to his first captain; 3rd tour, in the same division under Capt. Samuel Higginbotham, James Ware, Lt., Joseph Staples, Ensign—privates James Gulland, Howard & John Cash (deponent's brothers), etc. (same testimony as John Cash). He was taken sick at Malbon Hills and never recovered until Christmas after Cornwallis surrendered. Dr. John Rose attended him. Called out under Capt. Daniel Tucker, Henry Ballinger, Lt., John Taliaferro, Ensign, William Taliaferro, Orderly Sergt., Gen. Mathews, Commander, against the insurgents of Penn.; three months tour lacking nine days and discharged. After the Revolution, lived one year in Rockbridge Co., with Jo. Alexander and one year at widow McDowell's, mother of Col. James McDowell, until April, 1827, removed to Ga. Claim was rejected for lack of proof of six months service.

CASHWELL, HENRY,[71]—Amherst Co., Va., Sept. 17, 1832: b. Amherst Co., 1757; enlisted fall 1779 as Corpl. under Capt. John Sale as guard to British prisoners at Albemarle Barracks; enlisted Feb., 1781 as Orderly Sergt. marched under Capt. James Franklin, arriving at Guilford day after the battle. Capt. Franklin resigned and Capt. Young Landrum, of Col. John Holcombe's Regt., Lawson's Brig., took command; discharged at Deep River, N. C. 1781, Orderly Sergt. under Col. Hugh Rose, escorting from Amherst C. H. a small body of British prisoners and delivering them on board a British vessel in James River below James Town. Benjamin Higginbotham, William Hartless, William Lavender and William Cashwell testified they were with Henry Cashwell on the Guilford Expedition. His claim was allowed.

---

[71]The printed list of Pensioners, 1834-35, erroneously gives his service as with "North Carolina militia."

CASHWELL, WILLIAM,—Amherst Co., Va., Sept. 17, 1832: b. Feb., 1762; private, 1779, under Capt. David Woodroof, marched to Albemarle Barracks; vol. 1780, in Capt. John Morrison's Rifle Corps, marched to Richmond and stationed about three miles from Petersburg at Long's Ordinary; here were 1500 men under Gens. Lawson & Steuben. In Feb. drafted under Capt. James Franklin on Guilford Expedition; reached there in time to hear the guns at the battle of Guilford; fellow soldiers: William Hartless, Philip Smith & Benjamin Higginbotham. Drafted under Capt. John Stewart & was in the Siege of York Town; marched with the prisoners taken in the siege to Winchester Barracks. He d. June 9, 1847. Betsy (Penn) Cashwell, pensioner's widow, aged 77, applied July 18, 1848; they were m. Nov. 7, 1791, by Rev. Crawford.

CAWTHORN, RICHARD,—Fluvanna Co., Va., 1832, aged 69: 1779 enlisted in Amherst by Lt. Woodroof, private in Capt. Garland Burnley's Co., Ambrose Pollard, Lt. Roberts, Major, Col. Francis Taylor's Regt.; 18 mos. service & discharged at Albemarle Barracks; vol. 1781, in Col. Mathews' Rifle Regt. & was at the Siege of York Town; two years service. His claim was allowed.

CHEATHAM, JOSIAH,—Nelson Co., Va., March 18, 1839, Lucy Cheatham, widow, aged 69, applied stating her husband served as private under Capt. Samuel Cabell and Lt. Archer Perkins; battle of Saratoga, Buford's Defeat and Siege of York. They were m. Nov. 5, 1786, by Rev. Martin Dawson. He d. Feb. 13, 1813. Richard Hare, a fellow soldier at Siege of York, testified Cheatham enlisted under Capt. Samuel Cabell at the beginning of the war. Her claim was allowed.

CHILDRESS, ABRAHAM,—Perry Co., Ky., Oct. 17, 1832: b. Nov. 15, 1752; enlisted 1777 under Capt. Saml. Cabell; placed in the 4th or 5th Regt.; made a cook under Gen. Washington & served him as such 18 mos. & was then under Capt. Pamplin and Col. Meriwether for 3 years; discharged at Winchester 1 mo. after Cornwallis surrendered. Was in the battle of Brandywine and in hearing of the guns at Guilford. Stephen Arthur, J. P., Powell Co., Ky., testified Nov. 28, 1856, he is applicant for a pension; b. March 8, 1760, Bedford Co., Va., and raised near Abraham Childress in adjoining county. "I was present when most of my acquaintances left Liberty. At the same time Abraham Childress marched, went William Childres, Moseby Childres, Moses Fleetwood, John Fleetwood, Joseph Vurman & Thomas Arthur. Some time after they left the county under Capt. Cabell's command, I heard of the battle of Brandywine & that Moses Childres was shot down by the side of his brother. Abraham Childres & William Childres were taken prisoners of War, and William never returned. Abraham Childres re-

Amherst County, Virginia, in the Revolution 115

turned home with the Fleetwoods, my brother being killed. I entered service before the battle of Guilford, under Capt. Thomas Leftwich, Lt. Walters, 9th Regt. commanded by Col. Trigg."

William Childress, Owsley Co., Ky., son of Abraham Childress who d. May 6, 1849, in Letcher Co., Ky., declared he left the following heirs: William, Francis, Polly, Dicy, Abraham, Jr., Elizabeth, Goldsby & Seley. His mother, Elizabeth Childress, d. Feb. 17, 1833. Rejected.

CHILDRESS, BENJAMIN,—Albemarle Co., Va., Nov. 13, 1850: b. April 3, 1764; entered service as a private Oct., 1780, 2 mos. in Capt. Christian's Co.; 1781 2 mos. & 1 week under Capt. James Pamplin; two weeks later was ordered to Yorktown; furloughed on account of illness by Major Wm. Harris & Col. Hugh Rose. Before he recovered the army was disbanded. Samuel Childress declared that in 1781 his elder brother, Benjamin Childress, was called into service. Rejected as he did not serve six months.

CHILDERS, HENRY,—Grant Co., Ky., Feb. 11, 1833, aged 68: b. in Albemarle Co., Va., removed to Ky. 34 or 35 yrs. ago; vol. in Amherst Co., Va., and served 3 mos. as private in Capt. Samuel Higginbotham's Co. Next tour substituted for William Knight Bowles for 3 mos. as private in Capt. William Tucker's Co., Col. Dabney's Va. Regt., was in slight skirmish with the British near "Half Way House" and was discharged a short time before the British entered Yorktown. Placed on Pension Roll Feb. 28, 1833.

CHILDRESS, JOHN,—Knox Co., Tenn., Jan. 9, 1833: b. Albemarle Co., Va., Dec. 2. 1759; moved to Amherst Co., Va. while a child; vol. Aug., 1778, served as private in Capts. Roger Shackleford's & Richard Gaffert's companies, under Col. Broadhead; marched through Staunton, Va. & crossed the Allegheny Mts. at Braddock's old trace & crossed the Monongahela River at a place called the boat yard; from there the army marched to the Ohio River & built Fort McIntosh, which was occupied a few months when they crossed the Ohio River to Muskingum River. Discharged Feb. 20, 1779, having served 6 mos., enlisted fall 1779, under Capt. Richard Woodroof, Col. Taylor's Va. Regt. Spring of 1781 substituted for William Davis in Capt. William Tucker's Co., marched to Malbon Hills. Here our company lay about a week then marched to the "Half Way House" between Old Hampton and Little York, where we met the main army of militia under Gen. Nelson; marched under Gen. Nelson to Little York where we met the regular army under Gen. La Fayette. While we lay at Little York, Gen. La Fayette gave them a sham battle and then reviewed their troops. Moved to Burke Co., N. C. 1785 or '86, remained one year, then moved to Wilkes Co., N. C., where he resided 7 or 8 years, then to Knox Co., Tenn. Placed on Pension Roll May 3, 1833.

CLARKE, JOHN,—Washington Co., Ky., Aug. 14, 1834: b. Henrico Co., Va., Feb. 27, 1764; enlisted 1780 in Amherst Co., Va., as private in Capt. Christian's Co.; marched under Capt. James Dillard and joined Gen. Greene's Army a few days after the battle of Guilford; attached to a division of 500 riflemen commanded by Col. Lynch, who, after the battle, kept in pursuit of Cornwallis. He d. Jan. 25, 1839. Oct. 16, 1845, Ann Clarke, pensioner's widow, applied from same county aged 73. They were m. by Rev. John Bailey, May 19, 1791, at the home of her mother, Mrs. Ann Whitten, Lincoln Co., Ky. She d. Nov. 25, 1845.

COFFEE, REUBEN,—Wayne Co., Ky., Aug. 28, 1832: b. Albemarle Co., Va., Sept. 16, 1759. His father moved to Amherst 1764. He testified that he vol. under Capt. Moses Guest, Major Winston, Col. Benjamin Cleveland & was in the battle of King's Mountain. Moved with his father to Wilkes Co., N. C.; settled in Bucks Co., N. C. & after 22 years moved to Wayne Co., Ky. His claim was allowed.

COFFEY, OSBORN,—Casey Co., Ky., Feb. 8, 1830, "aged about 71": enlisted Feb. 14, 1776, under Capt. Samuel J. Cabell, Col. Mordecai Buckner's 6th Va. Regt., Contl. Line; later attached to Col. Morgan's Regt. Discharged Feb. 14, 1778; served as Sergt. at battles of Guilford, Eutaw Springs & Camden. William Montgomery testified Dec. 8, 1829, he was with Coffey under Capt. Samuel Cabell at Trenton, Princeton & Saratoga (where we took Burgoyne after two hard battles) and White Marsh. They were marched home to Amherst by Capts. Rose & Barnett. Served 1 yr. as Sergt. under Col. Greene in the South. Coffey has been neighbor to him in Ky. since 1797. He d. March 13, 1840, and Polly Coffey, pensioner's widow, applied same place April 8, 1844, aged 83. Ezra Morrison, Lincoln Co., Ky., Sept. 2, 1844, aged 88, & Patrick Hyght, aged 79, Casey Co., Ky., Nov. 2, 1844, testified they were at the marriage of Osborn Coffey & Mary Nightingale, in Amherst Co., Va., Feb. 15, 1783. Two children, Lucy & Jesse Coffey, living in Middleburg, Ky., Sept., 1844.

CONNER, DANIEL,—Nelson Co., Va., Oct. 4, 1820, "aged about 72": enlisted Feb., 1776 as private in Capt. Samuel J. Cabell's Co., Contl. Estabmt., Col. Daniel Morgan's Regt. for 3 years; transferred to Capt. John Stokes's Co. of Infty., Col. Thomas Parke's Regt. Battle of Saratoga under Capt. Cabell & Stony Point under Capt. Stokes, Gen. Wayne commanded at last named place. Discharged, Phila., 1779. He has no children & his aged wife lives with her children by a former husband. John De Masters & Charles Jones, fellow soldiers, testified Daniel Conner was at the taking of Burgoyne at Saratoga. Placed on Pension Roll Jan. 9, 1822; d. March 4, 1822. His widow, Mary (Hurt) Conner, applied April

Amherst County, Virginia, in the Revolution 117

30, 1853, aged 80. They were m. in Patrick Co., Va., Aug. 30, 1785, by Major Brett Stovall, J. P. Her claim was allowed.

COTRELL, JAMES,—Pikes Co., Ohio, June 9, 1841: b. Oct. 14, 1748; summer of 1776 private under Capt. Sale to guard deserters from Amherst Court House to Williamsburg; discharged after 6 weeks; Sept. 1, 1777 1 mo. under Capt. John Dawson, Col. Taylor; Jan., 1781 under Capt. Richard Ballenger, Lt. Thomas Jones, John Mathews, Ensign; vol. 1782 under Capt. John Sale. Rejected as he failed to furnish proof of six months service.

CREWS, JOSEPH,—Bedford Co., Va., May 11, 1832, aged 75: enlisted 1777, in Capt. Nicholas Cabell's Rifle Co., Col. Edward Carrington, on Contl. Estabmt. Discharged, Jamestown—2 yrs. 6 mos. service. In no battles except a scrimmage at Craney Island, where he received a ball in his left leg. His family consisted of wife & two daus. aged 3 & 7. Placed on Pension Roll, July 28, 1832; d. May 26, 1843. His widow, Nancy (Eubank) Crews, applied July 31, 1855, aged 66, stating they were m. in Bedford by Rev. John Sledd, Jan. 4, 1822.

CRITTENDEN, RICHARD,—Bartholomew Co., Ind., Nov. 12, 1832: b. Charles City Co., Va., March 6, 1761; March 15, 1778, substituted for his father who was drafted from Amherst Co., Va., as private under Capt. James Dillard, Lt. William Martin, Col. Patrick Rose; in battle of Guilford Court House. Served 18 mos. under Capt. Isaac Parker & Col. Nicholas Cabell in the Virginia troops on Cherokee Expedition; battles of Island Ford & Big Catawba; Siege of Yorktown under Capt. Charles Christian, Col. Bullitt, Gens. Washington & Greene. His last discharge, given him by Gen. Washington, was burned in 1789. After the Revolutionary War lived 5 years in Botetourt Co., Va.; 1 year in Salem, N. C.; 9 years in Union Co., S. C.; 20 years in Ky.; then removed to Ind. His claim was allowed. He d. June 22, 1841. His widow, Sally Crittenden, applied Oct. 9, 1843, aged 75, stating her husband was a lieutenant in the Revolution. Martha Le Master, Johnson Co., Ind., testified March 7, 1845, Sally, widow of Richard Crittenden, was her dau. The wedding took place at her father's Josiah Tanner, Spartansburg, S. C. Patsey Tanner, Decatur Co., Ind., testified she was m. to Lucius Tanner Jan. 15, 1793. Her sister, Sally Crittenden, was m. four years previously & they were daus. of Josiah and Martha Tanner.

Family Record:
Richard Hazelwood Crittenden, b. March 6, 1761:
 Sally Tanner, b. Oct. 30, 1773
Richard Hazelwood Crittenden and Sally, his wife,
 was married Feb. 12, 1789
Josiah Crittenden, b. Oct. 24, 1789

John Crittenden, b. Dec. 23, 1790
Charles Worde Crittenden, b. Jan. 11, 1793
Mary W. Crittenden, b. Dec. 15, 1794
Matthew Tanner Crittenden, b. Jan. 14, 1797
Samuel Crittenden, b. Dec. 24, 1798
Martha Crittenden, b. June 22, 1801
Nancy Crittenden, b. Aug. 16, 1803
Richard Hazelwood Crittenden, b. Jan. 7, 1806
James H. Singer, b. July 20, 1819 (no relation to the family shown)

Deaths:
Josiah Crittenden, d. July 22, 1796
Nancy Crittenden, d. Dec. 23, 1818
Matthew Tanner Crittenden, d. Aug. 5, 1798

Mary W. Singer & Richard Crittenden, Jr., Bartholomew Co., Ind., testified the above leaf was torn out of their father's Prayer Book and was in his handwriting.

NOTE. Martha Lemaster applied for a pension Aug. 14, 1843, aged 87; m. to Josiah Tanner, Dec. 1, 1771, in Mecklenburg Co., Va. They had the following children:

Sally Tanner, b. Oct. 30, 1773
Lucy Tanner, b. April 25, 1775
Martha Tanner, b. Aug. 7, 1777
Matthew Tanner, b. Jan. 11, 1779
Samuel Tanner, b. Aug. 15, 1780
Ann Tanner, b. Oct. 11, 1783
Elizabeth Tanner, b. Feb. 18, 1786
Creed Tanner, b. Feb. 24, 1788
Mary Tanner, b. Dec. 16, 1789
Kezia Tanner, b. April 29, 1792
John Tanner, b. ....
Eleanor Tanner, b. March, 1797
Thomas Tanner, b. Dec. 3, 1802

Josiah Tanner d. Oct. or Nov., 1807, Jefferson Co., Ky. His widow, Martha, m. Sept., 1826, in Oldham Co., Ky., Abraham Lemaster; he d. Nov. 3, 1837 in Ind. Martha Lemaster was allowed pension on account of the service of her former husband, Josiah Tanner, who served as lieut. in Capt. Cardry McBee's Co. of Horse under Cols. Roebuck & Williams in the S. C. troops; he was wounded in his right arm at the battle of King's Mountain.

CRUTCHER, WILLIAM,—Williamson Co., Tenn., Dec. 7, 1846, Elizabeth Crutcher, aged 83, applied, widow of William Crutcher who while residing in Amherst Co., Va., served 6 years in the Va. State Line of the Revolutionary War. They were m. in Amherst Co. in 1782. Their banns were published in 3 churches. He d. in Williamson Co., Tenn., Dec. 13, 1833. Henry G. Padgett, aged 50, deposed that as a child he lived neighbor to them in Amherst Co., Va. His father's 2nd wife was a dau. of William & Elizabeth Crutcher. The deponent moved to Williamson Co., Tenn. about 1819 & 5 years later William Crutcher & his wife moved to sd. Co. & State & he was frequently in their home. They had the following children: Polley, m. Beverley Padgett, Sarah, m. John Hudson, Robert, Elizabeth, m. Allen Buggs, William, Willis, Henry L., & Parker. Samuel M. Garland, Clerk of the Circuit Court, Amherst Co., Va., stated that no record of their marriage could be found in Amherst.[72] Rejected for lack of proof of marriage. She d. Jan. 14, 1848.

Bible Record:

Polley Crutcher, b. March 13, 1785
Sarah Crutcher, b. May 15, 1786
Robert Crutcher, b. Sept. 22, 1788
Elizabeth Crutcher, b. May 21, 1790
William Crutcher, b. Dec. 30, 1792
Willis Crutcher, b. April 25, 1795
Henry Lawson Crutcher, b. Jan. 25, 1798
Parker Crutcher, b. May 17, 1800

DAVIS, EDMUND,—Nelson Co., Va., May 6, 1818. In 1775 enlisted under Capt. Thomas Pinckney, of Charleston, S. C. In battles of Stono, Fort Moultrie, Siege of Savannah & Charleston. He applied again Aug. 28, 1820, aged 84; 1775 enlisted in Thomas Pinckney's Co., Col. Charles C. Pinckney's Regt. for 18 mos.; discharged 1779. In battle of Savannah under Gen. Lincoln, battle of Stono & Siege of Charleston taken prisoner, escaped & was taken prisoner at Camden & after eight weeks escaped & joined Gen. Thomas Sumter & was with him in battle of Hanging Rock, & battle of Fishing Creek where he was defeated & the force got scattered & he joined Capt. Samuel Richardson's Co. in Goochland, Va., Col. Hopkins' Regt. to end of War. His family consisted of wife aged 53, dau. aged 24, son aged 14. Nov. 24, 1818, Gen. Charles Cotesworth Pinckney Late Col. 1st Contl. Regt. S. C., testified Edmund Davis was a soldier Light Inft. 1st Contl. Regt., S. C. & was taken Prisoner at Surrender of Charleston 1780 & he escaped from prison & returned to his native State Virginia & resided ever since in Nelson Co. Placed on Pension Roll June 30, 1818; d. May 8, 1835. His widow, Milley Davis, applied same place, Oct. 15, 1838. They were m. in Amherst Co., Va., by Rev. Ezekiel Campbell, Sept. 4, 1793. Consent of her father, James Fitzgerald.

---

[72]William Crutcher & Elizabeth Pollard. Married by Rev. Joseph Ballenger, Jan. 16, 1784. (Order Book 1782-1784, p. 210). William Montgomery Sweeny's *Marriage Bonds & Other Marriage Records of Amherst Co., Va.*, 1763-1800, p. 23.

DAVIS, WILLIAM,—Fayette Co., Va., July 15, 1832, aged 77: enlisted early part of Revolution as private under Capt. Gabriel Penn, Va. Contl. Line, 8 mos. service; Capt. Penn not having a full company, his men were united with those of Capt. Nicholas Cabell's who also had an imperfect company, and the whole was placed under command of the latter. Tour 1781 under Capt. James Dillard. In battle of Guilford Court House, Siege of Yorktown and at the surrender of Cornwallis. He d. Jan. 20, 1846 & his widow, Benedicta Davis, applied Nov. 16, 1848 from the same county, aged 78. M.L.B. Amherst Co., Va., Jan. 1, 1787, William Davis & Benedicter Milstead. Waller Sandidge, Amherst Co., testified April 2, 1849, aged 74, "he was present at their marriage when a boy; they were married by Rev. Benjamin Coleman. Among their children were Polly, Nancey & William. He understood they went from this county and settled in Greenbrier Co., Va." Henry Peyton, Sr., Cabell Co., Va., testified he served two tours with William Davis—one under Capt. James Franklin, 1781. Her claim was allowed.

DEMASTER, EDWARD or EDWARD D. MASTERS,—Nelson Co., Va., Aug. 16, 1828, aged 65: enlisted 1779, served under Capts. Jacob Brown, Samuel Booker & William Johnston, Col. Samuel Hawes' Va. Regt., and was discharged at the close of the war at which time he was corporal of Continental Dragoons. Daniel Conner testified he enlisted same time as Masters (or Demasters) in Capt. Jacob Brown's Co., and both enlisted for during the war. His claim was allowed. Soldier's widow, Sally Demasters, was allowed pension on her application executed Oct. 18, 1848; she was b. Aug., 1775, dau. of Thomas Carter. They were married Aug. 23, 1794, in Amherst Co., Va., by Rev. Ezekiel Campbell. Her husband d. Nov. 24, 1837.

Children:

Betsey Demasters, b. September, 1797
Nancy Demasters, b. December, 1801
Polly Demasters, b. January, 1803
John Demasters, b. March, 1805
George Demasters, b. April, 1808
Wiatt Demasters, b. November, 1809
Cornelius Demasters, b. December, 1811
Sarah Ann Demasters, b. August, 1817
Elvira Demasters, b. December, 1819

DEMASTER, or MASTERS, JOHN,—Nelson Co., Va., July 23, 1842, Martha Demasters, age 82, widow of John Demasters (brother of Edward) who enlisted 1776 under Capt. Samuel J. Cabell, and was taken prisoner on Long Island, applied. They were m. July 29, 1779, by Parson Waddell, in Augusta Co., Va. Shortly afterwards her husband left on another tour, was taken sick and after forty days returned home. She was living in Nelson Co., Va., formerly part of Amherst Co., in 1848, where she had lived since she was six years old. Her maiden name was Martha (Patsy) Moran.

Bible Record:

John De Masters, b. Oct. 14, 1754; Martha Moran, b. July 17, 1760
Winifred De Masters, b. Feb. 6, 1781
Nancy De Masters, b. April 27, 1783
James De Masters, b. Oct. 18, 1785
Nicholas De Masters, b. Feb. 18, 1788
Jane De Masters, b. Oct. 13, 1791
Jesse De Masters, b. March 19, 1793
John De Masters, b. Dec. 15, 1796
Moris De Masters, b. Oct. 29, 1801
Polly De Masters, b. Dec. 4, 1804

A John Masters applied from Franklin Co., Ind., claiming Virginia service, which made it necessary for Martha De Masters to furnish the following proof: Edmund S. Coffee, Nelson Co., Va., March, 1845, aged 72, testified he was intimately acquainted with John De Masters who died in Nelson Co. several years since, & his widow, Martha. He frequently heard him speak of his service and of having been taken prisoner on Long Island & he thinks also at White Plains; the British officers wished him to swear allegiance to the King of England, which he refused to do. He spoke frequently of Gen. Washington, his commander. The said De Masters lived his whole life on Tye River, Nelson Co., and never was in Indiana. He d. about 1830 or '31. Mary Coffee, daughter of John De Masters, testified her father d. March, 1831, the same day one of her children was born. Pension was allowed.

DENNEY, JOHN,—Wayne Co., Ky., Nov. 22, 1841: b. Amherst Co., Va., Aug. 24, 1766; vol. as private under Col. William Cabell, with about 200 others, to prevent the British from crossing James River in order to take the British Prisoners at the Barracks in Albemarle Co. & marched to Lynch's Ferry. After 30 days watching for the British and in detachments getting all the water crafts several miles up & down the river they were marched back to Amherst Court House & discharged. Served 4 mos. at Albemarle Barracks & 1 mo. as guard to the British Prisoners when they were moved for safety. Discharges were lost when his home burned. Moved with his father to Fayette Co., Ky. & lived with him 6 years then moved to Wayne Co. Rejected as he failed to prove he served six months.

DICKERSON, THOMAS,—Henry Co., Va., Oct. 29, 1845, Jeremia Dickerson, aged 83, widow of Thomas Dickerson who served 2 years under Capt. Samuel Cabell, applied. At the capture of the Hessians at Trenton Christmas Day, 1776, and battle of Germantown. He moved from Amherst Co. about the close of the Revolutionary War to Henry Co., Va., where they were m. Oct. 2, 1782, by Rev. Guilliam. He d. Nov. 7, 1806. Oct. 30, 1845, James Thomas, Pittsylvania Co., Va., testified he became acquainted with Thomas Dickerson at Valley Forge. "He was a tolerable tall man and played the fiddle." He married Jeremia, dau. of Capt. John Wells, of Henry Co., Va. Pension was allowed.

DILLARD, JAMES,*—Amherst Co., Va., April 28, 1809, aged 53: enlisted from Amherst, Feb., 1776, as a Cadet in Capt. Samuel J. Cabell's Co. of Riflemen, and the same year was appointed Lt. in Capt. James Franklin's Co. of Infantry, belonging to the 10th Va. Regt. on Contl. Estabmt. "Owing to Capt. Franklin's resignation in 1777, his command devolved on me, which office I filled for six months." Nov. 28, 1809, Col. Samuel J. Cabell testified that "Capt. James Dillard joined my company of Riflemen as a Cadet in the month of Feb., 1776, after which he was appointed a Lieut. in Capt. James Franklin's Co. of Infantry belonging to the 10th Va. Regt. on Contl. Estabmt. and commanded by Col. Edward Stevens and I do further certify that the sd. Capt. Dillard acted as Commandant of a Company for several months whilst I was Brigade Inspector to the Brigade to which the 10th Va. Regt. was attached."

Aug. 15, 1828, Capt. James Dillard applied for a pension due him for his service in the Revolutionary War, under the act of May 15, 1828 and Dec. 15, 1829 sent additional proof of his service:

Amherst Court House of Virginia
15th Dec. 1829.

Sir,

Received your favor under date of 27th of November, 1828, and mark its contents as to its long delay and am much surprised when you inform me the Books of the War Department does not corroborate with my declaration and claim under the above Act. It might be expected they would not be perfect but did not suppose they would have been so much lacking as through your information I believe they are.

I now say that I know of no cause why they should not correspond with my declaration and claim under the above Act.

I should regret very much to think after serving my country through the war of the Revolution, that I should dishonor myself by sending forward a declaration and claim

---

*Capt. James Dillard was a grandson of James Dillard, (d. in Amherst Co., 1768) Captain of a Company of Rangers in the French & Indian War.

under the above Act that I was not only legally, but honorably entitled to under the above Act.

I did not know when I sent forward my claim that further proof would be necessary as I fully expected the Books of the War Department kept in time of that war would have justified my declaration and claim under the above Act. Agreeable to your advice I now send you the Deposition of Moses Wright, one of my old and reputable soldiers who enlisted with me when I was a Lieut. and also a certificate from the Virginia Land Office showing that I had drawn my bounty land as a Capt. in the Continental Line, which I hope will prove satisfactorily my service and rank in that Army. You will please to write on to Amherst Court House, Virginia, as heretofore. The branch of the United States Bank in the City of Richmond, Virginia, is the most convenient to me.

Hope you will write on as soon as convenient if I am to receive anything for my youthful service. Now at the age of seventy four can expect to enjoy it but a short time.

My hand has got very unsteady—fear you will hardly read it.

I am, Sir,
Respectfully your Obedient Serv't.,
James Dillard

Hon. Richard Rush,
Secretary of Treasury
Washington.

Jan. 20, 1829, Moses Wright, Buckingham Co., Va., testified that he enlisted under Capt. James Dillard of Amherst, for 3 years, when he joined the 10th Va. Regt. commanded by Col. Edward Stevens. Feb. 5, 1810, a Warrant was issued to James Dillard for 4000 acres of land as Capt. Contl. Line. Capt. James Dillard d. April 4, 1832. His widow, Jane Dillard, was allowed pension on her application executed April 7, 1840. She d. Sept. 3, 1843. April 7, 1840, Mrs. Mary London, of Amherst Co., Va., aged 89, testified she had lived in the county 67 or 68 years and became acquainted with Mrs. Jane Dillard in the spring of 1782. In March, 1782, she had seen the sd. James Dillard, decd., recruiting men in sd. county for the U. S. service in the Revolutionary War. They were married in Hanover Co., and moved to Buckingham Co., 1782 and in 1784 or '85, returned to Amherst Co., Va., where they lived together until his death. April 8, 1840, Micajah Pendleton, aged 82, Nelson Co., testified he was a guest at the infare which took place at the home of the bride's father, Major John Starke, in Hanover Co., 1782; the same year they moved to Buckingham Co., and thence to Amherst Co., Va.

Family Record:

James Dillard was born the 29th day of October, 1755, and married to Jane Starke the 3rd day of April, 1782. The said Jane Starke was born the 12th day of December, 1759

Joseph Starke Dillard, b. March 19, 1783
Mary Ann Hunt Dillard, b. Sept. 13, 1784
Nancy Wiatt Dillard, b. April 2, 1787
Jane Chane Dillard, b. April 11, 1789
James Spotswood Dillard, b. Nov. 29, 1791
Fanney Horsley Dillard, b. April 10, 1793
John Dillard, b. January 11, 1795
William Dillard, b. March 4, 1797
Elizabeth Dillard, b. Jan. 10, 1799
Washington Dillard, b. March 15, 1801
Salley Dillard, b. June 20, 1804

My father, James Dillard, was born 15th Oct. 1727, and married to my mother, Mary Ann Hunt, the 8th of July, 1748. The said Mary Ann Hunt was born 28th April, 1734 (old style). My mother, Mary Ann Dillard, departed this life 26th August, 1787, aged 53; my father, James Dillard, departed this life 24th August, 1794, aged 67. My youngest son, Washington Dillard, departed this life the 4th of April, 1814.

NOTE. Mary Ann (Hunt) Dillard was a daughter of John Hunt, Sr., and wife, Ann.

EADS, CHARLES,—Logan Co., Ky., July 22, 1833: b. Amherst Co., Va., March 10, 1755; enlisted 1775, one year under Capt. William Fontaine, Lt. John Marks, Ensign Wilson; ordered to join Gen. Scott and helped drive Lord Dunmore from his fortifications near Norfolk; discharged at Little York. Enlisted under Capt. Jordan Cabell; marched north to the Jerseys; was attached to Col. Morgan's Regt. of Riflemen, who had orders to join Gens. Gates & Arnold at Still Water, which was a forced march, and was there in time to assist in the capture of Burgoyne & had the pleasure after the battle was over of seeing 5700 proud Captives stack their guns on Saratoga plains. After the surrender Col. Morgan returned to Gen. Washington's head-quarters at White Marsh; a few days after we arrived the British sallied out from Philadelphia & took a stand on Chestnut Hill Ridge & Col. Morgan with 500 Riflemen (of whom this deponent was one), attacked them and greatly annoyed them, driving them frequently from the ravine, but we were compelled to give back. After two years was discharged. Capt. Cabell was promoted Major. On returning home visited my brother, Abraham Eads, in Henry Co., and while there attached myself to a troop of horse & served two years under Capt. Levins

Shelton. Returned to Amherst as his services were not needed & was invited by Col. Gaines to take command of a company as captain, which he did, & had the satisfaction of seeing Lord Cornwallis with all his proud host stack their arms on Pigeon Hill, at Little York. He generally acted as a supernumerary officer; in service four & one-half years. His claim was allowed; d. July 27, 1833. George Blakey, Logan Co., Ky., Sept. 10, 1833, aged 83, testified he enlisted in Capt. Patterson's Co. and was transferred to Capt. Samuel Cabell's Co.; attached to Morgan's Regt. of Riflemen.

EDMISTON, WILLIAM,—Wilkes Co., N. C., Aug. 2, 1844, aged 84: served 1 mo. under Capt. John Jacobs, Col. Taylor's Regt., Albemarle Barracks; substituted for brother, Robert Edmiston, Oct. 1, 1780, as private in Capt. Samuel Higginbotham's Co.; Joseph Higginbotham Morrison, Lt.; marched to Richmond; after tour of 3 mos. returned to the home of my father, James Edmiston, upon the headwaters of Pedlar River, Amherst Co.; following March emigrated to Lower Creek, Burke Co., N. C. On the eighth day after my arrival was again called into service, this time as Sergt. under Lt. James Blair, Capt. William Sumpter, Col. Charles McDowell's N. C. Regt. Discharged Sept. 15, 1781. Twentieth of that month went home to Amherst. Called into service in two weeks under Capt. Richard Ballinger to go to Little York. We were ordered to rendezvous at Amherst C. H. On my way there I met Charles Ison who informed me Lord Cornwallis had surrendered. Sept., 1782, returned to Burke Co., N. C., where he lived until about 1841, then moved to Wilkes Co. March 22, 1853, John T. Edmiston, Wilkesboro, Wilkes Co., N. C., applied for a pension for the heirs. Susannah Blair, Watauga Co., N. C., testified she was a dau. of William Edmiston, Revolutionary soldier, who d. Oct. 21, 1847, aged about 88, leaving thirteen children: Susannah Blair; Sally, Robert, Lucy, Emanuel, William, Betsy, Allen, Abraham, Thomas, Suthard, Belinda & John T. Edmiston. Rejected for lack of proof of 6 mo. service.

EVANS, JAMES,—Amherst Co., Va., Jan. 21, 1828, aged 70: enlisted 1779 or '80 & served as private in Capt. Stribling's Co., Col. Samuel Hawes' Va. Regt., until close of the War. Wife dead, and his only children, two married daus. were living in another State. Sept. 24, 1827, James Dillard testified: "Some time in March, 1781, a few days after the battle of Guilford C. H., on the retreat of the enemy, I was a Captain in the Army, and was ordered in front with my company to attack the enemy at Deep River, and as I marched through our army, which had opened for me to pass, I stopped at our ammunition waggons to get some powder and a few flints that my company was lacking; at that time James Evans came to me and shook hands, being well acquainted, as we lived in the same county; he was equipped as a soldier, but I have no knowledge of the company or regiment to which he belonged, as we only halted a few moments. James Dillard, formerly a Capt. in the 10th Va. Regt. of U. S." Placed on Pension Roll March 22, 1828.

FORBES, ALEXANDER,—Lincoln Co., Tenn., Oct. 19, 1832: b. Amherst Co., Va., March 3, 1760; enlisted 1777, for 3 years as private under Lt. Clough Shelton, Major Hawes, Col. Stevens, 10th Va. Regt. Contl. Line, Gen. Muhlenberg's Brig. which was reduced to the 6th commanded by Col. Green, Gen. Scott's Brig. of which troops Lord Stirling was Major-General. Marched to White Marsh Camp, Penn., thence to Valley Forge, where the troops took up Winter quarters; storming of Paulus Hook, where the watchword for the Americans was "Stony Point," as that battle had been recently fought. Deponent was not at the battle of Stony Point, but in hearing of the guns. As reward for the bravery of the troops in taking Paulus Hook, each soldier received $20; his term of enlistment had well nigh expired, for which reason he was sent as guard over the British prisoners to Philadelphia where he was discharged by Col. Gist. Noel Battles, St. Clair Co., Ala., was a fellow soldier. After the war moved to Madison Co., Ky., then to Adair Co., from there to Jackson Co., Ala., then moved to Lincoln Co., Tenn. Placed on Pension Roll May 11, 1833.

FORTUNE, JOHN,—Rockbridge Co., Va., Feb. 18, 1834, aged 71: enlisted for 18 mos. as private under Capt. Barrett, Col. Baylor's Regt. on Contl. Estabmt. He and his wife lived with his son, Zachariah T. Fortune, who, owing to his growing family, was financially embarrassed. Nancy Fortune, pensioner's widow, applied from Kanawha Co., Va., Feb. 11, 1839, aged 69, stating that her husband d. March 16, 1834. "John Fortune & Nancy Henderson, m. by Rev. Wm. Irvin, Nov. 1, 1785, Albemarle Co., Va." (M.R.). Her claim was allowed.

FOSTER, JAMES,—Nelson Co., Va., March 31, 1853, Nancy McClure, aged 85, former widow of James Foster who enlisted 1777 as private under Capt. Samuel J. Cabell for five years, applied; battles of Schuylkill or Red House, Monmouth & various engagements with Gen. Washington, Cols. Campbell, Gaines & other officers; was taken prisoner with Col. Cabell, 1780, and held at Haddrell's Point; exchanged about 1781. He d. April 15, 1795, and his widow m. Alexander McClure, July 15, 1799, who d. Oct. 15, 1850. Susan Roberts testified James Foster & his wife, Nancy Shepherd, moved to Albemarle Co., where he died. They were m. Dec. 30, 1785. Alexander McClure d. in Orange Co., Va.

Bartholomew Cyrus, Appomattox Co., Va., Sept. 10, 1853, Revolutionary pensioner, was in the battle of Schuylkill or Red House with James Foster until taken prisoner at Haddrell's Point. Zachariah Morris, Wood Co., Va., Aug. 7, 1854, aged 94, testified he and James Foster enlisted under Capt. Samuel Jordan Cabell about the commencement of the War, 1776, and that Foster was taken prisoner while in service. Wingfield Norvell, Nelson Co., Va., May 2, 1853, aged 79, testified that since 1797 he had known Nancy, widow of James Foster, by whom she had several children. Her claim was allowed.

FRANKLIN, JAMES,—Capt. 10th Va. Regt. Contl. Line, in fall of 1776, recruited his whole company and joined the main Army; in battles of Brandywine, Germantown & Guilford Expedition. Warrant No. 7290, for 3750 acres of land issued 14th Dec. 1832, to the heirs-at-law: Henry Landon Davies & Anna C., his wife, formerly Anna C. Franklin; Sarah W. (Franklin) Davies, widow of Samuel R. Davies; Elizabeth H. Franklin; Nancy Franklin, widow of James Franklin, decd., and Admx. of John R. Franklin, who departed this life since the said James Franklin. James Franklin's will proved in Amherst, March 10, 1813. Edward Stevens, formerly Col. of the 10th Va. Regt. Contl. Line, made affidavit Sept. 20, 1811, that James Franklin served under him as Captain and was an excellent officer; he was a volunteer on the Guilford Expedition. July 12, 1832, Thomas Jones, Nelson Co., testified he enlisted in the 10th Regt. Va. Contl. Line, Dec., 1776, under Capt. James Franklin; Franklin's Co. and affiant were at Brandywine. Joseph Thomas's declaration: b. Buckingham Co., 1759; enlisted by Lt. Clough Shelton in Capt. James Franklin's Co., which was raised in Amherst, Buckingham & other counties; was attached to the 6th Regt. Va. Regulars under Col. Edward Stevens; Franklin resigned and Shelton appointed Captain; remembers Col. Green, of Culpeper.

FRANKLIN, SAMUEL,—Bedford Co., Va., April 22, 1833: b. Amherst, Dec. 29, 1762, where he entered service 1778, as substitute for Cornelius Sale, under Capt. John Jacobs, Lt. David Davis, Ensign John Burnette, as guard at Albemarle Barracks; drafted, 1780, tour under Capt. Samuel Higginbotham, James Ware, 1st Lt., Joseph Staples, 2nd Lt., Travis Chambers, Ensign. Two companies marched at the same time under Capts. Harris & Christian. Drafted, 1781, out of the company commanded by Capt. Samuel Higginbotham, and marched under Capt. John Stewart to Little York & was attached to Gen. Washington until the surrender of Cornwallis & marched then under Capt. Stewart guarding prisoners; taken sick on the way in Md. & discharged. Francis Wood, aged 70, testified he served 3 mos. under Capt. John Stewart & was in the Siege of York Town & served on other tours stated by declarant. Placed on Pension Roll, May 22, 1833.

FRAZER, MICAJAH,—Jackson Co., Mo., May 2, 1836: b. Albemarle Co., Va., Dec. 25, 1753; private under Capt. Richard

Ballinger, Col. Taylor's Regt., 1 mo. at Albemarle Barracks. Enlisted, 1780, in Capt. Samuel Cabell's Co. for 18 mos.—Major William Cabell, Col. Pope, marched to Hoods Fort; then marched under Capt. Richard Ballinger, Major Hardeman & Col. Dabney to Little York and engaged in making breastworks against Cornwallis under Gen. La Fayette until Cornwallis surrendered; then put in a detached company commanded by Capt. Green, Major Hardeman & guarded Cornwallis's men to Winchester. Discharge given him by Capt. Taliaferro was destroyed by his home burning in Amherst many years ago. John Witt, Littleberry Witt, John Hardy, Alexander Miller, Benjamin Fry, Benjamin Gerrell and many others, making about twenty, were discharged same time and returned with me to Amherst. Adam Crum, Revolutionary soldier, old and blind, testified he was acquainted with Micajah Frazer during the Revolutionary War & saw him in service at Williamsburg & Little York; saw John & Littleberry Witt at the same places. Henry Peyton, Cabell Co., Va., testified he was a fellow soldier of Micajah Frazer's at York Town. One year after the Revolution Frazer removed to Wilkes Co., N. C.; after two years went to Amherst, married and moved to Pittsylvania Co.; there two years and moved to Western part of Va. on Sand River; thence to Jackson, Mo. Susan (Hamilton) Frazer, Wayne Co., Va., Oct. 13, 1846, testified she was 89 years of age, and was b. in Orange Co., Va. When 12 years of age removed with her parents to Amherst Co. Was married to Micajah Frazer in Staunton, by Rev. Jones, she thinks. He d. in Lawrence Co., Ky., Nov. 9, 1843. John Thompson testified Wayne Co., Va., Oct. 14, 1846, aged 71, that he was acquainted with Micajah Frazer, late of Lawrence Co., Ky., Revolutionary soldier & with Susan Frazer, his widow, and knew their daus. Nancy & Susan Frazer. Deponent further saith that a grandchild of said Micajah & Susan, a son of Nancy, died at Norfolk as a soldier in the War of 1812. Josiah Marcum testified that he was a fellow soldier under Capt. Richard Ballinger, Major Wm. Cabell & Col. Pope at Hoods Fort & was with him at Yorktown. Claim was allowed.

FROST, JOSEPH,—Coles Co., Ill., June 2, 1834; b. Amherst Co., Va., Dec., 1753; vol. 4 mos. as private under Col. Joseph Cabell; they marched as two companies, one under Capt. Higginbotham, the other under Capt. Nicholas Cabell; 3 mos. under Capt. Charles Taliaferro. Afterwards vol. under Col. William Cack against the Cherokee Indians & fought against them at Holston River. He served this tour from Bedford as his brother resided there: all other tours from Amherst, where he resided during the Revolutionary War. He d. Dec. 31, 1840, and Anna (Brooks) Frost, pensioner's widow, applied July 25, 1843, "Aged 86 last Sept." She was m. to Joseph Frost by Rev. John Frost, Washington Co., Va., July 20, 1786. Her claim was allowed.

FULCHER, RICHARD,—Barren Co., Ky., Sept. 17, 1832: b. Caroline Co., Va., March 9, 1756; enlisted Goochland Co., Va., 1777, as Corpl. under Capt. Richard Bibb, 1st Lt. James Ware, 2nd Lt. Walter Johnson, Ensign Obediah Smith, Gen. Alexander Nelson. One tour hired a substitute, John Conner, under Capt. Richard Taliaferro, Major William Cabell, Col. John Pope; enlisted Amherst fall of 1781, under Capt. John Woodroof, Lt. John Watson, Major Hardeman, Col. Meriwether, Gen. Stevens' Brig. In battle of James Town. Placed on Pension Roll, Aug. 17, 1833.

GATEWOOD, JOHN,—Allen Co., Ky., Sept. 17, 1832: b. Culpeper or Spotsylvania Co., Va., July 10, 1761; while a resident of Amherst Co. enlisted as private Feb., 1778 or 1779 in Capt. Christian's Co. guarding prisoners at Albemarle Barracks until April following, when his father learning of his illness went for him, had him released from duty & returned home with him; enlisted fall 1780, served 2 mos. & 20 days in Capt. James Montgomery's Co.; enlisted Jan. 1, 1781 under Capt. William Tucker as substitute for Thomas Powell, marched to the Half-Way House & while there the British slipped in & barbariously murdered Col. Mallory at his own house a little below where we lay. We pursued them and took 13 prisoners & guarded them to Williamsburg & returned to the army. May, 1782, in Capt. James Pamplin's Co., Col. Lindsey's Regt.; fifth tour under Capt. John Stewart at Siege of Yorktown and assisted in guarding the prisoners on the march to Winchester, Va., and on to the "New Barracks" on the South Branch of the Potomac. "I had certificates but thinking they would be no service to me I sold them to Moses Higginbotham, for three wool hats." He was placed on Pension Roll Aug. 17, 1833; d. Oct. 6, 1835. Soldier's widow, Nancy, was allowed a pension on her application executed Aug. 16, 1839, while a resident of Allen Co., Ky. Samuel Carpenter, J. P., testified that the following record was taken from a Bible showing great age:

John Gatewood, b. July 10, 1761: Nancy Gatewood,
b. Feb. 5, 1765
John Gatewood and Ann Gatewood were married
Aug. 22, 1782

Births:

Dotia Gatewood, b. Dec. 21, 1783
Amelia Gatewood, b. Dec. 21, 1785
Arstiley Gatewood, b. Jan. 11, 1788
Roland Gatewood, b. April 12, 1790
Wiley Gatewood, b. Sept. 16, 1792
Richard B. Gatewood, b. Jan. 5, 1795
Miarah Gatewood, b. June 9, 1797
Maria Gatewood, b. April 4, 1799

John F. Gatewood, b. Oct. 17, 1801
Fletcher Gatewood, b. Jan. 30, 1805

Deaths:
Wiley Gatewood, d. Aug. 14, 1806
John F. Gatewood, d. April 2, 1802
Fletcher Gatewood was living in Allen Co., Ky., in 1839.

GILES, JOSIAH,—Prince Edward Co., Va., Sept. 17, 1832: b. Chesterfield Co., Va., 1756; served 3 mos. under Capt. Jacobs guarding prisoners Albemarle Barracks, Col. Burley & Major Meredith commanded; 2nd tour under Capt. Richard Ballenger; 3 mos. under Capt. John Christian & Gen. Lawson, at Richmond, Hobb's Hole, Bottom's Bridge, Chickahominy; 3 mos. under Capt. John Phillips; 5th tour, his father's wagon being impressed by Col. Gabriel Penn, he was assured by said Penn that if he went with the wagon it would answer a tour of duty; tour included Siege of York Town. Substituted for Robert Hudson one tour. Placed on Pension Roll, June 21, 1833. He d. July 16, 1837. Patsey Giles, soldier's widow, was allowed pension on application executed Feb. 17, 1840, aged 68. They were married in Buckingham Co., Va., by Rev. Wm. Flowery, "Aug. 15, 1793, Josiah Giles & Patsey Abbott." (M.R.)

GREGORY, THOMAS,—Thomas Gregory, Jr., Lyon Co., Ky., April 24, 1854, aged 63, testified his father was b. in Amherst Co., Va. & d. in Caldwell, now Lyon Co., Ky., June 10, 1814. While a resident of Amherst Co. he enlisted June, 1776 as a private in Capt. Samuel J. Cabell's Co. & was in the battles of Brandywine, Monmouth & Siege of Yorktown; taken prisoner once and held for 6 mos. before he was exchanged. He remembered hearing a conversation between Justinian Cartwright (who d. in this county many years ago) and his father that they served five years together; then his father served in the place of his brother, Jeremiah Gregory, two years. "My mother Sally Gregory told me she was raised in Halifax Co., Va., and her brother, Joseph Staples, was opposed to her marriage, her father being dead." They were married in the fall, 1787, in Amherst or Halifax Co., Va. Children of Thomas & Sally Gregory: Samuel, Betsey, m. Jacob Fowler, Joseph, Thomas, Jeremiah, John W., Abigail, Mary Ann, m. Samuel Henderson. John W. Gregory, Lyon Co., Ky., 1854, aged 33, grandson of the soldier and son of Thomas Gregory, testified his grandmother d. about March 7, 1842, as he distinctly remembers, on that day "Jacob Fincannon and I cut our names on a beech tree: I cut 'John' and he 'Jack'; it was the day she was buried." The following children were alive in 1854 & were allowed the pension due their mother: Thomas Gregory, Joseph Gregory, and Mary Ann Henderson, a widow.

Amherst County, Virginia, in the Revolution 131

GUTHRIE, (or GUTTRY), NATHANIEL,—Madison Co., Ky., Aug. 13, 1832: b. Hanover Co., Va., Dec. 23, 1763; living in Amherst 1778, where he served as private under Capt. Ambrose Rucker, 1 mo. Albemarle Barracks; 1780 marched under Capt. William Tucker & his brother, Lt. Joseph Tucker to Hampton Roads, and stationed at a place called "The Half-Way House"; also stationed some time at Little York; Col. Dabney & Gen. Lawson were Commanding Officers; 1781 under Capt. John Loving, Lawson's Brig., and was at the Siege of York; discharged a few days before Cornwallis surrendered. Placed on Pension Roll March 27, 1833.

HALL, JOHN, Sr.,—Daviess Co., Ky., Oct. 11, 1832: b. 1746; served as private in 1st Division, Amherst Co. Militia under the following officers: fall 1779 in Capt. William Harris' Co. 8 weeks guarding prisoners at Albemarle Barracks, which was under command of Col. Charles Lewis; marched in Capt. John Diggs' Co. to Warwick & was stationed at Gillie's Landing on James River to prevent the enemy's vessels ascending the river; 1779 under Capt. William Harris, Col. Meriweather's Regt. marched below Richmond, Va.; 1781 marched in Capt. James Montgomery's Co. to James Town, & was one of Col. Meriweather's guards at the Battle of James Town. In Capt. John Loving's Co. at Siege of York; furloughed on account of illness & was not present at the surrender of Lord Cornwallis. Moved to N. C. 1798, after two & one half years moved to Ky. Placed on Pension Roll Dec. 21, 1833. He d. Jan. 3, 1837.

HAMILTON, JAMES,—Lee Co., Va., Feb. 18, 1833: b. Orange Co., Va., Jan. 15, 1757; removed to Amherst, age 15, where he took the oath of Allegiance to American government. "The Whigs were divided into ten classes, and every Whig in the county came forward to the Court House, drew a number, and according to number drawn was placed in one or the other 10 classes. He drew No. 6, and was called out a few months before Richmond was taken by Cornwallis, as private under Capt. Richard Ballenger, Lt. Thomas Jones, Ensign Richard Prior, marched to Richmond where the Rope works, Magazine, Smith shops & all public works were destroyed & guns spiked & rolled down into James River by Cornwallis; 2nd tour under Capt. John Diggs, Lt. Eads, Col. Pope; 3rd tour substituted Edward Masters, then apprentice with him at the hatting business, gave him $1000 in Continental money & a blanket; next tour under Capt. Watson, Lt. Watts, Albemarle Barracks; next tour guard to British Tories to Augusta Co., under Capt. John Jacobs; he understood the Tories were taken to Nova Scotia. After the Revolution moved to Augusta Co. & learned the hatter's trade, where he married; thence to Botetourt Co., from there to Wythe Co. thence to Russell Co. & then to Lee Co., Va.

His eldest dau. Mrs. Doughty, is 55 years old. May 23, 1835, he appeared in McMinn Co., Tenn., Court & declared he was the same James Hamilton who was placed on the Virginia Pension Roll & wished to be transferred to above State as his wife died & he had come to live with his children. He d. Feb., 1844 leaving an only child, Wyatt Hamilton.

HANSBROUGH, JOHN,[73]—Hampshire Co., Va., Jan. 29, 1833: b. Amherst Co., Va., 1762; private 1781 for 6 mos. under Capt. James Barnett, Lts. Lewis Neville & Woodroof, Lt.-Col. Pope, Col. Charles Dabney, Major Hardeman, Gen. Stevens; marched to Hampton, Va., to repel Benedict Arnold's Invasion. Charles Lavender was substitute one tour. Since the Revolution lived in Culpeper & last 40 years in above county. Pensioner d. August 9, 1844, and his widow, Fanny Hansbrough, same Co., applied Sept. 24, 1853, aged 72; m. in Culpeper, Sept., 1820. Claim allowed. Living May 25, 1869.

HANSBROUGH, WILLIAM,—Sarah, widow of William Hansbrough, applied Culpeper Co., Va., Sept. 18, 1845, aged 77; he enlisted 1775, private Capt. Fontaine's Co., 2nd Va. Regt.; at battle of Great Bridge when Capt. Fordyce was killed. He kept his discharge until his death. Married to Sally, dau. of William Vaughan, by Rev. John Woodville, Culpeper, Nov. 2, 1786. Two years in regular military service. Referred to brother, John Hansbrough, for proof. Same place & date, his dau. Mrs. Patsey Wale, aged 57, testified to seeing her father's discharge & hearing his conversation of the Revolutionary War. He d. in Culpeper, Oct., 1815. His brother, Samuel Hansbrough, Nelson Co., testified he was too young to be a soldier in the Revolutionary War; that his brother was under Capt. Fontaine for two years. Bransford West & George Purvis, two respectable old gentlemen, testified while living they knew my brother was a soldier under Capt. William Fontaine. Claim was allowed.

HARDY, ANDREW,—Simpson Co., Ky., Aug. 11, 1823, aged "about 71": enlisted Charlottesville, Va., 1775, private under Capt. William Fontaine, Lt. Marks, Col. Woodford, for one year. In battle of Great Bridge & assisted in taking three British vessels at Gwynn Island, where he lost his hearing by the firing of the guns; discharged in Amherst Co. by Col. Gaines. Next tour marched to Georgia under Capt. Pannel, Col. Samuel Elbert's Regt. & placed in Capt. Mosbey's Co.; discharged after three years by Capt. John Morrison, Albemarle Co., Va. Sept. 25, 1891, Andrew Hardy, Breckinridge Co., Ky., applied for a pension stating he was the son of the only child of Andrew Hardy, decd., a Revolutionary pensioner. Rejected.

---

[73]The list of Pensioners printed in 1834-35, erroneously gives his name as John *Harisbrough*.

HARE, RICHARD, Sr.,—Nelson Co., Va., March 18, 1833: b. "Kingdom of Great Britain, 1750"; served five tours as private, one under Col. Richardson; two under Capts. John Loving & James Pamplin at Albemarle Barracks; another tour under Capt. Jacobs & a fifth under Capt. Harris at Siege of York. After the Revolution lived in Albemarle, Amherst & Nelson counties. James Kidd was a fellow soldier on 3 tours. William Harris fellow soldier. Placed on Pension Roll Sept. 11, 1833. Last payment June 28, 1842.

HARGROVE, HEZEKIAH,—Nelson Co., Va., Sept. 25, 1832: b. Caroline Co., Feb. 21, 1748; enlisted Amherst, 1775, fifer, under Capt. Nicholas Cabell, Va. State Troops, or as they were usually called "Minute-men," attached to Col. Samuel Meredith's Regt. & marched to James Town. Detached under Lt. James Pamplin to Halifaxtown, N. C., as guard to ammunition; delivered same, returned to James Town & with his Regt. went to Richmond on board a schooner, where, after 16 mos. service was discharged by Capt. Cabell. On returning home was ordered West under same captain against the Indians; rendezvoused at Lynch's Ferry, 15 or 20 days & discharged owing to the great indisposition of many of the company. After two weeks at home, marched under same captain to Williamsburg. Next tour marched under Capt. James Pamplin, successor to Capt. Nicholas Cabell, to S. C.; attached to Gen. Gates near Charleston, where Capt. Pamplin left him & his officer he can't remember. After a few days was in Gates's Defeat & was put to rout, after which a part of said army called at Yadkin River, N. C. Discharged by an officer named Leftwich who merely told the soldiers "they had as well go home"; 2 mos. service. Again called out under Capt. James Pamplin, Lt. James Stewart, marched to Hood's Ferry; 4 mos. service. Next tour, 4 mos. under Capt. Azariah Martin, marched to a place called "The Half Way House," between Hampton & Williamsburg; that night was attacked by the enemy; tour of 12 mos. under Capt. James Franklin, joined Gen. Stevens at Williamsburg. At home a short time when he marched under Major Pope to Lynch's Ferry & waited for some time for prisoners taken at the Cowpens, and upon their arrival marched with them as guard to Rockfish Gap, where he received orders to march in a day or two under Capt. James Franklin to Petersburg & join Gen. Scott. Next tour his company had become so reduced he was enrolled in the Militia under Capt. Young Landrum; joined Gen. Lawson, Col. Holcombe & Major Skipworth at Cumberland C. H., and marched to Guilford & joined Gen. Greene. An engagement issued about 11 o'clock one morning, which waxed hot for about three hours when Gen. Greene was compelled to give ground, it was then said by 800 N. C. Militia having fled from the left wing. After burying our dead the enemy left their position & we pursued them 8 days & nights & they took shipping at Cross Creek. After

4 mos. tour discharged and returned home. Called out under Capt. John Loving, Sept. or Oct. to go to the Siege of York; marched to Buckingham Co., where he was bitten by a rattlesnake, after which accident he hired a substitute & that was the end of his military service. Placed on Pension Roll July 16, 1833.

HARPER, HENRY,—Nelson Co., Va., March 27, 1834: b. Amherst Co., Va., March, 1757; private spring of 1778, marched under Capt. James Dillard, Contl. Army, Valley Forge; inoculated for smallpox. After he recovered marched to White Plains; from there taken to a hospital at Danbury; when recovered was placed under Capt. Clough Shelton, 10th Va. Regt. & went into Winter Quarters at Bound Brook until Spring. 1780-81, in Militia under Capt. James Franklin marched from Amherst under Col. Peter Rose to N. C. and joined Gen. Greene. Thomas Jones testified Nov. 27, 1833, he was in Contl. service 1778, and while at West Point Henry Harper joined his company there. Benjamin Hawkins, alias Fitzgerald, Nelson Co., April 15, 1834, pensioner under Act of 1818, testified he marched North in Contl. Army & saw Henry Harper, whom he was acquainted with in Amherst, at White Plains, 1778; they belonged to the same brigade; also saw him in service in N. C. William Cashwell testified he marched with him under Col. Peter Rose to Guilford Court House. Placed on Pension Roll April 28, 1834.

HARRALL, WILLIAM,—Daviess Co., Ind., Sept. 2, 1832: b. Albemarle Co., Va.; when 13 years old his parents moved to Amherst. Aug., 1776 (1775) two companies were raised by voluntary enrollment, at a general muster of the Militia of Amherst Co., one commanded by Capt. Higginbotham, under whom he enlisted & the other by Capt. Joseph Cabell. They marched by way of Richmond to Williamsburg where the troops rendezvoused & the company to which he belonged was attached to Col. Mason's Regt. & Major Cabell's Battalion (sd. Joseph Cabell being promoted from rank of Capt. to Major) & his brother Nicholas Cabell commandant of company. After 3 mos. troops were discharged & returned home. Aug. or Sept., 1777 enlisted as private 6 mos. under a recruiting officer, Thomas Morrison & marched by sd. Morrison to Staunton & placed in Capt. Alexander Henderson's Co., Cols. Gibson & Boyer, Gen. McIntosh, & marched into what is now Ohio until they reached Tuscarawa River where they built Fort Lawrence; Col. Gibson was left with a detachment of the Army in command of the Fort & Gen. McIntosh with the rest of the troops including Capt. Henderson returned to Fort McIntosh; discharged & returned home March, 1778. Aug., 1780, vol. under Capt. John Morrison, joined Col. Randal, Major Holcombe, Gen. Lawson's Brig. Early in Jan., 1781, an express arrived at Amherst informing the citizens of the approach of the British under Gen. Arnold & of the destruction of public stores at Richmond, a Foundry & powder Magazine at Westham. With 15 or 16 other men he enlisted under Lt. James Montgomery, marched to Richmond (which the British had left 2 or 3 days previous), thence to Fredericksburg & at Williamsburg joined the militia & attached to Capt. David Shelton's Co.; vol. Sept., 1781 under Capt. John Loving marched to Richmond & Williamsburg where the Virginia Volunteers & Militia rendezvoused; placed under Cols. Richardson & Randal, Major John Martin & was in the Siege of Yorktown; discharged after Lord Cornwallis surrendered. In 1784 moved to Union Co., S. C. & 1809 to Daviess Co., Ind. Placed on Pension Roll April 6, 1833.

HARRIS, WILLIAM,—Nelson Co., Va., Oct. 22, 1832: b. Goochland Co., Va., July 13, 1748; vol. Sept., 1776, 4 mos. under Col. Joseph Cabell, Capt. Nicholas Cabell, Lt. Nathan Crawford; private April, 1777, under Capt. Christian, Lt. [Col.] James Higginbotham, Col. Lindsey; stationed at Malbon Hills where he was discharged; 1780, under Col. Richerson, Capt. James Pamplin, Lt. Joseph Staples, Ensign Thomas Smith; 1781, under Capt. John Loving, Lt. Abraham Seay & was at the Siege of York Town. Nathan Crawford testified he marched with William Harris as stated on a tour of duty as volunteer, two companies from Amherst being regularly ordered. Placed on Pension Roll May 31, 1833.

HARRISON, JAMES,—Amherst Co., Va., Sept. 3, 1832: b. Sept. 4, 1755, Culpeper Co., Va., "the year of Braddock's Defeat"; enlisted in Rockbridge, 1774, private under Capt. John Paxton; marched to Point Pleasant against the Shawnee Indians. "Whilst there witnessed the death of Cornstalk, the Shawnee Indian King, and his son, Ellenepsico, and two of his warriors, Red Hawk and Petello. Applicant can not recollect the length of time he served in this tour, he can only say that he went early in the fall, having slept comfortably in open barns when he started, and returned a short time before Christmas. Officers remembered: Col. Dickerson, from Bath, Col. Skillern, from Botetourt, both now dead. Was drafted from Amherst, spring 1779, under Capt. Shelton, now dead, as guard to British Prisoners at Albemarle Barracks; chief commander at the Barracks was Col. Taylor, of Orange." Winter 1779 served 3 mos. under Capt. Ambrose Rucker, Col. Taylor, Albemarle Barracks; June, 1780 called out by Col. Hugh Rose to exchange British prisoners at Jamestown, and deliver deserters from the American rank then at New London, Bedford Co., Va., to American Recruiting officers. In service 6 mos. then 6 mos. patrolling the county twice a week. His pension was allowed.

HARTLESS, WILLIAM,—Amherst Co., Va., Sept. 17, 1832: b. Caroline Co., Va., 1754; moved to Amherst Co. when 23; 1779 served as private under Capt. Philip Thurmond at Albemarle Barracks; 1781 marched under Capt. James Dillard to N. C., joined Gen. Greene's Army; Siege of York and surrender of Cornwallis under Capt. Christian; guard to British prisoners to Winchester Barracks then discharged. Placed on Pension Roll May 14, 1833.

HEIGHT, MATHEW,—Nelson Co., Va., April 22, 1833: b. Hanover Co., Va., March 10, 1763; served a tour 1779, as a vol. for James Bibb, Albemarle Barracks, under Capt. Rucker, Lt. Ware; 1780, while visiting a relative in Pittsylvania Co., vol. as private under Capt. Williams & was in Gates' Defeat at Camden; his company escaped to the swamps pursued by the enemy, where many were killed. He, with two comrades, concealed themselves in the swamp, until night, then made their way to Salisbury, joined some officers, marched to Hillsborough where he was taken ill and discharged, Nov., 1780. Detached from the militia, 1781, as guard to British prisoners taken at the Cowpens. Claim allowed.

HIGGINBOTHAM, BENJAMIN,[74]—Amherst Co., Va., Sept. 17, 1832: b. Amherst, 1757; called out 1779 private Amherst militia under Capt. Richard Ballinger, guarding British prisoners at the Barracks in Albemarle Co.; 1781, on Guilford Expedition under Capt. James Dillard; discharged at end of 3 mos. & returned home to Amherst. Same year was on a tour under Capt. Samuel Higginbotham, driving cattle from Amherst to Williamsburg for the Army. Officers remembered: Col. Taylor, Capts. Porter & Price at the Barracks, and when attached to Gen. Greene's Army remembers seeing Gen. Greene, Commander-in-Chief, Col. Lynch & Capt. Dillard, under whom he served. Same date James Smith, Sr., testified that in 1781 Benjamin Higginbotham & Philip Smith were on a tour of duty 4 mos. Va. militia driving beeves for the main army. William Hartless testified he was well acquainted with Benjamin Higginbotham & knew he performed the tours stated in his declaration. Henry Cashwell, William Cashwell & Philip Smith testified they performed a tour of duty with him in 1781; they all marched from Amherst to join Gen. Greene in N. C. His claim was allowed.

HIGGINBOTHAM, JACOB,[75]—April 21, 1855, John Higginbotham, applied from Elbert Co., Ga., for a pension for the heirs of Jacob Higginbotham, decd. (d. Jan., 1836), stating that his father served in the War of the Revolution as Capt. Amherst Co., Va., Militia. Claim was rejected for lack of proof. He stated that his father married Oct. 18, 1772, Anne———, & that they had the following children:

---

[74]The list of Pensioners printed in 1834-35 erroneously states his service was with "Connecticut militia."
[75]June Court, 1780, Amherst Co., Va., Jacob Higginbotham took the oath as Lieut., & at a Court held July 5, 1784 he was recommended as Captain.

COL. JOSEPH CABELL HIGGINBOTHAM
1782-1842

Silhouette in possession of his great-great-grandson
Dr. Leo Kasehagen

Hannah, b. Aug. 27, 1773; James, b. Feb. 13, 1775; Jacob, b. July 6, 1776; John, b. Jan. 9, 1778; Elizabeth, b. Jan. 14, 1780; Jane, b. March 3, 1782; Joseph, b. Feb. 27, 1784; Benjamin, b. Feb. 27, 1784; Caleb, b. April 3, 1787; Anne, b. Dec. 11, 1788; William, b. Sept. 13, 1790; Riley, b. Sept. 22, 1793; Frances G., b. Dec. 11, 1796.

HIGGINBOTHAM, COL. JAMES,[76]—Amherst Co., Va., Dec. 17, 1832: On the application of Joseph C. Higginbotham, of Bedford Co., & George W. Higginbotham, James Higginbotham & Joseph Dillard & Judith his wife, of Amherst Co., it satisfactorily appears to the Court from the testimony of Capt. Benjamin Higginbotham, Frederick Padget & Capt. Anderson Thompson; from a receipt of the late Col. James Higginbotham of the said County of Amherst for a recruit by the name of Thomas Oglesby, enlisted as a soldier in the regular Army of the United States for 18 months during the War of the Revolution; as also a commission bearing date the 1st day of Nov., 1775, appointing the said James Higginbotham Major of the Militia of Amherst County, from the Committee of Safety for the Colony of Virginia: That Major James Higginbotham was stationed part of the year 1776 at Williamsburg and in 1778 was promoted to Colonel in the Virginia State Line on Continental Establishment in which capacity he continued to serve, principally as a Recruiting Officer, until the close of the War. He died March, 1813.

Benjamin Higginbotham, Dec. 6, 1832, aged 75, b. Amherst Co., deposeth that his uncle, Col. James Higginbotham, entered service as a Major of militia 1776 & was stationed part of that year at Williamsburg, Va. 1778 was promoted, and bore the title of Colonel in one of the regular Regiments (he thinks the 9th) of the

---

[76]He was born Dec. 25, 1729, and died March 14, 1813. The following record of payment to him is found in the Virginia State Library: "Sept. 27, 1777. Capt. James Higginbotham for pay &c of his Comp. of Amherst Militia Pr. Accot., £189 7s. 4½d." *War*, 23 (1777). Col. James Higginbotham's sword, carried by him through the War of the Revolution, by his son Lieut. George W. Higginbotham through the War of 1812, and by his grandson Capt. William A. Higginbotham through the Civil War, is now in possession of his descendants in Virginia. His three sons served in the War of 1812: Col. Joseph Cabell Higginbotham was stationed at Norfolk. He was b. Aug. 9, 1782, and d. Nov. 18, 1842, "Fairy Dale," Bedford Co. Lieut. George Washington Higginbotham, 90th Regt. 3rd Brig. 2nd Division, Amherst County Militia, was called into active service 12th Jan. 1814 and was stationed at Lambert's Point. He was b. Dec. 20, 1783, and d. April 30, 1862, and is buried in Mount Pleasant Cemetery, Amherst Co. James Higginbotham, Jr., enlisted July 27, 1814, and marched under Capt. Hudson M. Garland to Norfolk, Va. He was b. Nov. 22, 1789, and d. in Warren Co., Ky., Aug. 15, 1852. Joseph Dillard also served in the War of 1812, in Capt. Hudson M. Garland's Co. and was stationed at Norfolk. *William & Mary Quarterly*, XXVI, No. 3, pp. 205-209, XXVII, No. 1, pp. 48, 49; *Virginia Magazine of History & Biography*, XLVI, No. 2, pp. 246-253, No. 4, pp. 329-338.

State line, raised in pursuance of an Act of the Legislature of said State, and continued to act in that capacity from the time of his said promotion to the end of the War. He knows that said James Higginbotham was in the last mentioned service, at Albemarle Barracks, in the year 1779 acting in the capacity of Col. in the said State line, as also at Williamsburg & York town in the year 1781. He the said Benjamin being in the service himself at that time, and placed on a detachment to collect Beef Cattle for the use of that portion of the army to which the said Col. Higginbotham belonged. He knows also that the said James Higginbotham served regularly in the War of the Revolution from the year 1776, nearly the whole of the time until its close—that he has known him to be from home in the said service more than 18 mos. at a time. He is positive in this, because in his absence, and at his request, he superintended his plantation affairs in the said County of Amherst. That the said James Higginbotham was chiefly engaged in the Recruiting service, in which he was more than ordinarily successful—has seen him recruiting men for the Army of the Revolution at the Court house of the said County of Amherst, for the term of 18 mos., and during the War—he remembers particularly of having seen him enlist the same Frederick Padget now residing in the County of Bedford, whose testimony has been taken to that effect, in support of the application of the heirs of the said James Higginbotham for the compensation due him for military services. That he has often heard the said James Higginbotham say, the Country was largely indebted to him for Military services as a colonel in the State line, that he had never received the compensation due to him, but had confidence that the State, when she could would do him justice, as he had served her faithfully, and much to the detriment of his private affairs. That the station of the said James Higginbotham in the army of the Revolution was matter of perfect notoriety at the time & for many years after the close of the War, but the men of that time have so nearly passed away, but few are left, who can testify with certainty any thing about it he knows of none who are now alive, except the said Padget and himself. The said Col. James Higginbotham at the time of his death had four children only towit: Joseph C. Higginbotham, Geo. Washington Higginbotham, James Higginbotham & Judith who had intermarried with Joseph Dillard—all of whom are now alive and reside in the said County of Amherst, except the said Joseph C. Higginbotham who resides in the County of Bedford in said State. The Wife of Col. Higginbotham departed this life before him. Deponent after the close of the Revolutionary War was commissioned Capt. of Militia, attached to the 90th Regt. Va. Militia of the said County of Amherst, but he does not know that the said Col. James Higginbotham performed any military duty after the close of the Revolutionary War, he does not think he did—because at that time he must have been nearly 60 years of age, being advanced towards 50 when he first entered the service, but remarkably active, hardy and athletic, and so continued to a very advanced age.

Frederick Padget, Bedford Co., Va., Nov. 16, 1832, aged 80: Sayeth that he knew the late Col. James Higginbotham of Amherst Co. & State of Virginia as a Col. in the Virginia Continental & State line, he also received Soldiers in the War as regulars for 18 months and during the War, which will show from a Recpt. now in my possession as follows: Amherst County St: This day I have received from James Harrison, Frederick Padget who acknowledges himself to be regular enlisted for the 32nd division to serve as a Soldier for during the War in the Army of the United States of America. Given under my hand this 10th day of March 1779. James Higginbotham, C. C. And when I was enlisted under Col. James Higginbotham I was sent on with the regulars, and was soon after wounded in the army and did not get well until the War ended; the term of enlistment was as stated in the Rect. the said James Harrison as above was the Orderly Serjeant.

Capt. Anderson Thompson, Bedford Co., Va., same date, aged 78: Sayeth that in 1776 he saw the late Col. James Higginbotham of the County of Amherst & State of Virginia in actual service as a Major at Williamsburg in said State, and as I understood & do believe, he the said Higginbotham was in the Continental & State line service, to what Regiment I do not recollect he belonged.

Amherst County, towit: "This day I received from James Henderson, Thomas Oglesby who acknowledges himself to be regularly enlisted for the 13th division to serve as a Soldier in the army of the United States of America for eighteen months. Given under my hand this 6th day of March 1779. James Higginbotham, C.C."

"The Committee of safety for the Colony of Virginia, to James Higginbotham Esqr.

By virtue of the power and authority invested in us by the Delegates and Representatives of the several Counties and Corporations in general convention assembled, we, reposing especial trust and confidence in your patriotism, fidelity, courage and good conduct, do by these presents constitute and appoint you to be Major of the Militia of the County of Amherst; and you are therefore carefully and diligently to discharge the trust reposed in you, by disciplining all Officers and Soldiers under your command. And we do hereby require them to obey you as their Major. And you are to observe and follow all such orders and directions as you shall from time to time receive from the convention, the Committee of safety for the time being, or any Superior Officers, according to the rules and regulations established by the Convention. Given under our hands, at Williamsburg this 1st day of November, Anno Domini 1775.

        Edm^d Pendleton
        John Page
        Thos Lud Lee
        P. Carrington
        Dudley Digges
        J^s Mercer"

HIGGINBOTHAM, WILLIAM,—Hardin Co., Tenn., Jan. 31, 1829: enlisted Amherst Co., Va., Jan. 6, 1777, as Sergt. in Capt. Samuel J. Cabell's Co., 6th Va. Regt.; again enlisted Dec., 1778, and served to the end of the war in Capt. James Mabon's Co., 2nd Va. Regt. Certificate of Capt. James Mabon, May 28, 1783: "Sergeant William Higginbotham enlisted with me for the war in Dec. 1778, in the 2nd Va. Continental Regiment." Certificate of Col. Samuel J. Cabell: "I do hereby certify that William Higginbotham enlisted in my Company of Riflemen attached to the 6th Va. Regt. in the month of Jan. 1777, for the term of three years. after which he re-enlisted for the War and was taken prisoner at Buford's defeat South or North Carolina, in the month of May, 1780, and I do further certify that the sd. William Higginbotham acted as a Sergeant and that during his term of service which generally came under my observation he conducted himself as a good Citizen and a brave soldier. Given under my hand this 25th day of Feb'y, 1810. Sam. J. Cabell, late Lt. Col. Virga. Line on Contl. Establishment." June 19, 1811, Edward Ware, James Ware & Caleb Higginbotham, Elbert Co., Ga., testified: "we knew William Higginbotham as a soldier and Lieutenant in the late Revolutionary War with Great Britain; he entered service 1776, and served until the end of the war in the Va. Contl. Line." Warrant was issued to him for 455 acres, March 9, 1793, as Sergt. & Feb. 28, 1810, one for 2666-2/3 acres as Lieut.

HOGG, JOHN,—Declaration of Susannah Hogg, Henry Co., Tenn., March 3, 1849, aged 88, widow of John Hogg who enlisted 1779 or early in 1780 under Capt. or Col. McKee, in the Virginia Troops & was discharged 1782. They were married by Rev. Crawford April 14, 1779, in Amherst Co., Va., & moved to the frontiers of Va. & stationed at a fort on the Kanawha River where they both stood guard. He died in Garrard Co., Ky., June 12, 1802. Goolsby Childress testified he served as mess-mate of John Hogg in the infantry during the Revolutionary War. In 1823, Susannah Hogg was living in Logan Co., Ky. Her claim was allowed.

  Children of John & Susannah Hogg (leaf out of Bible):
    Cele Hogg, b. March 31, 1780
    Luke Hogg, b. Dec. 4, 1781

Lucy Hogg, b. Aug. 15, 1783
Lucelia Hogg, b. April 12, 1785
Sally Hogg, b. April 12, 1787
Lucas Hogg, b. Jan. 30, 1796

HOSICK, WILLIAM,—Ulster Co., N. Y., June 22, 1810, aged 65: enlisted in Amherst Co., Va., fall 1776 as private for 3 years in Capt. James Franklin's Co., Col. Stevens' 10th Va. Regt. on Contl. Estabmt. After the Va. Regts. were reduced he served in Capt. Clough Shelton's Co. & the 6th Va. Regt. commanded by Col. Green, Lt. Col. Samuel Hawes. Battles of Monmouth, Germantown & Stony Point. Discharged Nov. 23, 1779. Placed on Pension Roll April 23, 1819. He died May 3, 1819.

HOUCHENS, CHARLES,—Edmondson Co., Ky., May 31, 1836: b. March 20, 1761; enlisted as private in Capt. Woodroof's Co. guard at Albemarle Barracks; served 2 years under Capt. Clough Shelton. Rejected for lack of proof of service.

HUFFMAN, JOHN,—Edgefield Dist., S. C., Aug. 4, 1818, aged 61: enlisted Amherst Co., Va., July, 1780, joined Capt. F. Cowherd's Co., Major Sneed's Battalion, Col. Hawes' 2nd Va. Regt. on Contl. Estabmt. Battles of Guilford Court House, Camden, Siege of 96 & Eutaw Springs. Placed on Pension Roll, Jan. 4, 1819. Dropped under Act of May 1, 1820. Restored, commencing Nov. 14, 1825. He sent additional proof of his service June 2, 1823 & testified his wife was aged 62; they had 3 children; one having died leaving them the care of two grandchildren now "tender in years." Nov. 14, 1825 he testified that he was wounded twice in the battle of Eutaw Springs by a bullet which entered in at his left arm & came out near his shoulder blade & the other entered near his collar bone & came out by the shoulder blade. From effect of wounds he has not been able to work & unless he receives help from the Government for which he has fought to gain freedom the land where his youngest dau. and grandchild lies buried will be sold for debt.

Amherst County Virginia April 22, 1782. I do hereby certify that the Bearer John Huffman during his Residence in this County has behaved himself as a good Citizen in Manifestation whereof he has lately served eighteen months as a regular Soldier in this States Continental Troops under Command of Gen. Greene & is at present free from any Militia Incumbrance. Hugh Rose C. L.
—of S. C.
Camden Vistr. Oct. 22, 1784
Wm. Murrell, J. P.

He died July 25, 1827. His widow, Lucretia Huffman, applied for a pension same place, Nov. 20, 1838. They were m. Feb. 18, 1785. Claim allowed.

ISON, ELIJAH,—McMinn Co., Tenn., July 24, 1846, aged 89: entered service as private 1775 or '76 for 3 mos. under Capt. David Chadwell. His messmates were William Small, Ned North & John Hodges; 1779 served 1 mo. under Col. Taylor, Albemarle Barracks; drafted again 1779 served 3 mos. in Washington's army. His messmates were William Edmondson & James Hartless. Rejected.

JOHNS, THOMAS,—Harrison Co., Ohio, Oct, 8, 1819, aged 77: enlisted Amherst Co., Va., 1776, for 2 years as private under Capt. Samuel Cabell, 6th Va. Regt. commanded by Col. Buckner on Contl. Estabmt. When Col. Buckner was broke, Capt. Cabell's Co. joined the Regt. commanded by Col. Daniel Morgan. Was at Stillwater, White Marsh, Trenton, Princeton & taking of Burgoyne at Saratoga. Discharged spring of 1778 in Penn. by Gen. George Weedon & Col. Parker. John Kendall, of same county, testified he had not seen Thomas Johns since he started with Col. Morgan's Regt. to Quebec until they both came to Ky. He was living in 1834, aged 92. Claim allowed.

JOHNSON, WILLIAM,—Wayne Co., Ky., Sept. 24, 1832: b. Aug. 2, 1757; vol. for 6 mos. 1775, under Capt. James Buford, in Bedford Co., Va., as Sergt. and marched to Williamsburg & the company was soon marched back to the frontiers under Col. William Christian, and burnt several Indian towns on the Tenn. River. While a resident of Bedford, enlisted 1776 in Amherst as Sergt. under Capt. James Franklin, Lts. Clough Shelton & James Dillard, 10th Va. Regt. commanded by Col. Edward Stevens. In battle of Brandywine, Gen. Weedon's Brig., after which Capt. Franklin resigned & our company was commanded by Clough Shelton. Battles of Germantown & Monmouth. Discharged at Petersburg, Va., after serving 3 years. Served 3 mos. as Sergt. under Capt. Jeremiah Pate, of Bedford Co. & was at battle or siege of 96; enlisted again from Amherst Co. as Sergt. under Capt. Charles Christian as substitute for Ballinger Wade. Placed on Pension Roll Sept. 2, 1833.

JONES, JOHN,—Calloway Co., Ky., Nov. 27, 1832: b. Albemarle Co., Va., Feb. 1, 1760; drafted as Orderly Sergt. Dec., 1779 under Capt. Richard Ballinger, Albemarle Barracks. May, 1781, vol. under Capt. James Barnett, Lt. John Gilmore, in a horse company raised for the purpose of opposing Col. Tarleton, who was approaching Charlottesville. He found his own horse & arms & immediately proceeded with the company toward Charlottesville. They pursued Col. Tarleton & were in a skirmish with the British at Burnt Tavern. Aug., 1781, vol. under Capt. Loving, Col. Sampson Mathews, Major Duvall. Next tour substituted for James Bibb, Capt. James Stewart's Co., Lt. Charles Eades, Major Duvall, Col. Mathew's Regt., Generals Lawson & La Fayette. In service during the Siege labouring most of the time in the intrenchments, and after the surrender of Cornwallis proceeded under his captain as guard to the prisoners to Winchester Barracks, 184 miles, then discharged. "He never received any pay for his service except, perhaps, a few dollars as substitute, which then was good only to light a pipe with." He moved to Ky. 1787. Claim allowed.

JONES, JOSIAH,—Anderson Dist., S. C., March 4, 1833: b. Cumberland Co., Va., about 1752; enlisted 1775, served 2 years under Capt. Cavill (Cabell), Col. Buckner, Gen. Lewis, in no engagements, after which he vol. with a company all of which deserted except 3 to go on an expedition to Stono; served 3 mos. under Col. Hampton, Gen. McDowell & was in an engagement upon Packolet near the line of North & South Carolina with the British & Tories; again vol. & served 40 days in a scouting party under Capt. Kirkendale in the Light Horse. He served as an Armorer repairing arms, making swords and shoeing horses for 2 years under Gen. McDowell & never received any remuneration for his services; vol. again for 26 days against the Cherokees under Capt. Watson. John Looney testified he served with him in 1776 in the 6th Va. Regt. The printed list of 1832 gives cause of rejection as "Proof required of his enlistment and service under Capt. *Cavil*."

JONES, NICHOLAS,—Declaration of Amarella Jones, widow of Nicholas Jones, Rockbridge Co., Va., April 4, 1838: "Her husband, Nicholas Jones, private Va. Contl. Line in Capt. Franklin's Co.; was in battles of Brandywine & Germantown, and was wounded in the thigh in one of the battles and allowed to return home on furlough." They were married in Amherst at the home of her father, John Camden, July, 1783, by Rev. Coleman, a Baptist minister, who removed to Ky. and is probably now dead. They had 10 children; survivors: Nancy, m. James McDaniel, lives in Kanawha Co., Va.; Lavina C., m. John Buntan, lives in Ky.; Winston J. lives in Ohio; Susan L., m. Halbert McAllison; William P., and John Nicholas, live in Rockbridge Co., Va. Feb. 4, 1845, Mrs. Amarella Jones, aged 79, was living in Rockbridge Co., Va.

 Bible Record (in possession of Winston J. Jones, Ohio):
 Nicholas Jones born July 3, 1760; Anna R. C. Jones,
  born March 20, 1765
 Nancy Jones, b. June 19, 1784
 Sally T. Jones, b. April 3, 1786
 Elizabeth W. Jones, b. March 25, 1788
 Lavina C. Jones, b. May 1, 1790
 Susan L. Jones, b. Sept. 26, 1792
 Winston J. Jones, b. March 28, 1795
 Rhoda L. Jones, b. Aug. 14, 1797
 William P. Jones, b. Jan. 9, 1800
 Wesley C. Jones, b. Dec. 3, 1802
 John Nicholas Jones, b. Jan. 28, 1804

Deaths:

Wesley C. Jones, July 9, 1813
Elizabeth W. McCluer, March 17, 1830
Rhoda L. McCluer, May 7, 1827
Nicholas Jones, Sr., April 7, 1831

Affidavit of Johnston Lane Jones, a younger brother of Nicholas Jones, Jan. 29, 1845, that he was 7 or 8 years of age when his brother returned from the army; he had been wounded in the thigh at Brandywine; was present when the ball was extracted by James Tooley, some years after he returned home. His brother was at Princeton & in battle with the Indians. Claim was allowed.

JONES, WILLIAM,—Elizabeth J. Jones, Sumter Dist., S. C., Feb. 2, 1854, applied for a pension for the heirs of her father, William Jones, who died Feb. 12, 1809, leaving her mother a widow with nine children, all dead except herself & brothers, Leonard & Wiley Jones, of Marengo Co., Ala. Her father served in the Revolution from Amherst Co., Va., and accompanied Gen. Greene's troops from Virginia to Sumter Dist., S. C., serving at various times from sometime prior to 1780, until June, 1782, as private under Capts. Long, Malone, Joseph Hill, George McCauley, and Cols. Marshall, Anderson, Peter Horry & Richard Richardson, and was in the battles of Guilford Court House & Eutaw Springs. He d. Feb. 12, 1809. Her mother who d. June 3, 1847, m. second, Dec. 1, 1811, John Parker, who d. Nov., 1831.

Family Record:

James Jones, b. Oct. 17, 1782
Elizabeth Jones, b. Dec. 5, 1784
Mary Jones, b. Dec. 1, 1786
Peggy Jones, b. May 11, 1789
Nancey Jones, b. Dec. 14, 1791
Eli Jones, b. Jan. 15, 1794
William Jones, b. April 11, 17—
Leonard Jones, b. June 18, 1798
Wiley Jones, b. Oct. 7, 1—
Betsey Ann Jones, b. Sept. 3, 1805
James Jones, married Jan. 8, 1806
Mary Jones, married Nov., 1805
William Jones, married Feb. 12, —9
Elizabeth Jones departed this life July ——
Sara Jones, b. Dec. 23, 1807
Susanah Jones, b. Jan. 26, 1810
Margaret Jones, b. June 30, 1812

John R. Pollard, Sumter Dist., S. C., April 25, 1855, aged 68, testified he was well acquainted with William Jones who married Ann, dau. of James & Ann Freeman, Jan. 24, 1780. William Vaughan, same place, June 9, 1855, a Revolutionary pensioner, aged 90, testified he served under Capt. Malone in S. C. on a scouting party against the Tories, with William Jones, Joshua Stafford & John Pollard, of Va. John Brandford, William Broadway, Abraham Nicholson & Obediah Spears were other soldiers remembered in same company. We surprised a large party of the enemy, killed two & captured ten and delivered them to Capt. Postell. Rejected for lack of proof of service.

JONES, THOMAS,—Mercer Co., Ky., July 6, 1818, aged 73: in 1832, a resident of Putnam Co., Ind.; enlisted Amherst Co., Va., 1775 as private under Capt. William Fontaine, Col. Stevens' 10th Va. Regt., Gen. Weedon's Brig.; afterwards placed in Capt. Clough Shelton's Co.; battles Brandywine, Germantown; discharged, 1779. Claim allowed.

JONES, THOMAS,—Nelson Co., Va., Sept. 25, 1832, aged 77: enlisted 1776, served as Sergt. in Capts. Samuel J. Cabell's, James Franklin's and Clough Shelton's Va. Cos. and in Cols. Edward Stevens' and Samuel Hawes' Va. Regts. In battle of Brandywine under Capt. Franklin, Lts. Clough Shelton & James Dillard, Ensign William Powell. Was often at Capt. Franklin's side in the battle & his conduct was that of a brave officer. Shortly after the battle of Brandywine, Franklin left his company and was said to be sick. Clough Shelton was promoted Capt., James Dillard 1st Lt., declarant Orderly Sergt., and were in the battle of Germantown where one of our company was killed & several (including declarant) wounded & removed to Reading. About 1 month later, Franklin called at the hospital & told him he was on his way home as his constitution would not stand the fatigue of the army. Discharged Dec., 1779, having served 3 years. Again enlisted Nov., 1780, 1st Lt. under Capt. Richard Ballinger, who was taken sick & returned home, & he commanded the company the remainder of the 6 mos. About a month later he again entered the service & was a commissioned officer in Col. Linsey's Va. Regt. until after the surrender of Cornwallis. He m. Oct. 17, 1780, Catherine Clarkson (b. June, 1760). Placed on pension roll, May 31, 1833. He d. July 8, 1835, Jonesboro, Nelson Co., Va. His widow Catherine Jones was allowed pension on application executed Oct. 19, 1838. Benjamin Childress, Albemarle Co., testified he lived in Amherst during the Revolution & served two tours under Capt. Thomas Jones. A leaf of Bible containing ages of eldest children accompanies declaration:

Hezekiah Jones, b. March 3, 1782
Clarkson Jones, b. Dec. 9, 1783
        d. Nov. 12, 1785
Shelton Jones, b. Jan. 21, 1785

Joshua Jones, b. Jan. 28, 1787
John C. Jones, b. July 1, 17—

Hezekiah Jones was living in Nelson Co. in 1840. Feb. 13, 1841, Mrs. Frances Carter testified she had known Catherine Jones from infancy. On Thomas Jones' return from his first tour in the militia he stopped at her house & took breakfast. This was March before the birth of her son, Henry Carter, March 26, 1781. A leaf torn out of her family Bible is enclosed to prove same: ("John Clarkson" on reverse side of page.)

>   Elizabeth Lilly, dau. of William Lilly, b. Aug. 27, 1766
>   Thomas Lilly, b. March, 1769
>   John Lilly, b. May 17, 1771
>   Gabriel Lilly, b. July 25, 1773
>   James Lilly, b. Nov. 20, 1776
>   Lindsey Lilly, b. Jan. 5, 1778
>   William Lilly, b. June 10, 1782
>   Sally & Mary, daus. of Henry Carter & Fanny, his wife, b. Aug. 13, 17—
>   John Carter, b. Aug. 11, 1780
>   Henry Carter, b. March 26, 1781

JOPLING, THOMAS,—Nelson Co., Va., April 29, 1832, aged 73: enlisted Feb. 9, 1776, Capt. Walker, Col. Russell's 9th Va. Regt., Gen. Muhlenberg's Brig.; discharged at Valley Forge, Feb. 9, 1778. He d. March 29, 1837, and Molly Jopling, pensioner's widow, applied same place, April 27, 1840, aged 69. Marriage bond accompanies declaration: "Nov. 22, 1790, Thomas Jopling, Jr., bachelor & Mary Stephens, spinster, both of Amherst Co. Consent of her father, James Stephens, Sr." Her claim was allowed.

KEY, GEORGE,—Callaway Co., Mo., June 5, 1833, aged 80: enlisted March, 1776 under Capt. Cabell, Alexander Rose, 1st Lt., Benjamin Taliaferro, 2nd Lt., marched to Williamsburg where we remained some time, thence to Gwynn Island against Lord Dunmore. After a month returned to Williamsburg. In the fall started to Cross Creek, N. C., having taken our baggage over the river at James Town, we were ordered to return to Williamsburg & about the 10th of Oct. ordered to join Gen. Washington in the Jerseys. Christmas eve we crossed the Delaware River & marched most of the night towards Trenton, suffering much, but were told we were going for new clothes. We reached Trenton between daylight & sunrise, attacked the Hessians, & after they surrendered we started for our camping ground & reached the Delaware River the same evening, which we crossed the next morning, when we discovered that two of our men had froze to death that night. Shortly after this affair, we recrossed the Delaware & by a stolen march in the night, surprised a small body of the British army at Princeton and defeated them. After this, was ill for 3 mos. When fit for duty was attached to Morgan's Rifle Regt. & marched beyond Albany to oppose Burgoyne's Army at Stillwater. Here a party of Morgan's troops were scouting & were attacked by enemy. The British killed one man at the first fire, and the party retreated. Morgan rallied his men & was joined by Gen. Gates. An attack was brought on between the two armies about 10 o'clock & the action ended when night parted them. The British kept their ground & we retired to our old encampment, about two miles off. Here we lay for some days and Morgan's men went out of the encampment in the afternoon & were met by the British. A fight issued between the armies & we beat the enemy back to their temporary encampment or fort. The British spiked a part of their cannons, threw some into the river & endeavored to retreat to Saratoga, to cross the river by night, but when they reached the river they found a part of our army on the other bank ready to oppose their crossing. After a slight skirmish, the British finding themselves enclosed, surrendered. We then returned to Penn. two miles above Philadelphia. After 2 years discharged by Col. Butler. Returned to Amherst, joined Capt. John Rogers, Light Infty., Nov., 1779. From Bedford we marched to Pittsburgh, and in spring of 1780 crossed the Mississippi River to Illinois where the Indians, about 400 strong, had killed 50 persons at a place called Strawberry Patch. Here we were joined by Col. Geo. R. Clark. On returning home we were compelled to kill a horse for subsistence; about two pounds came to my share, which then I thought was pretty good eating. Discharged after 2 years by Lt.-Col. Montgomery. Placed on Pension Roll, Oct. 17, 1833. He d. Jan. 15, 1836, and his widow, Susannah Key (dau. of John Craighead) applied, April 16, 1840, aged 74; they were married in Bedford Co., Va., Oct. 12, 1785, by Rev. Salesberry. Her brother, Robert Craighead, also moved to Callaway Co., Mo. Claim allowed.

KIPPERS, JOHN, Sr.,—Monroe Co., Mo., April 29, 1835: b. March 4, 1751; enlisted 1778 or '79 with Lt. Jordan, Major Riddle, Col. Heath, Col. Parker, Gen. Charles Scott; marched to S. C. in Col. Hawes' Regt. On the arrival of Col. Buford in S. C., was placed under his command & was in the engagement at Waxhaws. Col. Buford was defeated by Tarleton. Deponent was wounded by three saber cuts on the head & two thrusts of the bayonet, one in the right & the other in the left shoulder. He was taken prisoner & paroled by Col. Tarleton, which said parole was lost. While in said service he was at different periods under Capts. Stubblefield, Pain, Hoard & Adam Wallace who was killed at Buford's Defeat. He was at the Battle of Point Pleasant under Capt. Matthew Arbuckle; discharged by Gen. Hand. July 21, 1835, Charles Crutcher, Monroe Co., Mo., testified John Kippers came to his father's house, 1780, in Henry Co., Va., just after Buford's Defeat, with two or three cuts on his head, & remained 6 mos., until his wounds had almost healed. Afterwards, he removed to Greenbrier Co., Va., and several years afterwards returned to his father's home in Henry Co., and he is the same John Kippers who settled in Missouri 2 years ago. Rev. Lewis Allen Anderson, Greenbrier Co., Va., testified he was raised in the neighborhood of Capt. John Kippers & knew him to be a Revolutionary soldier. Affidavit of George Lee, Marion Co., Mo., Jan. 2, 1835, aged 80, a soldier of the Revolution. Claim allowed.

KNIGHT, AUSTIN,—Amherst Co., Va., July 19, 1843, Elizabeth (Ham) Knight, aged 70, widow of Austin Knight who d. Sept., 1817, applied. He served as private in Capt. Landrum's Co., Col. Holcombe's Regt. on Guilford Expedition; 1779 or '80 under Capt. William Tucker; under Capt. Stewart, Col. Holcombe at capture of Cornwallis. They were m. in Amherst Co., Va., Feb. 24, 1789 by Rev. Dameron. She d. Dec. 25, 1844, & her son, William, Admr. of her estate, applied, stating that Ann Mays & deponent were the only surviving children of Austin & Elizabeth Knight. Matthew Rickets testified he served in Capt. William Tucker's Co. with Austin Knight & his brother, William Knight, & in 1781 was at Guilford C. H. He was under Capt. LeRoy Upshaw & Knight was in Capt. James Dillard's Co. of Riflemen. Claim allowed.

LAIN, CHARLES,—Roane Co., Tenn., Sept. 10, 1832, aged 73: substituted for Hendrick Arnold, 1780, Corpl. under Capt. John Jacobs, Major Roberts, Col. Taylor, as guard to Burgoyne's prisoners at Albemarle Barracks. Next tour, Orderly Sergt. under Capt. James Pamplin, John Horsley, Lt. Major Roberts, Col. Taylor; tour under Capt. Richard Ballinger; 4th tour under Capt. John Woodroof, Col. John Pope, Col. William Cabell, joined Col. Meriwether & Gen. Stevens. Thomas Robertson, John Bowman & Joseph Lain were fellow soldiers. Thomas Robertson testified he served with him in Capt. Richard Ballinger's Co. & under Capt. John Woodroof, Major Hardeman & Col. Meriwether. He was placed on the Pension Roll Feb. 15, 1833; d. Nov. 6, 1843. His widow, Sally Lain, applied Oct. 14, 1853, Bradley Co., Tenn., aged 76. Marriage bond accompanies declaration: "Charles Lane & Sally Leister, Cocke Co., Tenn., Jan. 6, 1801." They raised 6 children. She was living Feb. 6, 1866. Claim allowed.

LAYNE, JOSEPH,—Roane Co., Tenn., Sept. 10, 1832: aged 76; while residing in Amherst Co., Va., enlisted in Albemarle Co. under Capt. John Jacobs, 2 mos. guarding prisoners at Albemarle Barracks; same year 2 mos. at same place under Capt. James Pamplin; next tour under Capt. William Tucker, Lt. Joseph Tucker & Ensign Daniel Tucker, Regt. commanded by Col. Dabney &

Major Hardeman; marched from Amherst through Richmond Town, Williamsburg & to the Half-Way House; 3 mos. under Capt. John Woodroof, Col. Stevens' Regt.; next tour substituted for Charles Rodes; at Siege of Yorktown & surrender of Cornwallis in Capt. John Wear's Co. Charles Lain & John Bowman of Roane Co., Tenn., were fellow soldiers. The latter testified that Joseph Layne married his sister, Rebecca Bowman. He also stated that there were two Joseph Laynes living in Amherst Co., Va., at the same time. Placed on Pension Roll, Feb. 19, 1834. He d. in Bradley Co., Tenn., March 15, 1846 & his widow applied, Nov. 3, 1849, aged 94. They were m. about 1775. Their eldest child, Anderson Layne, was b. 1782. Claim allowed.

LANDRUM, REV. JAMES,—Green Co., Tenn., Sept. 4, 1832, aged 70: served 2 tours of 3 mos. each under his father Capt. Young Landrum as guard to British prisoners at Albemarle Barracks; vol. 1781 under Capt. Young Landrum, Lt. Stephen Watts, Ensign Robert Horsley, marched South against Lord Cornwallis, joined Gen. Lawson, Col. Holcombe, Major Hubbard & was in the battle of Guilford; Thomas Trail who served in said company with Rev. Landrum and Vincent Jackson of Green Co., Tenn. testified to his service. Placed on Pension Roll Jan. 5, 1833. He d. Jan. 15, 1840 and his widow applied from the same place, Nov. 4, 1843, aged 70. M.L.B. Amherst Co., Va.: "Dec. 13, 1787, James Landrum, bachelor & Mary Clark Alford, spinster."

LAVENDER, CHARLES,—Lucy Lavender, applied Sept. 18, 1845, Jackson Co., Ga., aged 79, widow of Charles Lavender, who d. May 5, 1802, Edgefield Dist., S. C. He served a tour of military duty as a substitute at Albemarle Barracks, Col. Meriwether's Regt., Major Goodall; enlisted under Capt. Samuel Cabell, Contl. Line, and was gone so long that on his return his mother did not know him. They were m. in Amherst Co., Va., by Rev. David Patterson. Claim was allowed.

Charles Lavender, Jr., Jackson Co., Ga., Feb. 22, 1853, applied for a pension for the heirs of Charles & Lucy Lavender. He was Admr. of the estate of his mother, who d. June 14, 1846, leaving three children: Deponent, Simeon Lavender of Lowndes Co., Ala., & Willis Lavender of Choctaw Co., Miss. M.L.B Amherst Co., Va.: "Dec. 21, 1785, Charles Lavender, Jr., bachelor & Lucy Ballew, spinster." Joseph Ballew, McDowell Co., N. C., Aug. 20, 1852, testified he knew Charles Lavender in Amherst. Deponent had a brother, John Ballew, and Charles Lavender had a brother, William Lavender, and all three enlisted in the Continental Army. Charles Lavender moved to S. C. about 1787.

LAVENDER, WILLIAM,—Amherst Co., Va., May 17, 1830, aged 70: entered service as a private 1778 under Capt. Jesse Allen,

Col. Francis Taylor's Regt. Family consists of wife, dau. & grandchild. Hardin Woodroof, Buckingham Co., testified he was in same Regt. with Lavender & they served 18 mos. He d. Jan. 17, 1835, and his widow, Sarah Lavender applied May 19, 1838, aged 71; they were m. April 4, 1781, by Rev. Holmes. Both pensions were allowed.

LEAKE, JOHN M.,—Rutherford Co., Tenn., Oct. 21, 1833: b. Albemarle Co., 1758, in that part later Amherst Co., Va.; 1777 served as private on 3 tours of 1 mo. each at Albemarle Barracks: substitute for William Johnson under Capt. David Shelton; Capt. John Diggs' Co.; substitute for Josias Dodd under Capt. John Christian. About the time Arnold burnt Richmond marched under Capt. Richard Ballenger to Albemarle Old Court House & joined a company commanded by Capt. Joseph Tucker. The corps were transported in canoes from the river 18 miles of Richmond, disembarked & marched to the City. Capt. Tucker was ordered to Williamsburg & Capt. Ballenger to Hood's Fort. Drafted Aug. 1, 1781 under command of Col. Daniel Gaines. The corps was 200 strong. Marched to Williamsburg. The French had marched to that place & the corps under Col. Gaines haulted until they passed in front & the whole command marched to York—while stationed at York declarant was dispatched part of the time to drive a wagon for the purpose of transporting bread from Williamsburg for Gen. Lawson's Brig. After the capture of Lord Cornwallis declarant marched with the Army to Pages Warehouse on Pamunkey & discharged. Moved to Rockbridge Co., Va., 1795, then to Knox Co., Tenn. 1811 & in 1821 to Nelson Co. & then to the present Co. Placed on Pension Roll Nov. 19, 1833; d. Aug. 24, 1840. Nov. 14, 1840, his son Mark Leake, Admr. of his estate, applied for a pension.

LOCKARD, WILLIAM,—Amherst Co., Va., Jan. 4, 1821, aged 70: private 1779 for 18 mos., Capt. Call, Col. Baylor's Regt. Va. State Line on Contl. Estabmt.; discharged 1781; then enlisted in a company of cavalry under Capt. George Bowyer, at Buckingham C. H., commanded by Col. Wm. Washington, later by Col. Jones. Siege of Charleston & taking of Cornwallis & several minor engagements. Discharged 1783 in S. C. Family consists of wife, aged 61, and children all grown & married. Patrick Rose, formerly Lt. Col. of the Lower Regt. of Amherst, testified William Lockard served under Col. Wm. Washington. John Spitfathom stated he served in the 4th Va. Regt. & during that time he was personally acquainted with William Lockard who belonged to another corps. Claim allowed.

LUTTRELL, JAMES,—Knox Co., Tenn., Sept. 9, 1837: b. Westmoreland Co., Va., Feb. 12, 1755. When 9 years of age removed to Amherst Co. Drafted as a minute-man, 1780; rendezvoused at home of Abraham Warwick & under Capt. James Dillard, Lt. Thomas Morrison, Col. Peter Rose marched to Hillsborough, N. C. Gen. Gates was defeated before they reached Camden. Drafted under Capt. Charles Christian, Lt. Stephen Watts, Ensign Elijah Christian, Guilford Expedition; they were in sight of battle, after which they joined Col. Charles Lynch & pursued the British. Moved to Knox Co., Tenn., 1795. Joseph Lane, Bradley Co., Tenn., testified they both served as privates in Amherst Co. Militia & marched to N. C.

LYON, EDWARD,—Abbeville Dist., S. C., Oct. 16, 1820, aged 68: enlisted fall of 1775 for 1 year in Capt. William Fontaine's Co., Col. Adam Stephen's 2nd Va. Regt., & participated in battle of Great Bridge. Family consists of wife, aged 65, son aged 16 & children living in distant parts of the country. His brother-in-law, Henry Harper, testified to the truth of his statement. Placed on Pension Roll March 5, 1819; d. Jan. 12, 1823.

LYON, WILLIAM,—Nelson Co., Va., Oct. 9, 1837, Frances Lyon, aged 89, widow of William Lyon who d. March 30, 1811, applied under Act of June 7, 1832, stating that they were m. 1766. He served 3 tours of 3 mos. each & was discharged from the 4th after being in service a short time. John Pugh testified he served a 3 mos. tour with him in the Revolution. She d. April, 1838.

"Amherst Co. This day Thomas Ewers made oath Before me, that he has two Different Times been in Company with Wm. Lyon which particular times he saw the said Lyons knee Easily put out of Joint, or at least complained & applied to him to put in Place. Certified by me this 13th day of Sept. 1781. John Diggs."

"Wm. Lion a Soldier of Col. Gaines Regiment having an Empediment in One of his Legs is hereby Dischd. and tis hopd. that no Officer will attempt to send sd. Lion in the field any more Given under my hand at Goochland Court house this 21 day of Sept. 1781, Jno. Woodroof Capt."

The claim was not allowed as there was no satisfactory proof of 6 mos. military service.

MARTIN, AZARIAH,—Clay Co., Ky., Aug. 27, 1832, aged 68: vol. in militia summer of 1780; stationed at Amherst C. H., private under Ensign Jonathan Reid, guarding deserters; fall of 1780, vol. under his uncle, Capt. Azariah Martin; "marched 30 miles to Tye River where we met Gen. Morgan's Riflemen with prisoners taken at the Cowpens; we took charge of them, marched to Amherst, from there were taken by Rockingham & other militia to Winchester." Feb., 1781, vol. under Capt. James Dillard, Col. Rose's Regt., marched to Old Iron Works or Troublesome Iron Works, N. C. & joined Gen. Greene; discharged at Ramsey's Mills, on Deep River. On reaching home vol. under Capt. James Barnett an officer in Contl. Army under command of Col. Hugh Rose, marched to Richmond & joined Gen. Lafayette in battle of Jamestown & Siege of York until on account of illness obtained leave of absence a few days before Cornwallis surrendered. Placed on Pension Roll, Aug. 21, 1833. Lucy Martin, pensioner's widow, applied Madison Co., Ky., Feb. 28, 1840, aged 74; they were m. in Amherst Co., Va., April 20, 1791, at the house of her father, Charles Rodes; moved to Ky. same year. William Martin of same place testified he went to school with Lucy Roades. She m. his brother Azariah & they raised 6 children. March 2, 1840, Liberty B. Martin, aged 28, testified his father d. April 15, 1834, at Rockcastle, Ky. Claim allowed.

MARTIN, HUDSON,—Nelson Co., Va., Nov. 26, 1832: b. Albemarle Co., Va., May 14, 1761; entered service Feb. 15, 1779, under Lt. Goodwin, Albemarle Barracks, Col. Taylor. May following substituted for his brother, William Martin, who was ill, as Sergt. under same officers. Commissioned Ensign, Nov. 3, 1780, and served under Capt. James McAlexander, Lt. Tilmon Walton, Richmond, Va. Drafted, May 19, 1781, Fluvanna Co., marched to Louisa Co., where they joined Gen. La Fayette's Army, and from there to Burnt Ordinary & Old James Town, where an engagement took place brought on by Gen. Wayne, in which there was a right smart loss sustained & the enemy maintained their ground & afterwards went on board their vessels. Placed on Pension Roll May 31, 1833.

MASSEY, JOHN,—Nelson Co., Va., Sept. 24, 1853, Thomas Massey, aged 67, son of John Massey who d. in Amherst Co. Oct. 20, 1800, and Admr. of the Estate of Susanna Massey, who d. Dec. 1, 1847, widow of decd. soldier, applied for a pension under Act of July 4, 1836, due the heirs of John & Susanna Massey: Edmond, Jesse & Thomas Massey, Nelson Co.; William W., John & Charles Massey, Amherst Co.; Elizabeth Gill, formerly Elizabeth Massey & Mary Campbell, formerly Mary Massey, Rockbridge Co. His father, John Massey, served 4 or 5 years as Cornet in the Revolutionary War. He moved from Albemarle to Amherst during the war, where he married Susanna Wright, Jan. 1, 1779. Landon S. Gowing, aged 87, a schoolmate of John Massey, made affidavit as to his service. Rejected for lack of proof of marriage.

MATHEWS, JOSEPH,—Nelson Co., Va., Dec. 24, 1832: b. Fauquier Co., 1754; vol. as private under Capt. Joseph Cabell, Lt. Nicholas Cabell, Ensign Crawford; 2nd tour, under Capt. John Christian; 3rd tour, Capt. James Pamplin, Lt. Joseph Staples, Col. Lindsey's Regt.; 4th tour, Capt. John Loving, Ensign Abram. Seay. William Harris, a fellow soldier, & Capt. John H. Mosby testified as to his service. Placed on Pension Roll May 20, 1833.

Amherst County, Virginia, in the Revolution 153

MAYS, BENJAMIN,—Iredell Co., N. C., Aug. 7, 1832: b. Stafford Co., Va., 1757; entered service as private under Capt. Ballinger, Albemarle Barracks; 2 mos. under Capt. Samuel Higginbotham, Richmond; 3rd tour, early part of 1781, was in the Foot under Capt. Higginbotham, Col. Gaines, at New Glasgow; under Capt. Woodroof & Col. Gaines at Siege of York Town & Surrender of Cornwallis. Placed on Pension Roll June 21, 1833. Leutitia Mays, Davidson Co., N. C., Dec. 4, 1851, widow of pensioner, applied.

MAYSE, CHARLES,—Amherst Co., Va., July 15, 1833: b. Amherst, 1763; private 1779 or '80 in Capt. William Turner's Co., Albemarle Barracks; next tour under Capt. Young Landrum, joined Gen. Greene & was in battle of Guilford. Claim allowed.

McALEXANDER, ALEXANDER,—Nelson Co., Va., Aug. 27, 1834: b. Albemarle Co., May 1, 1756; enlisted spring 1778, Corpl. under Capt. John Higginbotham, Lt. Linsey Coleman, Albemarle Barracks; autumn, 1780, vol. Orderly Sergt. under Capt. John Morrison, Lt. Ewers, Ensign William Barnett, Col. Randolph's Va. Regt.; Jan., 1781, vol. under Lt. James Montgomery, marched to Williamsburg, where we joined Capt. James Barnett's Co., Col. Dabney's Va. Regt.; next tour, under Capt. William Tucker; 70 men were detached under Capt. Tucker by a forced march to Hampton, but found the enemy had gone to their shipping. Returned to York & The Half Way House, and erected new pine huts. Micajah Wheeler, a Rev. soldier, testified he knew the soldier in the winter of 1781 at The Half Way House. Charles Rhoades, fellow soldier in Capt. John Morrison's Co. He d. Jan. 30, 1840, and his widow, Martha McAlexander, applied from same place, May 4, 1844, aged 75. They were m. by Rev. Irving. She was living in 1849. Both pensions were allowed.

Family Bible Record:

Alexander McAlexander & Patsey Burnett were married March 2, 1786
Jane McAlexander, b. Jan. 14, 1787
William McAlexander, b. Jan. 1, 1789
John McAlexander, b. April 24, 1791
James McAlexander, b. Nov. 23, 1793
Edmund Tucker McAlexander, b. Feb. 22, 1796
Alexander Waugh McAlexander, b. July 28, 1798
Patsey Burnett McAlexander, b. Nov. 8, 1800
Amelia Carlisle McAlexander, b. Dec. 28, 1802
Samuel Ramsey McAlexander, b. April 5, 1804
David Robinson McAlexander, b. Dec. 6, 1806
Joseph Roberts McAlexander, b. May 1, 1809

McANALLY, DAVID,—Grainger Co., Tenn., June 7, 1833: b. Albemarle Co., Va., Aug. 5, 1748; enlisted under Capt. John Higginbotham, guard to British prisoners taken under Burgoyne, Albemarle Barracks, Col. Taylor in command; 1780, vol. Orderly Sergt. under Capt. John Morrison, attached to Col. Meade's Regt. in Petersburg, Gen. Lawson's Brig.; spring, 1781, under Capt. Barnett, Lt.-Col. John Pope, joined Gen. Lafayette; furloughed on account of illness; on recovering, joined the Army against Cornwallis; served 9 mos. in all, 5 mos. as Ensign. He d. Dec. 24, 1835. Nancy McAnally, widow of pensioner, applied April 6, 1840, same place. They were m. March 18, 1790, by Rev. Benjamin Burger, a Baptist minister in Amherst Co., Va. James McAnally testified the following is a leaf from the Family Bible of David McAnally: David McAnally, Sr., was born Aug. 5, 1748 & married Nancy Kyle March 18, 1790. She was b. March 15, 1765. Claim allowed.

McCARY, RICHARD,—Edgefield Dist., S. C., May 3, 1819, aged 56: enlisted 1778 or '79, under Charles Yarborough, Capt. Cavalry, Va. Contl. Line, Lt.-Col. Thornton, Col. William Washington; discharged, Richmond, Va., 1781, by Col. Davis. Applied again, June 2, 1823, stating his family living with him consisted of wife, children: Louisa 16, William 15, Kitty 13, Richard 11, Benjamin 9. Rejected, lack of proof of six months service.

Amherst, May 18th, 1781.

NOTE. "I do hereby certify that Richard McCary Junr. this Day Substituted himself to serve 18 months as a soldier in the room of James Bayly.

Hugh Rose C. Lt."

MILSTEAD, ZELUS,—Lincoln Co., Tenn., Oct. 22, 1832: b. Amherst Co., Va., 1756; drafted as private under Capt. Richard Ballinger, Va. Militia, Gen. Harris' Brig.; drafted again 6 mos. under Capt. Richard Ballinger, Albemarle Barracks; 12 mos. service. Removed to Spartansburg, S. C., then to Hancock Co., Ga.; after 15 years to Logan Co., Ky.; Williamson Co., Tenn.; thence to Muscle Shoals; thence to Maury Co. and to Lincoln Co. Placed on Pension Roll March 5, 1833.

MONTGOMERY, JOHN,—Adair Co., Ky., Oct. 8, 1833: b. April 3, 1762; private May, 1779, 18 days under Capt. Burras, guard Albemarle Barracks; 1780, vol. under Capt. John Morrison, Col. Meade's Regt., Gen. Lawson's Brig.; Jan., 1781, under Capt. James Barnett marched to Richmond, Williamsburg & York & there attached to Col. Dabney's Regt., thence to Hampton, back to Half Way House between York & Hampton then moved to York & there heard the British had surrounded the encampment they recently left. We expected them at York the Regt. paraded in front of York & some horsemen came & informed us the British had turned back.

Major Campbell called for volunteers to march against them & he was one that vol. & pursued the British to Hampton but did not overtake them; marched back to the Half Way House, to Williamsburg & discharged by Capt. Barnett; served another tour under Capt. Taliaferro, Col. Meriwether. In 1789 removed to Ky. Claim allowed.

MONTGOMERY, WILLIAM,—Marion Co., Mo., Sept. 4, 1832, aged 75: enlisted 1776 under Capt. Samuel J. Cabell, 6th Regt., Contl. Line. Capt. Cabell's Co. was drafted into Col. Morgan's Regt. Affiant was in 3 battles, Trenton, Princeton, Saratoga & taking of Burgoyne & had a hard engagement at White Marsh; discharged Feb. 14, 1778. In 1779, commissioned Lt. in State militia & appointed Recruiting Officer by Joseph Cabell & James Higginbotham. His wife d. prior to him & shortly after he was pensioned he d. Nov. 22, 1832. His son, John J. Montgomery, was living in Palmyra, Mo., April 25, 1845.

MORRISON, EZRA,—Lincoln Co., Ky., Aug. 30, 1832: b. Albemarle Co. in that part later Amherst Co., Va., 1756: "There is a record of his age in the lower part of Kentucky at the house of his sisters"; enlisted Nov. 9, 1776, in the 2nd Georgia Regt. Contl. Line, under Samuel Elbert, Col., John Stirk, Lt.-Col., Major Moseby, Capt. Joseph Pannel, afterwards George Hancock was Capt. & afterwards Shem Cook was Capt. Served 3 years. Was engaged in several skirmishes with the Florida Scout. He marched through Savannah, Augusta, Forts on Ogeechee River & was a good deal at Fort Howe. He had his discharge until some years ago when he gave it to the late Thomas Montgomery, then a Member of Congress, for the purpose of getting his portion of the land which had been allowed to the soldiers of the Revolution, and it was by him mislaid. April 22, 1833, Jacob Warriner, William F. Lee, William Dinwiddie, Archibald Huston & Benjamin Briggs, swear that they are well acquainted with Ezra Morrison, that he is reputed & believed in the neighborhood where he resides to be a soldier of the Revolution, and that they concur in that opinion. Claim allowed. He d. Nov. 1, 1844.

NOTE. For Ezra Morrison's service in the 2nd Va. Regt. see application of Susannah Welch, widow of Joseph Welch.

NEWMAN, JOHN,—Davidson Co., Tenn., April 19, 1826: enlisted in Buckingham Co., Va., Oct., 1776 as private under Capt. John Moseley & on his march enlisted in Georgia Troops under Col. Elbert. In battle of Savannah, Dec. 29, 1778 where his right arm was shot off near the shoulder by a cannon ball; taken prisoner and after wound healed he was sent aboard a prison ship 15 miles below Savannah; exchanged Aug., 1779 & went to Augusta, Ga., where he applied to Gen. McIntosh for a discharge. "Damn you!"

he said, pointing to declarants shoulder "a better discharge than I can give you. I have no right to discharge you, as you were enlisted for during the War." This declarant at that time was doing nothing for the service, was receiving no clothing or pay, nor had he received any since the battle of Savannah. He then applied to Gen. Elbert for a discharge who told him he could not give him one until the War was over. He left Augusta, Ga., about Dec. 1, 1779, and reached home in Amherst Co., Va., about Christmas. In 1784 declarant received from Gen. Elbert a discharge. Placed on Pension Roll May 9, 1826.

NEWMAN, JOSEPH,—Rutherford Co., Tenn., Oct. 9, 1828: enlisted 1776 for 3 years as private under Capt. Clough Shelton, 10th Regt. Va. Line; again enlisted 1778, Col. Posey's 3rd Regt. William Knight, Franklin Co., Tenn., Oct. 27, 1828, aged 70, testified he knew Newman served in Capt. Clough Shelton's Co., 1776. Claim allowed.

NEVIL, THOMAS,—Rutherford Co., Tenn., Nov. 18, 1832: b. Amherst Co., Va., 1761; drafted Nov., 1781; served 7 mos. as private under Capt. Ned Garland, guard at Albermarle Barracks to prisoners taken in the defeat & capture of Lord Cornwallis at Yorktown; furloughed on account of illness; fall of 1782 called out under Capt. James Mathews & rendezvoused at Thomas Jopling's in Amherst Co. The company was ordered to go out & collect beef for the use of prisoners at Albemarle Barracks & the Garrison at Irvine's Store in Albemarle Co. Placed on Pension Roll Oct. 16, 1833.

OGLESBY, JESSE,—Madison Co., Ky., Oct. 1, 1832, aged 72: b. Fluvanna Co., Va.; served 3 mos. tour under Capt. James Barnett, Col. Dabney, as substitute without any reward or fee, for his nephew, Richard Perkins, a man of family. I was drafted in my absence & said Perkins went in my place. Vol. 1781, under Lt. Young Landrum, Col. Pope, and was in battle of Jamestown. Removed to Ky. 15 years since. Robert Dinwiddie, aged 70, Madison Co., Ky., testified he was well acquainted with Jesse Oglesby. He d. March 23, 1852. Celia (Witt) Oglesby, pensioner's widow, applied May 21, 1855. They were m. in Amherst Co., Va., by Rev. B. Berry, Sept. 25, 1794. Claim allowed.

PADGETT, FREDERICK,—Bedford Co., Va., July 2, 1828: b. Essex Co., Va., 1753 or '54; 1779 enlisted in Amherst Co., Va., as private under Capt. James Harrison, marched by Lt. Jordan to Fredericksburg & placed under command of Capt. Howard. After a few weeks the company marched in Col. Buford's Regt. to Williamsburg, thence to James River & crossed at Cedar Point to Petersburg, where we took up winter quarters. In the spring marched under same officers to Charleston, S. C. & arrived within 12 miles of this place the very day the enemy surrounded the town. He distinctly heard the firing of the cannon. Col. Buford immediately ordered a halt & they lay that night on their arms & next morning retreated to Camden to the Waxhaw settlement & were engaged in a bloody battle with the British. The Americans were about 400; a great many were killed & wounded. The British forces far exceeded the Americans who were here defeated & taken prisoners of war, and were put in a barn that night & guarded. Next morning all who were able to walk marched as prisoners with the British & the others left upon the ground; among the latter men was the applicant. All left were placed by Tarleton, the British commander, on their parole. July 2, 1828, William Padgett, Bedford Co., Va., testified Frederick Padgett enlisted, March, 1779 in Capt. James Harrison's Co., 3rd Va. Regt. Contl. Line & served faithfully until May, 1780, on which day the sd. Regt. with exception of 2 men were all killed or wounded in the battle called "Buford's Defeat" in the state of N. C.; deponent & his brother Frederick Padgett were wounded & unable to travel with the British troops; they were paroled by Col. Tarleton May 30, 1780 in an old barn which served as a hospital for the wounded men. As soon as he & his brother recovered they joined the 11th Regt. July 22, 1833, Frederick Padgett, Bedford Co., Va., applied for a pension due him for his service in the Revolutionary War, under Act of June 7, 1832. He testified that he received a certificate 4 or 5 years ago which he placed in the hands of Charles Whitley for the purpose of obtaining a pension which he forwarded to the War Department. He testified further that he was defrauded by Charles Whitley, Leroy Jordan & Anthony Evans, Jr., late of this Co. in relation to his claim for a pension. He submitted the following additional proof of his service & his name was placed on the Pension Roll Nov. 2, 1832:

> Amherst County St: This day I have received from James Harrison, Frederick Padget who acknowledges himself to be regular enlisted for the 32nd division to serve as a Soldier for during the War in the Army of the United States of America. Given under my hand this 10th day of March 1779.
>
> James Higginbotham, C. C.

This is to certify that Fredk. Padgett private, Prisoner of War.

Wax haws, May 30th, 1780.   B. Tarleton

PANNEL, BENJAMIN,[76]—Todd Co., Ky., June 10, 1833: b. Albemarle Co., Va., March 1, 1755, in that part later Amherst Co.;

---

[76] The list of Pensioners printed in 1834-35 erroneously gives his name as Benjamin *Parmel.*

vol. 1777 under Capt. Joseph Cabell, Lt. Nicholas Cabell, Ensign Abraham Seay; July, 1778, under Capt. James Pamplin, Col. Reuben Lindsay, Lt.-Col. Holt Richeson; July, 1779, under Capt. William Tucker, Col. Lindsay, Lt.-Col. Richeson; June 1, 1781, under Capt. Loving who was taken ill in Richmond & Capt. James Barnett took command, Major Overstreet, Adj. Campbell, Col. Lindsay, Lt.-Col. Richeson; discharged a few days before the surrender of Cornwallis. In battle of Hot Water when Gen. Wayne was in command. Placed on Pension Roll Oct. 18, 1833.

PENDLETON, RICHARD,—Nelson Co., Va., Aug. 20, 1844: Mary Pendleton, aged 82, widow of Richard Pendleton, who d. May 20, 1829, applied, stating they were m. in Culpeper Co., Va., by Rev. Herdsman, Jan. 4, 1784. He enlisted Amherst Co. as private or non-commissioned officer of the cavalry under Lt. William Penn[77] in early part of the Revolutionary War with James Clements & William Tucker and marched North with Lt. Penn. In battles of Brandywine, Germantown & Monmouth in Capt. Spotswood Dandridge's Co. Served 2 yrs. & 9 mos.; discharged by Col. Jameson. He took the smallpox while in service, marks of which were apparent to the day of his death. Lt. Penn d. at Trenton, N. J., of smallpox. Mrs. Mary Carter, Amherst Co., Va., July 31, 1844, deposed when her uncle James Clements returned from the North he stopped at the home of her father, Joseph Roberts, in Amherst, now Nelson Co. He had the smallpox while in service. William Cashwell testified he frequently conversed with Richard Pendleton and heard him say he was in battles of Brandywine, Germantown, Monmouth & Edge Hill under Gen. Washington; they were hard run at times to get food for the cavalry. Col. Samuel Cabell who recruited & marched a company from Amherst about the same time was also at battle of Edge Hill. John Shelton, Nelson Co., Va., Aug. 28, 1844, aged 85, testified Lt. William Penn was recruiting officer of the Cavalry in Amherst Co. 1776, and Richard Pendleton, William Tucker & William McDaniel enlisted & marched to the North. William McDaniel d. of smallpox. Pendleton returned home 1779. He served two tours after his return, one with his brother Reuben Pendleton. James Tinsley, Bedford Co., Va., Sept.

---

[77]William Penn, b. in Caroline Co., Va., April 7, 1745 (son of George & Ann Penn), commissioned 1st Lt. Virginia Dragoons, 10th June, 1776: Capt. 1st Continental Dragoons, 25th Nov. 1776; d. 15th March, 1777, of smallpox at Trenton, N. J. Heitman's *Historical Register of Officers of the Continental Army*, p. 435. His will, dated Aug. 13, 1776, mentions himself as "going into Service;" proved in Amherst Co., Va., July 7, 1777. (Will Book 1, p. 355).

July 4, 1776, a Warrant was issued to his brother Gabriel Penn, commissioner of Buckingham District, for the use of Wm. Penn, Lieut. in Capt. Jameson's Troop of Horse, for £250 upon acct. for purchase of horses, Arms, accouterments. *Calendar of Virginia State Papers*, VIII, 236.

3, 1844, aged 81, testified he became acquainted with Richard Pendleton early in 1776 at the home of his father, William Tinsley, in Albemarle Co., while Pendleton was on his way to headquarters at the North as an enlisted soldier of the cavalry; said Pendleton, William McDaniel & others of the same company under command of Capt. Franklin stopped at their house for breakfast. After Pendleton returned home he served 1 mo. at Albemarle Barracks; deponent served a tour at said Barracks in winter of 1779 & 1780. William Tinsley, Madison Co., Va., Sept. 26, 1844, aged 76, testified he was Exor. of his father's will & paid said Pendleton the proportion which was the share of his wife, Mary Pendleton. Abraham Tinsley, Madison Co., Va., in a letter to his sister, Mrs. Mary Pendleton, Oct. 10, 1844, says: "I rode to Culpeper C. H., to obtain a copy of the marriage bond & found many of the old papers had been destroyed by worms." June 2, 1845, Col. John Pryor, Amherst Co., aged 57, declared he heard Richard Pendleton & Francis Slaughter[78] tell about their service in the North, under command of Spotswood Dandridge. Her claim was allowed.

PETERS, JAMES,—Nelson Co., Va., May 6, 1818, aged 52: enlisted in Amherst Co. sometime after Gates' Defeat as a private by one Mays, Recruiting officer for the Southern Army; marched under Capt. James Pamplin to Hillsborough, N. C., where he was attached to Capt. Ewell's Co., Col. Hawes' 2nd Regt., Contl. Estabmt. for 18 mos. & served in sd. Regt. in Capt. Cowherd's Co. until the capture of Cornwallis; battles of Guilford, Camden, Eutaw Springs & several skirmishes under Maj. Gen. Greene. Discharged by Capt. Cowherd at Salisbury, N. C. His family consisted of wife & 13 children. He was placed on Pension Roll Sept. 20, 1819; dropped under Act of May 1, 1820; applied again Nov. 29, 1821; d. Nov. 1, 1823. His widow, Elizabeth, applied Nelson Co., Va., Jan. 28, 1839. Fall of 1841 she moved to Rockbridge Co. where she applied Feb. 27, 1844, aged 77, under Act of March 3, 1843, which was allowed. M.L.B. Amherst Co., Va.: "March 11, 1793, James Peters, bachelor & Elizabeth Stevens, spinster. Consent of her father, Barnett Stevens."

POWELL, FRANCIS,—Wilkes Co., Ga., March 28, 1854, Joseph T. Burdett, aged 43, made the following declaration in order to obtain pension for the only living children of Francis Powell, decd.: Mary Powell, Joseph Powell & Elizabeth Burdett,

---

[78] Among the miscellaneous Court papers I found in 1931 was the following application for a pension. There is no record of this declaration in the National Archives, Washington, D. C.: SLAUGHTER, FRANCIS,—Amherst Co., Va., March 21, 1828, aged 73: enlisted 1776 in Capt. John Jameson's Co. 1st Regt. of Light Dragoons commanded by Theodorick Bland in the Va. State Line, Contl. Estabmt. Discharged at Winchester, Va., 1778. Living with dau., Lucy Spencer.

Wilkes Co., Ga.; Nancy Jackson, Chambers Co., Ala.; Jane Wortham, Coweta Co., Ga.; Sarah Wortham, Caroline Wells & Benjamin Powell, Meriwether Co., Ga.; Thomas Powell, Talbot Co., Ga. Deponent married a dau. of the sd. Powell, decd. over 20 years ago. Francis Powell vol. in Amherst Co., Va., the place of his nativity, under Gen. Washington at the beginning of the War; in battles of Bunker Hill, Brandywine, Camden, Cowpens, Guilford, Siege of Yorktown. He moved to Wilkes Co., Ga., and d. "about 16 years ago." Rejected for lack of proof of service.

PHILIP (PHILLIP), GEORGE NICHOLAS,—Mercer Co., Ky., Aug. 1, 1832, aged 75; enlisted in Amherst Co., Va., July, 1780, under Capt. Estang & marched North. In May, 1781, marched from White Plains to Philadelphia & Alexandria, and attached to Col. Washington's Regt. of Horse & was at the surrender of Cornwallis. Resided in Amherst Co. after the Revolutionary War until 1812, removed to Ky. Vol. in Col. Johnson's Regt. & marched to Canada. Francis Adams, Revolutionary soldier, testified to his service. Placed on Pension Roll Oct. 16, 1832.

James Davis, Livingston Co., Mo., Aug. 28, 1875, grandson of the Revolutionary soldier, stated his grandfather came with the French Army under Gen. Lafayette, in 1780, and after the war remained in America & was pensioned. He m. Sarah Bloom in Ky., and located in Floyd Co., Ind. They had a dau. Americus Phillips, who m. William Davis, deponent's parents, and three other children.

POLLARD, JAMES,—Spencer Co., Ind., Aug. 13, 1833: b. Culpeper Co., Va., 1762; private under Capt. Booker, Lt. Miller, Col. Kirkerdall, Gen. Muhlenberg's Brig. Absalom Pollard, Garrard Co., Ky., testified he was present when his brother, James Pollard, enlisted in Va. State Troops, and saw him receive his bounty & march with Capt. Booker's Co. from Amherst, and after 3 years he returned to deponent's house in Amherst. Placed on Pension Roll Oct. 1, 1833; d. July 4, 1840.

PRYOR, WILLIAM,—Amherst Co., Va., Oct. 15, 1832: b. Pedlar River, Albemarle Co., about 1752 or '53, for he well recollects the war of 1755, or what was then called "Braddock's War"; removed to the Great Kanawha River, Western Va., in autumn of 1773, and next spring planted a crop of corn, but was driven back to Amherst by the Indians; again visited that river and was at Point Pleasant in the spring of 1775, and saw Capt. Isaac Shelby, later Governor of Ky., who had been left with the wounded after the battle of Point Pleasant, 10th Oct. 1774; was again there occasionally and in Amherst until early in 1776, when the Indians compelled him and many others to take shelter in the fort; was then substitute for James Frazer under Capt. Matthew Arbuckle, commander of the fort, and whose subaltern officers were Lts. Andrew

Wallace & James Thompson, Ensigns Samuel Woods & James McNutt; served out Frazer's time (about 8 mos.) and then enlisted under Capt. Arbuckle for 2 years; about that time Capt. William McKee with Lt. James Gilmore with many private soldiers came to said place and were stationed there under Capt. Arbuckle; whilst there he (Pryor) performed many duties: was often detailed with others to go up the Kanawha River to the plantations above the Point for corn; was often stationed as guard on the Ohio River above the fort and often acted as a spy. In the fall of 1777, Cols. Dickerson & Skillern came to the fort with a number of men under their command on an expedition against the Shawnee towns; I served on this expedition with James Harrison, Micajah Goodwin and many others. When we arrived at the fort, a Lt. Gilmore went over the Kanawha to shoot turkeys and was killed by some unknown Indians, and as soon as his body was brought into the fort and was seen by his men, they immediately murdered Cornstalk, his son Nepseki, and another principal Indian then in the fort as hostages. Gen. Hand, of the U. S. Army, came to the fort from Pittsburgh and ordered the officers & men to return into the settlement, saying it was too late in the season to go over the Ohio & attack the Indian towns, the principal of which was Chilicatha. Hand ordered Arbuckle & McKee to shorten the pay & daily allowances of their men, saying they feasted too high; when this order was put into execution, almost every man shouldered arms and girted on their knapsacks and started home, when Col. McDowell, then in the fort, stated to Hand the impolicy of such a measure and obtained Hand's permission to follow & speak to the men, which he did, and promised them their former pay and allowances & the men returned. This deponent himself took no part in the mutiny.

In consequence of the massacre of Cornstalk, the Shawnees mustered all their strength in the spring of 1778, and besieged the fort at Point Pleasant for several days and killed one man, Paddy Shearman, & wounded Lt. Gilmore. Finding they could not take the fort, they killed off all our stock & marched to attack the forts & settlement in Greenbrier. We obtained information of this fact from Grenadier Squaw, said to be sister of King Cornstalk, who had taken shelter in the fort & when her stock was killed with ours, she obtained leave of Capt. McKee to go out to the Indians; she went out with some spirits and soon became intoxicated & although in that state she overheard the intentions of the Indians & when sober she came in & informed the officers of the designs of the Indians. Capt. McKee made a proposition that if any two men would carry the news to Greenbrier that, although he could not discharge them, yet he would extend their furloughs as would be paramount to a discharge; John Intchminger & John Logan volunteered & set out, but becoming alarmed returned the same evening. Philip Hammond & myself then agreed to go, when my older brother, John

Pryor, said that he should go as he was more experienced in Indian warfare, & as Hammond preferred that he should go, I gave way & they were dressed as Indians by the Grenadier Squaw & followed the Indians & passed them at the meadows, 10 or 12 miles from Donnelly's Fort, & were in the fort but a short time when the Indians arrived & attacked it, & a dreadful conflict ensued. Capt. Arbuckle was in Greenbrier visiting his family at the time, & hearing of the coming of the Indians & hearing the firing at the fort he, with Capt. Lewis, raised a company, forced their way into said fort & finally drove off the Indians, after many of them had been killed & wounded. Thus Greenbrier was saved. The Indians were so discomfited they abandoned their expedition & returned home. During this expedition Gen. Clark, of the U. S. Army, stopped at Point Pleasant on his way to take possession of a place then called the O Post, but now Vincennes.

During the autumn of 1778, there was a man named Morgan in the fort, who had been prisoner for many years with the Indians & who had a squaw with him said to be his wife. Morgan was held & ironed by the officers in order to take him to his father who had offered a large reward to any one who would bring his son to him. Finding himself but slightly guarded, he ran away with his wife & was never more heard of. The officers fearing that he would reach the Indian towns and inform them that our time had nearly expired, & that a great many of us would leave the fort in a few days, discharged myself, Zedekiah Shumaker & many others & we left the fort a few days before my two years had actually expired. After my return to Amherst at the close of 1778, I was the following year drafted in the militia to serve a tour of 3 mos. below Richmond under Capt. Samuel Higginbotham, Col. Christian's Regt., & served this tour with Zedekiah Shumaker, William Brown, Samuel Allen & many others. In 1780, served another tour of 3 mos. at Fort Powhatan, on James River below Richmond, now called Fort Jefferson, under Capt. Richard Ballinger; he served with Richard Tankersley, Nicholas Pryor (an elder brother), & many others. Certificates as to his character & services sworn to by Rev. John Davis, Abram Carter, Zedekiah Shumaker & Bartlett Cash. Placed on Pension Roll Sept. 6, 1833.

PUGH, JOHN,—Nelson Co., Va., Oct. 2, 1832: b. Amelia Co., Nov. 18, 1762 or '63; substituted for his father, John Pugh, Jan., 1781, under Capt. James Barnett, Major Campbell; drafted June, 1781, Capt. James Pamplin, Lt. Joseph Staples, joined Gen. Lafayette's Army. Some time after returning home visited his cousin, Burke Co., N. C., where there was a requisition for troops to go against the Indians. In Oct. or Nov., 1781, Capt. John McDowell came to his cousin's & said one of them would have to go against the Indians & he consented to go. After this tour returned to Amherst where he lived 2 years; then returned to N. C.; thence to S. C. After 2 years returned to Amherst & in 1800 removed to Monroe Co., where he resided 1 year, then moved to Amherst, now Nelson Co., Va. Polly Chewning testified she remembered when her brother left on a 3 mos. tour as a substitute for their father, John Pugh. Placed on Pension Roll May 31, 1833.

PURVIS, GEORGE,—Nelson Co., Va., Sept. 25, 1832: b. Caroline Co., Oct. 19, 1757; vol. 1775 in a company commanded by Capt. James Higginbotham, Lt. Joseph Cabell, Ensign Nicholas Cabell. We met at sd. Nicholas Cabell's & marched to Williamsburg by way of Richmond. He was standing guard when Gov. Dunmore made his way to the British shipping. A guard was placed at his house to take him in case he should return. After 3 mos. we were marched back to Amherst & discharged. Vol. 1776, under Capt. James Montgomery, Lt. Tilman Walton; 1777, served under Capt. John Diggs, Lt. Morrison, Col. Meriwether, Major John Pope; same year tour under Capt. John Christian, Lt. James Pamplin, Lt. Samuel Bell, Ensign Samuel Allen, Col. Daniel Gaines, marched to Hickory Run Meeting House, below Richmond, between Jamestown & Williamsburg. Next tour under Capt. John Jacobs, Lt. James Reid, Col. Tompkins; 1780-81, Capt. Tilman Walton, Lt. James Roberts, Gen. Lafayette; vol. in Capt. James Morrison's Co., Lt. Reid, marched from Warwick's Gap, then called Key's Gap, & joined Lafayette. We were directed to run 30 bullets at Jamestown & placed as foot guard to the artillery. Our company was in the advance & the company should fire & file to the right & left & let the artillery come into play. Before daylight an officer rode up & ordered a halt, but the army continued to march. When in sight of Jamestown found Cornwallis & his force had taken shipping. Charles Purvis, aged 66, & Hezekiah Hargrove testified Nov. 20, 1832, to his service. He d. Oct. 15, 1838, & his widow, Elizabeth (Murphy) Purvis, applied Jan. 26, 1852. They were m. Oct. 25, 1795, Amherst Co., Va. Both claims allowed.

RAY, WILLIAM,—Franklin Co., Ga., March 7, 1821, aged 64: enlisted Jan. 6, 1777, Capt. Samuel J. Cabell, Col. Morgan's Regt., Contl. Estabmt.; discharged Jan., 1780, Fredericktown, Md., by Col. Buford. At storming of Stony Point, battle of Monmouth. William Aaron testified he served 9 mos. with William Ray, was furloughed, & Ray remained the time stated. John Ray, Union Co., Ga., July 23, 1853, aged 46, applied stating deponent & sister, Suca Ray, were only children of William Ray who was placed on the Pension Roll Jan. 29, 1825 and d. April 6, 1833. His parents, William Ray & Patty Wilson, were m. in Oglethorpe Co., Ga., March 15, 1804.

REID, ALEXANDER,—Gerrard Co., Ky., May 1, 1833: b. Albemarle Co., Feb. 11, 1752, in that part later Amherst Co., Va.

Enlisted in Amherst Co. against the Indians, 1774, under Capt.
Alexander McClanahan, Col. Charles Lewis; joined the troops at
Staunton & marched to Big Kanawha, where a severe engagement
took place in which Col. Lewis was killed; vol. in Botetourt Co.,
Va., 1780, under Capt. James Barnett, Col. Hugh Crockett, for 3
mos. against the Tories; vol. again the same year in Amherst Co.
under Capt. Barnett & marched to Big Island on Holston River
against the Cherokee Indians in Col. William Campbell's Regt.
Spring, 1781, in service in Capt. Barnett's Co., mounted Infty.
Placed on Pension Roll Sept. 2, 1833.

ROBERTSON, THOMAS,—Monroe Co., Tenn., Sept. 17, 1832,
aged 70: drafted 1780, 6 mos. as private under Capt. Richard
Ballinger, Lts. Thomas Jones & Absalom Pollard, Ensign John
Mathews; marched from Amherst Jan. 1, 1781; reached Richmond
a few days after it had been burned by Arnold. On returning home,
Col. Rose called for volunteers for 20 days, & declarant vol. under
Capt. Woodroof, Col. Cabell, Lt. Col. Pope. Removed to Cocke
Co., Tenn., 30 years ago; after 6 years moved to Knox Co.; 14
years there, then to Monroe Co. Charles Lane & Joseph Lain testified they were Robertson's neighbors in Amherst Co., Va., during
the Revolution; Charles Lane was Robertson's messmate on both
tours, & Joseph Lain messmate on tour under Capt. Woodroof.
Claim was allowed.

ROYALTREE, (ROYALTY, RIALLY), JOHN,—Casey Co.,
Ky., Aug. 21, 1832: b. Stafford Co., Va., 1759; Feb., 1781, substituted for Thomas Waugh, private in Amherst Co. Militia, under
Capt. Wallace, 4th Va. Regt.; joined Gen. Lawson, marched to
Guilford; next tour under Capt. James Pamplin as substitute for
Thomas Waugh, Col. Lindsey's Regt., Gen. Lawson's Brig. In
engagement at old Jamestown. Discharged at Malbon Hills by Gen.
Lawson. Aug., 1781, marched under Capt. Landrum & served during Siege of York & was at surrender of Cornwallis & guard to
prisoners on their march to Winchester; taken sick and discharged,
8 mos. service. He d. Dec. 16, 1844, & March 30, 1857, Sally
Royalty, aged 87, widow of pensioner, applied from Collin Co.,
Texas, stating they were m. Jan. 25, 1803, by Jeremiah Vardeman,
M.L.B. "John Rially & Sally Sage, Lincoln Co., Ky., Jan. 24,
1803." She testified they were illiterate & could not write & the
Clerk of the Court misspelled their name. Rejected for lack of
proof of marriage.

RYAN, HARRIS,—Rhea Co., Tenn., Feb. 4, 1834: b. Amherst
Co., Va., Nov. 4, 1764; enlisted fall 1779 6 mos. in Capt. John
Morrison's Co., Lts. Samuel Yours & Thomas Ewers, Col. John
Pope's Regt., & was in skirmish at Petersburg under Gen. Lawson.
After the Revolution removed to Wilkes Co., Ga., then to Campbell

Co., Tenn., then to present county. Edward Demaster of Nelson Co., Va., was a fellow soldier in Capt. John Morrison's Co. Harris Ryan was living in McCracken Co., Ky., Aug. 11, 1843, when he requested that his name be transferred from the Tenn. Pension Roll to that of Ky., as his wife had died & his youngest dau. Unity was married to George Burnett & he lives with them.

RYAN, PHILIP,—Nelson Co., Va., Oct. 22, 1832: b. Albemarle Co., Dec., 1756, in that part later Amherst Co. & then Nelson Co., Va.; drafted out of his division on three tours: under Capt. William Harris, Lt. John Martin, Albemarle Barracks. After 1 mo. service taken with white swelling in his limbs & furloughed. On recovering, served 2 mos. in same company; 6 mos. in Capt. Richard Ballinger's Co. Edward Demaster, soldier of the Revolution, testified that during the War a certain John Morrison raised a volunteer company for 6 mos. service in Amherst Co., Va., that deponent & Harris Ryan were privates in sd. Co., they marched to Petersburg where sd. Philip Ryan was taken sick and brought home to Amherst in a wagon. Claim allowed.

SCRUGGS, SAMUEL SCOTT, Sr. (or SCOTT MARTIN),—Nelson Co., Va., March 27, 1828, aged 70: enlisted under name of Scott Martin, 1777, for 2 years under Capt. Samuel Jordan Cabell, in Regt. commanded by Col. Stevens, Va. Line, Contl. Estabmt. One dau. aged 20 living with him. Thomas Jones testified he served as stated. A copy of a deed dated Dec. 9, 1826, from Samuel S. Scruggs, & Jane his wife to their son, Samuel S. Scruggs, Jr., conveying a tract of land in Amherst Co., Va., is with his application papers. Placed on Pension Roll June 20, 1828.

SHUMAKER, ZEDEKIAH,—Amherst Co., Va., Oct. 15, 1832: b. Henrico Co., about 1754; went to the Great Kanawha & there resided until driven back to Amherst by the Indians in 1775; enlisted autumn of 1776 for 2 years under Lt. Moore of Rockbridge, some comrades being John Hogg, John Finney, Samuel Peters & William Ricks; marched to Point Pleasant. Other officers were Capt. William McKee, Lt. James Thompson & Ensign James Gilmore. Matthew Arbuckle was in command of the fort, his subalterns being Lts. Andrew Wallace & Samuel Woods, & Ensign James McNutt. Served 2 tours under Capt. Samuel Higginbotham & Capt. Anthony Rucker, guarding British prisoners at Charlottesville; fellow soldiers were Moses Sweeney, William Cook & others. (The greater part of this declaration is merely a repetition of that of William Pryor, & for that reason is omitted). His claim was allowed.

SIMMONS, JAMES,—Hawkins Co., Tenn., Aug., 1818: b. July 10, 1758; enlisted Jan., 1777, under Ensign William Powell, Capt. James Franklin, 10th Va. Regt., Gen. Weedon's Brig.; Capt.

Franklin resigned & Clough Shelton took command; discharged by Col. Febiger, Philadelphia 1780; battles Brandywine, Germantown, Monmouth, storming of Stony Point & two skirmishes under Col. Stevens & Gen. Wayne, Gen. Scott's Brig. Gave his discharge to his father, who lived in Rutherford Co., N. C. Placed on Pension Roll Sept. 30, 1819.

SMITH, AUGUSTINE,—Nelson Co., Va., Nov. 1, 1832, "aged about 80"; b. Westmoreland Co.; enlisted under Capt. Samuel Jordan Cabell, marched to Williamsburg, promoted Sergt., returned to Amherst on recruiting service; remained at Amherst C. H. for several weeks, during which time he enlisted 4 men: Austin Smith, James Weeks, Josiah Jones & David Barnett, & marched with them to Williamsburg. The troops were ordered to Sandy Point to guard flour & provisions. Capt. Hopkins & Lt. Williams were also there. One morning two British tenders made their appearance & fired on the troops with grape shot & cannon balls. One of the latter struck near the spring where he was standing & tore up the ground, throwing dirt on him. The firing continued during the day & they captured our flour & provisions. Militia from adjoining counties were in the engagement; the arm of one of their men was broken by a grape shot. Capt. Cabell's Co. returned to Williamsburg. Deponent was sent to Richmond with a wagon for flour. On his return the negro driver turned the wagon over & some of the barrels of flour fell on him & broke his back. He was taken by a man named Harris to Capt. Bowers a doctor who lived in a fine house opposite. While there a neighbor of Dr. Bowers', named Corbin, who owned many slaves came to see him. After 20 days was taken to Williamsburg & when able to travel was furloughed; purchased a parcel of cotton & put it into a bag to ride on. Was aided home by his brother, John Smith, & Joel Thompson (both now dead). Never recovered until several years after his enlistment expired. Claim allowed; d. Dec. 1, 1832. His sister, Mary Smith, applied March 24, 1835, for the balance of his pay for his heirs: sisters, Mary & Judith Smith & Sally Lowe, wife of William Lowe. Cert. paid in favor of Mary Smith, Extrx.

SMITH, PHILIP,—Amherst Co., Va., Oct. 15, 1832: b. Albemarle Co., 1755, in the part later Amherst Co., Va.; drafted 1781 as private under Capt. James Franklin & marched to N. C. Joined Gen. Greene's Army the day after battle of Guilford; summer of 1781, 4 mos. under Caleb Higginbotham driving cattle to Williamsburg for Contl. Army. Capt. Benjamin Higginbotham testified to seeing declarant on the Guilford Expedition. Bartlett Cash testified he marched with declarant in Capt. James Franklin's Co. & joined Gen. Greene after the battle of Guilford. Rejected—remarks in case: Only proved 3 mos. service, 6 mos. required under act he applied.

SMITH, THOMAS,—Washington Co., Ind., Oct. 12, 1818, aged 69: enlisted as private under Samuel Jordan Cabell, Col. Buckner's 6th Va. Regt. Was in battle near Albany when Johnson's Indians were made prisoners & carried into Albany; White Marsh and Saratoga. Discharged March 4, 1778, at the Sign of the White Horse, on Lancaster road 36 miles from Philadelphia. Wife, Hepsibah, aged 53. Placed on Pension Roll July 12, 1819; d. Feb. 27, 1829.

SMITH, WILLIAM,—Augusta Co., Va., Feb. 25, 1833: b. Staunton, July 22, 1763; his father moved to Amherst when declarant was young; declarant returned to Augusta in 1825; drafted latter part of 1777 or early in 1778 & marched from Amherst as private under Capt. David Shelton to guard British & Hessian prisoners captured at Saratoga; served another tour of 1 mo. at the Barracks; 1781, under Capt. James Barnett, Lt. John Woodroof, Col. Charles Dabney of Hanover. While stationed at Williamsburg, a soldier at the Half Way House announced that he had seen the British a few miles from camp, when declarant's & several other companies marched out & captured 70, who surrendered without making any resistance. They were delivered to Gen. Steuben at Williamsburg, where declarant was discharged. Drafted late in April under Capt. Richard Taliaferro, Lt. Charles Eades, Col. Meriwether, Gen. Stevens' Brig., & while stationed at Malbon Hills marched to Hot Water to reinforce Gen. Wayne; arrived during the fight & was in the battle. Was not discharged until after harvest. Claim allowed.

STRATTON, ISAAC,—Tazewell Co., Va., Jan. 22, 1822: b. June 22, 1754; vol. as private under Capt. John Overton, Col. William Davis' 14th Va. Regt., Contl. Estabmt., & in 1778 marched to Valley Forge where he joined the Grand Army. Battles of Monmouth, Storming of Paulus Hook, last named place under Major Henry Lee, where 300 men or upward were taken prisoners by the American Army. Served under Col. Morgan for 4 mos., then joined his former 14th Va. Regt. Discharged at Fredericksburg after 2 years & 6 mos. service. His family consisted of wife & 3 daus. Placed on Pension Roll Sept. 12, 1819; d. Jan. 16, 1831.

SWEENY (or SWEENEY), JOSEPH,—Washington Co., Ky., May 15, 1828: b. Feb. 28, 1760; enlisted Amherst Co., Va., Oct., 1780, under Capt. Joseph Yarbour for during the War, Va. Line, Contl. Estabmt., & received Cert. of reward for $80 to which he was entitled under Act of May 15, 1778; marched to Richmond & was appointed Waggon Master with a command of 9 waggons, which was called a brigade of waggons, under Gen. Russell. In Siege of York & surrender of Cornwallis; discharged by William McGraw, officer under Gen. Russell. On his way home sold his Cert. to a

Mr. Brown for a little mare to ride home. Battles of Camden, under Capt. White; Eutaw Springs, Guilford, under Capt. Harris. He d. June 7, 1846. Nancy Sweeny, widow of pensioner, applied from Mercer Co., Ky., May 8, 1851. Her maiden name was Nancy Whitten, & they were m. Dec., 1781, in Amherst, Va., by Rev. Coleman. Children, William, Elizabeth & Moses Sweeny, born prior to 1790. Charles Sweeney, Casey Co., Ky., June 6, 1851, aged 84, younger brother of Joseph Sweeney, testified they lived in Amherst Co., Va., during the war with their parents. His brother came home on furlough, sick. When he recovered he took him to the army. Claim was not allowed as no record of her marriage could be found.

Note. Their marriage is recorded in Amherst Co. Order Book, 1782-1784, p. 73, as follows: "Joseph Swenney & Nancy Whitten, Dec. 5, 1782, by Rev. Benjamin Coleman."

TALIAFERRO, RICHARD,—Pickens Co., Ala., Oct. 31, 1837, Mildred Taliaferro, aged 74, widow of Richard Taliaferro, who died intestate in S. C., April 15, 1806, applied. He served as Captain & Recruiting Officer, Va. Contl. Line; for nearly 2 years he was stationed at Amherst C. H. near her father's home & she well recollects his zeal & great success in the recruiting service. M.L.B. Amherst Co., Va.: "Richard Taliaferro, bachelor & Mildred Powell, spinster, July 18, 1780." William Cashwell, Amherst Co., Va., July 7, 1838, testified Capt. Richard Taliaferro was Recruiting Officer, sometimes marching his recruits Northward; other times to the Carolinas. William Lavender stated he saw Capt. Taliaferro in the Northern Army, 1777, & at Jamestown just before the Siege & Surrender of York. William Taliaferro declared that about 1783 his brother, Richard, moved with his wife Mildred to S. C., where they lived until his death, which took place years ago. His widow & many children survive. John Thompson, Jr., of Amherst C. H., now in Richmond, Nov. 16, 1838, wrote to the Pension Office & sent the declaration of his aunt, Mrs. Mildred Taliaferro, who applied under Act of July, 1836. Her claim was allowed.

Warrant No. 7624 for 4000 acres of land issued Feb. 27, 1834, to the following named heirs, children of Capt. Richard & Mildred Taliaferro: William, Elizabeth, wife of John Pitcher, Rebecca, wife of James M. Black, Richard, Benjamin, John, Roderick, Emily, wife of John Terry, & James P. Taliaferro, all living Jan. 20, 1834, except William, who died since the death of his father, leaving one dau. Rutha, who m. Abraham Smith.

TAYLOR, GEORGE,—Schuyler Co., Ill., Oct. 15, 1833: b. Oct. 12, 1762; enlisted in Amherst Co., Va., Sept., 1777, in Capt. Samuel Shackleford's Co., Col. Broadhead's Regt. attached to the command of Gen. McIntosh, for the purpose of marching to Detroit against the British. We left our county at Rockfish Gap in the Blue Ridge & moved on to Fort Cumberland, then took Braddock's Road &

went to a place called The Shades of Death; crossed the Monongahela River from there to Loganstown on the Ohio River. There built Fort McIntosh. From there turned a northwest course, piloted by Delaware Indians, until we struck the Muskingum River at the mouth of a creek called Tuscarawa, crossed the river & built Fort Defiance; were there met by about 70 Indians, which occasioned great joy amongst them—they fired one round & the troops fired two. That evening it commenced snowing & fell 3 feet deep, which covered the Gaps and everything on which our beeves could subsist; we then had to turn in & slaughter the beeves to keep them from starving; about the same time our flour gave out & left us in a starving condition & a sickness in camp, of which about 40 of our men died. We were liberated from the place by companies to make the best of our way to Fort McIntosh or starve. I saw several who had starved; others dead & some speechless; some with raw tugs or hides in their mouths endeavoring to chew or eat them. When we got back to McIntosh we got plenty provisions. A Major Lockhart, being Commissary, issued out plenty provisions without weight or measure. We lived at a high head on our way home. When that gave out our Captain would some days call for victuals as many as five times & give his certificates for same. I reached my Father's home about the middle of Jan., 1778, & discharged. In March, 1779, called out 5 weeks under Capt. Sherrard Clasby, of Albemarle, to guard prisoners in the Barracks at Albemarle that were taken at Saratoga with Burgoyne. Served 5 weeks under Capt. James Barnett, guard to prisoners in Richmond jail. Our company was relieved by Capt. Harris' Co. In spring of 1779, was called out by a division under command of Capt. [Lt.-Col.] James Higginbotham, to guard the Seaboard; was stationed part of the time at Williamsburg; 1780, marched under Capt. William Tucker to Hampton & Portsmouth, then back to Wiles or "Half-Way House," & took up winter quarters. That evening we took 80-odd British prisoners & marched them to Wiles' Barn & next morning marched with them to Williamsburg & then returned to the "Half-Way House." In February we were called out to pursue some British that were out on a foraging party, & Col. Mallory & two privates were killed. The British had 12 miles start on us. We pursued them 26 miles from Little York to Hampton. They made their escape & we returned to Little York. In March, 1781, Col. Dabney & Col. Ennis were our Field Officers, & both were present when I got my last discharge by Capt. William Tucker.[79] Oct. 15, 1833,

---

[79]In a letter written by Lt. Col. Dabney to Gov. Harrison March 23, 1781, from Hampton—Halfway House he "recommends, that the two companies from Amherst, and one from Albemarle Co., who have so long been on duty, be discharged, especially as they have behaved so well, and are now unfit for duty for want of shoes and clothing." *Calendar of Virginia State Papers*, 1, 590.

Benjamin Carpenter, Schuyler Co., Ill., testified he became acquainted with George Taylor while at Richmond guarding the Tories taken at the Battle of King's Mountain. He was Orderly Sergt. in Capt. Harris' Co., who relieved the company George Taylor was then doing duty in. His next acquaintance with him was at the taking of 80-odd British prisoners; they were both detailed to guard them to Williamsburg. Record of his age kept by his father (Will Taylor) now at his brother's in Ky. Claim was allowed.

TAYLOR, JOHN,—Washington Co., Ky., Aug. 14, 1834: b. Albemarle Co., Va., April 15, 1752; removed to Amherst where he vol. as private under Capt. Lewis, Dr. Gilmore, Capt. or Major in the Contl. Army; marched to Col. Nelson's in Hanover Co. Some time after receiving his discharge served 3 tours of 1 mo. each at Albemarle Barracks under Capt. John Higginbotham & Col. Taylor; 3 mos. under Capt. John Franklin, Maj. Gabriel Penn & Col. Hugh Rose, 7th Div. Va. Militia; marched to Stovall's Ferry on James River, to Moore's Tavern, Pr. Edward Co., where they rendezvoused & marched to Guilford, which they reached after the battle; the British retreated & the Division pursued them till they took shipping near the mouth of Haw River. The British sailed around & landed at Jamestown. On returning home was drafted under Capt. John Woodroof & Col. Pope & marched to Drinking Spring, near Williamsburg, where they joined the Main Army under Gen. Lafayette & other generals. Removed to Ky. about 40 years ago. Turner Smith, Clergyman, & John Clarke, neighbors of declarant for many years, testified to his good character and veracity. John Clarke served with him on the Guilford Expedition. Claim was allowed.

TEMPLE, JOHN,—Edgefield Dist., S. C., July 23, 1818, aged 60: enlisted in Capt. Samuel Jordan Cabell's Rifle Co., 6th Va. Infty. commanded by Col. James Hendricks, shortly after the battle of Bunker Hill; in service 6 years and in garrison 6 mos. until peace concluded his service; battles of Trenton, Brandywine, Amboy & taking of Burgoyne at Still Water. Oct. 4, 1820, he appeared in court & testified he was very deaf, defective in sight & helpless & weak in body, & had neither wife nor children living with him, & depends altogether on his pension or charity for subsistence. He testified Aug. 4, 1830, in Montgomery Co., Ala., that he was the same John Temple who was on the Pension Roll in S. C. & wished to have his name transferred to Alabama, as his son & many of his old friends reside there & he desires to live near them.

THOMAS, JOHN,—Albemarle Co., Va., May 6, 1833: b. Albemarle Co., April 8, 1757, in that part later Amherst Co., Va., where he resided until 1778, when he moved to present residence. Spring

1779, Ensign, Albemarle Militia, under Capt. John Martin, Lt. Nathaniel Garland. Again called into service Jan., 1781, by Capt. James Garland, who was killed by a sentinel & the command during the remainder of the tour devolved upon declarant; Sept., 1781, under Col. Nicholas Lewis gathering cattle sent to York Town. John Garth, Scott Co., Ky., testified he served at Albemarle Barracks at same time John Thomas served as Ensign. Micajah Wheeler, Sr. & John Wingfield testified they served several tours as guards at Albemarle Barracks & that John Thomas was serving at the Barracks as an officer. Rejected for lack of proof of 6 mos. service.

THOMPSON, JAMES,—Union Co., Ohio, June 28, 1833, aged 73: enlisted Amherst Co., Va., 1777 as substitute for a man by occupation a weaver, private under Capt. G. Burley, Col. Francis Taylor, Major Roberts, Albemarle Barracks; next tour drafted & marched against Cornwallis at Petersburg. Claim was allowed.

THURMOND, WILLIAM,—Amherst Co., Va., April 18, 1831, Philip Thurmond, son & heir-at-law of William Thurmond who entered service as Sergt.-Major during the War in Regt. commanded by Col. Samuel Hawes, Va. Contl. Line, applied for the heirs of William Thurmond, decd.: Sally Jones, wife of Tandy Jones, late Sally Thurmond; Lucy A. Turner, formerly Thurmond; Judith Beck, wife of Jesse Beck, late Judith Thurmond; Philip & William J. Thurmond; Elizabeth D. Crawford, wife of David Crawford, formerly Elizabeth Thurmond—Children of William Thurmond, decd., also Claiborn A. Tucker; Susan W. Christian, who was Susan Tucker, now wife of Charles Christian; Mary Tucker; Elizabeth D. Tucker; John C. Tucker—Children of Polly (Thurmond) Tucker, dau. of William Thurmond. Bounty Land Warrant No. 1996 for 100 acres.

TRAIL, JAMES,—Green Co., Tenn., Sept. 5, 1832, aged 75: 1779 private under Ensign Mathews, Col. Hatcher's Regt. of Regulars as guard to prisoners taken at Burgoyne's Defeat; Jan., 1781, drafted & enrolled at Amherst Co., Va., under Capt. Young Landrum of Virginia Militia & marched to Guilford where his company joined Gen. Lawson, Col. Holcombe & Major Hubbard, & was in the battle of Guilford; discharged after 4 mos.; again drafted & served under Capt. James Loving. Placed on Pension Roll Jan. 5, 1833.

TRUSLER, JOHN,—Franklin Co., Ohio, July 3, 1833: b. Albemarle Co., Va., 1758, in that part later Amherst Co.; entered service March 1, 1781. On Guilford Expedition as private under Col. Hugh Rose, Major William Penn, joined Gen. Greene; 4 mos. service. Siege of York under Capt. Loving; discharged after 5 mos. He d. Aug. 16, 1838. Elizabeth (Dunning) Trusler, widow of pensioner, applied from Union Co., Ohio, April 9, 1853, aged 78; m.

in Amherst Co., Va., April 22, 1803, by Rev. William Crawford. Both were pensioned.

TUCKER, JESSE,—Bedford Co., Va., July 25, 1843, Nancy King, aged 70, former widow of Jesse Tucker, applied. M. Amherst Co., Jan. 26, 1791, by Rev. Charles Crawford. He d. March, 1817, Bedford Co.; m. 2nd Powell Ownsley, Nov., 1819; he d. Jan., 1820, & she m. Nov., 1822, Gilliam King. He d. Jan. 9, 1830. Her husband Jesse Tucker enlisted in the early part of the Revolution under Capt. Franklin or Capt. Ballinger.

Family Record:

Parmelia A. Tucker, b. Nov. 16, 1791
Francis S. Tucker, b. Oct. 25, 1793
Henry L. Tucker, b. Feb. 7, 1795
Creed Haskins Tucker, b. Sept. 1, 1798
Mary C. Tucker, b. Dec. 2, 1800
Susanah L. Tucker, b. Feb. 16, 1803
Nancy Leftwich Tucker, b. April 16, 1805
Elizabeth F. Tucker, b. June 15, 1807
Sophia W. Tucker, b. Aug. 15, 1809
Martha R. Tucker, b. Sept. 17, 1811
Claudius L. Tucker, b. Sept. 16, 1813
Bueil G. Tucker, b. Nov. 16, 1815

Abraham Carter, Amherst Co., July 14, 1843, aged 80, stated his brother, William Carter, served several tours with Jesse Tucker & his brothers, Isaiah & Drury Tucker. William Cashwell was a fellow soldier on Guilford Expedition, in Capt. James Dillard's Co. of Riflemen, Col. Holcombe's Regt. Mrs. Betsey Ann Hurt, Bedford Co., Oct. 7, 1843, aged 78, declared that George Hurt & Harry Robenson served in the Revolutionary War with Jesse, Isaiah & Drury Tucker. Aug. 3, 1851, Nancy King testified further that "in the early part of the Revolution, while under age, Jesse Tucker enlisted under Capt. Richard Taliaferro & after serving 3 or 4 mos. at the Barracks his father got him off because of his age; when of age he enlisted again under the same officer." About ten years after their marriage she visited her brother, William Lane, in Albemarle, with her husband & passed by the Old Barracks, just outside of Charlottesville. He showed her the standing chimneys of the old Barrack house where he served under Capt. Taliaferro & said while there he was inoculated for smallpox. The Army roll at Cumberland C. H., 1782, shows enlistments from Amherst for 3 years of the following: "Jesse Tucker, enlisted Dec. 1, 1782, age 18 years, 6 ft., light hair, grey eyes, fair complexion; William Thurmond, enlisted Oct. 10, 1782, age 16, 5 ft. 10 inches, light hair, grey eyes, fair complexion." (From the Register of the first volume of papers concerning the Army of the Revolution, on file in First Auditor's

Office, Richmond, Va., Dec. 29, 1851.) Nancy King was living in Botetourt Co., Va., April 17, 1855. She was allowed a pension on account of the service of her first husband, Jesse Tucker.

TUGGLE, CHARLES,—Madison Co., Ga., Sept. 24, 1832, aged 79: enlisted Nov. 6, 1776, as private under Capt. Clough Shelton, Col. Stevens' 10th Va. Regt., Contl. Line; discharged 1779. On guard at battle of Brandywine & in hearing of the guns at Germantown, but being sick prevented from being in battle. He was marched to Baltimore, inoculated for smallpox; thence to Middle Brook to Winter Quarters; from there to Morristown & Valley Forge & again took up winter quarters; thence to Morristown, West Point, White Plains & was at storming of Stony Point under Gen. Wayne. March 15, 1842, Charles Tuggle appeared in Lowndes Co., Ala., Court & asked to have his certificate transferred from Ga. Agency to Ala., as his wife had died & being old & infirm desired to spend the remainder of his days with his only relative, a dau., in Ala. Last payment to May 6, 1842.

TURNER, HENRY,—Pike Co., Mo., June 13, 1849, Rachel Turner, aged 89, widow of Henry Turner who furnished a substitute 1779 in Amherst Co., Va., Militia, and in 1780 served as Lt., applied. Their son, Stephen B. Turner, same place, June 7, 1852, applied for a pension for the heirs of his father who he thought was a Captain in the Revolution. His parents were married 1777 in Bedford Co., Va. Father d. in Amherst Oct. 23, 1829; mother d. Jan. 4, 1850. Rejected.

Bible Record:

Sally Turner, b. Feb. 19, 17—
George Turner, b. Aug. 14, 1779
Terisha Turner, b. Dec. 10, 1784
Martha Turner, b. Oct. 27, 178—
Betsey Turner, b. May 21, 17—
Henry Turner, b. April 17, 1787
Samuel C. Turner, b. May 20, 1789
Ruth Turner, b. Oct. 10, 1790
Thomas Turner, b. Oct. 23, 1792
Stephen B. Turner, b.

On the first page of the Bible record: "Miss Kitty Turner was b. Sept. 29, 1795."

TURNER, WILLIAM,—Amherst Co., Va., Aug. 21, 1832: b. Albemarle Co., 1760; enlisted under Capt. Philip Thurmond, 3 mos. at the Barracks in Albemarle; "While there Capt. James Garland was killed by a sentinel on duty"; Orderly Sergt. under Capt. Young Landrum, Gen. Lawson's Brig., in battle of Guilford. Remembers seeing Gen. Edward Stevens removed from the battle ground badly wounded. Again drafted as Sergt. under Capt. Benjamin Higginbotham & on the line of march to York Town was appointed Ensign in said company, which commission in the great lapse of time he has lost. He & his Capt. were discharged as supernumerary officers a few days before the capitulation of Yorktown. Charles Stewart, Bedford Co., testified May 27, 1833, he served 3 mos. under Capt. Christian & William Turner. Placed on Pension Roll Sept. 11, 1833; d. Sept. 30, 1834. His widow, Sarah Turner, applied Nov. 19, 1838, aged 77 "on March 4th next." They were m. Aug. 20, 1780, by Rev. Samuel Irvine.

TYLER, DANIEL,—Bedford Co., Va., Aug. 23, 1819, aged 64: enlisted March 4, 1776, under Capt. Samuel J. Cabell, Col. Buckner's 6th Va. Regt. Contl. Estabmt. The company afterwards was attached to Col. Daniel Morgan's Regt. of Riflemen. In battles of Saratoga, capture of Burgoyne, Chestnut Hill & many skirmishes; discharged Feb. 20, 1778. John Jordan, Lt. Capt. Cabell's Co., testified Aug. 18, 1819: "Daniel Tyler enlisted as pvt. from Amherst, 1776, in Capt. Samuel J. Cabell's company attached to Col. Buckner's Regt. & joined Gen. Washington. The company was afterwards transferred to Col. Daniel Morgan's Regt. & sent to join Gen. Gates at that time opposed to the British Army commanded by Gen. Burgoyne. He was at the surrender of that army & in many severe actions, & behaved as a Brave & good soldier. After the reduction of the army, which went into Winter Quarters at Valley Forge, he was discharged." Daniel Tyler appeared in Bedford Court, Sept. 28, 1831 & testified all his children, except one son living in Indiana, lived in Logan Co., Ohio, & desired to remove there & have his pension transferred to that place. He d. in Highland Co., Ohio, where he had lived 14 years, March 10, 1845, and his widow, Sarah Tyler, applied from that place Feb. 2, 1848, aged 85. They were m. 1784 or '85 at the home of her grandfather, Stephen Cash, Amherst, Va. She d. Dec. 20, 1849, and on Feb. 6, 1856, Johannah Brown (m. Thomas W. Brown, Oct. 3, 1826), aged 50, and Nancy Tyler, aged 55, Highland Co., & their brother, Samuel Tyler, Boone Co., Ind., only living children, applied for a pension.

Family Bible Record:
Elizabeth Wade Tyler, b. Dec. 30, 1783
Anna Cash Tyler, b. Dec. 28, 1785
John Tyler, b. Jan. 30, 1788
Samuel Tyler, b. Jan. 18, 1790
Keziah Tyler, b. March 2, 1792
Nelson C. Tyler, b. Aug. 11, 1794
Zachariah Tyler, b. Oct. 3, 1796
Susannah Tyler, b. Nov. 30, 1798
Johannah Tyler, b. Jan. 10, 1801

Polley Tyler, b. July 1, 1803
Nancy Tyler, b. Dec. 16, 1805

TYLER, JOHN,—Amherst Co., Va., April 21, 1845, Elizabeth Tyler, aged 81, widow of John Tyler who died Aug. 19, 1830, aged 69, applied. Affidavit of William Cashwell, Amherst, May 4, 1846: was well acquainted with John Tyler, whose widow is an applicant for a pension. He marched with him in Capt. John Christian's Co. about the last of August, 1781, to York Town, & after the surrender under Capt. John Stewart & Col. Samuel Vance's Va. Regt., were two of the guards to British Prisoners to Winchester. John Tyler was also in service at Guilford Court House. Said Tyler married Miss Betsy Dillard, dau. of William Dillard. M.L.B. Amherst Co., Va.: "John Tyler, bachelor & Elizabeth Dillard, spinster, Feb. 2, 1789." Eaton Carpenter, son of Benjamin Carpenter, testified his father was drafted in the Amherst Militia, Siege of York & capture of Cornwallis. He heard his father say John Tyler was in same service.

May 19, 1846, Col. George W. Higginbotham, Amherst Co., Va., aged 63, "Recollects distinctly that in looking over his father's Revolutionary papers, he came across several Muster rolls containing the names of the soldiers that composed the several companies that were in service under deponent's father, Col. or Major Higginbotham, who was an officer in the Revolutionary War of the above grades; deponent has heard his father say that he was in service against the Indians & at Charlottesville, Williamsburg & Yorktown. Deponent cannot say positively the Captain's name, whose roll the name of John Tyler was on, but it is very clear in his recollection of having seen the names of John Tyler & Benj. Carpenter on the above rolls that were in the possession of his father, Col. James Higginbotham. The muster rolls are at the Court House or in Kentucky."

June 18, 1849, Lawson G. Tyler, Buckingham Co., Va., applied for a pension for the heirs of John Tyler, under Act of Feb. 2, 1848, as Admr. of Elizabeth Tyler, decd., who was a pensioner. She d. Feb. 5, 1849, leaving 7 children: George D., Lawson G., Tandy S., William H., John L. Tyler, Oney D. Joiner & Martha W. Briggs. Claim was allowed.

Bible Record:

George D. Tyler, b. June 3, 17—
Lawson G. Tyler, b. March 12, 1791
Charles Tyler, b. July 17, 1792
William Hudson Tyler, b. July ———
                d. Sept. 11, 1795
Tandy S. Tyler, b. June —, 1800
Oney D. Tyler, b. May 2, ———

Patsy W. Tyler, b. April 4, 18—
William Henry Tyler, b. Oct. ———
John L. Tyler, b. Sept. 12, 1808

UPSHAW, JOHN,—Elbert Co., Ga., July 16, 1833: b. Essex Co., Va., Feb. 22, 1755; while residing in Amherst Co., Va., enlisted as private in Va. troops on tours as follows: 1780, 3 mos. in Capt. William Tucker's Co., Col. Dabney's Regt.; during the year 1781, 1 mo. in Capt. Woodroof's Co., Col. Merriwether's Regt., marched to Hampton & discharged; 1 mo. in Capt. Dawson's Co., Albemarle Barracks; 1 mo. under Capt. Burrus, marched to York Town. Removed to Georgia "about 45 years ago." His claim was allowed. He d. in Elbert Co., Ga., 1834.

VIER, JOHN,—Franklin Co., Va., Jan. 24, 1834, aged 76: enlisted under Capt. Jesse Allen; transferred to Capt. Holeman Rice's Co. who resigned & he was placed under Capt. Burton, Col. Taylor, Albemarle Barracks. He d. March 7, 1834, & his widow, Sarah *Viah*, applied Jan. 21, 1843, aged 95; they were m. March 4, 1784. William Via, Floyd Co., Va., stated John *Via* was a pensioner. John Vier (or Via) m. Sarah Wright in Buckingham Co., 1784, & moved to Franklin Co. 40 or 50 years ago. Rev. Hawkins Landrum testified in Buckingham Co. that "he joined together John *Vyer* & Sarah Wright, 4th March, 1784."

VIA, WILLIAM,—Nelson Co., Va., Sept. 5, 1843, aged 92: enlisted under Jesse Allen of the Regular Army, Jan. or Feb., 1779, at Albemarle Barracks, having marched there in a militia company under Capt. Samuel Allen from Amherst Co.; served 21 mos. at Albemarle Barracks guarding British prisoners under Capts. Jesse Allen, John Woodroof & James Burton (of Orange Co.), Col. Taylor, until the prisoners were marched to Winchester for safer keeping, when he was discharged; 1781 served under Capt. William Tucker at York & Hampton, & later was at capture of Cornwallis, Oct., 1781.

It appears that there were two William Vias who served in the same regiment at Albemarle Barracks, & although the name of the above William Via is found on the Roll corresponding to his declaration, the claim was rejected on the presumption of fraud. He therefore produced the following additional testimony as to his services and his name was placed on the Pension Roll: Rev. Micajah Pendleton, Nelson Co., Va., aged 85, deposed Dec. 21, 1843, that he knew Samuel Arrington & William Via, of Nelson Co., who were both in the regular service in the Revolutionary War, under Capt. Jesse Allen, at Albemarle Barracks, in the year 1779 or 1780. That he, the said Micajah Pendleton, was in the militia service at the same time & place. Elijah Mays, same time & place, aged 80, deposed that he was in the militia at Albemarle Barracks; the regular troops & the militia were stationed separate & apart from each other, but the deponent frequently saw the said Via from time to time & conversed with him. The said Via may be said to be a tall man, say 5 feet 11 inches high, & is the only man by the name of William Via the deponent ever knew. Giles Davidson, aged 81, a Revolutionary pensioner, deposed he first became acquainted with William Via at Albemarle Barracks in Jan. or Feb., 1779; deponent enlisted from Buckingham Co., Va., in Capt. William Duiguid's Co.; John & Gideon Via were also in Capt. Jesse Allen's Co. at Albemarle Barracks. James Evans, Revolutionary pensioner, deposed that William Via was at the Barracks until fall of 1781 when the prisoners were marched to Winchester, Va., for safer keeping. William Via served 21 mos. in the regular army & 3 mos. in the militia. William Via d. in Nelson Co., Va., July 28, 1849, leaving no widow but children to wit: Rowland Via, Patsey Via & Elizabeth Cuningham. James Keith, Admr. of his estate, applied March 17, 1851, for pension for his heirs. Certificate of Pension was issued April 21, 1851, by Special Act of Congress.

VINES, THOMAS,—Rockbridge Co., Va., Nov. 6, 1832: b. Albemarle Co., 1756; drafted under Capt. John Loving 4 mos., Albemarle Barracks; 2nd tour under Capt. Azariah Martin, guarded prisoners taken in Carolina to Winchester; 3rd tour substituted for John Campbell, of Augusta, under Capt. Givings, Lt. William Robinson, Col. Huggart's Regt. This was when Tarleton plundered Charlottesville. Joined Gen. Lafayette's Army & was in battles of Hot Water & James Town. Tour under Capt. John Morrison of Amherst, Lt. Thomas Yores, Ensign James Bell. The company was to go south, Capt. Morrison having served there, but as Arnold was in Richmond, marched there, remaining 7 weeks. The enemy had gone after plundering, burning the rope-walks, etc.; discharged at Petersburg. Placed on Pension Roll May 14, 1833 & d. June 6, 1837. His widow, Mary Vines, applied, Augusta Co., April 28, 1846. M.L.B. Albemarle Co., Va.: "Thomas Vines & Mary Hill, aged 21, married by Rev. Allen Thomas, Oct. 20, 1795." She d. Dec. 24, 1862. Their son Nelson Vines applied March 27, 1876; William F. & Andrew Vines, sons of Nelson Vines, April 18, 1876, testified they were the only heirs of Nelson Vines, decd., & applied for a pension that may be due as grandchildren of Thomas Vines, a Revolutionary soldier.

WALKER, JEREMIAH,—Grainger Co., Tenn., Aug. 16, 1845, Mary Walker, aged 80, widow of Jeremiah Walker, a Revolutionary soldier who received a bounty warrant in Warren Co., Ky., for his services, applied. He also served in the War of 1812, & died from the effects of a wound received at River Raisin, a few days after the battle. They were m. in Pittsylvania Co., Va., 1787. "Ministers' return of marriages performed within the year: Jeremiah Walker

& Mary Mallicoat; Joseph Swensey & Ann Ditcher; John Kipee & Betsy Parsons; John Lawrence & Behethland Smith. Given under my hand this 10th day of September, 1788. Thomas Duglass, Minister of the Gospel."

"This is to certify that Jeremiah Walker enlisted under Clough Shelton, Lt., Dec. 2, 1776, for three years. He served that time and engaged for the war, served 3 months and furnished a substitute and was discharged by Nathan Gist. Given under my hand, Oct. 25, 1783. Samuel Hawes, Lt.-Col."

Jan. 26, 1849, Mary Walker appeared in Jackson Co., Ala., Court & asked to have her pension Cert. transferred to Jackson Co., Ala.

WALTON, TILMAN,—Burke Co., N. C., July 26, 1821, aged about 61: enlisted under Capt. James Franklin, Nov. 26, 1776, 10th Va. Regt. commanded by Col. Edward Stevens; while on march was transferred under command of Capt. Clough Shelton, Col. John Green's Regt. on Contl. Estabmt.; battles of Brandywine, Germantown, Monmouth & many skirmishes; discharged Dec. 6, 1779, in N. J. by Col. N. Gist, 2nd Va. Brig., after serving in capacity of private, Orderly Sergt., Lt. & Capt. He was a resident of Burke Co., March 18, 1818, & family residing with him were wife, aged 51, & two sons, 12 & 15. Judith Walton applied from same county March 10, 1843, & declared she was the widow of Tilman Walton who died Feb. 3, 1831. He received a pension of $96 per annum, commencing in the spring of 1822. They were m. in Cumberland Co., Va., April 12, 1787. She d. Aug. 31, 1846.

Family Record: Tilman Walton, son of William and Elizabeth Walton, was born January 9th, 1760. Judith Walton, dau. of Edward & Nancy Walton, was born February 19th, 1770. Tilman & Judith Walton were married April 12, 1787.

Children: Nancey Murrey Walton, b. Feb. 28, 1788, & m. James Askew, March 5, 1803; Elizabeth Tilman Walton, b. Feb. 15, 1790; William Orrell Walton, b. July 28, 1792; Judith Cox Walton, b. June 20, 1795; Edward Marshall Walton, b. March 20, 1798; Thomas Maddison Walton, b. Aug. 7, 1800, d. Sept. 21, 1801; Josias Wesley Walton, b. June 2, 1803, d. July 18, 1808; George Sidney Walton, b. Dec. 12, 1805, George Sidney Walton, b. Dec. 12, 1805 (so in record).

Jesse T. Walton, same place and date, aged 53, testified this is a true copy taken from the Bible of his parents, containing part of the names of the children.

WALTON, WILLIAM,—Green Co., Ala., Jan. 12, 1833, aged 68: spring of 1779, drafted by Capt. William Loving in the service

William Walton, son of William and Elizabeth Tillman Walton, born, Amherst Co., Va., Jan. 12, 1767; died Strawberry Hill, Green Co., Ala., May 18, 1844.
Courtesy of Miss Sara Elizabeth Mason of Gadsden, Alabama, great-great-granddaughter of William Walton.

of the State of Va. for purpose of packing wheat to Cabell's & Stevens' Mills to be ground into flour for the Army & corn & oats to a granary at Loving's Gap in Amherst. The part of the country where the grain was impressed is so mountainous that carriages could not be gotten to the farms; in this most disagreeable service I was compelled to continue 12 mos., finding my horse and fixtures, thinly clad in homespun furnished by my mother, one of the coldest winters almost ever known. In May, 1780, my father, William Walton, was drafted under Capt. John Loving to go to S. C. I vol., mounted a horse, armed with a small rifle, mustered into service at Amherst C. H., joined Major Franklin's Battalion at Lynch's Ferry on James River, & Col. Stevens' Regt. near Dan River, Gen. Gates' Army in S. C., & was in his defeat at Camden. Capt. Loving's Co. was left to return in any way they thought best for their own safety. My father & myself returned to Wilkes Co., N. C. Vol. Sept., 1780, with my father, under Capt. John Brown, Mounted Riflemen. We fell in with Ferguson's mounted British, routed them & took several Tories, among whom was William Mills, who Col. Cleveland & my uncle, Jesse Walton, hanged the next day. Marched to King's Mountain, joined the Regt. of Col. Campbell. Next morning an engagement took place, the Americans being commanded by Cols. Cleveland & Campbell & several other colonels, names not recollected, which resulted in the death of the British commander, Col. Ferguson, & many of his officers & men. The British killed & wounded was estimated at about 300; the Americans lost 30 or 40 killed & wounded. Between 700 & 800 British & Tories taken prisoners. The American forces, I believe, were between 1500 & 1600. Two or three days after the battle, 12 or 15 Tories, who had been notorious for killing many Whigs, were hung. The prisoners were marched off, I believe, to Charlottesville, Va.; March, 1781, vol. under Capt. William Cabell, Lt. Tilman Walton (my brother), mustered into service at Loving's Gap, marched to Charlottesville & under command of Baron Steuben marched to Point of Fork; driven from there by great loss of stores; some men killed, others wounded & some taken prisoners. Retreated to Albemarle old Court House. Joined the Army of Lafayette & marched to Richmond; soon afterwards to Williamsburg, joined the combined forces of the American Army under Gen. Washington & other distinguished officers, which resulted in the capture of Cornwallis on the last of Oct., 1781. Returned to my father's house in Amherst about the first of the year 1782. Served my country 2 years & 6 mos., found my own clothing & horse & never received One Dollar. Removed from Amherst, 1784. Gen. Samuel Dale testified he had known declarant for many years; they served in the Legislature of Alabama together. Placed on Pension Roll Jan. 16, 1833.

WARE, EDWARD,—Madison Co., Ga., Jan. 14, 1833: b. Amherst Co., Va., Oct. 18, 1760; vol. under Capt. James Higginbotham, Col. Fontaine's Regt., Aug., 1776 [1775], and served against Gov. Dunmore. Next tour, as Orderly Sergt. under Capt. Rucker, Col. Holt Richerson, Albemarle Barracks. Attached to the State Legion of Va., until after the capture of Cornwallis at York. The first tour in this service was 7 days under Capt. Samuel Higginbotham, guarding prisoners taken at King's Mountain; tour of 3 weeks as Sergt. scouting & endeavoring to retake some British prisoners who broke off from the Barracks at Charlottesville; next tour 6 weeks under Capt. Dillard, Col. Lynch's Regt. of Riflemen on Guilford Expedition & joined Gen. Greene. June, 2nd Lt. in Capt. John Loving's Co., Col. Holcombe's Regt., joined Gen. Lafayette's Army in King William Co. and marched to Williamsburg where Gen. Washington took command. He was in Gen. Lawson's Brig. at the Siege of York & surrender of Cornwallis. Removed to Elbert Co., Ga., 1791, in that part now Madison. Richard Bond, same place, testified he served with him on Guilford Expedition. Placed on Pension Roll July 30, 1833.

WARE, THOMAS,—Nelson Co., Va., Oct. 19, 1832: b. Amherst Co., Va., 1762 or '63; enlisted as private in Capt. Leak's Co., 1781, under Cols. Richardson & Lindsay, at Albemarle & marched to York; the French took Pigeon Hill on Sunday & he was called on to work in plain view of the enemy's breastworks for 4 days & nights. While there the enemy kept up a brisk cannonading with little injury—only one of our men being killed. After four days our army commenced a brisk cannonading & continued until the enemy was compelled to surrender, which they signified by hoisting a white flag; but their terms not being satisfactory to Gen. Washington, were rejected. Finally they offered acceptable terms, marched out & ground their arms. The day following we, with other militia troops, marched with prisoners to Nolan's Ferry on the Potomac River, where they were delivered to Maryland troops; 8 mos. service. He d. Dec. 26, 1851, & Mildred Ware, pensioner's widow, applied July 3, 1853; they were m. in Buckingham Co., Va., Oct. 15, 1787. M.L.B. Buckingham Co., Va.: "Thomas Ware & Milley Bryant, Oct. 8, 1787. Security, Randolph Jefferson." James Lyon, Nelson Co., March 3, 1854, aged 74, testified "he went to school with some of her children to a Mr. Holman Jopling, Thomas Ware & wife, Milley, raised 14 children." Mrs. Elizabeth Pugh is the eldest, John Thomas, Martha, Nancey, Malinda, Mildred, William, Edward, Peyton, Polly, Virginia, Almira & Robert. Her claim was allowed.

WATERS, MOSES,—Rutherford Co., N. C., Dec. 10, 1832: b. King William Co., Va., 1761; living in Amherst Co., Va., 1777, when he vol. in Capt. Warwick's Co., marched to Fort Warwick & placed under command of Lt. James Humfries, Col. Samuel Vance's Regt. 1779 vol. under Capt. David Crawford to go to Kentucky against the Indians & marched to Lexington, Ky. After his term of enlistment expired, vol. under Capt. Isaac Riddle to go to Licking Station where we were attacked by the British & kept the Fort after considerable struggle, several of the British were killed. On these two tours 9 mos. On returning home immediately numbered & placed on the Muster Roll at the time Tarleton marched his Army up the country & broke up the General Assembly that was sitting at Charlottesville in the State of Virginia. Marched under Capt. William Tucker to Richmond, Williamsburg & to Yorktown, placed under Gen. Weedon & ordered back to the Half Way House. That night the British landed a strong force at Yorktown. In the morning we were ordered back & followed them to Portsmouth. In the chase there was a skirmish in which Col. Mallory was killed; we took several prisoners. After the Revolution moved to Union District, S. C., then to Rutherford Co., N. C. Claim allowed.

WATKINS, SPENCER,—Jefferson Co., Tenn., Nov. 2, 1833: b. Albemarle Co., Jan. 15, 1750, in that part now Amherst Co., Va.; entered service Oct., 1779, under Capt. Young Landrum, Lawson's Brig.; later attached to Col. Holcombe's Regt. under Capt. Patterson. Feb., 1781, under Capt. Jack Woodroof, Lts. William & John Horsley, Ensign Robert Horsley, Major William Cabell, Col. John Meriwether. Four companies marched from Amherst, commanded by Capts. Woodruf, Pamplin, Diggs & Montgomery by way of Richmond to Bacon's Old Field, where they joined Gen. Stevens. In March, 1781, under Capt. Lewis Neville, Albemarle Barracks, & in Aug., 1781, 2 weeks under Nathaniel Dever. He moved to Tenn. in 1827 & d. in Jefferson Co. Sept. 28, 1849. Pensioner's widow, Sarah Watkins, applied same place, June 5, 1850, aged 76. They were m. Jan. 10, 1798 by William Flowery a Baptist Minister, at the home of her brother-in-law, Isaac Staples, in the presence of Jane & Ewell Staples, in Buckingham Co., Va. Ewell Staples d. in Jefferson Co., Tenn., about 2 years ago. Her claim was allowed.

WEBSTER, JOHN,—Rockingham Co., N. C., August 20, 1832, aged 73: enlisted 1776, for 3 years under Capt. Spotswood Dandridge, Lt. William Penn, Ensign Lindsey, Col. Theodorick Bland's 1st Va. Regt. Light Dragoons. At the same time 14 men enlisted in Amherst Co., among them: Richard Pendleton, William McDaniel, John Holeman (both d. with smallpox & were buried in same grave), Frederick Davies (d. at Little York) & William Tucker. Our company was organized at Fredericksburg, Va., marched to Williamsburg thence to Little York where we remained about 2 mos., marched to Baltimore thence to Philadelphia then to head Quarters at Morristown, N. J. In battles of Brandywine, Monmouth & White Plains. The winter the British lay in Philadelphia he was under command of Gen. Pulaski. We went into winter

Quarters at Trenton & was with Gen. Wayne at Paoli Tavern[80] when we were betrayed by one of our men & the Tavern Keeper who deserted & gave the British notice of our situation. We were surrounded by the British before we knew it & near 60 men were killed. Gen. Wayne by a stratagem made his escape. Discharged at Winchester, Va., which discharge was burned several years ago with his dwelling house. Mary Ray, widow of George Ray, Stokes Co., Tenn., Dec. 27, 1834, aged 80, deposed her brother John Webster, late of Rockingham Co., N. C., served as a private soldier in the cavalry & after 2 years returned to his home in Amherst Co., Va. John Crittenden, Stokes Co., N. C., Jan. 18, 1835, aged 70, testified that in his infancy his parents lived in Amherst Co., Va. neighbor to Richd. Webster, father of John Webster, decd., late of Rockingham Co., N. C., & he was well acquainted with John Webster when he enlisted in the Cavalry of the United States in Amherst Co. with Wm. Cook, David London, Richard Pendleton, Wm. McDaniel & others, & some of them never returned. John Webster returned home & with his family migrated to Guilford Co., N. C. a part of which is now Rockingham Co. & married Margaret Walker. Deponent moved from Va. to N. C. about the same time as Webster. Pleasant Webster, Rockingham Co., N. C., March 1, 1854, aged 62, son of John Webster, who d. July 31, 1833, & Admr. of the Estate of his mother, Maggie Webster, who d. March 15, 1842, applied for a pension for the heirs. The following children were living at the death of his mother: Polly, wife of William Hickman; Betsy, wife of James Carter; Sally Glenn; Richard, James, Pleasant, Joseph, Abner & Benjamin Webster; Rebecca Foy. His parents were m. in Amherst Co., Va., about 1779. His father made application under Act of July 7, 1832 for his services as a private in the Va. Cavalry & was suspended because the declaration was not satisfactory to the War Dept. He often heard his father speak of his service. At the battle of Brandywine a half-spent cannon ball struck during the cannonading, an officer of his company within 80 yards of the British Line. His father immediately dismounted raised the wounded soldier to his horse & escaped with him, amid showers of bullets from the enemy & shouts of applause from his countrymen. Judith Neal, same place, testified she lived near John Webster from his early manhood to his death. She often heard Theodrick Carter,

---

[80]*The Paoli* was one of the famous taverns on the old Lancaster turnpike" eight miles from West Chester, Pa., and about a mile and a half south from Gen. Anthony Wayne's residence. "One hundred and fifty Americans were killed and wounded in this onslaught, some of whom, it is said, were cruelly butchered after ceasing to resist, and while begging for quarter; and but for the coolness and skill of Wayne, his whole command must have been killed or taken prisoners. He promptly rallied a few companies, ordered Col. Hampton to wheel the line, and with the cavalry and a portion of the infantry, he gallantly covered a successful retreat." Lossing's *Pictorial Field-Book of the Revolution*, II, 369.

a Revolutionary soldier, say they were soldiers together & John Webster was a daring one.

WEBSTER, WILLIAM,—Washington Co., Ky., Aug. 28, 1833: b. Amherst Co., Va., 1764; Aug. 1, 1780, private under Capt. Ambrose Rucker; 3 mos. 1780 under Capt. William Tucker, Lt. Joseph Tucker & Sergt. William Stewart. His term expired at Hampton, Va., but at solicitation of his captain remained in service 1 mo. & 29 days more. After the Revolution moved to N. C. & 1788 or 1790 to Washington Co., Ky. His claim was allowed.

WELCH, JOSEPH,—Marion Co., Ky., Nov. 13, 1840, Susannah Welch, aged 77, widow of Joseph Welch who d. Feb. 27, 1825, applied. He enlisted 1776, in Capt. Samuel Cabell's Co. Elizabeth Welch stated her father belonged to Morgan's Rifle Corps. She remembers seeing the discharge given by Capt. Samuel Jordan Cabell for five years service. The following Bible record is in the handwriting of John Garland, a schoolmate of her father. After the record "Henry Harper was born March 3, 1783" begins the record of her parents' children:

Elizabeth Welch, b. June 25, 1787
Sherred Welch, b. Nov. 25, 1788
John Welch, b. Feb. 25, 179--
Susannah Welch, b. May 25, 1792
Margaret Welch, b. Jan. 19, 1795
Francis Welch, b. Aug. 29, 1797
Joseph Welch, b. Nov. 7, 1799

M.L.B. Amherst Co., Va.: "Joseph Welch, bachelor & Susannah Harper, widow, Dec. 15, 1785." Ezra Morrison, Lincoln Co., Ky., Nov. 20, 1840, testified he was well acquainted with Joseph Welch, a soldier in the Revolution from Amherst Co., Va., who enlisted in Capt. Samuel Cabell's Co., 6th Va. Regt. Deponent was at that time in a company commanded by Capt. Fontaine of the 2nd Va. Regt. In the fall of 1776, the Regt. lay at Springfield, & the Regt. Joseph Welch belonged to lay about 3 miles off at what was called College Camp, before they marched to the North. At this time deponent's time expired, & a short time after Joseph Welch marched North, he joined a regiment that marched to the South, where he was in service 3 years & did not see said Welch any more until he returned from the South. Joseph Welch removed to Lincoln Co., Ky., in 1789, & deponent moved to same place in 1790, & settled within half a mile of said Joseph Welch, who, after 30 years, moved with his family to Washington, now Marion Co., Ky., where he died. Deponent is a pensioner on the General Government for services rendered in the Revolutionary War. Her claim was allowed.

WEST, BRANSFORD,—Nelson Co., Va., Nov. 28, 1832: b. Chesterfield Co., Va., Aug. 26, 1754; enlisted 1775, under Capt.

Nicholas Cabell, Lt. James Pamplin, Ensign William Spencer. Called into service June 14, 1776, marched to Jamestown where Col. Edward Carrington was in command. While there the 6th Regt. U. S. Infty. arrived enroute to S. C., but the orders were countermanded. Vol. 1777, under Capt. Joseph Cabell, Lt. Nicholas Cabell, and marched with another company commanded by James Higginbotham to Manchester, thence to Richmond & Williamsburg; discharged after 2 mos. service. 3rd tour, drafted under Capt. James Barnett, Lt. Tilman Walton, marched to Richmond where he was made Sergt. Five captains with their companies were there from Amherst: Capt. Samuel Higginbotham & Capt. William Harris—he does not recollect the names of the others or of the field officers. 4th tour, Capt. James Barnett; 5th tour, 1781, drafted as Sergt. under Capt. Richard Taliaferro, Col. Meriwether, Major Hardeman, Brig.-Gen. Stevens. Hezekiah Hargrove testified Nelson Co., Sept. 24, 1832, he was on a tour under Capt. Nicholas Cabell to Jamestown with Bransford West. Joseph Mathews declared he served two tours with him, one under Capt. Nicholas Cabell, the other under Capt. Joseph Cabell. He d. Jan. 27, 1843, and Nancy West, pensioner's widow, applied from same place, Nov. 3, 1844, aged 80, stating they were married in 1792. Claim was allowed.

WILLIAMS, JOHN,—Buckingham Co., Va., Aug. 7, 1832, aged 81: marched from Amherst on Guilford Expedition under Capt. Landrum; next tour, under Capt. James Dillard. Born in Amherst where he resided until 3 years ago, when he moved to his present residence. The following neighbors in Buckingham testified to his character: A. Plunkett,[81] William P. Wright, Valentine Faris, Samuel Barton, W. B. Bell, Willis H. Plunkett, Thomas Day, Alford Hawkins, Leonard Wright, Edwin Lucas, James W. Crews & Taliaferro Plunkett. Claim was allowed.

WITT, ELISHA,—Estill Co., Ky.: b. Sept. 18, 1759, in Albemarle Co., Va. Enlisted in Amherst Co., Va., and served in Va. troops under Capts. Richard Ballenger, John Jacobs, John Biggs & William Harris, & Cols. Hugh Rose, Francis Taylor & John Pope. He was at the Siege of Yorktown & Surrender of Cornwallis. He m. July 17, 1781, Phebe Dodd. He d. Dec. 6, 1835, in Estill Co.,

---

[81]Ambrose Plunkett, b. Feb. 21, 1782; d. Buckingham Co., c. 1844; m. Jan. 13, 1801, Tabitha (b. Oct. 28, 1781) dau. of James & Ann Hill of Amherst. He was the son of Benjamin Plunkett (Ensign in Caroline Co., Va., Militia 1782) & his first wife, Winifred Rucker, dau. of Col. Ambrose Rucker (c. 1725-Dec. 21, 1807), & grandson of John Plunkett (d. 1758) of Orange Co. & his wife Mildred, & great-grandson of John Plunkett of King George Co., Va. (Loose papers 1755-1759, Orange Co., Va.). Willis H. & Taliaferro Plunkett were sons of Ambrose Plunkett. (Family Bible in possession of Adolphus Plunkett, Lynchburg, Va., in 1932.)

Ky. His children were William, Anne, Charles, Abner, Elisha, Nathan, Rachel, David, John & Silas. Placed on Pension Roll Jan. 16, 1833.

WOOD, WILLIAM,—Sumner Co., Tenn., Sept. 7, 1846, aged 83 years & 6 mos.: b. Amherst Co., Va.; entered service Aug., 1780, under Capt. James Gresham, Col. William Gaines, Va. State Troops, joined Gen. Morgan, Spartansburg, S. C., and was in the battle of the Cowpens, Jan. 17, 1781. Afterwards enlisted for during the war. Battle of Guilford, March 15, 1781, Siege of York & guard to prisoners taken there; discharged spring of 1782, which discharge was lost 50 years ago when his home in S. C. was destroyed by fire. Gave the following as references to his character & services: Col. William Martin, an old officer during the Creek & other Indian Wars; Major David Burford, David Hogg, Coleman Cornwell, Esq., Col. Overton & Judge Abraham Carathers. Rev. John Hill, aged 87, testified he was in the battle of Guilford where William Wood was wounded in the shoulder; they continued together until the Surrender of York. Claim was allowed.

WOODRUFF, HARDEN,—Buckingham Co., Va., May 17, 1833: Enlisted 1777 in Amherst Co. under Capt. Jesse Allen, Col. Francis Taylor's Regt. Married Oct. 11, 1784, Buckingham Co., Sally, dau. of Thomas Gunter. Claim was allowed.

WRIGHT, ANDREW,—Nelson Co., Va., May 31, 1844, Lucy Wright, aged 84, widow of Andrew Wright who d. Nov. 25, 1816, applied. He served in the Revolution 1779, as a waggoner hauling corn, wheat, flour & other produce to the Barracks; enlisted Oct., 1780, under Capt. John Christian, with his brother, Joseph Wright, Benj. Childress, Alexander McAlexander, & returned home at Christmas. Enlisted 1781, under Capt. James Pamplin, & was in battle of Jamestown. They were married in Charlottesville by Rev. Clay, of the Church of England, in a room full of British officers taken with Burgoyne; the license was obtained in Amherst. May 30, 1844, Benj. Childress, Albemarle Co., aged 81, testified the waggon Andrew Wright drove belonged to Robin Wright, a man of family, who usually drove his own waggon. Robin's waggon had been pressed into public service by the Quarter Master, who had bought up corn & wheat in Amherst to be taken to the mill to be ground & then hauled to the Barracks for the troops. Samuel Childress, aged 79, stated that Andrew Wright & his sister Lucy Childress were married 1779. His brother, Benjamin Childress, served a tour with Andrew & Joseph Wright & Alexander McAlexander. Her claim was allowed. Benjamin Wright, Nelson Co., May 30, 1844, testified the following family record were leaves taken from his parents' Bible. The marriage of Lucy, March 11, 1777, should read married to wife, Sarah S., who died at the birth of her dau. Sarah, Feb. 25, 1778, & his father married his second wife 12 months later.

 Andrew Wright, b. Dec. 25, 1748; Lucy, his wife, b. May 15, 1759

 Andrew Wright and Lucy, his wife, were married March 11, 1777

 Daughter, Sarah S. Wright, b. Feb. 25, 1778; m. Nov. 27, 1801

   Children of Andrew & Lucy Wright:

Jeaney Wright, b. Jan. 9, 1780,
   d. Feb. 16, 1780
Anney or Anna, b. March 8, 1782
Benjamin, b. June 2, 1783, m. Dec. 29, 1803, Jean ———, b. Aug. 18, '89
Esther Montgomery, b. July 30, 1785, m. March 26, 1830
Lucy, b. May 15, 1788, m. Jan. 31, 1811
Polley Wright, b. July 19, 1790
Betsey, b. March 6, 1793, m. July 9, 18 (blurred)
Matilda, b. Nov. 22, 1795, m. Jan. 9, 1817
Melinda, b. Oct. 26, 1798, m. Aug. 31, 1820
Peggy J., b. May 30, 1801

    Grandchildren:

Mehala Freeman, b. Aug. 18, 1799
Rebecca Freeman, b. May 25, 1802
Thomas Freeman, b. March 16, 1806
Polley S. Bowling, b. April 30, 1802
John W. Bowling, b. March 5, 1804
Salley Bowling, b. May 6, 1807
Robert M. Wright, b. July 4, 1817
James Wright, b. May 8, 1817
Andrew Washington, son of Benjamin & Jean Wright, b. Oct. 20, 1805
John B. Wright, b. Jan. 16, 1808; living in Nelson Co., Va., 1848
Elizabeth Jane Bennett Fortune, dau. of Thomas & Elizabeth Fortune, b. Sept. 12, 1813,
   d. Oct. 11, 1813
William M. Wright, b. Oct. 7, 1810,
   d. Jan. 30, 1811
Sarah J. Wright, b. Dec. 23, 1811
David H. Wright, b. May 24, 1814,
   d. Feb. 8, 1817
Lucy C. Wright, b. Oct. 20, 1816
Elonder Wright, b. Dec. 26, 1820
William H. Wright, b. Feb. 21, 1817

Lucy Wright d. Sept. 17, 1847, and May 18, 1850, Benjamin Wright, Nelson Co., applied for a pension for the heirs: Benjamin, Anna, Esther M. & Polley Wright; Lucy Kidd; Elizabeth Fortune; Matilda Woody; Melinda Griffith; Peggey Kidd.

WRIGHT, GEORGE,—Oldham Co., Ky., Dec. 4, 1833: b. Amherst Co., Va., 1763; served two tours, 1779-80, as private under Capt. Banks, Albemarle Barracks; Dec., 1780, under Capt. Richard Ballinger, Lt. Pollard, 3 mos. service; drafted 1781, Col. Meriwether, Gen. Lawson's Brig., & joined Gen. Lafayette near Williamsburg; while there saw Col. Cabell, Militia officer. Placed on Pension Roll, Feb. 4, 1834.

WRIGHT, MOSES,—Amherst Co., Va., Aug. 26, 1843, Elizabeth Wright, aged 84, widow of Moses Wright, who d. March, 1830, applied. He served under Capt. Samuel Cabell at Albemarle Barracks, fellow soldiers Benj. Camden, Jno. Campbell & Jas. Ramsey; served another tour with Jimmy Thompson. She was m. to Moses Wright 1775 & had 3 children: Benjamin, Nancy & Matilda during the War. Mrs. John Maddox, aged 67, remembers hearing a conversation between John Campbell, Moses Wright, William Campbell, & Edward & John Demasters about their Revolutionary service. Mrs. Sally Campbell, widow of Henry Campbell, Nelson Co., stated Moses Wright married Elizabeth Whitehead during the Revolution. William Thompson, aged 68, testified Moses Wright, Benj. Camden, John Campbell, James Ramsey & James Bonlief were fellow soldiers of his brother, Jimmy Thompson. Claim was allowed.

Soldiers of French and Indian War

Service proved in Amherst County Court in order to obtain bounty land allowed by proclamation of the King of Great Britain of 1763.

Order Book 1773-1782

Name of Soldier	Officers under whom service was performed	Year in which service was performed	
Richard Bailey	Col. William Byrd	1760	p. 404
Linn Banks (Serjt.)*	Col. William Byrd	1759-60	p. 397
Levy Baldock	Col. William Byrd	not stated	p. 396
Richard Baldock (Serjt.) (Levy Baldock heir-at-law)	Col. Stephen	not stated	p. 396
Henry Dawson	Col. William Byrd	1760	p. 404
James Fitzjarrel (Serjt.)	Col. William Byrd	1759-60	p. 398
William Forbus	Cols. Washington & Byrd	not stated	p. 397
Samuel Miller	Col. William Byrd	not stated	p. 397
Joseph Newman	Gen. Braddock	1755	p. 407
Gabriel Penn (Serjt.) (was granted 200 acres of land)	not stated	not stated	p. 389
Daniel Ryalty°	Cols. Washington & Byrd	not stated	p. 394
John Sale (Serjt. Major)	Col. Byrd, 1st Va. Regt.	1760	p. 381
John Stratton	Col. William Byrd	1760	p. 403
James Thompson	Gen. Forbes	1758	p. 404
William Thompson	Col. Washington	1757	p. 405
Thomas Upton	Col. William Byrd	1760	p. 403
Francis West	Col. William Byrd	1760	p. 403
James Wills†	Col. William Byrd	1760	p. 404

---

*Served as a soldier in 1759 and as a sergeant in 1760.
°Served five years.

†"Know ye that by virtue and in consideration of a Military Warrant under the proclamation of the King of Great Britain of 1763 No. 1089 and in consideration of a Land Treasury Warrant No. 5185 both issued the 31st day of May, 1783, there is granted by Edmund Randolph, Esq. Governor of the Commonwealth of Virginia unto James Wills a certain tract or parcel of land containing 150 acres by Survey bearing date 25th April 1785 lying and being in the County of Amherst on the North Branches of the South fork of Rucker's Run and bounded as follows, To Wit, Beginning at pointers in his own line thence etc. to the corner of James Thompson," etc. Dated February 7, 1787. (Virginia State Library, Archives Division, Land Office Grants 8, 1786-1787, p. 404).

Officers of Amherst Militia Before the Revolution

Court held June 2, 1766

Richard Shelton, Captain
Ambrose Rucker, Lieutenant
Thomas Montgomery, Ensign   Page 4

Court held September 1, 1766

George Seaton, Quarter Master   Page 71

Court held June 5, 1769

James Nevil, Esq., Colonel
George Stoval Jr., Esq., Lieut. Colonel
James Higginbotham, Esq., Major*   Page 498

Court held July 3, 1769

John Higginbotham, Captain
Gabriel Penn, Lieutenant
George Penn, Ensign   Page 503

Court held August 7, 1769

Aaron Higginbotham, Captain
Charles Tuley, Captain
Nathaniel Davis, Lieutenant
Samuel Higginbotham, Lieutenant   Page 519

The following is the form that was used in entering all these commissions as entered on the Order Book 1766-69:

"At a Court held for Amherst County at the Courthouse the seventh day of August 1769, and in the ninth Year of the Reign of our Sovereign Lord George the third now King of Great Britain etc.

---

*Captain in the French and Indian War. *The Pennsylvania Gazette*, of Dec. 8, 1763, contains an interesting letter from Capt. William Christian, dated "Roanoke, October 19, 1763," describing an affair with the Indians which took place Oct. 12th, from which we extract the following: "Being joined by Captain Hickenbotham, with 25 of the Amherst militia, we marched on Tuesday last to Winston's Meadows, where our scouts informed us, that they had discovered a party of Indians about three miles off. Night coming on, prevented our meeting them; and next day, being rainy, made it difficult to follow their tracks. As they were on their return, Captain Hickenbotham marched to join Captain Ingles down New River, etc." *William and Mary Quarterly*, XXVI, No. 3, 210; Withers's *Chronicles of Border Warfare* (1917), p. 99.

Before his Majesty's Justices, to-wit

| James Nevil | James Dillard | Gentlemen |
| John Rose | Henry Rose | |

Aaron Higginbotham produced his Commission to be a Captain, Charles Tuley produced his commission to be a Captain, and Nathaniel Davis and Samuel Higginbotham produced their Commissions to be Lieutenants of the Militia of this County who severally took the usual Oaths to his Majesty's person & Government, and the abjuration Oath, & Repeated & Subscribed the abjuration Oath & Test."

Page 519

Appendix

THE WILL OF SARAH HENRY

Will Book 2, page 229

In the name of God, Amen.

I Sarah Henry of Amherst County Widow of Sound sense and Perfect Memory—do—hereby make and ordain this my Last Will and Testament, in manner and form Following

I give to my son John Syme a Mourning Ring

I give to my son William Henry a Mourning Ring

I give to my son Patrick Henry a Mourning Ring

Item I give to my son Patrick Henrys daughter—Elizabeth Henry my negro man Reuben who is in the Possession of my Son in Law William Russell and my daughter Elizabeth Russell But it is my Desire that the negroe man Reuben may chuse at my decease whether he will belong to the said Elizabeth Henry or be sold to my Son in Law William Russell—if he chuses to be sold Then I desire my Executors may sett a price on him and that Price paid to the above said Elizabeth Henry

Item I give to my Son in Law Samuel Merediths daughter Jane Henry Meredith my negro Boy Simon

Item I give to my daughter Lucy Wood—a Mourning Ring

Item I give to my daughter Annie Christian a Mourning Ring—and to her daughter—Sarah Winston Christian I give my negro Boy Charles

Item I give to my daughter Susanna Madison my negro woman Fanny and I give to Her son John Henry Madison my negro Girl Cloe

Item I give to my daughter Susanna Madison a Mourning Ring—and I give to her daughter Sarah Madison £20 Current Money

Item I Lend to my daughter Elizabeth Russell The following Negroes—Simon and Aggy—Kiah and Delphia—and James Allen—dureing her naturall Life—and—at the decease—of my daughter—Elizabeth Russell the aforesaid negroes—except James Allen—to be equally divided between Every surviving Child of my daughter Elizabeth Russell—and James Allen to Descend to my Grandson Charles Henry Campbell

If my daughter Elizabeth Russell should decease without Children or Grand Children Or such Children or Grandchildren should die without Lawful Issue to Possess and Enjoy the aforesaid Gifts —In such a Case I Desire that the aforesaid negroes may be Equally divided among my Surviving daughters—

In Case Debts should arise against the Estate of my Deceased Husband John Henry that may Cause the aforesaid negroes to be

Sold, then it is my desire that my Children pay, Proportionably according to the number and Worth of the Mortgaged negroes in their Possession—and I Desire, that Simon and Aggy and Kiah may Chuse their Master and Mistress among my Children—their prices to be Sett by my Executors, hereafter named,—and their Value to go in my Estate Towards paying the debts and Legacies,—and all the Residue of my Estate I give to my daughter Elizabeth Russell and Her Children—as above—

Item I give to my Grandson Charles Henry Campbell and my Grand Daughter Sarah Buchanan Campbell Eight Thousand pounds of Tobacco—out of that I am to Reserve of Peter Rippeto for a Tract of Land which I sold the Said Rippeto Lying in this County—which Tobo when Received by my Exors. to be sold by them for money and Put out to Interest till my said Grandson and Granddaughter arrive to Lawful age or marry—at which Time each one of them shall be entitled to an Equall Part—in case either of them should die before they are of age or have Lawfull Issue—in such case it is my desire the survivor may have the whole of the money with the interest arising thereon—But in case Both of these my Grand Children should Decease before they are of age, or have Lawfull Issue, in such case it is my desire that the above mentioned Money should be Equally divided among my surviving sons and daughters—each one an equal part—

The Remainder of the Tobo arising from the Sale of the aforesaid Land sold to Rippeto I give to my Son in Law Samuel Meredith—on his paying John Lankester his Charges and for his improvements which he made on that Land, also the Expenses of Surveying the Land, after Lankester went to Live on it

I desire that my Wearing Apparrell may be divided among my daughters

and Lastly I appoint my Son in Law Samuell Meredith and my son Patrick Henry and my Son in Law William Christian and my son in Law Thomas Madison and my worthy friend Edmund Winston Executors of this my Last Will and Testament—and in Case of any Disputes—or misunderstandings should arise about my aforesaid Will—Then I appoint and desire my above mentioned Executors or any Three of them Shall Decide and Determine all such Disputes and misunderstandings—that may arise among my Legatees—That no Law Sutes shall be Commenced about My Will—

This 12th day of March 1784 I Sett my Hand and Seal

            Sarah Henry (seal)

acknowledged in presence of

 James Franklin
 James Higginbotham
 Jos. Barnett

At a Court held for Amherst County the Second Day of May 1785 This Last Will & Testament of Sarah Henry Deceased was this Day presented in Court by Edmond Winston one of the Executors therein Named & proved by the Oaths of James Franklin & Joseph Barnett two of the witnesses thereto whereupon the said Executor with Saml Meredith his Surety Entered into & acknowledged Bond in the penalty of Two Thousand Pounds Took the Oath Required by Law and Ordered to be Recorded

       Test Edm'd. Wilcox Clk.

INDEX

Aaron, Rebecca (Rudd), 94; William, 26, 94, 163
Abbott, Patsey, 130
Adams, Francis, 160
Adcock, John, 18, 20, 22, 23
Akin, David, 29, 30
Akins, Thomas, 26
Alexander, Lt. James, 52; Joseph, 113
Alford, John, 94; Mary, 49; Mary Clark, 149; Thomas, 49, William, 69
Alfred, Mrs. Susannah, 94, 95; Thomas, 15, 19, 94, 95
Ali, Hyder, 66
Allcock, Lt. Richard, 32, 33, 34
Allen, Andrew Jackson, 95; Barbara L., 95; Dolly, 95, 96; Elizabeth M., 95; Erasmus, 69; George W., 95; James M., 95; Capt. Jesse, 5, 97, 105, 112, 149, 176, 177, 185; Jesse J., 95; John, 96; Landon C., 95; Sally B., 95; Capt. Samuel, 69, 81, 162, 163, 176; William, 69, 95; William H., 95
Amminet (Amonnet, Ominate, Omminate), John, 26, 27, 28, 30, 96
Anderson, Col., 144; James, 69; Rev. Lewis Allen, 148; Samuel, 80
Anflay, William, 20
Arbuckle, Capt. Matthew, 147, 160, 161, 162, 165
Armistead, Mr., 67
Armstrong, Gen., 101
Arnold, Gen. Benedict, 124, 132, 134, 150, 164, 177; Benjamin, 96; Hendrick, 69, 76, 89, 92, 97, 148; Mary Ann, 96
Arrington, Samuel, 58, 95, 97, 176
Arter, John, 100
Arthur, Stephen, 114; Thomas, 114
Asburey, William, 55
Ashley, Charles, 76, 82
Askew, James, 178
Ayres, Sgt. Henry, 100; Nathan, 72; Sgt. Samuel, 9, 14, 17, 19, 21, 23, 69; Thomas, 9

Bailey, Ezekiah, 69; Rev. John, 116; Jonathan, 98; Josephus, 16; Philip, 97; Richard, 188; Thomas, 60; William, 26, 97, 98; Wyatt, 98
Baldock, Levy (Levi), 88, 98, 188; Richard, 98; Sgt. Richard, 188
Balew, Capt. Thomas, 96

Ballard, Cpl. William, 58
Ballenger (Ballinger), Lt. Henry, 113; Joseph, 93; Rev. Joseph, 119; Capt. Richard, 31, 32, 36, 69, 76, 84, 85, 93, 103, 107, 117, 125, 128, 130, 131, 136, 142, 145, 148, 150, 153, 154, 162, 164, 165, 172, 184, 187
Ballew (Ballou, Bellew), Lt. David, 108, 112; John, 149; Joseph, 149; Lucy, 149; Tabitha, 93
Banks, Capt., 187; Almirium, 99; Ann (Stanton), 50; Daniel P., 98; Elizabeth, 98 (2); Emily A., 98; Emily A., Jr., 99; Frances, 98; Gerrard, 50; John Smith, 99; Joseph R., 99; Sgt. Linn, 69, 81, 86, 188; Louisa, 99; Mary, 50, 98; Nancy, 98; Cpl. Reubin, 55; Wesley J., 98, 99; Lt. William, 33, 35, 36; Sgt. William, 98; William S., 98
Barbee, Sgt. Daniel, 100
Barnes, Ann, 87; John, 87
Barnett, David, 16, 166; Capt. James, 9, 94, 99, 100, 116, 132, 142, 151, 153, 154, 155, 156, 158, 162, 164, 167, 169, 184; James, Jr., 69; James P., 100; John, 58; Capt. John, 38, 69, 81, 88, 91, 100, 112; Joseph, 82, 192, 193; Marcey, 100; Nathaniel, 72; Robert, 69, 82; Capt. Robert, 100; Col. William, 107; Ens. William, 33, 69, 89, 107, 153
Barrett, Capt., 126
Barron, Capt. James, 77; Capt. Richard, 77
Barton, Samuel, 184
Bartor, Samuel, 100
Baskerville, Lt. Samuel, 28, 29
Battles, Noel, 26, 27, 28, 30, 126; Shadrack, 26, 27, 29, 30
Baylor, Col., 126, 150
Bayly, James, 154
Bean, Johnson, 69, 88; Richard, 60, 100, 101
Beard, Archibald (Archer), 21, 22, 23
Beaton, Neil, 77
Beck, Jesse, 171; Judith, 171
Beckham, William, 26, 27, 28, 30
Becknall (Becknal, Becknel), Elizabeth, 92; James, 15, 92; John, 92; Thomas, 15, 18, 20, 92 (2)
Bell, Capt. Henry, 69, 75, 78; Ens. James, 73, 177; John, 15, 17, 20;

Index

Lt. Samuel, 15, 17, 19, 21, 23, 52, 163; Thomas, 69; W. B., 184
Berry, Rev. B., 156
Bethell, John, 69
Bibb, James, 136, 142; John, 69; Capt. Richard, 129; Sarah, 69; Lt. William, 31, 32, 52, 69, 84, 86
Bibee (Bibe), Thomas, 58, 101
Bibey, Edward, 52
Biddle, Bee, 71
Biggs, Capt. John, 184; John, Jr., 63; Mary, 63, 64
Black, James M., 168; Rebecca, 168
Blackwell, Lt. Joseph, 28, 29
Blaine (Blain), George, 69, 82, 88, 101; Rachel, 101
Blair, Allen, 102; Lt. James, 125; John S., 102; Mary Ann (Staples), 102; Susannah, 125
Blakey, George, 18, 20, 22, 23, 125; William, 18, 20, 22, 23
Bland, Col. Theodorick, 159, 181
Bloom, Sarah, 160
Bolling, James, 77
Bond, Elizabeth, 102; Frances, 102; George (Bonds), 26, 27, 28, 30; Joseph, 112; Lindsey, 102; Nathan, 69, 102; Permele, 102; Sgt. Richard, 102, 180; Richard, Jr., 102; Sophia, 102; Susannah, 102
Bonlief, James, 187
Booker, Capt., 160; Capt. Samuel, 120
Booth (Boothe), Elizabeth, 86; Judith, 86; Nathaniel, 86; William, 86
Boulware, William, 52
Bowers, Dr., 166
Bowles, David, 17; William Knight, 69, 115
Bowling, Sgt. Edward, 102, 103; James, Sr., 103; John W., 186; Letty M., 103; Polley S., 186; Robert, 69; Salley, 186
Bowman, Barsheba (Hooper), 104; Drury, 72; John, 26, 27, 29, 30, 52, 103, 148, 149; Lewis, 104; Rebecca, 149; Sally, 104; William, 52, 54, 69, 102
Bowyer, Capt. George, 150
Boyer, Col., 134
Bracey, William, 91
Braddock, Gen., 188
Bradford, Will, Jr., 26
Brandford, John, 145
Bransford, James, 103
Branwood, John, 29, 30
Briant, Archer, 18; John, 58; Sgt. John, 58, 105, 106; Zachariah, 58, 105, 106

Briggs, Benjamin, 155; Martha W., 175
Bristoe (Bristow), Benjamin, 18, 20
Broadhead, Col., 115, 168
Broadway, William, 145
Brooks, James, 69, 89; John, 56; Robert, 69; William, 15, 18, 20, 22, 23, 69
Brown, Mr., 168; Rev., 109; Adam, 63, 69; Alexander, 7, 48; Anderson, 104; Elizabeth, 98; George, 104; Capt. Jacob, 83, 88, 101, 120; James, 18, 21, 22, 23; Johannah, 174; John, 49, 52, 60, 69; Capt. John, 179; Sgt. John, 51, 104; Joshua, 104; Leonard, 110; Lucinda, 104; Matilda, 105; Maurice, 104; Meredith, 105; Mordecai, 49, 73, 74; Nancy, 104; Nancy (Glenn), 104; Randolph, 25; Robert, 25, 57; Sally, 110; Stark, 15, 18, 20, 22, 23, 105; Sydney Scott, 104; Tabitha, 105; Terresa, 110; Thomas W., 174; Tutt, 110; William, 26, 105, 162
Brummit (Brummitt), Thomas, 26, 27, 29, 30; William, 26
Bryan, Ann Purkins, 84; Benjamin, 84; William, 84
Bryant, Benjamin, 52, 54, 86; Milley, 180; Nancy (Gragg), 54; Richard, 26; William, 86; Zacharias, 86
Buckner, Col. Mordecai, 10, 11, 99, 105, 110, 116, 142, 143, 167, 174
Buford, Col., 89, 109, 114, 140, 147, 148, 156, 157, 163; Capt. James, 142
Buggs, Allen, 119; Elizabeth, 119
Bullitt, Col., 117
Buntan, John, 143; Lavina C., 143
Burdett, Elizabeth, 159; Joseph T., 159
Burfoot, Sgt. Thomas, 14, 17, 19, 21; William, see Burford
Burford, Daniel, 69; Capt. Daniel, Jr., 69, 78; Major David, 185; John, 69; Margaret, 69; William, 15, 18, 20, 22, 69
Burfort, Tandy, 106
Burger, Rev. Benjamin, 154
Burgoyne, Gen., 12, 97, 99, 104, 105, 109, 116, 124, 142, 147, 148, 154, 155, 169, 170, 171, 174, 185
Burks, Charles, 69; David, 69
Burley, Col., 130; Capt. G., 171
Burnett, George, 165; Jeremiah, 26; John, 26, 62; Mary, 62, 63; Patsey, 153; Unity, 165
Burnette, Ensign John, 127
Burnley, Capt. Garland, 114

Index

Burras (Burrus), Lt., 97; Capt. Charles, 32, 36, 59, 70, 78, 82, 92, 154, 176; Sgt. Joseph, 55
Burrows, Mr., 67
Burton, Capt. James, 58, 59, 97, 176; Phillip, 55; William, 87; William, Jr., 87
Bush, John, 93
Buster, Lt. Claudeous (Claudious), 34, 73
Butler, Col., 105, 147
Bybie, Samuel, 50
Byrd, Col. William, 188
Byrnes, James, 25
Byron, Lt., 97

Cabell, Col. Edward A., 106; Elizabeth, 106; Mrs. Hannah, 106; Joseph, 106; Col. Joseph, 1, 2, 5, 6, 31, 32, 54, 61, 62, 63, 74, 75, 78, 79, 80, 81, 82, 83, 107, 128, 134, 135, 152, 155, 158, 163, 184; Joseph C., 106; Nathaniel Francis, 106; Col. Nicholas, 1, 4, 5, 6, 34, 35, 37, 54, 69, 70, 84, 85, 90, 92, 106, 107, 117, 120, 128, 133, 134, 135, 152, 158, 163, 164, 184; Col. Samuel Jordan, 9, 10, 12, 13, 14, 16, 17, 19, 28, 68, 71, 94, 99, 105, 110, 111, 112, 114, 116, 120, 122, 124, 125, 126, 127, 128, 130, 140, 142, 143, 145, 146, 149, 155, 158, 163, 165, 166, 167, 170, 174, 183, 187; Col. William, 2, 5, 7, 9, 67, 102, 106, 121, 148; Dr. William, 106; Major William, Jr., 37, 38, 61, 62, 63, 64, 69, 70, 72, 73, 75, 79, 80, 84, 91, 107, 128, 129, 179, 181, 187
Cack, Col. William, 128
Call, Capt., 150
Callaway, Frances (Walton), 4; Col. Richard, 4
Camden, Benjamin, 187; John, 143; William, 74
Cameron, Hugh, 25
Cammeron, Duncan, 70
Camp, Content (Ward), 50; Rev. Ichabod, 50, 75; John, 50; Mary, 50; Mary Anne, 50; Phoebe (Canfield), 50; Sgt. Samuel, 50, 70, 86
Campbel, Murdon, 77
Campbell, Adj., 158; Major, 155, 162; Anthony, 107; Benjamin, 107; Betsey, 107; Charles Henry, 191, 192; Rev. Ezekiel, 119, 120; Frances, 107; George, 15, 18, 20, 22, 49, 73, 78; Henry, 107, 187; Cpl. Henry, 57, 59; James, 26, 27, 29, 30; Joel, 71, 88; John, 49, 78, 81, 107, 177, 187; Lawrence, 60, 70, 81, 107; Mary, 152; Moses, 70; Nancy, 107; Neill, 71, 78, 82; Sarah Buchanan, 192; Mrs. Sarah (Sally), 107, 187; Tabitha, 70; William, 187; Capt. William, 100, 101; Col. William, 126, 164, 179; Wyatt, 107
Canterbery, Jidethon, 58
Canterberry (Canterbury), Joseph, 16, 22, 23, 62; Joseph, Jr., 16; McFarlane, 109; Mary, 109; Ruth, 61, 62
Carathers, Judge Abraham, 185
Carpenter, Sgt. Benjamin, 107, 170, 175; Eaton, 175; John, 15, 17, 19, 22, 23; Mary, 109 (2); Samuel, 129; Thomas, 70; William, 108, 109
Carr, Nathaniel, 50
Carrington, Col. Edward, 117, 184; Col. George, 106; Hannah, 106; P., 140
Carter, Abraham, 162, 172; Betsy, 182; Edward, 70; Mrs. Frances, 146; Henry, 146; Henry, Jr., 146; James, 182; John, 146; Landon, 93; Lane, 52; Mary, 146, 158; Micajah, 51; Lt. Peter, 34, 37, 39, 51, 70, 87, 91; Sally, 120, 146; Sarah (Williams), 110; Solomon, 71; Theodrick, 182; Thomas, 120; William, 93, 106, 109, 172
Cartwright, Bennett G., 110; Christian, 111; Frances, 110; Henry L., 110; James A., 110; John, 70, 86, 88; Justinian (Jesse), 17, 110, 130; Justinian, Jr., 110; Levin L., 110; Nancy S., 110; Peter, 110, 111; Rev. Peter, 110, 111; Polly, 111; Polly M., 110; Rosanna, 111; Sally, 110; Terresa, 110; Winnefred, 110
Casey, Roger, 70
Cash, Bartlett, 111, 112, 162, 166; Benjamin, 76; Elizabeth, 111 (2); Frances, 111; George, 113; Henry W., 111; Howard, 6, 112, 113; James, 113; Jefferson R., 111; Joel, 111; John, 6, 111 (2), 112, 113; Lucy (Campbell), 113; Mary, 113; Mary Ann, 111; Nancy, 76, 113; Nancy P., 111; Peter, 6, 112, 113; Robert Howard, 70, 76, 88, 92; Stephen, 70, 113, 174; Tamasen (Tamsey), 88, 92; William P., 111; Willis, 111
Cashwell, Betsy (Penn), 114; Sgt. Henry, 113, 136; Peter, 60, 70; William, 113, 114, 134, 136, 158, 168, 172, 175
Cawthan, Robert, Sr., 59

Index

Cawthorn (Caathan), James, 98; Richard, 57, 58, 114; Robert, 57, 58
Chadwell, Capt. David, 142
Chambers, Ensign Travis, 109, 127
Chandler, William, 26, 27, 29, 30
Chapple, William, 70
Charity, Charles, 28, 30
Chastaine, James, 93
Cheatham, Josiah, 15, 18, 20, 21, 23, 114; Lucy, 114
Chewning, Polly (Pugh), 163
Childres, Moseby, 114; William, 114
Childress, Abraham, 114, 115; Abraham, Jr., 115; Ann, 70; Benjamin, 115, 145, 185; Dicy, 115; Elizabeth, 115 (2); Francis, 115; Goolsby (Goldsby, Goolsbey), 93, 115, 140; Henry (Childers), 55, 115; John, 55, 115; Joseph, 70; Lucy, 185; Polly, 115; Samuel, 115, 185; Seley, 115; William, 115
Chisnal, Alexander, 80
Christian, Capt., 97, 115, 116, 135, 136, 174; Annie, 191; Capt. Charles, 35, 36, 54, 70, 86, 88, 113, 117, 127, 142, 151, 171; Ens. Drury, 35, 71, 82, 86; Ens. Elijah, 33, 37, 151; Capt. Henry, 26, 33, 70, 83; James, 72, 82; John, 83; Capt. John, 31, 32, 36, 59, 70, 86, 97, 109, 113, 129, 130, 150, 152, 163, 175, 185; Lt. Robert, 31, 32, 35, 37, 70, 84; Sarah Winston, 191; Susan W., 171; Col. William, 77, 100, 111, 142, 162, 189, 192; William Brown, 83
Church, Thomas, 27, 52
Clark, Benjamin, 16; Gen. George Rogers, 8, 100, 147, 162; Joseph, 27, 29, 30; Moses, 73; Nathaniel, 70
Clarke, Ann, 116; John, 116, 170
Clarkson, Catherine, 145; John, 146
Clasby, Capt. Sherrard, 169
Clay, Rev., 185; Joseph, 89
Clements, James, 158
Cleveland, Col. Benjamin, 96, 116, 179
Clifton, John, 52
Clinton, Gen., 12
Cloe, John, 52
Coats, George, 18, 21, 22
Cockburn, George, 70
Cocke, Bowler, 13
Coffee, Edmund S., 121; Mary, 121; Reuben, 116; Sgt. William, 9, 14
Coffey (Coffee), Jesse, 116; Lucy, 116; Ozborn (Osborn, Osburn), 15, 18, 20, 22, 23, 116; Polly, 116
Coke, Henry, 28, 30
Cole, Rev., 67

Coleman, Rev. Benjamin, 70, 91, 93, 107, 120, 143, 168; Elizabeth, 70; George, 70; James, 55; John D., 70; Cpl. Joseph, 28, 29; Lt. Lindsey, 33, 35, 36, 70, 74, 86, 153; Littlebury, 16
Collins, Lt. William, 54
Conner, Daniel, 15, 18, 20, 22, 62, 116, 120; James, 41; John, 129; Mary (Hurt), 116; Susannah, 62
Cook, Samuel, 56; Capt. Shem, 155; William, 165, 182
Cooper, Charlotte, 85; Coatney, 85; Phillip, 85; Robert, 85
Coper, Jesse, 100
Corbin, 166
Cornwallis, Lord, 12, 53, 54, 65, 66, 67, 94, 95, 96, 97, 98, 100, 108, 109, 112, 114, 116, 120, 125, 127, 128, 131, 135, 136, 143, 145, 148, 149, 150, 152, 153, 154, 156, 158, 159, 160, 163, 164, 167, 171, 175, 176, 179, 180, 184
Cornwell, Coleman, 185
Cottrell (Cotrell, Cottrel), Gilbert, 56; James, 107, 117
Cowherd, Capt. F., 141, 159
Cox, 96; Benjamin, 89; Clary, 89; Sgt. Edward, 14, 17, 19, 21, 23, 89; Margaret, 89; William, 28, 30
Craighead, John, 147; Robert, 147
Crawford, Rev., 114, 140; Ann, 70; Rev. Charles, 172; Capt. David, 2, 31, 69, 70, 75, 80, 81, 87, 88, 171, 180; Elizabeth D., 171; Joel, 83; Ens. John, 38, 152; Lt. Nathan, 70, 86, 92, 107, 135; Rev. William, 172
Crawley, Thomas, 26
Creasey (Creasay), Cpl. George, 14, 17, 19, 21, 23
Crews, Lt. Giddion (Gideon, Gidion), 18, 21, 22, 23, 33, 34; James, 18, 21, 22, 23, 70; James W., 184; Capt. Joseph, 33, 117; Nancy (Eubank), 117
Crider, John, 102; Sarah (Bond), 102
Crisp, William, 70
Crittenden, Charles Worde, 118; John, 118, 182; Josiah, 117, 118; Martha, 118; Mary W., 118; Matthew Tanner, 118; Nancy, 118; Richard Hazlewood, 117; Richard Hazlewood Jr., 118; Sally, 117; Samuel, 118
Crittendon, John, 70
Crockett, Col. Hugh, 164
Croker, William, 10
Croucher, Thomas, 25
Crow, John, 27

Croxton, Elizabeth, 73; Joanna, 73; Johanna, 73; John, 73; Nancy, 73; Samuel, 73
Crum, Adam, 128
Crutcher, Charles, 147; Elizabeth, 118, 119 (2); Henry Lawson, 119; Rev. Isaac, 104; Parker, 119; Polley, 119; Robert, 119; Sarah, 119; William, 56, 118, 119 (2); Willis, 119
Cumings, Lt. Alex., 100
Cuningham, Elizabeth (Via), 177
Cunningham, William, 26
Cyrus, Bartholomew, 126

Dabney, Col. Charles, 115, 128, 131, 132, 148, 153, 154, 156, 167, 169, 176
Dale, Gen. Samuel, 179
Dameron, Col., 54; Rev., 148
Damron, Daniel, 15; George, 18, 21, 22, 24
Dandridge, Capt. Spotswood, 12, 158, 159, 181
Davidson, Giles, 177
Davies, Anna C., 127; Frederick, 181; Henry Landon, 70, 74, 75, 78, 82, 92, 127; Samuel R., 127; Sarah W. (Franklin), 127
Davis, Benedicta (Benedicter), 120; Lt. David, 34, 127; Edmund, 119; Israel, 70; James, 160; Jane, 92; Rev. John, 74, 162; Milley, 119; Nancey, 120; Lt. Nathaniel, 189, 190; Polly, 120; Richard, 70; Robert, 70, 92; Capt. Samuel, 78; William, 55, 115, 120, 160; William, Jr., 120; Col. William, 154, 167
Davison, Capt. John, 50
Dawson, Henry, 188; Capt. John, 2, 70, 75, 78, 79, 81, 84, 117, 176; Rev. Martin, 70, 77, 83, 114; Lt. Pleasant, 37, 52; Robert, 50; Thomas, 83
Day, Thomas, 184
Deavenport, Achilles, 16; Edmond, 16; John (Davenport), 15, 18, 20, 22
Deaver, John, 17
Demasters, Betsey, 120; Cornelius, 120; Cpl. Edward (D. Masters), 120, 165, 187; Elvira, 120; George, 120; James, 121; Jane, 121; Jesse, 121; John (Master, Masters), 15, 18, 20, 21, 116, 120 (2), 121 (2), 187; Martha, 120, 121; Mary, 121; Moris, 121; Nancy, 120, 121; Nicholas, 121; Polly, 120, 121; Sally, 120; Sarah Ann, 120; Wiatt, 120; Winifred, 121

Denney, John, 121
Depriest, John, 69, 70, 78, 88; William, 82
Dever, Nathaniel, 181
Diamond, Peter, 25
Dick, Col., 99
Dickerson, Col., 135, 161; Jeremia (Wells), 121, 122; John, 16; Cpl. Thomas, 14, 17, 19, 21, 23, 121, 122; Lt. Thomas, Jr., 35, 36
Dickey, A., 17
Digges, Dudley, 140
Diggs (Digges), Capt. John, 2, 35, 36, 52, 70, 78, 79, 81, 83, 92, 107, 131, 150, 151, 163, 181
Dillard, Lt., 96; Betsy, 175; Elizabeth, 124; Elizabeth (Holliday), 51; Fanney Horsley, 124; Capt. James, 51, 122; Capt. James, Sr., 2, 31, 51, 72, 74, 75, 79, 80, 84, 92, 124, 190; Capt. James, Jr., 9, 10, 17, 25, 51, 82, 91 (2), 94, 96, 102, 104, 107, 109, 116, 117, 120, 122, 123, 124, 125, 126, 134, 136, 142, 145, 148, 172, 180, 184; Capt. James, 51, 70, 89, 151; James Spotswood, 124; Mrs. Jane, 123; Jane Chane, 124; John, 75, 77, 124; Joseph, 70, 81, 95, 137, 138; Joseph Starke, 124; Judith (Higginbotham), 137, 138; Mary Ann (Hunt), 124; Mary Ann Hunt, 124; Nancy Wiatt, 124; Salley, 124; Susannah, 95; Thomas, 51; Washington, 124; William, 70, 124, 175
Dinwiddie, Robert, 156; Samuel, 52; William, 155
Ditcher, Ann, 178
Dixson, William, 70
Doake, 79
Dodd, Josias, 150; Phebe, 184
Donelly, John, 100
Dooley, Jacob, 101
Doughty, Mrs., 132
Duglass, Cpl. George, 55; Rev. Thomas, 178
Duiguid, Capt. William, 177
Duncan, Cpl. David, 16, 79; John, 79
Dunlap, Rev. William, 10
Dunmore, Lady, 1; Lord, 1, 5, 11, 77, 100, 103, 124, 146, 163, 180
Dunn, Capt. Peter, 99
Du Val, William, 72
Duvall, Major, 142

Eads (Eades, Edes), Abraham, 124; Lt. Charles, 15, 18, 20, 21, 107, 108, 124, 131, 142, 167; Thomas, 70
Earle, Capt. David, 95

Index

Eddes, William, 50
Edmiston, Abraham, 125; Allen, 125; Belinda, 125; Betsy, 125; Emanuel, 125; James, 125; John T., 125; Lucy, 125; Robert, 125; Sally, 125; Suthard, 125; Thomas, 125; Sgt. William, 125; William, Jr., 125
Edmonds, Lt. Robert, 31; Samuel, 70
Edmondson, 142
Edmunds, John, 70
Edwards, Anne, 87; Lt. Joseph, 33, 34, 37, 70, 81, 87, 109; Nelly, 87; William, 87
Elbert, Col. Samuel, 50, 94, 132, 155, 156
Elliot, William, 70
Elliott, Col. Thomas, 10, 11
Ellis, Lt. Charles, 33, 35, 37, 70; Cpl. John, 28, 29; Capt. Josiah, 35, 36, 70, 84
Ennis, Col., 169
Estang, Capt., 160
Evans, Anthony, Jr., 157; Benjamin, 60; James (Evins), 59, 97, 125, 177; John, 29, 30; Thomas, 91
Everett, John, 57, 58, 100
Ewell, Capt., 100, 159
Ewers, Lt. Thomas, 34, 36, 151, 153, 164

Fair, Edman, 57
Farguson, James, 58
Faris, Valentine, 184
Farrar, Lt. Thomas, 34, 35
Fasharn, Edward, 50
Febiger, Col., 99, 101, 166
Ferguson, Col., 179
Fincannon, Jacob, 130
Findley, 80, 84
Finley, Major, 100
Finney, John, 165
Fisher, Mrs. Clyde W., 50
Fitzgerald (Fitzgerrell, Fitsgerrald, Fitzgerrald), James, 119; John, 15, 17, 20, 21; Milley, 119
Fitzjarrel, Sgt. James, 188
Fitzpatrick, Thomas, 70; William, 70
Fland, Mitchel, 17
Fleetwood, John, 114, 115; Moses, 114, 115
Fleming, Col. Charles, 9
Flowers, John, 58
Flowery, Rev. William, 130, 181
Floyd, Mitchell, 49
Fontaine, Rev. Peter, 67; Col. William, 3, 65, 67, 95, 103, 124, 132, 145, 151, 180, 183
Forbes, Gen., 188; Angus, 93

Forbus, Alexander, 27, 28, 29, 52, 126; William, 52, 188
Ford, Capt., 96
Fordyce, Capt., 4, 107, 132
Forsyth, Benjamin, 70
Fortune, Elizabeth, 186, 187; Elizabeth Jane Bennett, 186; John, 126; Nancy, 126; Thomas, 186; Zacha, 59; Zachariah T., 126
Foster, Ens. James, 38, 126, 127; Nancy, 126, 127
Fowler, Betsey, 130; Jacob, 130
Fox, Samuel, 71
Foy, Rebecca (Webster), 182
Francisco, Peter, 28, 30
Franklin, Anna C., 127; Elizabeth H., 127; Henry, 70; Henry, Jr., 70, 75, 93, 96; Capt. James, 25, 26, 70, 94, 96, 102, 109, 111, 112, 113, 114, 120, 122, 127, 133, 134, 141, 142, 143, 145, 159, 165, 166, 170, 172, 178, 192, 193; Major James, 6, 179; Joell, 70; Lt. John, 32, 70, 93; John R., 127; Mary Ann, 93; Nancy, 127; Samuel, 127; Sarah W., 127
Frazer, James, 160, 161; Micajah, 127, 128; Nancy, 128; Susan, 128; Susan (Hamilton), 128
Freeman, Ann, 144 (2); James, 144; Mehala, 186; Rebecca, 186; Thomas, 186
Frost, Anna (Brooks), 128; Rev. John, 128; Joseph, 128
Fry, Benjamin, 51, 70, 128
Fulcher, Cpl. Richard, 129

Gaffert, Capt. Richard, 115
Gaines, Bernard, 3; Col. Daniel, 2, 3 (2), 34, 35, 36, 70, 73, 74, 75, 76, 77, 80, 82, 83, 84, 86, 87, 88, 92, 100, 125, 126, 132, 150, 151, 153, 163; Elizabeth, 3; Mary, 3; Col. William, 185
Galaspie, George, 70; William, 70
Galdons, Julius, 82
Galliher, David, 21, 22, 24
Galloway (Gallaway, Galleway), Benjamin, 15, 17, 19, 22, 23
Galt, William, 71, 76
Gardner, John, 103
Garland, Major Edward, 50; Capt. Hudson M., 137; Capt. James, 95, 171, 173; John, 183; Lt. Nathaniel, 171; Capt. Ned, 156; Samuel M., 103, 119; Spotswood, 95
Garrett, Henry, 60
Garsh, Michael, 100
Garth, John, 171
Garvin, Christian, 111

Gates, Major-Gen. H., 12, 53, 54, 124, 133, 136, 147, 151, 159, 174, 179
Gatewood, Amelia, 129; Ann (Nancy), 129; Arstiley, 129; Dotia, 129; Dudley, 76; Fletcher, 130; James, 105; John, 56, 129; John F., 130; Sgt. Larkin, 55, 70; Maria, 129; Miarah, 129; Nancy, 129; Richard, 56, 83; Richard B., 129; Roland, 129; Wiley, 129, 130; William, 60
Gerrell, Benjamin, 128
Gibson, Col., 134; Griffin, 25
Gilbert, Ezekiel, 70, 84; George, 70, 74, 82, 86; Henry, 3, 74, 86; Josiah, 71, 82; Mary, 3; Mary (Wyatt), 3; Richard, 86; Thomas, 55, 86
Giles, Mr., 66; John, 6, 112; Joseph, 112; Josiah, 6, 130; Patsey, 130; Perrion, 77; William, 6, 112
Gill, Elizabeth, 152
Gillaspie, Frances, 110; Letty More, 103
Gillenwater, Joel, 50; John, 58
Gilliam (Gillam), Archer (Archibald), 18, 20, 22, 23; John, 17
Gilliland, Hugh, 56
Gillinwater, Elijah, 55
Gillinwaters, William, 17
Gilmer, Lt. John, 4, 70
Gilmore, Dr., 170; Lt., 161; Lt. James, 161, 165; Lt. John, 142
Gist, Col. Nathan, 126, 178
Givings, Capt., 177
Glenn, Nancy (Cloak), 104; Sally, 182; Tyra, 104
Godsey, Austin, 18, 21, 22, 24; Benoni, 20; William, 18, 21, 22, 24
Goff, Samuel, 28, 30
Golden, Jules, 27
Goldsmith, Bennoni (Benoni), 15, 18, 22, 23
Gollihorn, David, 19
Goodall, Major, 149; Sgt. James, 58
Goode, Dan, 55
Goodrich, Mary, 93
Goodwin, Lt., 152; John Henry, 87; Joseph, 77, 81, 84; Micajah, 81, 161; Richard, 56; William, 55
Goolsbey (Goolsby), James, 93
Gordon, 5; Armistead C., 14
Gowing, James, 26; Landon S., 152; Samuel, 16
Grady (Gready), Edmond (Edmund), 27, 28, 30
Grasse, Count de, 66
Grattan, Robert, 52
Graves, Clara, 96; Francis, Jr., 96; Francis, Sr., 96; Capt. John, 53, 54; Capt. Thomas, 96; William, 56

Green, Capt., 128; Col. John, 28, 29, 96, 126, 127, 141, 178; Joseph, 18, 21, 22, 23
Greene, Gen., 11, 53, 69, 102, 109, 116, 117, 133, 134, 136, 141, 144, 151, 153, 159, 166, 171, 180
Gregory, Abigail, 130; Betsey, 130; Jeremiah, 50, 130 (2); John W., 130 (2); Joseph, 130; Mary Ann, 130; Sally (Staples), 130; Samuel, 130; Thomas, 15, 18, 20, 22, 130
Gresham, Capt. James, 37, 70, 185
Griffin, John, 70, 90; Reuben, 17, 49; Sherrod, 50
Griffith, Melinda, 187
Griggory, see Gregory
Gue, John, 27, 93
Guest, Capt. Moses, 116
Guilliam, Rev., 122
Gulland, James, 113
Gunter, Sally, 185; Thomas, 185
Guthrie (Gutrey, Guttry), Nathaniel, 55, 131
Guttery (Guttry), John, 25, 49; William, 83

Habersham, John, 89
Hadrick, John, 26
Hall, James, 69; John, Sr., 131; Randall, 98
Hallyburton, James, 72
Hambleton, Archer, 70; James, 81; Luke, 70
Hamilton, James, 131, 132; Wyatt, 132
Hamm (Ham), John, 55; Stephen, 49, 70, 72, 80
Hammond, Philip, 161, 162
Hampton, Col., 143, 182
Hancock, Capt. George, 155
Hand, Gen., 147, 161
Handsbrough, Ptolemy, 16
Haney, James, 58
Hansbrough, Fanny, 132; John, 132; Kesiah, 70; Samuel, 132; Sarah, 132; William, 132; Lt. William, Jr., 32, 34, 35
Hardeman (Hardiman), Major, 103, 107, 128, 129, 132, 148, 149, 184
Harding, Edward, 70; Groves, 70
Hardwick, John, 80
Hardy, Andrew, 132 (2); Charles, 50; John, 128
Hare, John B., 57; Richard, Sr., 114, 133
Hargrove, Hezekiah, 43, 70, 133, 163, 184
Harisbrough, see Hansbrough
Hariston, Capt. George, 96

202 *Index*

Harloe, Nathaniel, 70
Harmer, John, 85
Harper, Henry, 27, 134, 151, 183; Susannah, 183
Harrall, William, 134
Harril, Bailey, 100
Harris, Gen., 154; Mr., 166; Lee, 70, 88; Mathew, 70; William, 133; 135, 152; Capt. William, 32, 33, 36, 59, 89, 97, 108, 127, 131, 133, 165, 168, 169, 170, 184; Lt. William, Jr., 31, 62; Major William, 115
Harrison, Gov., 68, 169; Battaile, 76; Col., 110; James, 135, 161; Capt. James, 139, 156, 157; Ens. Reuben, 36, 38, 76, 82; Cpl. Richard, 25, 27, 28, 29
Hartless, Henry, 70; James, 142; William, 113, 114, 135, 136
Hartshorn, Capt., 94
Harvie, 88; Col., 57; Daniel (Harvey), 70; Martha, 70; Richard, 70
Hatcher, Col., 171
Hawes, Lt. Col. Samuel, 28, 96, 120, 125, 126, 141, 145, 147, 159, 171, 178
Hawkins, Alford, 184; alias Fitzgerald, Benjamin, 134; John, 10; Marcey, 100; Nathan, 100; Ens. Thomas, 38, 82, 88
Hay, Lt. Charles, 35, 36, 38, 49; Gilbert, 77; James, 71; William, 77
Haynes, William, 58; Lt. William, 38
Hays, Cassie, 63; George, 63
Hazele, George, 26
Heath, Col., 147
Height, Mathew, 136
Helton, Edward, 59
Henderson, Capt. Alexander, 70, 134; Bennet, 52; Ens. James, 34, 36, 83, 139; John, 70; John, Jr., 78; Joseph, 52; Mary Ann, 130; Nancy, 126; Obediah, 70; Samuel, 130; William, 26
Hendricks, Lt. Col. James, 10, 11, 14, 17, 170; Sophia, 102
Henry, Elizabeth, 191; John, 191; Col. Patrick, 1, 95, 100, 191, 192; Sarah, 191, 192, 193; William, 191
Hensley, William, 15, 18
Herdsman, Rev., 158
Hickman, Polly, 182; William, 182
Higginbotham, Capt. Aaron, 70, 73, 83, 96, 108, 189, 190; Capt Aaron, Jr., 73; Anne, 136, 137; Benjamin, 137; Capt. Benjamin, 70, 78, 102, 111, 113, 114, 136, 137, 138, 166, 174; Ens. Caleb, 35, 70, 92, 140, 166; Caleb, 137; Clara (Graves), 73, 96; Elizabeth, 137; Frances G., 137; Frances (Riley), 9; Francis, 70; Col. George Washington, 73, 137, 138, 175; Hannah, 137; Lt. Jacob, 36, 70, 93, 136; Jacob, Jr., 137; James, 137; Col, James, 1, 31, 32, 59, 60, 72, 76, 81, 85, 86, 88, 101, 108, 128, 134, 135, 137, 138, 139, 155, 157, 163, 169, 175, 179, 184, 189, 192; James, Jr., 137, 138; Jane, 137; John, 9, 136, 137; Capt. John, 59, 60, 70, 153, 154, 170, 189; John, Jr., 82; Joseph, 137; Sgt. Joseph, 55, 70, 108; Col. Joseph Cabell, 137, 138; Mary Ann, 96; Moses, 70, 129; Nancey, 76; Rachel, 9; Riley, 137; Capt. Samuel, 6, 36, 70, 78, 82, 84, 89, 90, 92, 97, 108, 109, 112, 113, 115, 125, 127, 136, 153, 162, 165, 180, 184, 189, 190; Thomas Lee, 60, 73; Lt. William, 15, 16, 18, 20, 21, 140; William, 70, 93, 137; Capt. William A., 137
Hight, John, 70
Hill, Ann, 184; Cpl. James, 17, 19, 21, 23, 70, 75, 184; Capt. John, 35, 37, 39, 70; Rev. John, 185; Capt. Joseph, 144; Mary, 177; Tabitha, 184; Thomas, 70
Hilley, Daniel, 57, 58; Thomas, 70
Hilton, Lt. George, 31, 33, 71
Hite, Patrick, 50
Hix, Edward, 28, 29
Hoard, Capt., 147
Hockaday, Lt. Phillip, 17, 19
Hodges, Edmund, 112; John, 142
Hogg, Cele, 140; David, 185; John, 140, 165; Lucas, 141; Lucelia, 141; Lucy, 141; Luke, 140; Sally, 141; Susannah, 140
Holcombe, Col. John, 111, 113, 133, 134, 148, 149, 171, 172, 180, 181
Holeman, John, 181
Hollas, Basdel, 57
Holmes, Mr., 67; Rev., 150
Holston, Major, 67
Holt, Lt. William, 52
Hooker, William, 81
Hopkins, Capt., 166; Col., 119; James, 52, 53, 70; Dr. James, 2, 53, 84, 86, 91; Mary, 54; Reuben, 54
Hopson, Capt., 99
Horrell, Thomas, 69, 70; William, 70, 88
Horry, Col. Peter, 144
Horsley, Lt. John, 32, 33, 34, 70, 98, 148, 181; Lucinda (Horseley), 98; Lt. Robert, 5, 38, 39, 49, 149, 181;

Index

Lt. William, 2, 31, 32, 35, 36, 70, 74, 79, 80, 90, 92, 181
osick (Hosack, Hoesack), William, 26, 27, 28, 30, 141
ouchens (Hutchens), Charles, 57, 141
oustoun, J., 50
oward, Capt., 156; John, 51; William, 71, 72
ubbard, Major, 149, 171; Carter, 107
udson, John, 119; Joshua, 70, 88; Robert (Robin), 15, 18, 20, 21, 94, 130; Sarah, 119
uffman, John, 89, 141; Lucretia, 141
uggart, Col., 177
ughes, Moses, 70, 81; Lt. Thomas, 3, 103; William, 70, 82
umfries, Lt. James, 180
umphries, Thomas, 50
unt, Ann, 124; John, Sr., 124
unter, Titus, 55
urt, M⸺ ⸺ey Ann, 172; George, ⸺ald, 155
⸺), Jacob, 26, 27, 29, 30
, Patrick, 116

dians: Cornstalk, Shawnee Indian King, 135, 161; Ellenepsico (Nepseki), son of Cornstalk, 135, 161; Red Hawk, 135; Petello, 135; Grenadier Squaw, 161, 162
gles, Capt., 189
nes, Capt. James, 110
tchminger, John, 161
vin, Rev. William, 93, 126
vine, Rev. Samuel, 174
ving, Rev., 153; Charles, 70, 76
on, Lt. Charles, 32, 35, 70, 125; Elijah, 142

ck, Col., 100
ckson, Daniel Will, 74; Nancy, 160; Vincent, 149; William, 50
cobs, Capt. John, 36, 59, 79, 125, 127, 130, 131, 133, 148, 163, 184
meson, Capt. John, 158, 159
fferson, Governor, 68; Randolph, 180
nins, Caleb, 58
hns, Bartlett, 86; Francis, 86; Jesse, 26, 86; John, 44; John Alexander, 86; Martha, 86; Mary, 86; Nancy, 86; Robert, 86; Robert, Jr., 55, 86; Salley, 86; Thomas, 15, 17, 19, 21, 23, 76, 86, 142; William, 15, 17, 19, 21, 76, 86
hnson, Col., 160, 167; Benjamin, 56; Frances, 78; James, 29, 30; Jeremiah, 29, 30; Jonathan, 78; Mary, 78; Noell, 81, 82, 86, 88; Phillip, 78; Richard, 18, 21; Robert, 88; Snelling, 78; Lt. Walter, 129; William, 15, 17, 19, 83, 94; William, Jr., 26, 49, 70, 101, 150; Sgt. William, 25, 27, 28, 29, 142
Johnston, Col. George, 11; John, 70; Ens. William, 98; Capt. William, 120
Joiner, Oney D. (Tyler), 175
Jones, Col., 150; Mrs., 62; Rev., 128; Amarella (Anna R. C.), 143; Ann, 144; Betsey Ann, 144; Catherine, 145, 146; Lt. Charles, 25, 27, 28, 29, 38, 70, 94, 116; Clarkson, 145; Eli, 144; Elizabeth, 144; Elizabeth W., 143; Hezekiah, 145, 146; James, 144; Cpl. Joel (Joell), 17, 19, 21, 23; Lt. John, 100; Sgt. John, 100, 142; John C., 146; John Nicholas, 143; Johnston Lane, 144; Joshua, 146; Josiah, 16, 143, 166; Leonard, 144; Lavina C., 143; Margaret, 144; Mary, 70, 144; Nancey, 144; Nancy, 143; Nicholas, 25, 143, 144; Peggy, 144; Rhoda L., 143; Richard, 81; Sally, 171; Sally T., 143; Sara, 144; Shelton, 145; Susan L., 143; Susanah, 144; Tandy, 171; Thomas, 25, 27, 28, 30, 62, 145, 165; Cpl. Thomas, 55; Lt. Thomas, 25, 27, 28, 29, 107, 117, 127, 131, 134, 145, 146, 164; Wesley C., 143, 144; Wiley, 144; Sgt. William, 25, 27, 29, 30; William, 144 (2), 145; William P., 143; Winston J., 143
Jopling (Joplin), Mr., 108; Holman, 180; James, 70; John, 70; Josiah, 70; Molly, 146; Sgt. Ralph, 9, 14; Capt. Thomas, 70, 72, 74, 79, 85, 86, 92, 156; Thomas, Jr., 82, 146
Jordan, Lt., 147, 156; Benjamin, 73; Caroline Matilda, 2; Capt. John, 9, 12, 14, 17, 19, 21, 23, 174; Leroy, 157; Matthew, 9; Capt. Reuben, 38, 70, 107; Col. Samuel, 2, 9; Sarah, 2
Jorden, James, 58
Josling, Cpl. John, 14, 17, 19, 21, 23
Jouett, John, 3
Joyner, Peter, 75

Keith, James, 177
Kemp, Rev., 103
Kendall, John, 142
Kennady, Ensign William, 58
Kennedy, Jesse, 94, 95; Susanna, 95
Kenney, John W., 57
Kent, Alexander, 28, 30

Kerr, Armstrong, 107
Key, George, 15, 18, 20, 22, 23, 146; Martin, 81; Rice, 44; Susannah (Craighead), 147
Kidd, James, 133; Lucy, 187; Peggey, 187
King, Gilliam, 172; Nancy, 172, 173; Walter, 85
Kipias, John, 55
Kipee, John, 178
Kippers, Capt. John, Sr., 147, 148
Kirkendale, Capt., 143
Kirkerdall, Col., 160
Kirkum, Capt., 100
Knight (Night), Cpl. Andrew, 26, 27, 28, 29; Ann, 148; Austin (Orstin), 55, 148; Elizabeth (Ham), 148; John, 70; William, 55, 148 (2), 156
Kyle, Nancy, 154; William, 83

Lackey, John, Jr., 87; Samuel, 70, 89
Lafayette, Marquis de, 12, 96, 98, 99, 108, 109, 115, 128, 142, 152, 154, 160, 162, 163, 170, 177, 179, 180, 187
Lain (Laine, Lane, Layne), Anderson, 149; Sgt. Charles, 148, 149, 164; John, 15, 18, 20, 22, 23, 26, 58; Joseph, 55, 148, 149, 151, 164; Rebecca, 149; Sally, 148; Thomas, 15, 17, 20, 22, 23; William, 172
La Master (Le Master), Abraham, 74, 118; Martha, 117, 118; Richard, 74
Lambert, Ensign George, 100
Lamont, John, 51, 60
Landrum, Rev. Hawkins, 176; Rev. James, 149; Mary Clark, 149; Thomas, 60; Capt. Young, 33, 34, 35, 36, 102, 111, 113, 133, 148, 149, 153, 156, 164, 171, 173, 181, 184
Lankester, John, 192
Lavender, Charles, 58, 132, 149; Charles, Jr., 149; John, 75; Lucy, 149; Milley, 74; Sarah, 150; Simeon, 149; William, 74, 113, 149, 150, 168; Willis, 149
Lawrence, John, 84, 178
Lawson, Gen., 107, 112, 113, 114, 130, 131, 133, 134, 142, 149, 150, 154, 164, 171, 173, 180, 181, 187
Leak, Capt. John, 100, 180
Leake, John M., 150; Mark, 150
Lee, Ambrose, 83; Gen. Charles, 8, 13, 101, 105, 110; Francis, 60, 83; Ens. George, 35, 83, 148; Col. Henry, 8, 14, 96, 167; Mary, 93; Richard, 83; Thos. Lud, 140; William, 100; Capt. William, 37, 70, 86; William F., 155

Leftwich, Capt. Thomas, 115, 133
Leister, Sally, 148
Lesly, Gen., 66
Lewis, Capt., 162, 170; Gen. Andrew, 10, 11, 143; Col. Charles, 3, 5, 131, 164; James, 85; Col. Nicholas, 171
Lewton, Thomas, 89
Lilly, Elizabeth, 146; Gabriel, 146; James, 146; John, 146; Lindsey, 146; Thomas, 146; William, 146; William, Jr., 146
Lincoln, Gen., 101, 119; Abraham, 110
Lindsey (Lindsay), Ensign, 181; Col. Reuben, 94, 129, 135, 145, 152, 158, 164, 180
Lipford, John, 18, 20, 22, 24
Lively, Ann, 89; James, 74; Joseph 70 (2)
Livingston, John, 74
Lobbing, John, 52
Lockard, William, 150
Locke, Andrew 1⁁
Lockert, W
Lockhart, M
Loftis, Jol
Logan, Co..
London, David, .., 79, 86; Mrs. Mary, ...79, 80
Long, Capt., 144
Looney, John, 143
Lovday, Bassalius, 17
Loving, Capt., 158, 171; Capt. James, 171; John, 70; Capt. John, Jr., 31, 32, 36, 54, 73, 87, 89, 102, 107, 131, 133, 134, 135, 142, 152, 177, 179, 180; Capt. William, 69, 70, 73, 75, 77, 81, 89, 90, 91, 92, 178
Low, Sgt. Daniel, 17, 19, 21, 23; Jesse, 18, 20, 22, 23
Lowe, John, 28, 29; Sally, 166; William, 166
Lowry, Patrick, 93
Lucas, Ambrose, 58; Edwin, 184; Col. James, 52, 53, 54; Thomas, 70; Zacha, 58
Lumpkins, Thomas, 74
Luttrell, Mrs. Elizabeth, 109; James, 150; William, 109
Lynch, Col. Charles, 102, 116, 136, 151, 180
Lyon, Edward, 55, 151; Elisha, 70; Frances, 151; James, 180; John, 70, 80; Nicholas, 52, 55; Richard Tankersley, 80; William (Lion), 151

McAlexander, Sgt. Alexander, 153, 185; Alexander Waugh, 153; Amelia Carlisle, 153; David Robinson,

Index

153; Edmund Tucker, 153; James, 153; Capt. James, 70; Capt. James, Jr., 32, 33, 39, 152; Jane, 153; John, 153; Joseph Roberts, 153; Martha, 153; Patsey Burnett, 153; Samuel Ramsey, 153; William, 153
McAllison, Halbert, 143; Susan L., 143
McAnally, Ens. David, 34, 154; James, 154; Nancy, 154
McBee, Capt. Cardry, 118
McBride, Alexander, 26
McCalver, John, 26
McCary; Benjamin, 154; Kitty, 154; Louisa, 154; Richard, 6, 70, 112, 154; Richard, Jr., 154; William, 154
McCaskel, Allan, 77
McCauley, Capt. George, 144
McClain, Henry, 52, 54; James, 54; Thomas, 15, 18, 20
McClanahan, Capt. Alexander, 164
McCleod, Alexander, 77; Kennith, 77; Patrick, 77
McCluer, Elizabeth W., 144; Rhoda L., 144
McClure, Alexander, 126; Nancy, 126
McCommack (McCormack, McCormmack), John, 18, 20, 22
McCraw, John, 29, 30
McCriman, Peter, 77
McCuagg, Ronald, 77
McCue, John, 73
McCulloch (McCullock), Capt. Roderick, 2, 34, 45, 73, 75, 76, 78, 80, 81, 85, 87, 92
McDaniel, George, 78; James, 143; Nancy, 143; William, 158, 159, 181, 182
McDowel, Alexander, 77; Samuel, 16
McDowell, Col., 161; Gen., 143; Mrs., 113; Col. Charles, 125; Col. James, 113; Major James, 96; John, 29, 30; Capt. John, 96, 162
McFagin, Charles, 100
McGehee, Samuel, 70, 87
McGraw, William, 167
McIntosh, Gen., 134, 155, 168; Neil, 77
McKee, John, 50; Capt. William, 140, 161, 165
McKey, Alexander, 100
McLenin, Finley, 77
McLeor, Angus, 77
McManniway (McManaway, McMannaway), John, 26, 27, 29, 30; William, 26
McNeece, Ens. James, 112; Ens. William, 98

McNeely, Lt. Michael, 33, 34, 38, 70, 72, 92
McNutt, Ens. James, 161, 165

Mabon, Capt. James, 140
Maddox, Mrs. John, 187
Madison, John Henry, 191; Sarah, 191; Susanna, 191; Thomas, 192
Magann, Joseph, 81; Merritt, 49, 76, 80
Mahoon, William, 56
Maitland, Col., 101
Mallicoat, Mary, 178
Mallory, Col., 129, 169, 181
Malone, Capt., 144, 145
Manees, Ens. James, Jr., 36, 70
Mann, Ebenezar (Ebenezer), 18, 21, 22, 23; Robert, 18, 21, 22, 24
Mansfield, Lawrence, 95
Mantiply, Nathaniel, 75
Marcum, Josiah, 128
Marks, Lt. John, 3, 103, 124, 132
Marr, John, 70
Marshall, Col., 95, 144; Hon. John, 110; William, 52
Martin, Azariah, 70, 151, 152; Capt. Azariah, 34, 36, 52, 53, 54, 133, 151, 177; Giddeon (Gideon), 52, 54; Henry, 69, 70, 84, 86, 90, 91; Ens. Hudson, 35, 152; Hudson, P. M., 57, 95; James, 70; Jesse, 70; Capt. John, 171; Lt. John, 165; Major John, 135; Sgt. John, 52, 70; Liberty B., 152; Lucy (Roades), 152; Moses, 70; Nicholas L., 57; Scott, see Samuel Scott Scruggs; Sherod, 73; Stephen, 70; Lt. William, 37, 38, 81, 117, 152; Capt. William, 32, 33; Col. William, 100, 185
Mason, Col., 107, 108, 134
Massey, Charles, 152; Edmond, 152; Elizabeth, 152; Jesse, 152; Ens. John, 36, 152; John, Jr., 152; Mary, 152; Susanna, 152; Sylvanus, 72; Thomas, 152; William W., 152
Massie, Sarah (Cocke), 13; Capt. Thomas, 13; Major Thomas, 13; William, 13
Masters, Edward, 131; Eles Steven Rachel, 101; John, 121
Mathews, Col., 114; Ensign, 171; Gen., 113; James, 70; Joseph, 152, 184; Col. Sampson, 142
Matthews, Col. George, 3; Capt. James, 32, 33, 34, 81, 86, 156; Ens. John, 32, 77, 107, 117, 164; Nancey, 93
Maupin, Mr., 5

May, Lt. Col. Charles, 50; Capt. John, 100
Mayfield, Isaac, 70, 82; John, 82, 93
Mays, 159; Ann, 148; Benjamin, 45, 153; Charles, 94; Elijah, 176; George, 94; James, 70; Joseph, 70, 94; Leutitia, 153; William, 70
Mayse, Charles, 153
Meade, Col., 154
Meeky, Capt., 105, 109
Meggenson, Joseph Cabell, 83
Melton, William, 70
Mercer, Js., 140
Meredith, Major, 130; Jane Henry, 191; Margaret, 86; Rice, 86; Col. Samuel, 6, 70, 90, 91, 133, 191, 192, 193
Meriwether (Merriwether, Merriweather), Lt., 12; David, 9, 70; Francis, 2, 3, 70, 78, 79; Col. John, 97, 103, 107, 114, 129, 131, 148, 149, 155, 163, 167, 176, 181, 184, 187; Martha, 9; Mary (Harvie), 9
Merrit (Meritt), John, 81, 83
Miller, 52; Lt., 160; Alexander, 70, 89, 92, 128; Francis, 50; Robert, 16; Samuel, 188; Thomas, 82, 84, 85
Mills, Ambrose, 75; Mary, 75; William, 75; William, 179
Milstead, Benedicter (Benedicta), 120; Joseph, 77; Zelus, 154
Mitchell, Robert, 100; Stephen, 100
Moffitt, Thomas, 78, 80, 81, 82
Moilos, Thomas, 27
Móney, Nancy (Carpenter), 109
Montgomery, Col., 147; David, 70; James, 82; Capt. James, 108, 129, 131, 163, 181; Lt. James, 32, 33, 70, 135, 153; John, 70 (2), 88, 154; John J., 155; Joseph, 70; Mary, 82; Ens. Robert, 108; Thomas, 70, 155; Ens. Thomas, 189; Lt. William, 15, 17, 19, 21, 23, 33, 35, 37, 70, 99, 108, 116, 155
Moody, Thomas, 16
Moore, Lt., 165; Bartlett, 111; Ens. Benjamin, 35, 70, 81; Charles, 96; David, 111; Nancy P., 111; William, 19, 21, 22, 23, 111
Moran, Martha, 121; Ens. Nicholas, 34, 70, 86, 88
More, George, 50
Morgan, 162; Gen. Daniel, 7, 12, 13, 14, 19, 21, 22, 23, 53, 96, 99, 101, 104, 105, 110, 116, 124, 125, 142, 147, 151, 155, 163, 167, 174, 183, 185; Spencer, 100
Morison, John, 77

Morris, Major, 12, 105; Zachariah, 127
Morrison, Ezra, 116, 155, 183; Capt. James, 70, 163; John, 70; Capt. John, 70, 114, 132, 134, 153, 154, 164, 165, 177; Lt. Joseph Higginbotham, 71, 89, 91, 92, 125, 163; Rachel, 9; Lt. Thomas, 34, 70, 134, 151; William, 9, 87
Mosbey, Capt., 132
Mosby, Capt. John H., 152
Moseby, Major, 155
Moseley, Capt. John, 155
Moultrie, Gen., 101
Muhlenberg, Gen., 94, 98, 126, 146, 160
Munroe, George, 16
Murrah (Murray), John, 15, 18, 20, 22; Capt. Richard, 77, 78, 81; William, 52
Murrell, William, 141
Murrey, James, 70
Murrow, Richard, 70, 76, 86
Muter, Col. George, 51, 92

Nail, Joseph, 16
Neal, Judith, 182
Negro Will (Waggoner), 56
Nelson, Col., 170; Major, 69; Mr. Secy., 72; Gen. Alexander, 115, 129
Nevil, Col. James, 2, 5, 31, 70, 72, 73, 74, 75, 79, 80, 81, 84, 85, 86, 89, 91, 92, 189, 190; Capt. Lewis (Neville), 37, 38, 132, 181; Mary Ann, 61, 62, 63; Reuben (Nevill), 16, 61; Thomas, 70, 156
New, David, 56
Newman, John, 94, 155; Joseph, 15, 18, 20, 22, 26, 27, 29, 30, 156, 188
Nicholas, Charles, 100; John, 70; John, Jr., 73; Capt. John, 3, 12
Nicholson, Abraham, 145
Nightingale, Mary, 116; Mathew, 70, 81
North, Ned, 142
Northcutt, Francis, 26
Norvell, Wingfield, 127

Obryan, James, 52
O'Daniel, Sgt. Frederick, 100
Oglesby (Oglesbey), Celia (Witt), 156; Jesse, 156; John, 97; Richard, 71, 81, 82, 86; Thomas, 137, 139; William, 89
O'Hara, Gen., 65
Ohern, Owen, 52
Ore, Susan (Carpenter), 109
Overstreet, Major, 158
Overton, Col., 185; Capt. John, 167
Ownsley, Powell, 172

Index

Padgett (Padget), Beverley, 119; Frederick, 137, 138, 139, 156, 157; Henry G., 118; Phebee, 93; Polley, 119; William, 157
Page, James, 72; John, 140.
Pain, Capt., 147
Palmer, Ellis, 29, 30
Pamplin, Major James, 4, 5, 6, 31, 32, 36, 38, 39, 53, 54, 94, 98, 108, 112, 114, 115, 129, 133, 135, 148, 152, 158, 159, 162, 163, 164, 181, 184, 185
Pannel (Pannell), Capt., 94, 132; Benjamin, 157; Capt. Joseph, 155; Thomas, 73, 78
Parke, Col. Thomas, 116
Parker, Col., 142, 147; Capt. Isaac, 117; James, 1; John, 144
Parks, Mary, 83; William 83
Parmel, see Pannel
Parrock, Thomas, 63
Parsons, Betsy, 178
Pate, Capt. Jeremiah, 142
Patrick, Charles, 73
Pattern, Alexander, 52
Patterson (Patteson, Pattison), Capt., 181; Charles, 72; Rev. David, 149; Edward, 18, 21, 22, 23; James, 71; Sgt. Littleberry (Littlebury), 17, 19, 21, 23; Capt. Thomas, 3, 19, 125
Patton, Alexander, 71
Paxton, Capt. John, 135
Payton, James, 27, 28, 30; William, 88
Peasley, Hugh, 73
Pendleton, Edmd., 140; Edmund, 49; Mrs. Mary (Tinsley), 158, 159; Rev. Micajah, 123, 176; Reubin, 55, 158; Cpl. Richard, 55, 158, 159, 181, 182
Penn, Ann, 4, 158; Major Gabriel, 2, 4, 5, 9, 35, 36, 38, 39, 50, 61, 63, 65, 69, 71, 72, 74, 75, 78, 79, 80, 81, 83, 84, 87, 88, 89, 90, 91, 92, 102, 109, 120, 130, 158, 170, 188, 189; George 4, 158; Capt. George, 35, 36, 71, 80, 81, 83, 87, 88, 107, 189; Lt. John, 71, 75, 76, 77, 83, 90, 92, 97; Joseph, 71, 75, 77, 87; Cpl. Phillip, 55; Sarah (Callaway), 4; Thomas, 56; Capt. William, 97, 98, 158, 181; Major William, 171; Sgt. William, 55
Pentecost, Polly, 111
Perkins, Lt. Archer, 114; Capt. John, 96; Richard, 156
Perrow, Daniel, 71
Peter, Richard, 55
Peters, Elizabeth, 159; James, 159; John, 61, 62; Samuel, 165

Peyton, George, 25; Henry, Sr., 120, 128; James, 25, 56; John, 77, 82, 83; Philip, 77; Ens. Volentine (Valentine), 39
Phelps, John, 26; William, 26
Philip (Phillip), Americus, 160; George Nicholas, 160; John, 79
Phillips, David, 71; George, 15, 18, 20, 22; Ens. George, 35; Jacob, 71; John, 15, 18, 20, 22, 49, 82, 94; John, Jr., 15; Capt. John, 130; William (Philips), 49, 52, 71, 72; Zacharias, 71
Pierce, William, 52
Pinckney, Col. Charles Cotesworth, 119; Capt. Thomas, 119
Pitcher, Elizabeth, 168; John, 168
Plod, John Henry, 52
Plunkett, Adolphus, 184; Ambrose, 184; Ens. Benjamin, 88, 184; John, 184; John, Jr., 184; Mildred, 184; Tabitha, 184; Taliaferro, 184; Willis H., 184; Winifred, 184
Pollard, Lt., 187; Lt. Absalom, 52, 160, 164; Lt. Ambrose, 114; Benjamin, 72; Elizabeth, 119; James, 55, 160; John, 145; John R., 144; Robert, 16; William, 6, 61, 62, 63
Pope, John, 71; Lt. Col. John, Jr., 35, 37, 38, 89, 97, 107, 128, 129, 131, 132, 133, 148, 154, 156, 163, 164, 170, 184
Porter, Capt., 95, 136
Porterfield, Col., 54
Posey, Col., 156
Postell, Capt., 145
Powe, Thomas, 71, 90
Powell, Benjamin, 160; Lt. Edmund, 33, 35, 36, 71, 82; Francis, 56, 159, 160; Ens. James, 96; Joseph, 159; Lucas, 2, 9, 71, 84, 85, 86, 87; Luke, 54; Mary, 159; Mildred, 168; Obediah, 55; Lt. Richard, 35, 36, 71, 82, 88; Thomas, 55, 71 (2), 92, 129, 160; Lt. Wiatt, 32, 69, 71, 92; William, 55, 83, 84, 87; Ens. William, 25, 145, 165; Zachariah, 56
Pratt, Rebecca, 109
Price, Capt., 136; Joseph, 72; Thomas, 52
Pryor (Prior), John, 55, 162; Col. John, 159; Nicholas, 77, 162; Ens. Richard, 131; William, 160, 161, 165
Pucket, Jacob, 52
Pugh, Mrs. Elizabeth (Ware), 180; John, 151, 162, 163; John, Jr., 162
Pulaski, Gen., 181
Purkins, William, 52

Purvis, Charles, 163; Elizabeth (Murphy), 163; George, 1, 71, 90, 132, 163
Putnam, Gen., 11, 99

Quinn (Quin), John, 50, 89; Cpl. Richard, 58

Raines, Ignatious, 71
Ralls, Caleb, 81
Ramsey (Ramsay), Bartholomew, 77; Daniel, 15, 17, 20, 22, 23; James, 187; Joel, 15, 18, 20; Simn., 52
Randal, Col., 134, 135
Randolph, Col., 153; Gov. Edmund, 188
Ray, George, 182; John, 163; Mary, 182; Patty, 163; Suca, 163; William (Wray), 15, 18, 20, 22, 163
Reid, Capt., 101; Alexander, 163; Lt. Alexander, Jr., 32, 71, 75, 76, 79, 81, 82, 89, 90; Major Alexander, 2, 31, 32, 71, 82, 92; George, 25; Lt. James, 84, 163; Ens. Jonathan, 151; Martha, 71; Samuel, 73
Reoch, Edward, 55
Revere, Paul, 3
Reynolds, Absalom, 74; Charles, 71; Patrick, 55; Tabitha, 105; William Cannon, 74
Rice, Capt. Holeman, 176
Richardson (Richeson, Richerson), Col. Holt, 97, 98, 102, 107, 133, 135, 158, 180; John, 71, 86; Mary, 86; Col. Richard, 144; Capt. Samuel, 97, 119
Rickets (Ricketts), Matthew, 148; Thomas, 71
Rickitts, Stephen, 56
Rickman, Dr., 61, 62
Ricks, William, 165
Riddle, Major, 147; Capt. Isaac, 181
Ridgway, Thomas, 71
Rippeto, Peter, 192
Roach, Absalom, 58; Ashcraft, 71; David, 58; Jonathan, 58
Robenson, Harry, 172
Roberts, Henry, 71; Lt. James, 163; Major John, 59, 114, 148, 171; Ens. Joseph, 39, 71, 89, 158; Susan, 126
Robertson, Ens., 103; George, 29; Robert, 72; Thomas, 71, 148, 164; Ens. William, 3
Robinson, George, 28; Morgan P., 59; Lt. William, 177
Rodes (Rhoades, Rhodes), Charles, 71, 73, 149, 152, 153
Roebuck, Col., 118
Rogers, Andrew, 100; Capt. John, 147

Rose, Capt. Alexander, 9, 15, 99, 116, 146; Catherine, 2; Col. Charles, 2, 3, 35, 49, 71, 75, 76, 79, 81, 82, 84, 88, 113; Rev. Charles, 2, 10; Henry, 190; Hugh, 2; Col. Hugh, 2, 35, 36, 51, 60, 61, 62, 68, 71, 73, 74, 75, 79, 80, 84, 85, 86, 88, 89, 99, 106, 109, 113, 115, 135, 141, 152, 154, 164, 170, 171, 184; John, 2; Col. John, 2, 9, 31, 61, 71, 73, 74, 75, 78, 79, 80, 84, 87, 90, 190; Dr. John, 113; Margaret (Grant), 2; Lt. Col. Patrick, 33, 35, 36, 37, 71, 77, 84, 90, 102, 117, 150; Col. Peter, 107, 134, 151; Dr. Robert, 10; Rev. Robert, 2
Rowsey, John, 55
Royaltree (Royalty, Rially), John, 164; Sally (Sage), 164
Rucker, Lt. Col. Ambrose, 2, 3, 35, 36, 59, 69, 71, 72, 73, 74, 75, 76, 77, 79, 80, 81, 83, 84, 87, 88, 131, 135, 136, 180, 183, 184, 189; Anthony, 49, 71, 83, 92, 165; Capt. Benjamin, 2, 35, 37, 71, 78, 79, 80, 83; Lt. Isaac, 32, 35, 37, 71, 83; Isaac Jr., 71 (2); John, 71 (2), 88, 111; Reubin, 88; Susannah, 88; William, 71; Winifred, 184
Rush, Hon. Richard, 123
Russell, Elizabeth, 191, 192; Col. William, 27, 146, 167, 191
Ryalty, Daniel, 188
Ryan, Harris, 164, 165; John, 78; Philip, 81, 165; Unity, 165

Sale, Cornelius, 71, 127; Capt. John, 6, 71, 77, 81, 111, 112, 113, 117, 188
Salesberry, Rev., 147
Sandidge, John, 71, 77, 93; Pulliam, 71; Waller, 120; William, 46
Santin, Frances, 102
Saterwhite, John, 28, 30
Satterwhite, Francis, 71, 76, 77, 84
Saunders, Benjamin, 71; Capt. David, 39; William, 90
Savage, George, 26; James, 55, 71, 77; Lt. William, 98
Scott, Capt., 100; Charles, 72; Gen. Charles, 29, 30, 103, 107, 110, 124, 126, 133, 147, 166; Drury, 29, 30; Hannah, 73; John, 29, 30, 71; Thomas, 29, 30
Scrags, Sgt. Henry, 100
Scruggs, Jane, 165; Samuel Scott, Sr., 27, 29, 30, 165; Samuel S., Jr., 165
Seaton, George, Q. M., 189
Seay, Lt. Abraham, 32, 37, 71, 135, 152, 158
Seayres, Reuben, 15, 17, 20, 22, 23

Shackleford, Capt. Roger, 58, 107, 113, 115; Ens. Samuel, 35, 38, 168
Shannon, Thomas, 73
Sharp, Joseph, 26
Shasteen, James, 25
Shearman, Paddy, 161
Shelby, Capt. Isaac, 100, 160
Shelden, Thomas, 49
Shelton, Capt. Clough, 5, 25, 27, 28, 29, 30, 71, 94, 96, 103, 104, 126, 127, 134, 141, 142, 145, 156, 166, 173, 178; Capt. David, 32, 33, 36, 59, 71, 77, 94, 102, 135, 150, 167; John, 158; Capt. Levins, 125; Capt. Richard, 71, 76, 78, 80, 84, 189
Shenault (Shennault), John, 15, 18, 20, 21
Shepherd, Lt. David, 2, 4, 71, 85; Nancy, 126; Susan, 98
Shields, John, 69, 71, 73
Shoemaker, John, 55
Shumaker (Shoemaker), Zedekiah, 162, 165
Simmons (Simons), James, 26, 27, 28, 30, 55, 165
Simonton, Thomas, 103
Simpson, William, 71
Singer, James H., 118; Mary W., 118
Skillern, Col., 135, 161
Skipworth, Major, 133
Slaton, Henry, 55
Slaughter, Francis, 159
Sledd, Rev. John, 117
Small, William, 142
Smith, Abraham, 168; Sgt. Augustine, 16, 81, 166; Austin, 15, 17, 20, 22, 23, 166; Behethland, 178; Ellison, 100; Hepsibah, 167; Jacob, 71, 76; James, 26, 77; James, Sr., 136; John, 71, 112, 166; Johnson, 58; Judith, 166; Mary, 166; Ens. Obediah, 129; Philip, 71, 78, 114, 136, 166; Rutha, 168; Thomas, 15, 16, 18, 20, 22, 23, 28, 29, 49, 167; Ens. Thomas, 135; Sgt. Thomas, 58; Rev. Turner, 170; William, 15, 100, 167
Sneed, Major, 141
Snider, John, 71
Snooks, Matthew, 9, 10, 15
Sorrell, John, 71
Spears, Obediah, 145
Spencer, Lucy, 159; Lt. William, 5, 32, 60, 72, 76, 81, 82, 88, 89, 184
Spitfathom, John, 150
Stadner, John, 71
Stafford, Joshua, 145

Staples, Ewell, 181; Isaac, 181; Jane, 181; John, 71, 76, 84; Joseph, 15, 18, 20, 21, 130; Lt. Joseph, 6, 112, 113, 127, 135, 152, 162; Samuel, 16, 76
Stark, Adj. Joseph, 84
Starke, Jane, 124; Major John, 123
Statham, Charles, 76
Staton, William, 71
Steel, William, 17
Stephen, Gen. Adam, 11, 151, 188
Stephens, James, Sr., 146; Mary, 146
Steuben, Gen., 114, 167, 179
Stevens, Barnett, 159; Gen. Edward, 25, 53, 54, 94, 96, 102, 103, 104, 107, 112, 122, 123, 126, 127, 129, 132, 133, 141, 142, 145, 148, 149, 165, 166, 167, 173, 178, 179, 181, 184; Elizabeth, 159; James, 69, 71, 81; John, 18, 20, 22, 23
Stewart (Stuart), Charles, 174; James, 105; Capt. James, 133, 142; Sgt. James, 55; Capt. John, 71, 81, 97, 114, 127, 129, 148, 175; Sgt. William, 183
Stinnett, John, 56
Stirk, Lt. Col. John, 155
Stirling, Major-Gen. Lord, 126
Stith, John, 69
Stokes, John, 105; Capt. John, 116; Lt. John, 17, 19; Matilda, 105
Stovall (Stoval, Stovaul), Bartholomew, 98; Major Brett, 117; George, 71; Lt. Col. George, Jr., 72, 73, 189; James, 56; Sgt. Joseph, 55
Stratton, Abraham, 60; Absolem, 16; Henry, 60; Isaac, 60, 167; John, 71, 88, 188.
Street, Anthony, 71
Stribling, Capt., 125
Strickling, Mary, 109
Stuart, Charles, 1
Stubblefield, Capt., 147
Sullivan, Gen., 11
Summers, Adj. Simon, 10
Sumpter, Capt. William, 125
Sumter, Gen. Thomas, 97, 119
Sutherland, Phillip, 58
Sutlef, John, 50
Sweeny (Sweeney, Swenney, Swinney), Charles, 168; Elizabeth, 168; John, 77; Joseph, 167, 168; Moses, 71, 72, 165, 168; Nancy, 93, 168; William, 168
Swensey, Joseph, 178
Swindall, Peter, 89
Syme, Col. John, 14, 191

Talbert, Thomas Henry, 71
Taliaferro, Capt., 128, 155; Benjamin, 168; Capt. Benjamin, 4, 9, 12, 14, 17, 19, 21, 22, 23, 24, 113, 146; Capt. Charles, 71, 78, 128; Ens. Charles, Jr., 38; Elizabeth, 168; Emily, 168; James P., 168; John, 168; Ens. John, 113; Martha, 9; Mildred, 168; Lt. Nicholas, 27; Rebecca, 168; Capt. Richard, 38, 57, 71, 109, 129, 167, 168, 172, 184; Richard, Jr., 168; Roderick, 168; Rutha, 168; William, 168; Sgt. William, 113, 168; Capt. Zachariah, 2, 9, 31, 69, 71, 75, 79, 80, 84, 88, 92; Lt. Zacharias, Jr., 38
Tankersley, Reuben, 49; Richard, 49, 162
Tanner, Ann, 118; Creed, 118; Eleanor, 118; Elizabeth, 118; John, 118; Lt. Josiah, 117, 118; Kezia, 118; Lucius, 117; Lucy, 118, Martha, 118; Mary, 118; Matthew, 118; Patsey, 117; Sally, 117, 118; Samuel, 118; Thomas, 118
Tarleton, Col. B., 3, 53, 66, 69, 107, 108, 142, 147, 157, 177, 181
Tate, John, 16; Nathan, 15, 18, 20; Robert, 52
Taylor, Col. Francis, 49, 57, 58, 95, 97, 105, 107, 109, 112, 114, 115, 117, 125, 128, 135, 136, 142, 148, 150, 152, 154, 170, 171, 176, 184, 185; George, 56, 168, 170; John, 17, 56, 170; Capt. Richard, 100; Will, 170; Lt. Zachariah, 33, 34, 35
Temple (Temples), John, 15, 18, 20, 170
Tennison, John, 71
Terry, Emily, 168; John, 168
Thacker, Isham, 25; Petter, 71
Thomas, Rev. Allen, 177; Cornelius, Jr., 74; Capt. Cornelius, 5, 71, 72, 73, 74, 76, 78, 85; Elizabeth, 74; Cpl. Harrison, 25; James, 122; John, 74; Ens. John, 17, 19, 21, 23, 170, 171; Joseph, 26, 27, 28, 30, 127; Levi, 26, 27, 28, 30; Lucy, 74, 78; Michael, 71; Norborn, 74; Sgt. Reuben, 25; Salley, 74
Thompson, Capt. Anderson, 137, 139; James, 171, 187, 188; Lt. James, 161, 165; Joel, 166; John, 128; John, Jr., 168; William, 90, 91, 187, 188
Thornton, Lt. Col., 154
Threadgill, Capt. Thomas, 54
Thurman, Elisha, 110; Polly M., 110

Thurmond, Elizabeth D., 171; Judith, 171; Lucy A., 171; Philip, 171; Capt. Phillip, 33, 34, 36, 37, 71, 109, 135, 173; Sally, 93, 171; Capt. William, 103, 172; Sgt. William, 171; William J., 171
Tiller, William, 71
Tilman, Daniel, 71; Mary, 93
Tinsley, Abraham, 159; David, 71, 77; Edward, 71; Lt. Isaac, 32, 33, 36, 71; James, 158; John, 71, 88; Joshua, 71; William, 58, 159 (2)
Tomlinson, Ambrose, 76
Tompkins, Col., 163
Toner, James, 26, 27, 29, 30
Tooley, James, 144
Trail, James, 71, 171; Thomas, 149
Trent, Capt. Henry, 71, 77; Capt. John, 71, 106; Obediah Henry, 83; Peterfield, 78
Trigg, Col., 115; Lt. Daniel, 100
Trusler, Elizabeth (Dunning), 171; John, 171
Tucker, Bueil G., 172; Claiborn A., 171; Claudius L., 172; Creed Haskins, 172; Lt. Daniel, 32, 55, 113, 148; Drury, 172; Elizabeth D., 171; Elizabeth F., 172; Francis S., 172; Henry L., 172; Isaiah, 172; Jesse, 57, 85, 172, 173; John C., 171; Capt. Joseph, 32, 38, 39, 55, 74, 82, 83, 131, 148, 150, 183; Martha R., 172; Mary, 171; Mary C., 172; Mathew (Matthew), 71, 85, 87; Nancy Leftwich, 172; Parmelia A., 172; Polly (Thurmond), 171; Sophia W., 172; Susan W., 171; Susanah L., 172; William, 107; Capt. William, 55, 115, 129, 131, 148, 153, 158, 169, 176, 181, 183; Lt. William, 38
Tuggle, Charles, 26, 27, 29, 30, 173; Henry, 26, 27, 28, 30; Joshua, 15, 18, 20, 22; Cpl. Joshua, 52
Tuley, Capt. Charles, 189, 190
Turner, Betsey, 173; George, 173; Ens. Henry, 39, 71, 173; Henry, Jr., 173; Lt. James, 33, 34, 35, 54, 71; John, 71, 86; Kitty, 173; Lucy A., 171; Martha, 173; Rachel, 173; Ruth, 173; Sally, 173; Samuel C., 173; Sarah, 174; Stephen, 71; Stephen B., 173; Terisha, 173; Terisha, Jr., 71; Ens. Terisha, 37, 71; Thomas, 173; Capt. William, 102, 153; Ens. William, 173, 174
Tyler, Anna Cash, 174; Charles, 175; Daniel, 15, 17, 20, 21, 23, 174; Elizabeth, 175; Elizabeth Wade, 174; George D., 175; Johannah,

174; John, 174, 175; John L., 175, 176; Keziah, 174; Lawson G., 175; Nancy, 174, 175; Nelson C., 174; Oney D., 175; Patsy W., 176; Polley, 175; Samuel, 174; Sarah, 174; Susannah, 174; Tandy S., 175; William Henry, 176; William Hudson, 175; Zachariah, 174
Tylor, Daniel, 58
Tyra, William, 112
Tyree, Jacob, 49 (2), 71; John (Tyre), 15, 18, 20, 94; William, 49

Upshaw, John, 56, 176; Capt. Leroy, 33, 34, 52, 148
Upton, Thomas, 188

Vance, Col. Samuel, 97, 175, 180
Vardeman, Jeremiah, 164
Vaughan, Ann, 91; Cornelius, 51, 87, 91; James, 17; John, 87; Martin, 51; Mary, 87; Sarah, 132; William, 132, 144
Venison, William, 112
Via, Gideon, 58, 97, 177; John, 58, 97, 176, 177; Littlebury, 58; Patsey, 177; Rowland, 177; William, 97, 176 (2), 177
Viar (Via), David, 56; William, 56
Vier (Via), John, 176; Sarah, 176
Vines, Andrew, 177; Mary, 177; Nelson, 177; Thomas, 177; William F., 177
Vineyard, Rosanna, 111
Vurman, John, 114

Waddell, Rev., 120
Wade, Abigail Hardwick, 84; Ballinger, 71, 85, 142; Clary, 84; Dudley, 16; Jeremiah, 59, 85; Jeremiah, Jr., 59; Joshua, 59; Lucreasy, 84; Pearce, 49, 84, 85
Wale, Mrs. Patsey, 132
Walker, Capt., 146; Mrs., 67; Baylor, 74; Henry, 28, 30; Jeremiah, 25, 26, 27, 28, 29, 52, 177, 178; Margaret, 182; Mary, 177, 178; Saluda, 98
Wallace, Capt., 164; Capt. Adam, 147; Lt. Andrew, 161, 165; John, 51
Walls, Rev., 110
Walters, Lt., 115
Walton, Edward, 178; Edward Marshall, 178; Elizabeth, 178; Elizabeth Tilman, 178; George Sidney, 178 (2); Jesse, 179; Jesse T., 178; Josias Wesley, 178; Judith, 178; Judith Cox, 178; Nancey Murrey, 178; Nancy, 178; Thomas Maddison, 178; Lt. Tilman, 26, 27, 28, 29, 108, 152, 163, 178, 179, 184; Lt. William, 32, 37; William, 71, 81, 82, 178 (2), 179; William Orrell, 178
Ward, James, 71, 82; Capt. Meacock, 50; Nathan, 71
Ware, Almira, 180; Sgt. Edward, 71, 140, 179; Edward, Jr., 93, 180; James, 112, 140; Lt. James, 6, 33, 35, 36, 71, 85, 109, 112, 113, 127, 129, 136; Cpl. John, 25, 27, 28, 29; Ens. John, 39, 60; John Thomas, 180; Malinda, 180; Martha, 180; Mildred, 180 (2); Nancey, 180; Peyton, 180; Polly, 180; Robert, 83, 180; Thomas, 83, 180; Virginia, 180; William, 180; Capt. William, 33, 34, 37, 38, 39, 71, 92
Warren, Burrus, 56; James, 86; John, 105
Warriner, Jacob, 155
Warwick, Capt., 180; Abraham, 71, 84, 86, 151
Wash, Cpl. Benj., 25; James, 17; Sgt. Thomas, 25
Washington, Gen. George, 7, 11, 12, 13, 14, 51, 66, 67, 98, 99, 103, 104, 105, 114, 117, 121, 124, 126, 127, 142, 146, 158, 160, 174, 179, 180, 188; Col. William, 69, 96, 100, 101, 102, 150, 154, 160
Waters, John, 56; Moses, 55, 180
Watkins, Ens. Robert, 19, 21; Sarah, 181; Spencer, 181
Watson, Capt., 131, 143; James, 71, 84, 86; Lt. John, 55, 129
Watts, Caleb, 71; Capt. Steven (Stephen), 34, 38, 39, 131, 149, 151
Waugh, George, 104; Susannah, 104; Thomas, 164
Wayne, Gen. Anthony, 8, 14, 108, 116, 152, 158, 166, 167, 173, 182
Wear, Capt. John, 149
Weathered, Francis, 73
Webb, Capt., 53; Capt. Jacob, 78
Webster, Abner, 182; Benjamin, 182; Betsy, 182; James, 182; John, 181, 182, 183; Joseph, 182; Maggie, 182; Pleasant, 182; Polly, 182; Richard, 182; Richard, Jr., 182; Sally, 182; William, 55, 183
Weedon, Gen. George, 142, 145, 165, 181
Weeks (Weekes), James, 9, 15, 19, 21, 166

Welch, Elizabeth, 183 (2); Francis, 183; John, 15, 16, 18, 20, 22, 183; Joseph, 15, 17, 19, 22, 23, 155, 183; Joseph, Jr., 183; Margaret, 183; Samson (Sampson), 15, 18, 20, 22; Sherred, 183; Susannah, 155, 183 (2)

Wells, Caroline, 160; James (Wills), 71; Capt. John, 122

West, Sgt. Bransford, 71, 132, 183, 184; Francis, 15, 71, 188; John, 15, 71, 74; Nancy, 184; Thomas, 71

Wheeler, James, 18, 21; John, 18, 21; Micajah, 153, 171

Whilsett, William, 71

White, Capt., 168; James, 56; John, 25

White's Dragoons, 69

Whitehead, Elizabeth, 187; John, 48

Whitley, Charles, 157

Whitsill, William, 88

Whitten, Mrs. Ann, 116; Nancy, 168; Peggy, 93; William, 76

Whittle, John, 71

Whorley, William, 16

Wiatt, Major John, 38, 71, 85

Wilcox, Edmund, 61, 62, 71, 72, 74, 75, 76, 83, 84, 87, 88, 89, 193; Mrs. Sophia, 111; Thomas, 55

Wiles, 169

Wilkerson, Sarah (Bailey), 98

Williams, Capt., 136; Col. 118; Lt., 166; Arthur, 69; Francis, 58; John, 18, 21, 22, 23, 184; Katy, 93; Robert, 71; William, 77

Williamson, William, 56

Wills, James, 188

Wilson, Ens., 124; Patty, 163; William, 73

Wilton, Betty, 63; James, 63

Wingfield, 171

Winker, Thomas, 26

Winston, Major, 116; Edmund (Edmond), 192, 193

Witt, Abner, 49, 86, 185; Anne, 185; Charles, 49, 185; Conny, 97; David, 185; Elisha, 184, 185; George, 49; John, 71, 88, 128, 185; John, Jr., 91; Littleberry, 128; Nathan, 185; Rachel, 185; Silas, 185; William, 185

Wood, Dosha, 105; Francis, 127; James, 105; Col. James, 59; Josiah, 71; Lucy, 191; William, 185

Woodford, Gen., 4, 13, 67, 103, 132

Woodroof (Woodruff), Capt., 98, 164; Capt. David, 36, 59, 71, 77, 81, 84, 91, 97, 114, 141; Harding, 91; Cpl. Hardin (Hardan, Harden), 57, 58, 150, 185; Capt. Jack, 181; John, 49; Capt. John H., 57, 85, 97, 114, 129, 132, 148, 149, 151, 153, 167, 170, 176; Capt. Richard, 115; Richard, 91; Sally, 185

Woods, James, 3, 71; Capt. John, 100; Lt. Samuel, 71, 89, 161, 165

Woodson, John, 109

Woodville, Rev. John, 132

Woody, Matilda, 187

Wortham, Jane, 160; Sarah, 160; Thomas, 60, 71

Wren, Nicholas, 77, 86

Wright, Archillis, 71; Andrew, 71, 100, 185, 186; Andrew Washington, 186; Anney (Anna), 186, 187; Benjamin, 16, 71, 185, 186, 187 (2); Betsey, 186; David H., 186; Elizabeth, 187; Elonder, 186; Esther Montgomery, 186, 187; Francis, 55; George, 187; Isaac, 71, 88; James, 71, 186; Jean, 186; Jeaney, 186; John, 71, 75; John B., 186; Joseph, 185; Leonard, 184; Lucy, 185, 186 (2), 187; Lucy C., 186; Matilda, 186, 187; Melinda, 186; Moses, 26, 27, 28, 30, 84, 123, 187; Nancy, 187; Paul, 28, 30; Peggy J., 186; Polley, 186, 187; Lt. Robert, 32, 39, 71, 86, 88; Robert M., 186; Robin, 185; Sarah, 176; Sarah J., 186; Sarah S., 185, 186; Stark, 58; Susanna, 152; Thomas, 71; William, 107; William H., 186; William M., 186; William P., 184

Yarborough, Capt. Charles, 154

Yarbour, Capt. Joseph, 167

Yores, Lt. Thomas, 177

Young, John, 58

Yours, Lt. Samuel, 164; Cpl. William, 28, 29

www.ingramcontent.com/pod-product-compliance
Lightning Source LLC
Chambersburg PA
CBHW060129170426
43198CB00010B/1100